Ius Gentium: Comparative Perspectives on Law and Justice

Volume 116

Ius Gentium is a book series which discusses the central questions of law and justice from a comparative perspective. The books in this series collect the contrasting and overlapping perspectives of lawyers, judges, philosophers and scholars of law from the world's many different jurisdictions for the purposes of comparison, harmonisation, and the progressive development of law and legal institutions. Each volume makes a new comparative study of an important area of law. This book series continues the work of the well-known journal of the same name and provides the basis for a better understanding of all areas of legal science.

The *Ius Gentium* series provides a valuable resource for lawyers, judges, legislators, scholars, and both graduate students and researchers in globalisation, comparative law, legal theory and legal practice. The series has a special focus on the development of international legal standards and transnational legal cooperation.

Doron Goldbarsht • Louis de Koker
Editors

Financial Crime, Law and Governance

Navigating Challenges in Different Contexts

Springer

Editors
Doron Goldbarsht
Macquarie Law School
Macquarie University
Macquarie Park, NSW, Australia

Louis de Koker
La Trobe Law School
Melbourne, VIC, Australia

ISSN 1534-6781 ISSN 2214-9902 (electronic)
Ius Gentium: Comparative Perspectives on Law and Justice
ISBN 978-3-031-59546-2 ISBN 978-3-031-59547-9 (eBook)
https://doi.org/10.1007/978-3-031-59547-9

This Springer imprint is published by the registered company Springer Nature Switzerland AG
The registered company address is: Gewerbestrasse 11, 6330 Cham, Switzerland

To our wives, Erin and Jeanne, and our children, Arielle, Hallel, Allie and Louis. Without their continuing support and their sacrifices, our work would not be possible.

—Doron and Louis

Contents

Contributors

Abdullahi Bello Northumbria Law School, Northumbria University, Newcastle, UK

Ariel Burgess Royal Military College of Canada, Kingston, ON, Canada

Pompeu Casanovas La Trobe Law School, Melbourne, VIC, Australia
Artificial Intelligence Research Institute, Spanish National Research Council (IIIA-CSIC), Bellaterra, Barcelona, Spain

Elizabeth David-Barrett University of Sussex, East Sussex, UK

Louis de Koker La Trobe Law School, Melbourne, VIC, Australia

Doron Goldbarsht Macquarie University, Macquarie Park, NSW, Australia

Daniel Halpin Cybertrace, Sydney, NSW, Australia

Rhianna Hamilton The University of Adelaide, Adelaide, Australia

Hannah Harris Macquarie University, Macquarie Park, NSW, Australia

Jackie Harvey Northumbria Law School, Northumbria University, Newcastle, UK

Gary Hughes Barrister, Britomart Chambers, Auckland, New Zealand

Vince Hurley Department of Security Studies and Criminology, Macquaire University, Macquaire Park, NSW, Australia

Christian Leuprecht Royal Military College of Canada, Kingston, ON, Canada
Queen's University, Kingston, ON, Canada

Samuel Orchard Supreme Court of New South Wales, Sydney, NSW, Australia

Alfio Puglisi King's College, London, UK

Nicholas Ryder School of Law and Politics, Cardiff University, Cardiff, UK

Benjamin Scott Sydney, NSW, Australia

Corina Sheerin School of Business, National College of Ireland, Dublin, Ireland

Abdullahi Shehu ECOWAS Inter-Governmental Action Group against Money Laundering in West Africa (GIABA), Dakar, Senegal

Alex Simpson Department of Security Studies and Criminology, Macquaire University, Macquaire Park, NSW, Australia

Peter Sproat Northumbria Law School, Northumbria University, Newcastle, UK

Sheri Todd Sydney, NSW, Australia

Slobodan Tomic University of York, York, UK

Sue Turner Northumbria Law School, Northumbria University, Newcastle, UK

Tony Ward Northumbria Law School, Northumbria University, Newcastle, UK

Towards a Global Approach to Combating Financial Crime

Louis de Koker and Doron Goldbarsht

Abstract This chapter considers some of the main drivers behind the current globalised approach to combating financial crime. It traces the history behind the current global anti-money laundering and counter terrorism and proliferation financing framework that emerged over the past decades. It considers in particular key United Nations conventions, United Nations Security Council resolutions and the role of the Financial Action Task Force and also regional initiatives, with a particular focus on Europe.

1 Introduction

During the twentieth century, increasing international economic interconnectedness was accompanied by criminal interconnectedness, especially of organised crime. Serious criminal activities transcended borders with greater ease and frequency and hence informed the need for a more global approach to combating serious crime.[1,2]

An effective global approach to combating serious crime requires a sufficient level of harmonised laws and law enforcement measures across nations to prevent criminals from exploiting gaps in jurisdictions with lax regulations. A vulnerable regulatory system in one country could, depending on its infrastructure and context, potentially undermine the security of other jurisdictions.[3] By implementing agreed

[1] McClean (1988); Lewis (1989); Florez and Boyce (1990); Dorn and South (1990); Carter (1994); Solomon (1994); Shelley (1995); Myers (1995).

[2] Williams (1994); Naylor (1995); Van Duyne (1995); Mittelman and Johnston (1999).

[3] Goldbarsht and de Koker (2024); Goldbarsht (2022), p. 46; FATF (2013).

L. de Koker (✉)
La Trobe Law School, Melbourne, VIC, Australia
e-mail: l.dekoker@latrobe.edu.au

D. Goldbarsht
Macquarie University, Macquarie Park, NSW, Australia

D. Goldbarsht, L. de Koker (eds.), *Financial Crime, Law and Governance*, Ius Gentium: Comparative Perspectives on Law and Justice 116,
https://doi.org/10.1007/978-3-031-59547-9_1

standards for defining crimes, prosecuting offenders, and recovering illicit gains, nations can close legal loopholes that transnational criminals often exploit. Such consistency also supports mutual legal assistance, enabling efficient cooperation in investigations and prosecutions.

While the benefits of international cooperation against transnational crime are evident, hurdles arise from the complexities of diverse legal systems, political considerations, and variations in capacity and resources. Striking a balance between respecting national sovereignty and fostering collaboration is a delicate endeavour, further hindered by the constant evolution of criminal tactics. Geopolitical tensions and increasing concerns about data privacy and cybersecurity add further layers of complexity.

What are the main drivers of the global crime combating approach that are relevant to the field of financial crime today? This chapter considers this question by revisiting some of the key elements of the history of global crime combating coordination in response to transnational financial crime. It traces the main challenges posed by globalisation to international cooperation and enforcement and considers the web of international conventions, intergovernmental bodies, and regional organisations that represent the modern global approach to combating financial crime.

2 History and Development of the Global Anti-Financial Crime Framework

Global cooperation in respect of transnational criminal enterprise emerged in the twentieth century in response to the proliferation of drugs and the flow of illicitly obtained funds across traditionally defined borders. In the financial crime space, this collaboration expanded to the financing of terrorism and the proliferation of weapons of mass destruction.[4] Today, key elements of the global response to international financial crime are embodied in several United Nations (UN) conventions. These generally standardise key elements of the predicate offences and also address related financial flows. Elements of offences relating to the financing of terrorism and the laundering of proceeds of crime, for example, are addressed in the UN instruments. These are further detailed and supplemented by the standards set by the Financial Action Task Force (FATF). The FATF is an intergovernmental body responsible for setting the international standards in anti-money laundering (AML), counter-terrorism financing (CTF) and counter-proliferation financing (CPF) regulation. The FATF recommendations have received normative status, outside the formal sources of Article 38(1) of the Statute of the International Court of Justice, through compliance and international cooperation.[5]

[4] De Koker (2024).

[5] Abass (2013), pp. 62–63; Goldbarsht and Michaelsen (2017), p. 199.

2.1 UN Conventions

It is well over a century since the International Opium Commission convened in Shanghai from 5–26 February 1909, marking a significant milestone in the development of international narcotics control.[6] The initiative for convening the Commission emerged from US President Theodore Roosevelt's administration, which sought collaboration among nations including the United States, Austria-Hungary, China, France, Germany, the United Kingdom, Italy, Japan, the Netherlands, Persia, Portugal, Russia and Siam. The Commission focused on the pressing issue of the Chinese opium problem, which led to an imperial edict in 1906 prohibiting opium cultivation and use in China over a 10-year period.[7] Beyond regional concerns, the Commission recognised the broader global challenge of narcotics, including addiction to manufactured opiates. Although the Commission was not intended to adopt binding measures, it did adopt resolutions calling for the incremental suppression of opium smoking, combating narcotics smuggling, and encouraging cooperation with governments overseeing foreign concessions in China. The Commission also stressed the need for control over the production and distribution of opiates such as morphine to address the growing issue of addiction.[8]

The Commission accelerated international narcotics control efforts which—only 3 years later—led to the adoption of the Hague Opium Convention of 1912, establishing narcotics control as an institution of international law on a multilateral basis.[9]

As time progressed and the organised drug trafficking threat increased, the focus of narcotics control broadened from drug control measure to include the laundering of proceeds of drug offences. In 1988, the UN adopted the Convention against Illicit Drugs and Psychotropic Substances[10] (the Vienna Convention), the first intergovernmental agreement to provide for the criminalisation of money laundering by state parties. The Vienna Convention embedded a new transnational crime strategy disrupt criminal enterprises. This strategy, adopted to respond to the evolution of drug markets and the growth of organised criminal activity and cartel behaviour, viewed crime syndicates as businesses whose activities can be curtailed by disrupting their application and enjoyment of proceeds of crime. The strategy comprised the uniform criminalisation of the laundering of proceeds of crime and the implementation of a regime allowing the confiscation of proceeds of crime,

[6] Wright (1909). Wright (1912); UN Office on Drugs and Crime (2009), pp. 33–49; Barop (2015).

[7] For the linkages the actions of colonial powers and especially with the Opium Wars, see Collins (2021), UN Office on Drugs and Crime (2009), p. 22.

[8] UN Office on Drugs and Crime (1959).

[9] Convention Relating to the Suppression of the Abuse of Opium and Other Drugs, 23 January 1912, 8 LNTS 187. See UN Office on Drugs and Crime (1959); de Koker and Turkington (2016), p. 243.

[10] UN Convention against Illicit Traffic in Narcotic Drugs and Psychotropic Substances (opened for signature 20 December 1988, entered into force 11 November 1990) 1582 UNTS 95 (Vienna Convention).

combined with a raft of due diligence and surveillance obligations for regulated institutions.

Article 1(b) of the Vienna Convention requires state parties to criminalise money laundering, in particular:

1. The conversion or transfer of property, knowing that such property is derived from any offence or offences established in accordance with the Convention, or from an act of participation in such offence or offences, for the purpose of concealing or disguising the illicit origin of the property or of assisting any person who is involved in the commission of such an offence or offences to evade the legal consequences of his actions; and
2. The concealment or disguise of the true nature, source, location, disposition, movement, rights with respect to, or ownership of property, knowing that such property is derived from an offence or offences established in accordance with article 1(a) of the Convention or from an act of participation in such an offence or offences.

Each country must also, subject to its own laws, criminalise the acquisition, possession or use of property, knowing at the time of receipt that it was derived from a drug offence, regardless of the location of the predicate offence.[11]

The Convention defines 'proceeds' as meaning any kind of asset formed or generated, either directly or indirectly, through the commission of an offence. Notably, the Convention provides that 'knowledge', for purposes of the money laundering offence, could be inferred from objective factual circumstances.[12]

The Convention also addresses the identification, freezing and seizing of criminal proceeds primarily to undermine the profitability and viability of criminal enterprise and to satisfy the financial claims of victims, regardless of the jurisdiction in which they reside. The Convention's confiscation regime enables domestic law enforcement bodies to freeze (pending sentencing) and seize proceeds derived from drug offences (or property of the same value), as well as drugs and instruments of drug offences. In addition, it requires state parties to empower their domestic courts and competent authorities to order the production of bank, financial or commercial records, and state parties are not allowed to refuse cooperation with these obligations on the ground of bank secrecy.[13]

The Vienna Convention also promotes international cooperation by strengthening mutual legal assistance, including extradition.

Though confined to drugs and drug trafficking, the 1988 Convention set the pattern for international cooperation in criminal matters that was soon adopted by other instruments too. In 2000, for example, the UN Convention against Transna-

[11] Vienna Convention, art 1©(i).

[12] Vienna Convention, art 3(3).

[13] Vienna Convention, art 5(3) and 7(3).

tional Organised Crime[14] (the Palermo Convention) was adopted with the intention of promoting cooperation among states in combating 'transnational' activities, including human trafficking, people smuggling, and smuggling and trafficking in firearms and ammunition.

Importantly, the Palermo Convention expanded the UN's definition of 'money laundering' to include several predicate offences, including 'participation in, association with or conspiracy to commit, attempt to commit and aiding and abetting, facilitating and counselling the commission of any of the offences established in accordance with this article'.[15] The Palermo Convention also expanded the ambit of 'proceeds of crime' beyond drug-related offences to proceeds of 'serious' offences. Furthermore, the Convention defined the term 'organized criminal group' as a 'structured group of three or more persons, existing for a period of time and acting in consort with the aim of committing one or more serious crimes or offences ... in order to obtain, directly or indirectly, a financial or other material benefit'.[16] A group can however be a 'structured group' without having formally defined roles for its members, continuity of its membership or a developed structure. This broad definition of a 'structured group' further extended the scope of the Convention.

In addition, the Convention introduced a responsibility for ratifying states, when acting on a request from another state, to give priority consideration—to the extent permitted by law—to returning assets to enable victim empowerment.[17]

The 2004 UN Convention against Corruption[18] (UNCAC) adopted similar measures relating to the laundering and confiscation of proceeds of corruption, strengthening the global use of the financial system to combat serious transnational crime.[19] UNCAC requires ratifying parties to implement effective anti-corruption policies and to have an independent body or bodies to implement those policies. They are further required to expand the sphere of money laundering activity to include the 'concealment or continued retention of property' known to have been generated from a predicate offence.[20] In addition, UNCAC introduced two mandatory criminal offences—offering or soliciting a bribe and embezzlement or misappropriation by a public official[21]—alongside several optional offences, including trading in (undue)

[14] UN Convention against Transnational Organized Crime (opened for signature 12 December 2000, entered into force 29 September 2003) 2225 UNTS 209 (Palermo Convention).

[15] Palermo Convention, art 6.

[16] Palermo Convention, art 2.

[17] Palermo Convention, arts 13–14.

[18] UN Convention against Corruption, opened for signature 9 December 2003, 2349 UNTS 41 (entered into force 14 December 2005) (UNCAC).

[19] UN Convention against Corruption (adopted 11 December 2003, entered into force 14 December 2005) 2349 UNTS 41.

[20] UNCAC, art 24.

[21] UNCAC, arts 15–17.

influence,[22] abuse of position to obtain an advantage,[23] illicit enrichment and private sector bribery, and embezzlement.[24] Relevantly, UNCAC requires ratifying states to ensure that their money laundering offences apply the 'widest possible range' of predicate offences that result in the generation of proceeds, including those occurring outside of a state's jurisdiction.[25]

While the UN's money laundering and asset confiscation was taking shape, work was also progressing on international consensus regarding the combating of terrorism.

With regard to terrorist financing, it should be noted that, prior to the attacks of 11 September 2001 on the USA, the international community did not assign a high priority to combating terrorist financing.[26] This is despite it being addressed by the 1999 International Convention for the Suppression of the Financing of Terrorism.

For decades sensitivity regarding the definition of terrorism formed a substantial barrier to effective cooperation on counter-terrorism. Agreement on the definition of the concept was difficult to reach in a post-colonial phase where many countries gained independence after violent struggles for freedom from colonialism and oppression.[27] Consensus could, however, be reached on action against specific acts that were deemed as beyond redemption regardless of the political context and motivation. However, as terrorism has gained prominence internationally, a 'working' definition has solidified through state legislation, decisions from various geographical organisations, and international bodies like the UN (Goldbarsht 2020, 19). International conventions were therefore adopted to address specific acts, such as airplane hijacking,[28] hostage taking,[29] causing harm to diplomats,[30] and bombings,[31] among many others.[32] What many of these conventions have in

---

[22]UNCAC, art 18.

[23]UNCAC, art 19.

[24]UNCAC, arts 20–22.

[25]UNCAC, art 23(2)(a).

[26]Roth et al. (2004), p. 4.

[27]Boaz (2002), Schmid (2023).

[28]Convention for the Suppression of Unlawful Seizure of Aircraft (opened for signature 16 December 1970, entered into force 14 October 1971) 860 UNTS 105.

[29]International Convention against the Taking of Hostages (opened for signature 17 December 1979, entered into force 3 June 1983) 1316 UNTS 205.

[30]Convention on the Prevention and Punishment of Crimes against Internationally Protected Persons, including Diplomatic Agents (opened for signature 14 December 1973, entered into force 20 February 1977) 1035 UNTS 168.

[31]International Convention for the Suppression of Terrorist Bombings (opened for signature 15 December 1997, entered into force 23 May 2001) 2149 UNTS 284.

[32]Convention on Offences and Certain Other Acts Committed On Board Aircraft (opened for signature 14 September 1963, entered into force 4 December 1969) 704 UNTS 219; International Civil Aviation Organization, Convention for the Suppression of Unlawful Acts against the Safety of Civil Aviation (opened for signature 23 September 1971, entered into force 26 January 1973) 974 UNTS 177; Convention on the Physical Protection of Nuclear Material (opened for signature 26 October 1979, entered into force 8 February 1987) 1456 UNTS 101; Convention for the Suppression of Unlawful Acts Against the Safety of Maritime Navigation (opened for signature

common is that they first declare the illegal act to be a criminal one and detail the elements of the offence (establishing the *mens rea* and *actus reus*), then establish legal jurisdiction, the rights of the defendant, an obligation to extradite or prosecute, and international cooperation. From a law enforcement perspective the values of these measures were limited by their focused scope and by their reactive nature: they could only be used once the crime has been committed. It was not until the 1990s that the international community developed a convention to deal with terrorism as a phenomenon that was more than a mere list of specific criminal activities.

On 17 December 1996, the UN General Assembly adopted a resolution[33] that urged all member states to take steps to prevent and counteract, through appropriate domestic measures, the financing of terrorists and terrorist organisations, whether such financing is direct or indirect, through organisations which also have, or claim to have, charitable, social or cultural goals or which are also engaged in unlawful activities such as illicit arms trafficking, drug dealing, and racketeering, including the exploitation of persons for the purposes of funding terrorist activities.[34]

France proposed the development of a draft UN convention on terrorist financing and this was endorsed at a G8 London Conference on Terrorism on 7 and 8 December 1998.[35] Drafts of the convention were considered at meeting of European Union (EU) member states and at G8 meeting, before being tabled at the UN.[36] The draft was first considered by an ad hoc committee of the UN from 15 to 26 March 1999 and then by a working group that recommended adoption of the convention by the General Assembly.[37] On 9 December 1999, the General Assembly adopted the International Convention for the Suppression of the Financing of Terrorism (the Terrorism Financing Convention).[38] This was the first international treaty to deal directly and explicitly with terrorist financing. Despite its adoption very few signatory countries had taken steps to ratify the Convention prior to the attacks of 11 September 2001 on the USA. Only Botswana and Sri Lanka ratified the Convention in 2000, followed by the United Kingdom and Uzbekistan by mid-2001.[39] Many more signatories and ratifications poured in after the September

10 March 1988, entered into force 1 March 1992) 1678 UNTS 221; and Convention on the Suppression of Unlawful Acts Relating to International Civil Aviation (opened for registration 10 September 2010, entered into force 1 July 2018) 3307 UNTS.

[33] Resolutions of the UN General Assembly are not legally binding on member states per se. However, this resolution led to the drafting of the Convention.

[34] *Measures to Eliminate International Terrorism*, GA Res 51/210, UN Doc A/RES/51/210 (17 December 1996), para 3(f).

[35] G8 Justice and Interior Ministers (1998).

[36] Aust (2001), p. 286. The G8 was a political forum comprising the world's eight wealthiest nations. It became the G7 in 2014, after the suspension of Russia.

[37] Aust (2001) p. 287.

[38] International Convention for the Suppression of the Financing of Terrorism, opened for signature 10 January 2000, 2178 UNTS 197 (entered into force 10 April 2002).

[39] UN Treaty Collection (2023).

2001 attacks and on 10 April 2002 the Terrorism Financing Convention entered into force.

The Convention filled an important gap in international law by expanding the legal framework for international cooperation in the investigation, prosecution and extradition of persons who engage in the financing of terrorism.[40] It introduced the concept of terrorism financing in article 1:[41]

> Any person commits an offence within the meaning of the Convention if that person by any means, directly or indirectly, unlawfully and wilfully, provides or collects funds with the intention that they should be used or in the knowledge that they are to be used, in full or in part, in order to carry out:
>
> (a) An act which constitutes an offence within the scope of and as defined in one of the treaties listed in the annex to the Convention; or
> (b) Any other act intended to cause death or serious bodily injury to a civilian, or to any other person not taking an active part in the hostilities in a situation of armed conflict, when the purpose of such act, by its nature or context, is to intimidate a population, or to compel a government or an international organization to do or to abstain from doing any act.

The Terrorism Financing Convention adopted a broad definition of 'funds' to include 'assets of every kind, whether tangible or intangible, moveable or immovable, however acquired, and legal documents or instruments in any form, including electronic or digital, evidencing title to, or interest in, such assets, including, but not limited to, bank credits, travellers cheques, bank cheques, money orders, shares, securities, bonds, drafts, letters of credit'.[42] In addition, article 8 authorise the identification, detection and freezing or seizure of any such funds.

2.2 UN Security Council

After bombing attacks on the US embassies in Kenya and Tanzania in 1998, international efforts to fight terrorism intensified. A year later, the UN Security Council (UNSC) adopted, under Chapter VII, SC Resolution 1267, which required UN member states to restrict the activities, and freeze the assets, of individuals and entities identified as being linked to the Taliban. In 2000, UNSC Resolution 1333[43] added a 12-month arms embargo over the territory of Afghanistan under Taliban control and expanded the financial sanctions to cover Osama bin Laden and Al-Qaida.

[40] United States Department of State (2000).
[41] Terrorism Financing Convention, art 2.
[42] Terrorism Financing Convention, art 1.
[43] UNSC Res 1333, UN Doc S/RES/1333 (2000) (19 December 2000).

The sophistication of the attacks perpetrated on the USA on 11 September 2001 signalled a need for greater international cooperation to fight terror and the financing of terrorism. In response, UNSC Resolution 1373 was adopted on 28 September 2001.[44] The resolution contains three sets of general obligations for states, the first two of which are phrased as mandatory ('*The Security Council* ... *Decides*') while the third is in hortatory terms ('*The Security Council* ... *Calls* upon all States to ...').[45] Of the mandatory obligations, one deals entirely with financing, requiring states to criminalise the collection of funds that support terrorism in any form; to freeze the resources of persons who commit, or attempt to commit, terrorist acts, as well as those of any entities controlled by such persons or acting under their direction; and to prevent their nationals and any person in their territories from providing any form of financial or related service to terrorists, attempted terrorists, or any entities under their control or direction.

The second obligation requires states to refrain from providing any form of support to terrorists, and to prevent terrorist acts from occurring though a number of steps set out in the paragraph. These steps include suppressing recruitment to terrorist groups, denying safe haven to anybody connected to terrorism, prosecuting terrorists and punishing them in a manner that reflects the seriousness of their crimes, and ensuring that their border controls prevent terrorists from moving between states. There is a strong emphasis on international cooperation, with states being required to exchange information in order to provide early alerts of planned acts of terrorism and to aid each other in criminal investigations.[46]

UNSC Resolution 1373 consists largely of language taken from the Terrorism Financing Convention, which for some time lacked sufficient ratification to come into force.[47]

On 29 July 2005, the UNSC unanimously adopted UNSC Resolution 1617,[48] which strongly urged all member states to implement the comprehensive international terrorism financing standards embodied in the FATF recommendations. This call was reiterated more recently by UNSC Resolution 2462, adopted on 28 March 2019.[49]

[44] UNSC Res 1373, UN Doc S/RES/1373 (2001) (28 September 2001).

[45] UNSC Res 1373, UN Doc S/RES/1373 (2001) (28 September 2001), paras 1–3.

[46] UNSC Res 1373, UN Doc S/RES/1373 (2001) (28 September 2001), para 2.

[47] By 1 December 2000, it had been signed by 35 states, of which only two had ratified it. See the discussion above in 2.1. By 11 September 2001, the number of ratifications had increased to four. By early 2004, 132 states had signed the convention and 112 had ratified it.

[48] UNSC Res 1617, UN Doc S/RES/1617 (20 July 2005).

[49] UNSC Res 2462, UN Doc S/RES/2462 (28 March 2019).

2.3 Financial Action Task Force

UN Conventions create binding obligations for ratifying parties while UNSC resolutions in general are considered as binding on members of the United Nations. They tend to be high level instruments and may not provide sufficient detail to ensure appropriate implementation. The FATF was established as a technical body to provide the required level of technical detail within the scope of its mandate.

The FATF is responsible for setting international standards and supporting policies to mitigate the risks of money laundering, terrorism financing and the financing of proliferation of weapons of mass destruction. Formed in 1989, it now comprises 38 members[50] and two regional bodies, representing major financial economies and hubs. Additionally, the FATF has 9 'associate members', comprising FATF-style regional bodies. They are tasked with promoting and enforcing the FATF's mandate on a regional basis. More than 200 countries and jurisdictions are committed to implementing the FATF's standards in their domestic laws, regulations and practices.

The FATF promotes a coordinated global response to organised crime, corruption, terrorism and proliferation by maintaining global standards (known as the Forty Recommendations) and continuous peer review of compliance with the standards through a mutual evaluation process. This process reviews the technical compliance levels of countries with the FATF standards as well as the level of effectiveness of their domestic measures.

The FATF standards support the implementation of the Vienna Convention, Palermo Convention, UNCAC and the Terrorism Financing Convention. The FATF interprets the 'inevitable constructive ambiguity in politically negotiated documents',[51] and thereby facilitate the incorporation of standards into national legal frameworks. The FATF Recommendations are complemented by a set of Interpretive Notes and a Glossary. The FATF also publishes extensive non-binding guidance and best practice publications which are aimed at assisting member states in updating their AML/CTF/CPF frameworks to adequately address significant risks.

In consultation with regional and representative bodies and observer organisations—including the International Monetary Fund, the World Bank and UN agencies—the FATF standards are revised and updated consistently to reflect new and emerging money laundering, terrorism financing and proliferation financing risks to financial markets. Increasingly, the FATF consults publicly on changes to its standards or guidance.

Failure to implement effectively the FATF standards may result in the FATF issuing a public warning, identifying the risks posed to the international financial system. The FATF may place a state with strategic AML/CTF/CPF deficiencies on either the 'grey list' or the 'black list'.[52] In this way, the FATF pressures

[50] The FATF suspended membership of the Russian Federation on 24 February 2023.

[51] UN General Assembly (2019).

[52] De Koker et al. (2023); Goldbarsht (2017).

non-compliant states to speedily address the deficiencies in order to maintain their position in, and access to, the global economy.[53]

2.4 *The Role of Intergovernmental and Regional Bodies*

While the FATF standards are 'soft law', in the sense that they are not legally-binding on states, they support elements of the 'hard law' resolutions of the UNSC. They also enjoy wide-spread political support at a global level.[54] The FATF standards have, for example been endorsed by the UN, by several key regional bodies, including the EU, and by international financial institutions like the International Monetary Fund, and the World Bank. In addition, compliance with the standards is enforced by leveraging the power of the international financial system through the FATF's black and greylisting process. The FATF's standards are therefore viewed and experienced as a particularly hard form of soft law and this has ensured a high level of technical compliance with the standards by countries.[55]

The EU and the FATF operate independently but share a common goal of combating money laundering and the financing of terrorism and proliferation, contributing to the global financial anti-crime framework as assessor bodies through mutual evaluation processes and follow-up procedures.[56] The EU and its bodies provide a good example of regional initiatives in relating to global combating of financial crime.

Europe has demonstrated a long-standing commitment to combating money laundering and terrorism financing in combination with the UNSC and the FATF. In 1991, the then European Economic Community issued Council Directive 91/308/EEC, introducing the term 'money laundering' and requiring member states to prohibit money laundering. Organisations within the financial sector were required to implement measures to adequately identify their customers, maintain appropriate records, and, importantly, report suspicious transactions.

In 2001, the European Parliament issued Council Directive 2001/97/EC, which extended the scope of the EU directives to several predicate and laundering offences. In 2005, the EU issued Directive 2005/60/EC, updating procedures for the adequate identification of customers, known as 'customer due diligence' and adopting a risk-based approach to the gathering of client information and identification materials. In 2015, the EU issued Directive (EU) 2015/849, requiring, for example, the reporting of transactions, outside of a regular business relationship, totalling €10,000 or more and incorporating e-money products under AML/CTF regulations. In 2018, the EU issued Directive (EU) 2018/843, aimed at increasing the transparency of the financial

[53] De Koker and Goldbarsht (2024); Goldbarsht and Harris (2022), p. 530.

[54] SC Res 1617, UN Doc S/RES/1617 (20 July 2005), para. 7.

[55] Goldbarsht (2022), p. 215.

[56] FATF (2019).

sector, including through the requirement for publicly available beneficial ownership registries for companies and limiting the anonymity of virtual currencies and digital wallets, and Directive (EU) 2018/1673, which, for example, introduced stricter penalties for money laundering-related offences and 22 predicate offences.

3 Consideration of Globalisation Challenges

The increase in globalisation and the advancement of technology have eroded the relevance of national borders to the financial services ecosystem. The characteristics of transnational crimes are articulated in the Palermo Convention and specifically include money laundering, terrorism, and bribery as crimes that occur in one jurisdiction but may have extraterritorial effects. The ease and immediacy with which value and funds can be transferred across traditional borders—for example, via virtual assets such as cryptocurrencies—have dramatically heightened the nature of money laundering and terrorism financing as transnational crimes. Indeed, the proliferation of decentralised finance has established a free-flowing currency market without any regard for jurisdictional boundaries, requiring only an internet connection. In this regard, the gatekeeper role traditionally played by large financial institutions—maintaining AML/CTF controls, such as customer due diligence measures—can be evaded by peer-to-peer virtual asset transactions or by using cloud-based decentralised service providers, not tied to a single jurisdiction or (potentially) subject to appropriate regulatory controls.[57] Accordingly, AML/CTF regulatory efforts have shifted some of the regulatory role from individual governments towards the private sector. Whether that will succeed and, if so, at what price, is not clear at the moment. These challenges and approaches have however increased the need for a coordinated approach across the global financial system.

4 Collection

Applying a multidisciplinary lens, the chapters in this collection explore the complex interrelationship between financial crime, technology, law, governance, sustainability and international cooperation in jurisdictions around the world. Each double-blinded peer reviewed chapter offers a unique perspective on combating financial crime in a global context. Together, the chapters comprehensively investigate a range of innovative strategies and emerging trends in addressing financial crime.

In their chapter (*Non-Conviction-Based Asset Recovery in Nigeria: An Additional Tool for Law Enforcement Agencies?*)[58] Peter Sproat, Tony Ward, Jackie Harvey,

[57] De Koker et al. (2022).

[58] Sproat et al. (2024).

Sue Turner, Abdullahi Shehu and Abdullahi Bello dissect Nigeria's approach to combating financial crime, focusing on AML and asset recovery powers granted to established agencies. The chapter highlights the country's struggle to successfully prosecute cases of grand corruption and to recover assets, while kleptocrats exploit legal loopholes to hide stolen wealth offshore. The authors explore the concept of non-conviction-based asset recovery as an innovative approach for Nigerian law enforcement agencies, considering its existence within the legal framework and dissecting the barriers to its effective implementation. Through this analysis, the chapter contributes to the ongoing discourse on refining strategies for financial crime prevention and asset recovery in Nigeria.

Louis de Koker and Pompeu Casanovas examine over compliance and de-risking drawing on experiences in South Africa's banking industry. Their chapter (*'De-risking', De-banking and Denials of Bank Services: An Over-compliance Dilemma?*)[59] identifies the drivers of conservative compliance decisions and reflects on drivers of decisions by banks to terminate customer relationships. Drawing from experiences in a rule-based context, the authors assess the influence of these drivers and their relevance in a risk-based environment. Following a thorough examination, the chapter concludes that the key drivers remain pertinent in a risk-based context and should be considered by regulators seeking to limit de-banking. The authors call for a balanced approach that neutralises over-compliance drivers while maintaining effective compliance measures.

Focusing on New Zealand's property market, Gary Hughes investigates the intersection of money laundering and foreign investment. His chapter (*Money Laundering through Real Estate: Why, and How, New Zealand Has Sought to Regulate It*)[60] sheds light on the challenges involved, particularly in relation to real estate booms. The chapter explores how gatekeeper professions—such as real estate agents, lawyers, and accountants—addressed these challenges through expanded AML regulations. The chapter highlights that, despite regulatory efforts, there remain persistent challenges in the wake of endeavours to regulate the sector by neighbouring Australia.

The nexus of environmental crime, illicit gains, and AML/CTF efforts in Australia is the focus on Ben Scott's chapter (*Environmental Crime and Money Laundering in Australia*).[61] The author examines international and Australian perspectives on environmental crime, including their intersection with AML/CTF practices. The chapter provides an overview of Australia's risk profile and examines recent instances of waste trafficking and water-related crime. By highlighting these issues, the author underscores the need for comprehensive approaches in addressing the financial aspects of environmental crime.

In their chapter (*Giving Shape to Finance and the City of London: Permissive Regulation and Minimalist Governance*),[62] Alex Simpson, Corina Sheerin and

[59] De Koker and Casanovas (2024).

[60] Hughes (2024).

[61] Scott (2024).

[62] Simpson et al. (2024).

Vince Hurley, considers the culture and role of the financial industry of the City of London and its embodiment of capital supremacy and market ideology. Analysing the fallout from the 2008 financial crisis and its implications for systemic harm, the chapter highlights how lenient regulations and corporate greed fostered a culture of risk and aggression. By exploring the ethical implications of this environment, the author focuses on the city's governance and the intricate interplay between finance, regulation, and societal impacts.

Doron Goldbarsht and Hannah Harris explore the governance challenges posed by the FATF Recommendations in addressing money laundering and terrorist financing. Their chapter (*Enhancing Integrity in the Implementation of FATF Recommendations: Robust Governance Frameworks to Combat Financial Crime in an Age of Intergovernmental Rulemaking*)[63] uses Australia as a case study. The authors explore the potential role of an integrity branch of government in upholding strong processes and procedures amid the growing power of intergovernmental organisations such as the FATF. By examining the Australian context, the chapter offers insights into how an integrity branch could enhance legitimacy, maintain good governance, and navigate the evolving landscape of global financial crime.

The United Kingdom combats terrorism financing by implementing global measures from the UN and the FATF. This has pushed financiers to shift away from traditional sources, forcing terrorists to resort to fraud for funding, often going unnoticed. In his chapter (*To Report or Not to Report? An Analysis of the Relationship between Defence against Terrorism Financing Suspicious Activity Reports and Fraud in the United Kingdom*),[64] Nicholas Ryder undertakes a groundbreaking investigation. He identifies a new typology of terrorism financing through fraud. This discovery promises to enhance our comprehension of how terrorists raise and utilise funds, shedding light on the deficiencies within the United Kingdom's counter-fraud and counter-terrorism financing reporting mechanisms.

Ariel Burgess, Rhianna Hamilton and Christian Leuprecht examine the intersection of cryptocurrency-enabled crimes and terrorism. Their chapter (*Terror on the Blockchain: The Emergent Crypto-Crime-Terror Nexus*)[65] challenges the one-size-fits-all approach to addressing these issues. The authors demonstrate how terrorist groups are exploiting cryptocurrency, alongside traditional financial systems, for fundraising and financial transfers. Critiquing the adequacy of existing regulations, the chapter underscores the need for nuanced recommendations that account for the evolving crypto-crime-terror nexus and advocates for effective interagency collaboration to combat these threats.

Focusing on the risks associated with non-fungible tokens (NFTs), Samuel Orchard's chapter (*Money Laundering Risks: The Case of Non-Fungible Tokens: Key Recommendations for Australia*)[66] explores their potential use for money

---

[63] Goldbarsht and Harris (2024).

[64] Nicolas (2024).

[65] Burgess et al. (2024).

[66] Orchard (2024).

laundering and illicit financial activities. The chapter examines Australia's regulatory landscape in relation to NFTs and provides recommendations for reform to address emerging vulnerabilities. By examining the technical and normative aspects of NFTs, the chapter offers a comprehensive understanding of the challenges posed by this evolving digital asset class.

Slobodan Tomic and Elizabeth David-Barrett's chapter (*The Legal Design of Domestic MLA procedures in Southeast Europe: A Comparative Analysis of Serbia, North Macedonia and Bosnia and Herzegovina)*[67] examines the legal design of Mutual Legal Assistance (MLA) procedures in Southeast Europe, specifically in Serbia, North Macedonia, and Bosnia and Herzegovina. They analyse various forms of MLA, including extradition, takeover of prosecution, and execution of foreign judgments. The study assesses how two key components of legal design, institutional discretion, and checks and balances systems, impact MLA policy. While these countries share similarities in their legal frameworks, differences exist in certain forms of MLA, including discretion and the presence of checks and balances.

In their chapter (*Public–Private Collaboration for Combating Cyber Fraud*),[68] Daniel Halpin and Sheri Todd address the growing threat of cyber fraud in Australia. The chapter emphasises the importance of collaboration between government, law enforcement, and the private sector. The authors highlight the escalating losses due to scams and examine the current state of cooperation between various stakeholders. By discussing benefits and barriers to collaborative efforts, the chapter proposes ways to enhance asset recovery for victims and mitigate the impact of fraudulent activities through strengthened cooperation.

Alfio Puglisi's chapter (*Policy Conservatism and the WireCard Scandal*)[69] focuses on the WireCard scandal, investigating Germany's financial policy approach and its impact on innovation and financial crime. The author analyses the historical context and policy decisions that led to regulatory avoidance, revealing the role of regulatory architecture in concealing financial misconduct. By shedding light on this scandal, the chapter underscores the influence of policy conservatism on financial technology and the importance of balancing regulatory innovation with effective oversight.

In their concluding chapter (*Global Standard-Setting on Financial Crime: Navigating Challenges*),[70] Doron Goldbarsht and Louis de Koker identify some of the questions that global standard-setting for financial crime combating faces. These include addressing the plight of jurisdictions that do not have the resources to meet the increasingly sophisticated standards, and navigating the risks of increased geopolitical and economic fragmentation.

As demonstrated in these chapters, a global approach to combating crime is not only a strategic choice but also a necessity. By fostering collaboration, harmonising

[67] Tomic and David-Barrett (2024).

[68] Halpin and Todd (2024).

[69] Puglisi (2024).

[70] Goldbarsht and De Koker (2024).

regulation, and embracing technology, the global community can build a more robust defence against the evolving landscape of criminal activities and ensure the safety and security of its citizens across borders. The challenges to be navigated to ensure effective and efficient action should however not be underestimated.

References

Abass A (2013) International law. Oxford University Press, Oxford

Aust A (2001) Counter-terrorism — a new approach: the International Convention for the Suppression of the Financing of Terrorism. Max Planck UNYB 5:295–296

Barop H (2015) Building the 'opium evil' consensus – the international opium commission of Shanghai. J Modern Eur Hist 13(1):115–137

Boaz G (2002) Defining terrorism: is one man's terrorist another man's freedom fighter? Police Pract Res 3(4):287–304. https://doi.org/10.1080/1561426022000032060

Burgess et al (2024) Chapter 8: Terror on the Blockchain: The Emergent Crypto-Crime-Terror Nexus. In: Goldbarsht D, de Koker L (eds) Financial crime and the law: Navigating Challenges in Different Contexts, Ius Gentium: comparative perspectives on law and justice, vol 116. Springer, Cham

Carter DL (1994) International organized crime: emerging trends in entrepreneurial crime. J Contemp Crim Justice 10(4):239–266

Collins J (2021) Legalising the drug wars: a regulatory history of UN drug control. Cambridge University Press

Convention for the Suppression of Unlawful Seizure of Aircraft (opened for signature 16 December 1970, entered into force 14 October 1971) 860 UNTS 105

Convention for the Suppression of Unlawful Acts Against the Safety of Maritime Navigation (opened for signature 10 March 1988, entered into force 1 March 1992) 1678 UNTS 221

Convention on Offences and Certain Other Acts Committed on Board Aircraft (opened for signature 14 September 1963, entered into force 4 December 1969) 704 UNTS 219

Convention on the Physical Protection of Nuclear Material (opened for signature 26 October 1979, entered into force 8 February 1987) 1456 UNTS 101

Convention on the Prevention and Punishment of Crimes against Internationally Protected Persons, including Diplomatic Agents (opened for signature 14 December 1973, entered into force 20 February 1977) 1035 UNTS 168

Convention on the Suppression of Unlawful Acts Relating to International Civil Aviation (opened for registration 10 September 2010, entered into force 1 July 2018) 3307 UNTS

De Koker L (2024) The FATF's combating of financing of proliferation standards: private sector implementation challenges. In: Goldbarsht D, De Koker L (eds) Financial crime and the law: identifying and mitigating risks. Springer, Cham

de Koker L, Casanovas P (2024) Chapter 3: De-Risking, De banking and Denials of Bank Services: An Over-complince Dilemma. In: Goldbarsht D, de Koker L (eds) Financial crime and the law: Navigating Challenges in Different Contexts, Ius Gentium: comparative perspectives on law and justice, vol 116. Springer, Cham

De Koker L, Goldbarsht D (2024) FATF's risk-based approach: has the pendulum swung too far? In: Goldbarsht D, de Koker L (eds) Financial crime and the law: identifying and mitigating risks. Springer, New York, pp 47-262. https://doi.org/10.1007/978-3-031-59543-1_10

De Koker L, Turkington M (2016) Transnational organised crime and the anti-money laundering regime. In: Hauck P, Peterke S (eds) International law and transnational organised crime. Oxford University Press, Oxford

De Koker L, Ocal T, Casanovas P (2022) Where's Wally? FATF, virtual asset service providers, and the regulatory jurisdictional challenge. In: Goldbarsht D, De Koker L (eds) Financial technology and the law. Law, governance and technology series, vol 47. Springer, Cham, pp 151–183. https://doi.org/10.1007/978-3-030-88036-1_7

De Koker L, Howell J, Morris CN (2023) Consequences of greylisting by the Financial Action Task Force. Risks 11(5):81. https://doi.org/10.3390/risks11050081

Dorn N, South N (1990) Drug markets and law enforcement. The British Journal of Criminology 30(2):171–188

FATF (2013) Effectiveness has moved to the top of the FATF agenda: statement by FATF President Bjørn S. Aamo at the EU Conference 'Fighting Money Laundering and Terrorist Financing – New Framework, Future Challenges'. Brussels, 15 March 2013. http://www.fatf-gafi.org/publications/fatfgeneral/documents/effectivenesshasmovedtothetopofthefatfagenda.html. Accessed 29 Aug 2023

FATF (2019) High level principles and objectives for FATF and FATF-style regional bodies http://www.fatf-gafi.org/publications/fatfgeneral/documents/high-levelprinciplesfortherelationshipbetweenthefatfandthefatf-styleregionalbodies.html. Accessed 29 Aug 2023

Florez CP, Boyce B (1990) Colombian organized crime. Police Stud Int Rev Police Dev 13:81

G8 Justice and Interior Ministers (1998) Virtual meeting on organized crime and terrorist funding backgrounder, 15 December. http://www.g7.utoronto.ca/terrorism/terror98.htm

Goldbarsht D (2017) Who's the legislator anyway? How the FATF's global norms reshape Australian counter terrorist financing laws. Fed Law Rev 45(1):127–151

Goldbarsh D (2020) Global counter-terrorist financing and soft law: multi-layered approaches. Edward Elgar Publishing, Cheltenham, UK

Goldbarsht D (2022) Multi-layered approaches to counter terrorist financing: norm development and compliance. Edward Elgar, Cheltenham

Goldbarsht D, De Koker L (2024) Global standard-setting on financial crime – navigating challenges. In: Goldbarsht D, De Koker L (eds.), Financial crime, law and governance, Ius Gentium: Comparative Perspectives on Law and Justice. Springer, Cham.

Goldbarsht D, De Koker L (2024) Chapter 13: Global Standard-Setting on Financial Crime: Navigating Challenges. In: Goldbarsht D, de Koker L (eds) Financial crime and the law: Navigating Challenges in Different Contexts, Ius Gentium: comparative perspectives on law and justice, vol 116. Springer, Cham

Goldbarsht D, Harris H (2022) Check the balance: is the doctrine of separation of powers sufficient in the context of intergovernmental organisations? A case study of Australia's AML/CTF financing framework. Fed Law Rev 50(4):527–557

Goldbarsht D, Harris (2024) Chapter 6: Enhancing Integrity in the Implementation of FATF Recmmendations: Robust Governance Frameworks to Combat Financial Crime in an Age of Intergovernmental Rulemaking. In: Goldbarsht D, de Koker L (eds) Financial crime and the law: Navigating Challenges in Different Contexts, Ius Gentium: comparative perspectives on law and justice, vol 116. Springer, Cham

Goldbarsht D, Michaelsen C (2017) International legal and quasi-legal approaches to combatting money laundering: an Australian perspective on norm-development. In: van Duyne PC et al (eds) The many faces of crime for profit and ways of tackling it. Wolf Legal Publishers, Oisterwijk

Halpin D, Todd S (2024) Chapter 11: Public-Private Collaboration for Cyber Fraud. In: Goldbarsht D, de Koker L (eds) Financial crime and the law: Navigating Challenges in Different Contexts, Ius Gentium: comparative perspectives on law and justice, vol 116. Springer, Cham

Hughes G (2024) Chapter 3: Money Lanudering thoNon-conviction-BasedAsset Recovery in Nigeria: An Additional Tool for Law Enforcement Agencies. In: Goldbarsht D, de Koker L (eds) Financial crime and the law: Navigating Challenges in Different Contexts, Ius Gentium: comparative perspectives on law and justice, vol 116. Springer, Cham

International Civil Aviation Organization, Convention for the Suppression of Unlawful Acts against the Safety of Civil Aviation (opened for signature 23 September 1971, entered into force 26 January 1973) 974 UNTS 177

International Convention against the Taking of Hostages (opened for signature 17 December 1979, entered into force 3 June 1983) 1316 UNTS 205

International Convention for the Suppression of Terrorist Bombings (opened for signature 15 December 1997, entered into force 23 May 2001) 2149 UNTS 284

Lewis R (1989) European markets in cocaine. Contemp Crises 13(1):35–52

McClean D (1988) Mutual assistance in criminal matters: the Commonwealth initiative. Int Comp Law Q 37(1):177–190

Mittelman JH, Johnston R (1999) Globalization of organized crime, the courtesan state, and the corruption of civil society. Glob Gov 5(1):103–126

Myers WH (1995) The emerging threat of transnational organized crime from the East. Crime Law Soc Change 24:181

Naylor RT (1995) From cold war to crime war: the search for a new "national security" threat. Trans Org Crime 1(4):37–56

Nicolas R (2024) Chapter 7: To Report or Not to Report: An Analysis of the Relationship between Defence against Terrorism Financing Suspicious Activity Reports and Fraud in the United Kingdom. In: Goldbarsht D, de Koker L (eds) Financial crime and the law: Navigating Challenges in Different Contexts, Ius Gentium: comparative perspectives on law and justice, vol 116. Springer, Cham

Orchard S (2024) Chapter 9: Money Laundering Risks: The Case of Non-Fungible Token: Key Recommendations for Australia. In: Goldbarsht D, de Koker L (eds) Financial crime and the law: Navigating Challenges in Different Contexts, Ius Gentium: comparative perspectives on law and justice, vol 116. Springer, Cham

Puglisi A (2024) Chapter 12: Policy Conservatism and the WireCare Scandal. In: Goldbarsht D, de Koker L (eds) Financial crime and the law: Navigating Challenges in Different Contexts, Ius Gentium: comparative perspectives on law and justice, vol 116. Springer, Cham

Roth J, Greenberg D, Wille S (2004) Staff report to the commission: monograph on terrorist financing. National Commission on Terrorist Attacks Upon the United States

Schmid AP (2023) Defining terrorism. International Centre for Counter-Terrorism. https://www.icct.nl/sites/default/files/2023-03/Schmidt%20-%20Defining%20Terrorism_0.pdf

Scott B (2024) Chapter 4: Environmental Crime and Money Laundering in Australia. In: Goldbarsht D, de Koker L (eds) Financial crime and the law: Navigating Challenges in Different Contexts, Ius Gentium: comparative perspectives on law and justice, vol 116. Springer, Cham

Shelley LI (1995) Transnational organized crime: an imminent threat to the nation-state? J Int Aff 48:463–489

Simpson A et al (2024) Chapter 5: Giving Shape to the Finance and the City of London: Permissive Regulation and Minimalist Governance. In: Goldbarsht D, de Koker L (eds) Financial crime and the law: Navigating Challenges in Different Contexts, Ius Gentium: comparative perspectives on law and justice, vol 116. Springer, Cham

Solomon JS (1994) Forming a more secure union: the growing problem of organized crime in Europe as a challenge to national sovereignty. Dickenson J Int Law 13:623

Sproat et al (2024) Chapter 2: Non-conviction-Based Asset Recovery in Nigeria: An Additional Tool for Law Enforcement Agencies. In: Goldbarsht D, de Koker L (eds) Financial crime and the law: Navigating Challenges in Different Contexts, Ius Gentium: comparative perspectives on law and justice, vol 116. Springer, Cham

Tomic S, David-Barrett E (2024) Chapter 10: The Legal Design of Domestic MLA procedures in SoutheastEurope: A Comparative Analysis of Serbia, North Macedonia and Bosnia and Herzegovina. In: Goldbarsht D, de Koker L (eds) Financial crime and the law: Navigating Challenges in Different Contexts, Ius Gentium: comparative perspectives on law and justice, vol 116. Springer, Cham

UN Convention against Corruption (adopted 11 December 2003, entered into force 14 December 2005) 2349 UNTS 41

UN Convention against Illicit Traffic in Narcotic Drugs and Psychotropic Substances (opened for signature 20 December 1988, entered into force 11 November 1990) 1582 UNTS 95

UN Convention against Transnational Organized Crime, opened for signature 12 December 2000, entered into force 29 September 2003) 2225 UNTS 209

UN General Assembly (2019) Promotion and protection of human rights and fundamental freedoms while countering terrorism: note by the Secretary-General. UN Doc A/74/35, 29 August 2019

UN Office on Drugs and Crime (1959) The Shanghai Opium Commission. https://www.unodc.org/unodc/en/data-and-analysis/bulletin/bulletin_1959-01-01_1_page006.html. Accessed 29 August 2023

UN Office on Drugs and Crime (2009) A century of drug control. https://www.unodc.org/documents/data-and-analysis/Studies/100_Years_of_Drug_Control.pdf

UN Treaty Collection (2023) International Convention for the Suppression of the Financing of Terrorism https://treaties.un.org/pages/ViewDetails.aspx?src=IND&mtdsg_no=XVIII-11&chapter=18&clang=_en

United States Department of State (2000) International Convention for Suppression of Financing Terrorism: message from the President of the United States. 3 October 2000. https://www.congress.gov/106/cdoc/tdoc49/CDOC-106tdoc49.pdf. Accessed 29 Aug 2023

Van Duyne PC (1995) The phantom and threat of organized crime. Crime Law Soc Chang 24:341–377

Williams P (1994) Transnational criminal organisations and international security. Survival 36(1): 96–113

Wright H (1909) The International Opium Commission. Am J Int Law 3(4):828–868

Wright H (1912) The International Opium Conference. Am J Int Law 6(4):865–889

Louis de Koker LLB LLM (UFS) LLM (Cantab) LLD (UFS) FSALS, is a Professor and Associate Dean: Research and Industry Engagement at the La Trobe Law School (Australia), an Extraordinary Professor at the Faculty of Law of the University of the Western Cape (South Africa) and a Board member of the Financial Integrity Hub (FIH) at Macquarie Law School. From 2014 to 2019 he was the national program leader of the Law and Policy research program of the Australian government-funded Data to Decisions Cooperative Research Centre. Louis is an expert on anti-money laundering and counterterrorist and proliferation financing, and especially the relationship between financial integrity and financial inclusion policies and regulations. Louis has worked with the Consultative Group to Assist the Poor, the World Bank, the OECD, the Asian Development Bank regulators and financial service providers on the design and implementation of appropriate integrity and inclusion over the past two decades. He has advised on a range of laws and regulations and his research on integrity laws and their impact on financial inclusion has been cited in publications of various international bodies including the World Bank, IMF, the Financial Action Task Force (FATF) and the Basel Committee on Banking Supervision.

Doron Goldbarsht LLB, LLM (HUJI), PhD (UNSW), is the Director of the Financial Integrity Hub (FIH) and an Associate Professor at Macquarie Law School, where he teaches banking and financial crime. He is an expert on anti-money laundering and counter-terrorist financing (AML/CTF) regulations, with expertise in the related fields of compliance and financial innovation, with over 20 years of experience in the field. His recent books *Financial Crime and the Law: Identifying and Mitigating Risks* (Springer 2024, co-edited), *Financial Crime, Law and Governance: Navigating Challenges in Diverse Contexts* (Springer 2024, co-edited), *Financial Technology and the Law: Combating Financial Crime* (Springer, 2022 co-edited), and *Global Counter-Terrorist Financing and Soft Law: Multi-Layered Approaches* (Edward Elgar, 2020), as well as journal and chapter publications, focus on international AML/CTF standards and the mechanisms for their effective implementation and compliance at the national level.

Non-Conviction Based Asset Recovery in Nigeria: An Additional Tool for Law Enforcement Agencies?

Peter Sproat, Tony Ward, Jackie Harvey, Sue Turner, Abdullahi Shehu, and Abdullahi Bello

Abstract Within Nigeria, anti-money laundering and asset recovery powers lie primarily with agencies established under the Corrupt Practices and Related Offences Act 2000, the Economic and Financial Crimes Commission Act 2004 and the Advance Fee Fraud and Other Fraud Related Offences Act 2006. International efforts to recover assets associated with serious and organised crime emanating from Nigeria frequently focus on the proceeds of corruption. Despite the powers of Nigerian authorities and extensive international efforts, relatively few cases of grand corruption are prosecuted successfully, and the value of the assets recovered from financially-motivated criminals are very low in comparison to the value of the proceeds they are said to generate. Kleptocrats and other Politically Exposed Persons have been able to exploit legal loopholes in the criminal courts to avoid or delay conviction, enabling them to conceal massive amounts of stolen wealth in offshore financial centres around the world. The aim of this contribution is to focus on non-conviction based asset recovery and its availability to the Nigerian authorities in their efforts to combat financial crime. Despite extensive debate over the existence of non-conviction based asset recovery-related legislation, we demonstrate such provisions are available, however, we also show that there are many barriers to their effective implementation which may obscure their usefulness.

Chapter drafted by the authors on behalf of the Northumbria Team leading 'Hiding the beneficial owner and the proceeds of corruption' https://ace.globalintegrity.org/projects/benowner/ supported by the FCDO-funded Global Integrity Anti-Corruption Evidence (ACE) Programme. Additional project team members comprise: Sam Sittlington, Alan Doig, Petrus van Duyne, Jan van Koningsveld and Sinan Gonul.

P. Sproat · T. Ward · J. Harvey (✉) · S. Turner · A. Bello
Northumbria Law School, Northumbria University, Newcastle, UK
e-mail: jackie.harvey@northumbria.ac.uk

A. Shehu
ECOWAS Inter-Governmental Action Group against Money Laundering in West Africa (GIABA), Dakar, Senegal

D. Goldbarsht, L. de Koker (eds.), *Financial Crime, Law and Governance*, Ius Gentium: Comparative Perspectives on Law and Justice 116,
https://doi.org/10.1007/978-3-031-59547-9_2

1 Introduction

Nigeria suffers from extensive financially-motivated crime. Indeed, its name is synonymous in certain countries with the advance fee fraud scheme which begins with 'a letter mailed, or e-mailed, from Nigeria [that] offers the recipient the 'opportunity' to share in a percentage of millions of dollars that the author—a self-proclaimed government official—is trying to transfer illegally out of Nigeria'.[1] Perhaps it is this ignoble practice that explains why contemporary Nigeria is a 'significant' centre for financial crime and cyber-crimes according to the U.S. State Department.[2] However, it would not explain Nigeria's ranking as amongst the worst on the African continent for organised criminality and criminal markets. These depressing rankings from the European Union-funded *Africa Organized Crime Index*[3] reflect Nigeria's 'infamous' human trafficking networks; non-renewable resources crimes (including extensive illegal oil bunkering); pervasive drug markets; and its position as a 'major transit hub' for wildlife trafficking.[4] Indeed in terms of the latter, Nigeria is one of only six 'Countries of Concern' for the U.S. State Department—a label that derives from the Department's belief that public and classified material indicate either high-level or systemic government involvement in the trafficking of endangered or threatened species.[5]

The involvement of public officials brings us to the crime of corruption, which is not measured by the *Africa Organized Crime Index,* but which is probably the most important financial, if not organised, crime in Nigeria, whether gauged by the value of the proceeds of crime generated or the impact of the crime on economic development and everyday life. It has been suggested that close to $400 billion was stolen from Nigeria's public accounts from 1960 to 1999 and Sani Abacha alone removed the equivalent of 2–3% of the country's GDP for every year that he was President.[6] Similarly Ibrahim Magu, the then acting chairman of Nigeria's main anti-corruption agency, the Economic and Financial Crimes Commission (EFCC), posited that the money stolen by 32 entities (human and corporate) between 2011 and 2015, was well over ₦1.3 trillion (approximately US$6.5 billion).[7] One wonders if it was

[1] The author of this definition—America's Federal Bureau of Investigation—goes on to note these 'Nigeria Letter or '419' Frauds' violate section 419 of the Nigerian criminal code.

[2] US Department of State, Bureau of International Narcotics and Law Enforcement Affairs (2022), p. 147.

[3] The ENACT Organised Crime Index is a multi-dimensional tool that measures both the level of countries' criminality and their resilience to organised crime. The latest report for 2021 ranks Nigeria with the second highest criminality score of all 54 countries of the continent.

[4] ENACT Organised Crime (2021), pp. 3–4.

[5] US Department of State, Bureau of Oceans and International Environmental and Scientific Affairs (2021).

[6] 'Anti-Corruption Climate Change: it started in Nigeria', Speech by UNODC Executive Director Antonio Maria Costa at sixth National Seminar on Economic Crime, Abuja, 13 November 2007.

[7] https://www.efccnigeria.org/efcc/news/3954, accessed 19/12/2023. Note these news bulletins are now apparently blocked on the EFCC website.

estimates like these that led the then Prime Minister of the United Kingdom David Cameron to describe Nigeria as 'fantastically corrupt'[8] in 2016.

Today, Nigeria ranks 150th of 180 countries in Transparency International's *Corruption Perception Index* 2022 with a score of 24/100.[9] Shehu[10] explained that the manifestations of corruption include crony capitalism, embezzlement, extortion and extortive corruption, facilitation payments, kickbacks, kleptocracy, lobbying/ campaign financing, patronage and regulatory capture, rent-seeking, systemic corruption and state capture, as well as tender and procurement fraud. Further details of such widespread contemporary (and historical) corruption can be found in literature such as the six (overlapping) versions of the Human Environmental Development Agenda's (HEDA) *A Compendium of 100 High Profile Corruption Cases in Nigeria*[11] or *A New Taxonomy for Corruption in Nigeria* by Page.[12] All of the proceeds of public embezzlement constitute monies that could have been used for the economic development of Nigeria.

Grand corruption[13] in Nigeria and elsewhere produces criminal assets that require laundering. Corrupt public officials protect themselves by using their positions to bribe others to ignore the law. Therefore, corruption not only constitutes a cause of money laundering (*i.e.* as a predicate offence), but corruption by politicians and public officials can become a major impediment to the rule of law. Over the years, kleptocrats and other Politically Exposed Persons (PEPs)[14] in Nigeria have been able to conceal massive amounts of stolen wealth in offshore financial centres around the world. In sum, corruption is the main source of proceeds of crime in Nigeria, and the main target for asset recovery in the country.

Despite Nigeria's accession to international treaties such as the United Nations Conventions on corruption, transnational organised crime and drug trafficking, and its adherence to the anti-money laundering (AML) recommendations or standards set by the Financial Action Task Force (FATF) and its regional body GIABA,[15] these, and other, financially motivated crimes continue on a large scale. Notwithstanding Nigerian efforts led by the current administration to combat money laundering, according to the U.S. State Department there have been 'minimal increases in arrests

---

[8] https://www.bbc.co.uk/news/uk-politics-36260193, accessed 19/12/2023.

[9] https://www.transparency.org/en/cpi/2022, accessed 19/12/2023.

[10] Shehu (2015).

[11] The most recent version of this document was produced in November 2022 available at https://hedang.org/compendiums/, accessed 19/12/2023.

[12] Page (2018).

[13] We define Grand Corruption as: '*Serious or large-scale perversion of a person's integrity in the performance of duty or work by inducement, where 'grand' refers to either the financial or person's scale of the seriousness of the activity, which may include the harm it inflicts*' as set out in Harvey et al. (2020).

[14] As may be defined with reference to FATF standards as an individual who is or has been entrusted with a prominent public function.

[15] GIABA is the French acronym for the Inter-Governmental Action Group against Money Laundering in West Africa.

and prosecutions'.[16] Relatively few cases of grand corruption are prosecuted successfully in Nigeria, and, consistent with other countries,[17] the value of the assets recovered from financially motivated criminals is very low in comparison to the value of the proceeds they are said to generate.

This chapter focuses upon a single form of asset recovery, that known as civil forfeiture, civil recovery or non-conviction based (NCB) asset recovery as a means of depriving kleptocrats and PEPs of the proceeds of their crimes and its (debated) legal basis within Nigeria.

The next part of this chapter considers the international legal framework relating to asset recovery, including the UN Conventions and best practice in applying NCB asset recovery in other jurisdictions (Sect. 2).[18] We follow this with an overview of the challenges faced within Nigeria with asset recovery in general, and particularly in connection with the proceeds of corruption (Sect. 3). The chapter then considers in detail the current legal basis for the use of NCB asset recovery and its application within Nigeria (Sect. 4) after which we present a summary of our reflections on whether NCB asset recovery can assist the Nigerian authorities in their efforts to combat financial crime (Sect. 5).

2 International Basis for NCB Asset Recovery

The origin of asset recovery in international treaties is often traced back to the United Nations Convention against Illicit Traffic in Narcotic Drugs and Psychotropic Substances, 1988 (Vienna Convention). This convention required state parties to adopt measures to enable the confiscation of proceeds derived from illicit drug production, trafficking and associated money laundering in order to eliminate the main incentive of those involved in the supply side of the problem. The Vienna Convention focused

[16] US Department of State, Bureau of International Narcotics and Law Enforcement Affairs (2022), p. 149 notes 'The EFCC investigated 2045 cases related to corruption and secured 38 money laundering convictions in 2021'. Referencing the most recent mutual evaluation report (see later), it states: 'The [international] experts also identified a need to improve coordination of money laundering investigations and prosecution of offenders' (p. 148).

[17] See for example, Levi et al. (2017), p. 324; Pol (2020), p. 82.

[18] In the United States, some statutes allow for confiscation on a civil basis, which entails a lower burden of proof, effectively placing an onus on the owner to establish legitimacy once the State has established probable cause or a probability that the property is the proceeds of crime (see 31 USC §5316), but this has also been strongly criticized as violating rights of property and the presumption of innocence. Italy allows for special administrative procedures for forfeiture and confiscation of assets independently of criminal conviction. There, property owned by any person suspected of participating in Mafia-type associations can be confiscated if it cannot be accounted for from legitimate sources or if it can be established by evidence that it derives from illicit sources, if the owner cannot establish legitimate origin (see Law #575 of 31 May 1965, article 2*ter*). The *EFCC Act* of Nigeria addresses this aspect of pecuniary resources in s.19(5) for the accused to prove that it does not represent proceeds of crime.

upon confiscation after a trial in a criminal court and did not specifically mention civil or NCB asset recovery, but it did suggest that parties to the convention 'may consider ensuring that the onus of proof be reversed regarding the lawful origin of alleged proceeds or other property liable to confiscation'.[19] This would mean that, rather than prosecutors being required to prove that the origin of proceeds was unlawful in order to allow confiscation, the individual would be required to prove the origin of the proceeds was lawful in order to avoid such confiscation.

Two years later, the G7 constituted a Financial Action Task Force on Money Laundering (FATF) that produced a Report[20] which would later be viewed as the first version of its standard-setting '40 Recommendations' to prevent money laundering. Amongst other things, the Report recommended that countries adopt measures similar to those set out in the Vienna Convention, to enable their national authorities to confiscate the proceeds of any (but primarily drug) money laundering offences (Recommendation 8). It did not mention NCB asset recovery but encouraged international cooperation on confiscation.

Going further, the United Nations Convention against Transnational Organized Crime 2000 (Palermo Convention) addressed recovery of the proceeds of transnational crime committed by a 'structured group'.[21] It required state parties to adopt measures to enable the identification, tracing, temporary freezing or seizure and permanent confiscation of the proceeds of criminal activities noted in this Convention. Like the Vienna Convention, it encouraged state parties, when requested, to conduct similar asset tracing and recovery activities on behalf of other state parties. It did not specifically name NCB asset recovery; however, Article 12(7) suggests that state parties may wish to 'consider the possibility of requiring that an offender demonstrate the lawful origin of alleged proceeds of crime or other property liable to confiscation' which seems similar to the Vienna Convention's suggestion that state parties consider reversing the onus of proof in regard to asset recovery.

Three years after this, the United Nations Convention Against Corruption (UNCAC, 2003) made the return of assets stolen through corruption a 'fundamental principle of the Convention' and declared that state parties 'shall afford one another the widest measure of cooperation and assistance in this regard.'[22] The Convention devoted Articles 51–59 to asset recovery, and while none of these Articles specifically mentioned NCB asset recovery, Article 54 suggested state parties 'consider' taking measures 'to allow confiscation of such property *without a criminal conviction* in cases in which the offender cannot be prosecuted by reason of death, flight or absence or in other appropriate cases' (our emphasis).

FATF updated its international AML standards in the same year. One of the 40 Recommendations encouraged countries to adopt measures similar to those set

[19] UN Convention Against Illicit Traffic in Narcotic Drugs and Psychotropic Substances (1988), Article 5(7).

[20] Financial Action Task Force (1990).

[21] UN Convention against Transnational Organized Crime (2000), Article 2.

[22] UN Convention Against Corruption (2003), Article 51.

forth in the Vienna and Palermo Conventions to enable their authorities to identify, investigate, restrain and ultimately confiscate the proceeds of money laundering or predicate offences. The preferred first route is to pursue a criminal prosecution, with asset recovery a part of that process. However, FATF also recommended that countries consider adopting measures that allow such proceeds 'to be confiscated without requiring a criminal conviction, or which require an offender to demonstrate the lawful origin of the property alleged to be liable to confiscation.'[23]

The current international AML standards appearing in 2012[24] also referenced the Vienna and Palermo Conventions alongside the 'Terrorist Financing Convention' and repeated ideas about asset recovery. Moreover, these standards used the term 'non-conviction based confiscation' on two occasions. The first was when recommending that countries consider adopting measures that allow proceeds of crime to be confiscated without requiring a criminal conviction, or which required an offender to demonstrate the lawful origin of the property alleged to be liable to confiscation. The second was when recommending that countries should ensure they had the authority to be 'able to respond to requests made on the basis of non-conviction-based confiscation proceedings' and related provisional measures, unless this was inconsistent with the fundamental principles of the domestic law of a state party.

FATF's 2012 best practice paper on confiscation and asset recovery provides eleven pages of guidance on these matters. It restates UNCAC Art.54 that, as a minimum, Recommendation 38 means countries should cooperate with NCB asset recovery requests when the suspect is unknown, unavailable by reason of death, flight, or absence; and that countries should explore ways to recognise the NCB confiscation orders of other countries, even if they do not have the same such orders.[25] FATF suggest also that NCB confiscation would be useful in numerous circumstances, including situations where property is found but: the person is immune from prosecution or there is no realistic chance of bringing a prosecution; a conviction could not be obtained for procedural or technical reasons (*e.g.* the statute of limitations is exceeded); the person has already been acquitted; or where there is insufficient admissible evidence to meet the burden of proof.[26]

The World Bank[27] has argued that ability to instigate civil proceedings for asset recovery should be 'affirmatively stated in the law', either incorporated within existing criminal codes or as part of a separate piece of legislation. The most recent edition of this report[28] noted the complexity of asset recovery particularly in states where there is widespread corruption, thus recommending consideration of all 'legal options'. In such circumstances, UNCAC's Intergovernmental Group on Asset

---

[23] FATF (2003), Recommendation 3.

[24] FATF (2012).

[25] FATF (2012), p. 6.

[26] *ibid.*, p. 6.

[27] Greenberg et al. (2009), p. 29.

[28] Brun et al. (2021), p. 2.

Recovery (IGGAR) noted, NCB asset recovery is effective in 'divesting the corrupt of the proceeds of their crimes and restoring those funds to the victim state' especially where assets have been moved or are located offshore. Indeed, where the corrupt are government officials, it may be the only available tool.[29] Despite this, the IGGAR also note that NCB asset recovery does not necessarily provide a simpler alternative to criminal investigation and prosecution, as it also requires investment in capacity to understand and unravel (often complex) financial structures and arrangements.

The fact that investigations can span multiple jurisdictions gives rise to additional potential barriers to the use of NCB asset recovery, which have been highlighted by the NGO Basel Institute on Governance.[30] For example, in some circumstances a decision in one jurisdiction to forego criminal action in favour of civil remedies, including NCB asset recovery, may have implications on another jurisdiction wishing to undertake criminal action on 'related matters'. Another barrier is that without appropriate non-conviction legislation, destination countries may not be able to respond to legal assistance requests. Further, it is recognised that even if both jurisdictions have in place appropriate NCB recovery legislation, the standards of proof can vary[31] making it difficult for the courts to enforce others' judicial orders.

Countries that are asked to enforce foreign NCB confiscation orders but do not have any NCB provision themselves may regard such a request as beyond the scope of co-operation in criminal matters under UNCAC.[32] Some such jurisdictions, however, are willing to interpret the 'essence and purpose' of the requesting country's civil or administrative proceedings widely enough to 'create an analogy to [their] own domestic proceedings'.[33]

In sum, despite some issues, NCB provision has been promoted as a means of combatting financially motivated crime, including corruption, through denial of economic gain. It thus plays a role in strengthening the international framework for prevention of money laundering, which alongside monitoring of PEPs (FATF's Recommendation 12) removes opportunity for or benefits of corruption.[34]

---

[29] Open-ended Intergovernmental Working Group on Asset Recovery (2019), p. 3.

[30] International Centre for Asset Recovery (n.d.), pp. 44–45.

[31] As between common law 'on a balance of probabilities' and civil law jurisdictions that usually rely on 'beyond a reasonable doubt'.

[32] Open-ended IGWG on Asset Recovery (2019), p. 9.

[33] Open-ended IGWG on Asset Recovery (2019), p. 9.

[34] Shehu (2014), p. 190.

3 Challenges with Asset Recovery in Nigeria

Having previously noted that the first choice of sanction should be criminal prosecution with criminal asset forfeiture, in common with other jurisdictions, Nigeria's legal system contains both civil and criminal law provisions. This means that, if a criminal prosecution in respect of assets derived from corruption cannot be pursued or fails, the alternative of NCB asset recovery can be considered.[35] There is debate in Nigeria, however, surrounding: (a) the very existence of relevant NCB asset recovery-related legislation; and (b) asset recovery more generally.

3.1 Legislative Basis for NCB Asset Recovery in Nigeria

Setting aside ethical criticism of the use of civil recovery in any criminal justice system and the potential for any government to use it (or any other anti-corruption tools) for partisan purposes, there remains a fundamental debate regarding whether provision allowing for NCB asset recovery exists within Nigeria's legal system. Legal scholars would normally be clear about the existence of such a distinctive power in law, and academic debate would usually focus upon legal minutiae such as its limitation, or on the consequences of using the power in practice. However, a review of the literature reveals there are academics (albeit not legal scholars) who imply or suggest NCB asset recovery does not exist in Nigeria and who propose its enactment.[36] Indeed, even the Nigerian government itself appears to have stated this on at least one occasion. In answer to a question[37] about asset recovery in a UN review of its implementation of certain articles of UNCAC, the official response was: 'The Proceeds of Crime Bill is currently before the National Assembly. When passed into law it will enable Non-Conviction-Based Asset Forfeiture and also provide a harmonized framework for managing recovered assets.'[38]

In complete contrast, Waziri-Azi noted that 'the assets of some ... high-profile individuals have already been recovered through the increased use of non-conviction based forfeiture orders'[39] going onto conclude that:

> Contrary to public opinion, non-conviction based forfeiture mechanisms, have always been provided for in Nigerian laws like the Corrupt Practices and Other Related Offences Act

[35] *ibid.* p. 196.

[36] Nwoba and Nwokwu (2018); Omoroghomwan (2018); Shehu (2014), p. 193 writes of a 'lack of comprehensive civil forfeiture provisions in Nigeria'.

[37] UN Office on Drugs and Crime (2019), p. 17. In answer to the question 'Please describe (cite and summarize) the measures/steps, if any, your country needs to take, together with the related time frame, to ensure full compliance with the chapters of the Convention that are under review, and specifically indicate to which articles of the Convention such measures would relate.'

[38] *ibid*, p.17.

[39] Waziri-Azi (2018), p. 67.

(2000), Advanced Fee Fraud and Other Fraud Related Offences Act (2006), Failed Banks (Recovery of Debts) and Financial Malpractices in Banks, Code of Conduct Bureau and Tribunal Act, Economic and Financial Crimes Commission (Establishment) Act (2004), Administration of Criminal Justice Act (2015), National Drug Law Enforcement Agency Act.[40]

As we will discuss, relevant legislative provisions do exist and have developed over time. However, there are many barriers to their effective implementation which may obscure their existence and usefulness.

3.2 *Asset Recovery Generally in Nigeria*

The legislative framework establishing the Nigerian law enforcement agencies (LEAs) provides them with a wide range of powers to identify, track and seize assets, and the ability to seek orders from the court to freeze, confiscate and forfeit the proceeds of crime. For example, powers of criminal forfeiture (sometimes regarded as a more effective method of asset recovery because of its preventative nature) are available through s.7(1)(b) of the Economic and Financial Crimes Commission (EFCC) Act (2004). This Act also makes the EFCC the coordinating agency for the enforcement of the provisions of various legislative acts related to economic crime.[41] Criminalisation not only allows national authorities to detect, prosecute and deter offences but also provides the legal basis for international cooperation among LEAs and judicial and administrative authorities. S.7(1)(b) EFCC Act also states that the 'Commission has power to cause investigations to be conducted into the properties of any person if it appears to the Commission that the person's lifestyle and extent of the properties are not justified by his source of income'. This section therefore grants the EFCC proactive powers to investigate any person (not just those convicted of a criminal offence), and in particular any PEP, who appears to be 'living beyond their means'.[42] Significantly, although 'it is not legally possible to enforce a foreign non-conviction-based confiscation order in Nigeria',[43] Nigeria has benefitted from the recovery of stolen assets that have been found in other jurisdictions that have NCB asset recovery provisions within their

[40] *ibid*, p. 76 Sections 37(1), 46, 47(1), 48(1); Sections 7, 17; Section 3(1); Section 23(2)(c); Sections 20, 21, 25; Sections 333, 334; Section 31 respectively.

[41] Variously The Money Laundering (Prohibition) Act 2011 (replaced by the Money Laundering (Prevention and Prohibition) Act 2022); The Advance Fee Fraud and Other Related Offences Act 1995; The Failed Banks (Recovery of Debt and Financial Mal-Practices in Banks) Act, as amended; The Banks and Other Financial Institutions Act 1991, as amended: Miscellaneous Offences Act; and other laws or regulations relating to economic and financial crimes, including the Criminal Code and Penal Code.

[42] Shehu (2014), p. 90.

[43] GIABA (2021), p. 268.

legislation.[44] More usually, however, international recovery efforts involve a range of sanctions and take time and commitment as illustrated in the following two high-profile cases:

3.2.1 The Abacha Case

General Sani Abacha was President of Nigeria from 1993 to 1998. During this period, he is alleged to have embezzled billions of US dollars with the proceeds laundered through bank accounts in several offshore financial centres, including Switzerland. The incoming President Obasanjo (1999–2007) sought assistance from a Swiss legal firm to assist with a request for MLA which successfully resulted in a general freezing order over Abacha's assets. As there was no available 'final forfeiture judgement in the Nigerian courts' at this time, 'the Swiss courts legally applied the organized crime provisions of the (then) Art 59 Swiss Criminal Code which mandated the confiscation of 'all assets, which are subject to the power of disposal of a criminal organization'. Deeming the Abacha clan 'a criminal organization', the courts declared the assets would be confiscated.[45] The World Bank was brought in to monitor the repatriation of funds totalling $1 billion which took place in a series of tranches between 2005 and 2017.[46]

3.2.2 The Ibori Case

James Ibori, former Governor of Delta State (1999–2007) used a network of associates and family members to move stolen funds through a series of companies located in offshore jurisdictions. He was charged with embezzlement in the Nigerian courts but the case was thrown out in 2009. However, in 2012 Ibori pleaded guilty in a London court to conspiracy to defraud the Nigerian state and to money laundering and was sentenced to a 13-year prison sentence. More recently in January 2020, the UK launched a fresh attempt to confiscate assets totalling £178 m.[47] As reported by Spotlight on Corruption[48] the confiscation process in the UK that commenced in 2007 has been far from straightforward. In March 2021 the UK returned £4.2 m ($5.8 m) to the Nigerian authorities, being the proceeds recovered from family members and from an associate who were separately convicted in the UK of

---

[44]Tope Adebayo (n.d.).

[45]Shehu (2014), p. 191.

[46]World Bank Monitoring of Repatriated Abacha Funds, December 4, 2017. https://www.worldbank.org/en/news/factsheet/2017/12/04/world-bank-monitoring-of-repatriated-abacha-funds, accessed 19/12/2023.

[47]Harvey et al. (2021).

[48]Spotlight on Corruption *James Ibori: Confiscating the corrupt assets of a Nigerian Governor* 25th March 2021 available at https://www.spotlightcorruption.org/james-ibori-confiscating-the-corrupt-assets-of-a-nigerian-governor/, accessed 19/12/2023.

money laundering. The return took place under a 2016 bilateral memorandum of understanding that required the proceeds to be used for development projects.[49]

International cooperation notwithstanding, the legal and institutional framework for asset recovery in Nigeria continues to evolve,[50] and the most recent evaluation of its effectiveness was carried out in the autumn of 2019 (published in the summer of 2021) by GIABA.[51] The two principal FATF Recommendations are 4 (measures to identify, trace and evaluate property which is subject to confiscation) and 38 (authority to take expeditious action in response to requests by foreign countries to identify property which may be subject to confiscation).[52] The 2021 evaluation report considered that Nigeria had addressed the deficiencies highlighted in its 2008 mutual evaluation and from a perspective of technical legal compliance was now compliant with Recommendation 4. It was found to be largely compliant with Recommendation 38[53] (partially compliant in 2008), so positive progress has been made in both cases.

The 2008 evaluation had stated that, in relation to Recommendation 38, Nigeria did not have 'comprehensive legislation on international cooperation' but that it had been able to negotiate multilateral and bilateral agreements on MLAs[54] that included asset restraint and confiscation. The most recent evaluation noted that the country still failed to 'demonstrate effective legal and operational frameworks for seeking international cooperation including the recovery and repatriation of assets' but that the enactment of the Mutual Legal Assistance in Criminal Matters Act, 2019 (MLACMA) had the objective of streamlining these processes.[55]

While significant efforts have been made in this direction and some assets have been seized, confiscated, or forfeited to government, there are problems arising from the management of these assets both while under interim forfeiture after seizure and when finally forfeited after due process. Over the years, there has been concern

---

[49] *James Ibori: UK returns $5.8m stolen by ex-governor to Nigeria* BBC news 18th May 2021 available at https://www.bbc.co.uk/news/world-africa-57161645, accessed 19/12/2023.

[50] GIABA (2008), on the FATF Recommendation 3 dealing with confiscation, Nigeria was found partially compliant. The report identified 'Significant legal gaps in the confiscation regime' (p.57). The reasons included the 'lack of definition of important concepts such as freezing, seizure, forfeiture and confiscation as well as inconsistency in the laws relating to freezing of assets; Insufficient legal protection for bona fide third parties; Absence of rules to manage and dispose of confiscated properties; and Weak coordination in the AML/CFT regime' (p. 57).

[51] GIABA (2021). For a fuller discussion of the results of this evaluation see Harvey et al. (2024). The mutual evaluation has been updated by the first enhanced follow up report, GIABA (2022).

[52] FATF (2012), p. 1.

[53] GIABA (2021), p. 268: 'Most requirements are met with exception of not having legal measures in place for the enforcement of foreign non-conviction-based confiscation orders'.

[54] GIABA (2008), p. 171. Also see Global Forum for Asset Recovery (2019), p. 10.

[55] GIABA (2021), p. 3.

because of fears of dissipation,[56] a lack of transparency[57] and chaotic management.[58] According to Nigeria's Open Government Partnership,[59] a 'lack of transparency has been exacerbated by a fragmented and inefficient legal and institutional framework' resulting in a failed process for asset identification, recovery, management and disposal (if required). Interestingly, the LEAs themselves seem to agree on the need for a strategy and / or mechanism for the management of such assets.[60]

Frustrated with the slow progress on asset recovery, President Buhari (2015–2023) had signed Executive Order No 6 (2018) on the Preservation of Suspicious Assets and Related Schedules.[61] This order appears to have been prompted by the frequent adjournment of cases due to perceived incompetence of public prosecutors, congested dockets of the courts, and dilatory tactics of defence counsels. However, the most frequent barrier is the continued abuse of interlocutory appeals which has frustrated attempts to expedite trial procedures in the Federal and State High Courts.[62] The Executive Order is mainly concerned with the provision of restraint pending criminal prosecution in order to prevent asset dissipation and was implemented as a 'stop-gap' for the long delayed (and now enacted) proceeds of crime legislation described below.[63] The order did not purport to create new powers of forfeiture but rather instructed the relevant authorities, under the direction of the Attorney General (AG), to use 'all available lawful or statutory means, including seeking the appropriate Order(s) of Court' (s.1(a)).

The following year, the Nigerian Government gazetted the new Asset Tracing, Recovery and Management Regulations, 2019, (the Regulations) providing a framework for asset management.[64] These stated that the Office of the AG would be responsible for the management of assets, regardless of whether they had been

---

[56] See for example Transparency International Blog Returning Nigerians' stolen millions August third 2018: https://www.transparency.org/news/feature/returning_nigerians_stolen_millions, accessed 19/12/2023.

[57] Also see current investigation into the suspended acting Chairman of the EFCC https://nairametrics.com/2020/07/11/magu-probe-new-facts-suggest-case-is-about-re-looting-of-previously-stolen-funds/, accessed 19/12/2023.

[58] Global Forum for Asset Recovery (2019), p. 7.

[59] https://www.opengovpartnership.org/members/nigeria/commitments/NG0008/, accessed 19/12/2023.

[60] Harvey et al. (2021), p. 52. During a public hearing on the recovery and management of looted funds at the House of Representatives in May 2021, Nigeria's Attorney General and Minister of Justice, Abubakar Malami, indicated that the problems associated with the management of recovered assets were attributable to the absence and/or delay in enacting the POCA.

[61] For details refer to https://www.proshareng.com/news/Doing-Business-in-Nigeria/Executive-Order-No.-6-On-Preservation-Of/40687#, accessed 19/12/2023.

[62] Harvey et al. (2020), p. 14.

[63] Also see Famsville Solicitors: President of Nigeria Signs Executive Order 6 of 2018 on the Preservation of Assets Connected With Serious Corruption and Other Relevant Offences, July sixth 2018, available from https://www.lexology.com/library/detail.aspx?g=e83d7e39-2a32-42e0-a61b-d5d23c441b27, accessed 19/12/2023.

[64] Replacing the Proceeds of Crimes Regulation, 2012.

restrained or permanently forfeited, and for the coordination of all asset recovery work being conducted by Nigeria's LEAs irrespective of whether the tracing and investigating took place within or outside of Nigeria.[65] In September 2020, the Ministry of Justice established a Central Database for Asset Recovery and Management for the storage of records of all recovered assets within and outside Nigeria, including for NCB forfeiture. Part 3, s.11(1–3) of the Regulations requires proceeds from the disposal of permanently forfeited assets to be paid into a designated 'Federal Government of Nigeria Asset Recovery Account' held at the Central Bank. S.11(4–6) sets out the time periods for firstly the AG informing the Minister for Finance of funds being paid into the account (15 days); and for the Minister to transfer such proceeds into the Consolidated Revenue Account (30 days); or to other tiers of government (45 days). S.1(7) provides for the Federal Government to receive at least 30% of the proceeds of asset recovered for other State and Local Governments.[66]

The explanatory note to the Regulations states that the provisions are in line with international best practice for management and disposal of assets in a transparent manner. As we were unable to locate any asset recovery database,[67] it is not clear if data (part 2 (s.3(c-e))) are being shared either within government agencies or (better) located in the public domain, or if there are plans for such sharing. Anecdotally, we heard that these Regulations were not being followed by LEAs and that a high court had declared the Regulations null and void.

It has been observed that the funds recovered internationally were as a result of the effort and investigations undertaken by agencies in external countries and not as a result of the action of domestic agencies.[68] Consistent with our observations, the mutual evaluation report notes that it is difficult to measure the volume of assets that have been recovered via forfeiture as there is little accessible in the way of a public record nor is there a central database of recovered proceeds.[69] Those asset recoveries that have been publicised have been vastly inflated for the benefit of the news media.[70]

A Proceeds of Crime Bill had been pending for over a decade, moving back and forth from the executive to the legislature, due to its political sensitivity and

[65]GIABA (2021), p. 95 notes that at the time the evaluation took place the focus of the Asset Recovery and Management Unit of the Ministry of Justice (ARMU) was on 'the confiscation, forfeiture, and management of foreign assets'.

[66]However, following the return of £4.2 million by the British government as part of the Ibori investigation, the AG said the money would be used for federal infrastructure development. This caused considerable aggravation, as following the precedence in the Dariye case, it was presumed that the proceeds would be given to the victim state, Delta State.

[67]Harvey et al. (2021) noted the existence of very basic charts, however, they no longer appear accessible.

[68]GIABA (2021), p. 3.

[69]*ibid*, p.96.

[70]van Duyne and Harvey (2022) also see Global Forum for Asset Recovery (2019), p. 8.

objections from the LEAs who feared dilution of their own powers.[71] The Bill sought to address the deficiencies inherent in the Nigerian asset recovery armoury already discussed and was eventually enacted as the Proceeds of Crime Recovery and Management (PCRM) Act (2022). While somewhat watered down from its original form,[72] the PCRM Act aims to construct an 'effective legal and institutional framework' for the recovery and management of the proceeds of crime or from benefits derived from unlawful activities and to harmonise and consolidate existing legislative provisions on their recovery. This latter objective is achieved through s.77 with respect to the management of finally forfeited assets which affords primacy of this PCRM Act over other relevant laws.

At its core are NCB confiscation powers, and the creation of individual Proceeds of Crime Management Directorates within existing LEAs. The relevant organisations will have the power to implement, enforce and duly administer the provisions of the Act in connection with asset recovery and management. The Act aims to 'strengthen collaboration' to improve criminal asset recovery specifically via 'non-conviction based forfeiture proceedings' (s.1(f)). Powers vested with individual organisations with respect to investigation, identification, tracing and recovery of the proceeds of unlawful activities appear to remain intact although each must also comply with the provisions of this Act (s.54). The Directorates must establish and maintain statistics on amounts recovered and managed (s.3(f)) with proceeds to be paid into a single account at the Central Bank—the Confiscated and Forfeited Properties Account (s.68(1)). This account is to be managed 'by the head of the relevant organisation' with reports provided to the Minister of Finance (s.68(2)). It also provides for the Federal High Court to designate special courts to hear and determine all cases under the Act (s.73(2)).[73]

There is evidence to support the fact that PEPs and other powerful officials in Nigeria have escaped prosecution and, as already mentioned, even when a case is brought to court there may be frequent delays, with other cases being thrown out for poorly prepared evidence.[74] This is where NCB forfeiture may prove useful as a potential additional tool, as it does not rely on first securing a criminal conviction. Nevertheless, while the PCRM Act aims to streamline asset recovery initiatives in Nigeria, there is no guarantee that efforts to use the powers contained in this Act will avoid existing systemic problems that undermine the effectiveness of implementation on the ground.

[71] Global Forum for Asset Recovery (2019), p. 4.

[72] The provision for Unexplained Wealth Orders has been removed as has the proposed creation of a single assets recovery agency.

[73] This is not new, Harvey et al. (2020), p. 44–45 discussed the need for specialist courts with the ICPC and noted that the Supreme Court in Abuja during the 2017/18 session directed their creation for hearing cases of corruption.

[74] Shehu (2014), p. 192. Also see Harvey et al. (2021).

4 NCB Asset Recovery in Practice

As discussed above, in Nigeria, AML and asset recovery powers lie primarily with agencies established under the EFCC Act. The earlier Corrupt Practices and Related Offences Act 2000 (CPA)[75] and the Advance Fee Fraud and Other Fraud Related Offences Act 2006 (AFF Act) contain additional provisions. The provisions are complex in their drafting and, in practice, overlap in their reach. Their use is varied and, at times, inconsistent. We will consider the EFCC Act and the CPA together as there is considerable overlap between them.

The CPA includes two provisions which allow limited forms of NCB forfeiture, although both are drafted in perplexing terms.[76] Sect. 47(1) is particularly puzzling:

> In any prosecution for an offence under this Act, the court shall make an order for the forfeiture of any property which is proved to be the subject-matter of the offence or to have been used in the commission of the offence where –
>
> (a) the offence is proved against the accused; or
> (b) the offence is not proved against the accused but the court is satisfied:
>
> (i) that the accused is not the true and lawful owner of such property; and
> (ii) that no other person is entitled to the property as a purchaser in good faith for valuable consideration.

The effect of subsection (b) is that the court is not merely authorised, but required, to order forfeiture in circumstances where the property in question is proved to be the subject-matter of, or used in, the offence charged, and yet that offence has not been proved against the accused. However, how can the link between the property and the offence be proved without proving the offence and identifying the offender? One possibility is that although the prosecution proves the relevant matters to the satisfaction of the judge, the trial fails to reach a verdict because, for example, the accused dies or absconds (similar in scope to Article 54 UNCAC). Another is that it might be clear that the alleged offence took place, despite the accused being acquitted of being a party to it (for example, they might innocently have received the property as a gift from the true culprit). It seems plausible, however, that the intention of the section is to create a form of interim forfeiture of property connected to the *alleged* offence, pending the outcome of the trial.[77] This reading is supported by the cross-heading of the section: 'Forfeiture of property upon prosecution for an offence'. Nigerian principles of statutory interpretation (like those in English law)[78]

---

[75] This Act was purportedly repealed by the Corrupt Practices Act 2003, but the 2003 Act was annulled, so the 2000 Act remains valid: *Nwankwoala v FRN* (2018) LPELR-43891(SC). Also See *the ICPC Act at 20! – Overview of the Act*, Independent Corrupt Practices & Other Related Offences Commission, June 13th, 2020 available at https://icpc.gov.ng/2020/06/13/the-icpc-act-at-20-overview-of-the-act/, accessed 19/12/2023.

[76] Page (2021) p.24 notes that vague and ambiguous drafting is a characteristic of Nigeria's anti-corruption laws.

[77] *ibid*, p. 15, Page interprets s.47 in this way, but does not explain his interpretation.

[78] *R v Montila* [2004] UKHL 50 [33-8] (coincidentally, a case on money laundering).

allow cross-headings to be taken into account where the wording is ambiguous.[79] If this reading is correct then s.47(1)(b) of the CPA has been largely superseded by the more clearly worded power of interim forfeiture contained in the EFCC Act at s.29.

S.29 applies to property that has been seized by the EFCC, which the EFCC is required to do under s.28 whenever a person is arrested under the EFCC Act. S.29 avoids the perplexing requirement for 'proof' under the CPA, and instead requires only '*prima facie* evidence that the property concerned is liable to forfeiture'. This has been defined in a series of Nigerian cases as evidence which if uncontradicted and believed will be sufficient to prove the offence.[80]

The EFCC Act (s.33) also provides more clearly than the CPA for the forfeiture of a defendant's property following an acquittal. When an accused is acquitted or discharged the court may either revoke or confirm the forfeiture of assets, according to what 'is considered just, appropriate or reasonable in the circumstances' (s.33(1)). S.33(2) specifically provides that forfeiture may be confirmed where the accused is discharged on 'merely technical grounds'. The availability of these powers since 2004 probably explains why, so far as we can discover, the ambiguous s.47 CPA has been little used.

The constitutionality of interim forfeiture has been challenged in several cases. In Nwaigwe *v FRN*[81] the Court of Appeal upheld such a challenge and ruled that s.29 EFCC Act was an unconstitutional violation of the presumption of innocence. In subsequent cases, however, the constitutionality of s.29 has been upheld.[82] The constitution expressly provides that forfeiture, whether by civil or criminal proceedings, does not violate the right to property (art 44(2)(b)), and interim forfeiture, as a measure to prevent assets from being dissipated prior to trial, can easily be defended against the charge that it violates the presumption of innocence.[83] A more difficult issue, however, is whether the presumption of innocence is violated by the power to confirm forfeiture following acquittal on the simple ground that it is 'appropriate, just or reasonable' to do so (s.33(1) EFCC Act). We have not been able to find a case which decides this point. Problems about the compatibility of forfeiture powers with the presumption of innocence are by no means unique to Nigeria.[84]

S.48 CPA deals with property that has been seized by the Independent Corrupt Practices Commission (ICPC) during an investigation, where that investigation does not result in prosecution or conviction. It allows the Chair of the ICPC to apply to the

[79]National Judicial Institute, Revisiting the Rules of Statutory Interpretation: Best Practices https://nji.gov.ng/wp-content/uploads/2019/03/REVISITING-THE-RULES-_OF-STATUTORY-INTERPRETATION-_BEST-PRACTICES.pdf accessed 29/04/2021.

[80]Tijani (2011), p. 129.

[81](2009) 16 NWLR (Pt. 1166) 169, discussed by Tope Adebayo, pp. 4–5.

[82]Dangabar v FRN (2012) LPELR-19732 (CA); FRN v Ikedinwa (2013) LPELR-21120(CA). Nwaigwe was subsequently disapproved by the Supreme Court in Jonathan v FRN.

[83]Tijani (2011), pp. 135–136.

[84]See for example Mahmutaj (2009).

High Court, within 12 months of the date of the seizure, for the property to be forfeited on the ground that it has been obtained in connection with, or as a result of, an offence under the Act.

It appears that under s.48(3) CPA, the initial burden of satisfying the court that the property was used in, or the subject-matter of, an offence rests (in accordance with common-law principles) on the ICPC. Under S.138(1) Evidence Act 2011, if the person alleged to have committed a crime is a party to the proceedings, the allegation must be proved beyond a reasonable doubt. This will not apply, however, where the alleged offender is not a party, for example because they have fled the country. Once the ICPC proves the crime and its connection with the property, the onus shifts to the person claiming the property to 'show cause' why it should not be forfeited (*e.g.* because they were not the offender and purchased the property in good faith).

One case where s.48 CPA was successfully used against an alleged embezzler involved the forfeiture of properties worth ₦124.5 million (about US$346,000) by a civil servant, Daniel Obah, who was alleged to have purchased them with money fraudulently drawn from his ministry's account.[85] Reports of the case do not say whether the criminal activity was proved to the criminal standard as the Evidence Act 2011 requires. Even assuming that civil courts strictly adhere to the criminal standard of proof, civil proceedings might be attractive as a way of avoiding the delaying tactics common in criminal proceedings.

The clearest provision for NCB forfeiture is to be found in the AFF Act at s.17[86]:

> Where ... any property in the possession of any person, body corporate or financial institution is reasonably suspected to be proceeds of some unlawful activity under this Act, the Money Laundering Act of 2004, the Economic and Financial Crimes Commission Act of 2004 or any other law enforceable under the Economic and Financial Crime Commission Act of 2004, the High Court shall upon application made by the Commission...upon being reasonably satisfied that such property is ...the proceeds of unlawful activity ... make an order that the property or the proceeds from the sale of such property be forfeited to the Federal Government of Nigeria.

As under the CPA, the court has to give notice inviting anyone with a claim to the property to come forward. The notice period is normally 14 days, but this can be varied by the High Court (s.17(4) AFF Act). Section 17(6) expressly provides that forfeiture under the section shall not be based on conviction. In *Ogungbeje v EFCC*,[87] the Court of Appeal stated emphatically:

> The sum total of the provisions of the law is that there is non-conviction based forfeiture of properties suspected to be derived from proceeds of crime, the submission by learned Counsel that there must be investigation, trial and conviction before an order of forfeiture is made by the Court is therefore a gross misconception and without foundation in law.[88]

[85] ICPC News Release, 15 Apr 2019; 'Civil Servant Loses N124.5 m Property to FG', *Guardian* (Nigeria) 16 Apr 2019.

[86] NCB forfeiture under s.17 of the Act is applicable in matters regarding unclaimed property and/or proceeds of unlawful activity under the Acts listed.

[87] (2018) LPELR-45317(CA).

[88] *ibid.*, p. 37.

This section is much easier to interpret and to apply than either s.47 or s.48 of the CPA. It applies to a wider range of offences and to any property that is the 'proceeds of unlawful activity', rather than being the subject matter of, or used in, a specific offence. Rather than requiring the court to be 'satisfied' of the criminal connections of the property, it requires only that it be *reasonably* satisfied. The term 'reasonably satisfied' is defined by the Evidence Act 2011 s.33(2) as meaning that the party bearing the burden of proof has adduced sufficient evidence to satisfy the court on the balance of probabilities in the absence of any contrary evidence.

The question whether such a low standard of proof is compatible with the presumption of innocence (Constitution of Nigeria art, 36.5) or with the Evidence Act 2011 s.135(1), which requires a court to apply the criminal standard of proof where the commission of a crime by a party to civil proceedings is 'directly in issue' was addressed by the Court of Appeal in *Jonathan v FRN.*[89] Drawing on case law from various jurisdictions, but primarily the US, the Court held in this case that s.17 AFF Act created an '*in rem*' procedure, based 'on the legal fiction that the property and not the owner has contravened the law', and the presumption of innocence had no place in such proceedings.[90] The effect of s.17 was to place the burden on the appellant (the wife of former President Jonathan) to prove that the funds in question were *not* the proceeds of unlawful activities, 'since it is the Appellant who is asserting that the funds came from legitimate source or origin'.[91]

The AFF Act creates a wide-ranging power of civil forfeiture wherever the EFCC can make out a *prima facie* case that assets are the proceeds of corruption or financial crime. At the time of the 2008 GIABA report, however, civil forfeiture appears to have been relatively little used. It is since 2015, according to Page, that its use has significantly increased, being viewed by prosecutors as a 'creative' response to the inefficiency of the criminal courts.[92] This does not explain why more recent academic contributions, discussed earlier, give the impression that NCB forfeiture does not exist. We can only ascribe this to the difficulty for scholars who are not lawyers[93] (and even those who are) of finding up-to-date and intelligible information about this area of law. In contrast to the earlier mutual evaluation of 2008, the 2021 report draws on s.17 AFF Act as providing evidence that there is a legal basis to apply NCB forfeiture where it has not been possible 'for justifiable reasons' to secure a money laundering conviction. However, they also note that the country did not show that it had followed this route,[94] which suggests that NCB asset recovery remains uncommon in Nigeria.

---

[89] (2018) LPELR-43505(CA).

[90] *Ibid.*, pp. 31–32. For a critical account of *in rem* proceedings as legal fiction see Barnet (2001).

[91] *Ibid.*, p.60; see also *La Wari Furniture and Baths v FRN*, (2018) LPELR-43507(CA), p. 64.

[92] Page (2021) pp. 26–27.

[93] *e.g.*, Nwoba and Nwokwu (2018); Omoroghomwan (2018).

[94] GIABA (2021), p. 93.

Tope Adebayo LLP describe 'civil forfeiture as an innovation birthed by necessity.'[95] It is an innovation that raises a difficult issue of principle, which is by no means unique to Nigeria.[96] Forfeiture of assets in cases of corruption looks very much like a punishment for a crime, which should only be imposed when the presumption of innocence is rebutted in a criminal trial. On the other hand, it seems perfectly reasonable that someone who is asking the state to uphold their right to certain assets (or to return those assets following seizure) should be asked to prove on the balance of probabilities that they have legitimately acquired such a right. This, rather than the legal fiction that an asset is somehow 'guilty', is the justification for civil forfeiture proceedings where the burden of proof is on the purported owner of the asset. By circumventing the protections afforded to criminal defendants, however, such a procedure creates a risk of abuse.

In their very useful discussion of civil recovery in Nigeria, Tope Adebayo LLP defend its constitutionality but add:

> It is conceded that the procedure could be abused by overzealous EFCC officials to unjustly deprive persons of their legitimate assets. There is therefore a duty on the Courts to ensure that when an application is brought pursuant to Section 17 AFFA, all persons with legitimate interest in the asset are served with the interim order. The court must ensure that significant opportunity is given to all parties to contest the application.[97]

It is too early to say what impact the newly-enacted PCRM Act will have on this debate. Part 5 of this Act specifically addresses NCB recovery of the proceeds of crime, subject to civil proceedings and as such to be proved on a balance of probabilities (s.8). The scope of its application is set out in s.7 and s.19 PCRM Act, and, in addition to the proceeds of crime, covers property used or intended to be used in criminal activity, and property that is abandoned or unclaimed that is reasonably suspected to the be the proceeds of crime. Such assets are to be subject to a court granted preservation order and, as with the AFF Act, a notice period of 14 days is provided to allow for interested parties to come forward. An important part of the PCRM Act, s.19(4), maintains the validity of a forfeiture order irrespective of the outcome of current or future criminal proceedings with which the property may be associated.

Concerns have been raised by the Policy and Legal Advocacy Centre[98] (PLA Centre) over s.74 which reverses the burden of proof:

---

[95] Tope Adebayo (n.d.), p. 8.

[96] See generally Ivory (2014); Hendry and King (2015); Rui and Sieber (2015).

[97] Tope Adebayo (n.d.), p. 5. It is perhaps questionable whether the period of 14 days between an interim and forfeiture order under the court may grant a final forfeiture order under the AFF Act s.17 gives a sufficient opportunity to contest it.

[98] Policy and Legal Advocacy Centre, *Proceeds of Crime Bill: Senate Imposes Burden of Proof on Defendant* March, 25th 2022, available at https://placng.org/Legist/proceeds-of-crime-bill-senate-imposes-burden-of-proof-on-defendant/ accessed 31/01/2023.

the defendant in any proceedings under this Act bears the burden of proving that he is the legitimate owner of the assets suspected to be proceeds of crime or derived from unlawful activity or that the assets are of legitimate origin and not proceeds of unlawful activity.

These concerns centre on the potential for the law to be abused against 'enemies of a government in power'. However, from our prior discussion, s.74 would seem to be consistent with both the Vienna and Palermo Conventions. The PLA Centre also argued that the section appeared inconsistent with the principles of common law and in contravention of s.131 of the Evidence Act 2011 and s.36(5) of the 1999 Nigerian constitution that provides for the presumption of innocence in a criminal prosecution, although our prior discussion would suggest that this has already been tested in the courts.

5 Summary of Reflections on NCB Asset Recovery in Nigeria

Given the difficulties encountered in securing successful convictions of kleptocrats and PEPs or in recovering illegally-gained assets to date, the aim of this chapter was to determine whether NCB asset recovery powers are usefully available to the Nigerian authorities in their efforts to prevent financial crime, in particular grand corruption. Our research shows that ample legal tools are indeed, and have been, available to enable NCB asset recovery in line with international norms and expectations, despite some suggestions to the contrary. However, it is also evident that there are challenges to be navigated if NCB provisions are be to effectively employed as in practice their application is complex and inconsistent. While this may in part reflect fundamental concerns among the wider international, legal and academic community about the appropriateness of NCB asset recovery for reasons of fairness, questions of standards of proof and uncertainties about its justification, there are significant barriers specific to Nigeria which also serve to hamper implementation. In common with Nigeria's criminal regime, much civil recovery power rests in the hands of multiple LEAs, which tend to compete for resources and influence, rather than collaborate. This serves to water down rather than strengthen the effectiveness of widely-applicable powers, such as those found in the AFF Act, in favour of agency-specific powers, such as those under the EFCC or the CPA.

The multiple-agency system has also generated a fragmented legislative picture, with overlapping and competing powers and vested interests frustrating attempts to deliver a single and effective proceeds of crime act. In fact, the latest legislative product, the PCRM Act, has been slow to appear and suffered dilution at draft stage, leaving yet another piece of legislation that muddies rather than clears the waters.

There is little doubt that too many opportunities continue to be presented to those in positions of authority to embezzle state resources for personal benefit and exploit overlap and inefficiencies in the investigative and legal systems, affording opportunity for the proceeds of corruption to be hidden away. In light of problems inherent in the Nigerian legal system, it is difficult to conclude that promising NCB asset recovery powers will be utilised in a fashion which will make a significant difference to the *status quo* any time soon.

References

Barnet T (2001) Legal fiction and forfeiture: an historical analysis of the civil asset forfeiture reform act. Duq Law Rev 40:77–110

Brun J-P, Sotiropoulou A, Gray L, Scott C, Stephenson KM (2021) Asset recovery handbook: a guide for practitioners, 2nd edn. World Bank, Washington, DC. https://openknowledge.worldbank.org/bitstream/handle/10986/34843/9781464816161.pdf?sequence=5&isAllowed=y. Accessed 19 Dec 2023

ENACT Organised Crime (2021). https://africa.ocindex.net/2021/country/nigeria. Accessed 19 Dec 2023

FATF (2003) 40 Recommendations October (incorporating all subsequent amendments until (October 2004). https://www.fatf-gafi.org/media/fatf/documents/FATF%20Standards%20-%2040%20Recommendations%20rc.pdf. Accessed 19 Dec 2023

FATF (2012) Best practices on confiscation (recommendations 4 and 38) and a framework for ongoing work on asset recovery. FATF, Paris

Federal Bureau of Investigation (n.d.) Scams and safety. https://web.archive.org/web/20211021030038/https://www.fbi.gov/scams-and-safety/common-scams-and-crimes/nigerian-letter-or-419-fraud. Accessed 19 Dec 2023

Financial Action Task Force on money laundering: Report (1990). https://www.fatf-gafi.org/media/fatf/documents/reports/1990%20ENG.pdf. Accessed 19 Dec 2023

GIABA (2008) Mutual evaluation report. Anti-money laundering and combatting the financing of terrorism: Nigeria. https://www.giaba.org/media/f/299_Mutual%20Evaluation%20Report%20of%20Nigeria.pdf. Accessed 19 Dec 2023

GIABA (2021) Anti-money laundering and counter-terrorist financing measures – Federal Republic of Nigeria, Second round mutual evaluation report

GIABA (2022) Anti-money laundering and counter-terrorist financing measures – Federal Republic of Nigeria, First enhanced follow-up report (November). Accessed 19 Dec 2023

Global Forum for Asset Recovery (2019) Progress report: Nigeria, developments Since December 2017 to June 2019. Civil Society Legislative Advocacy Centre/Transparency International Nigeria

Greenberg TS, Samuel LM, Grant W, Gray L (2009) Stolen asset recovery: a good practices guide for non-conviction based asset forfeiture, Stolen Asset Recovery (StAR) Series. World Bank, Washington, DC. https://openknowledge.worldbank.org/bitstream/handle/10986/2615/480920PUB0Stol101OFFICIAL0USE0ONLY1.pdf?sequence=1&isAllowed=y. Accessed 19 Dec 2023

Harvey J, Bello A, Doig A, van Duyne PC, Gonul S, van Koningsveld J, Shehu A, Sittlington S, Sproat P, Turner S, Ward T (2020) Tracking beneficial ownership and the proceeds of corruption: evidence from Nigeria, interim project report. Northumbria University, Newcastle

Harvey J, Bello A, Doig A, van Duyne PC, Gonul S, van Koningsveld J, Shehu A, Sittlington S, Sproat P, Turner S, Ward T (2021) Tracking beneficial ownership and the proceeds of corruption: evidence from Nigeria, final project report. Northumbria University, Newcastle

Harvey J, Sproat P, Turner S, Ward T (2024) Can FATF's focus on beneficial ownership aid anti-corruption efforts in a 'low-capacity' country? Challenges from the front line in Nigeria. In: Azinge-Egbuiri N, Esoimeme E, Ryder N (eds) Global anti-money laundering standards: developing countries' compliance challenges. Routledge, London. (in press)

Hendry J, King C (2015) How far is too far? Theorising non-conviction based asset forfeiture. Int J Law Context 11(4):398–411

International Centre for Asset Recovery (n.d.) Guidelines for the efficient recovery of stolen assets. https://baselgovernance.org/sites/default/files/2020-09/200902_AR_Guide_FINAL.pdf. Accessed 19 Dec 2023

Ivory R (2014) Corruption, asset recovery and the protection of property in public international law: the human rights of bad guys. Cambridge University Press

Levi M, Reuter P, Halliday T (2017) Can the AML system be evaluated without better data? Crime Law Soc Change 69:307–328

Mahmutaj K (2009) Cash forfeiture following acquittal: an "affront to public perception" or a breach of a fundamental human right? Crim Law Rev 11:783–793

Nwoba MOE, Nwokwu PM (2018) Appraisal of Economic and Financial Crimes Commission (EFCC) and the fight against corruption in Nigeria. Soc Sci 13(1):94–104

Omoroghomwan OB (2018) An appraisal of the activities of Economic and Financial Crime Commission (EFCC) on the Administration of Criminal Justice in Nigeria. Acta UnivDanubiensis 11(2):174–193

Open-ended Intergovernmental Working Group on Asset Recovery (2019) Mutual recognition of non-conviction-based freezing orders and confiscation judgments. Note prepared by the Secretariat 24th May, CAC/COSP/WG.2/2019/CRP.1. https://www.unodc.org/documents/treaties/UNCAC/WorkingGroups/workinggroup2/2019-May-29-30/V1903719e.pdf. Accessed 19 Dec 2023

Page M (2018) A new taxonomy for corruption In Nigeria. Carnegie Endowment for International Peace, Washington DC

Page M (2021) Innovative or Ineffective? Reassessing Anti-Corruption Law Enforcement in Nigeria (GI-ACE Working Paper 9). Foreign, Commonwealth & Development Office

Pol RF (2020) Anti-money laundering: the world's least effective policy experiment? Together, we can fix it. Policy Des Pract 3(1):73–94

Rui JP, Sieber U (eds) (2015) Non-conviction-based confiscation in Europe. Duncker & Humblot, Berlin

Shehu AY (2014) Key legal issues and challenges in the recovery of the proceeds of crime: lessons from Nigeria. Int Law Res 3(1):186–201

Shehu AY (2015) Nigeria the way through corruption to the well-being of a people. National Open University of Nigeria, Lagos

Tijani N (2011) Interim forfeiture of assets and the fundamental rights of accused persons. Niger Law Pract J 10:122–136

Tope Adebayo (n.d.) The jurisprudence of non-conviction based asset forfeiture (civil forfeiture) in Nigeria constitutionality of the new knight-errant innovated under the UNCAC (19th June). https://www.topeadebayollp.com/insights/display/33/. Accessed 19 Dec 2023

UN Convention Against Corruption (2003). https://www.unodc.org/unodc/en/treaties/CAC/. Accessed 19 Dec 2023

UN Convention Against Illicit Traffic in Narcotic Drugs and Psychotropic Substances (1988)

UN Office on Drugs and Crime (2019) Country Review Report of Nigeria: Review by Côte d'Ivoire and Myanmar of the implementation by Nigeria of articles 5-14 and 51-59 of the United Nations Convention against Corruption for the review cycle 2016-2021. https://www.unodc.org/documents/treaties/UNCAC/CountryVisitFinalReports/2019_12_16_Nigeria_Final_Country_Report.pdf. Accessed 19 Dec 2023

United Nations Convention against Transnational Organized Crime (2000). https://www.unodc.org/documents/treaties/UNTOC/Publications/TOC%20Convention/TOCebook-e.pdf. Accessed 19 Dec 2023

US Department of State, Bureau of International Narcotics and Law Enforcement Affairs (2022) International narcotics control strategy report, Vol II, Money Laundering. https://www.state.gov/wp-content/uploads/2022/03/22-00768-INCSR-2022-Vol-2.pdf. Accessed 19 Dec 2023

US Department of State, Bureau of Oceans and International Environmental and Scientific Affairs (2021) End wildlife trafficking report. https://www.state.gov/2021-end-wildlife-trafficking-report/. Accessed 19 Dec 2023

van Duyne PC, Harvey J (2022) Grand corruption in Nigeria: Nigeria's grabbing political elite. In: van Duyne PC, Larsson P, Harvey J, Antonopoulos G, von Lampe K (eds) Narrating organised crime stories and Aristotelian principles of drama. Eleven International Publishing, The Hague, pp 133–170

Waziri-Azi F (2018) Case for the establishment of specialized corruption courts in Nigeria: A panacea for the prosecution of high-profile corruption cases. J Law Policy Glob 80:67–77

Peter Sproat former Senior Lecturer in Financial Crime, Northumbria University. Peter is a research fellow at an investigative think tank which conducts forensic research and analysis on tax avoidance, tax policy, and tax law. Prior to that he was a senior lecturer in financial crime at Northumbria University and has extensive background in teaching aspects of financial crime, policing, and politics at a number of universities in the UK. Peter has published numerous academic articles on anti-money laundering, asset recovery and the policing of fraud and organised crime.

Tony Ward Professor of Law, Northumbria University. Tony is Convenor of the Northumbria Centre for Evidence and Criminal Justice Studies, and Co-Director of the International State Crime Initiative (ISCI). His main research interests are in the law of evidence and the criminological field of state crime (including grand corruption). With Penny Green, he is co-author of State Crime: Governments, Violence and Corruption (2004) and State Crime and Civil Activism (2019).

Jackie Harvey Emeritus Professor Northumbria University. Jackie is emeritus professor at Northumbria University's Newcastle Business School. She has had a varied career crossing from fiscal and macro policy economist, commercial banking and entering academia in 2000. She established her research reputation in the field of anti-money laundering, most recently being principal investigator on a UK FCDO funded project examining beneficial ownership and corruption in Nigeria.

Sue Turner Assistant Professor, Northumbria University. Sue is an Assistant Professor at Northumbria Law School with particular expertise in business and finance law and regulation. She leads numerous specialist modules across postgraduate, undergraduate and professional programmes and is a member of the Financial Crime Compliance Research Interest Group. Prior to joining Northumbria University, Sue was a banking and finance solicitor with a global law firm.

Abdullahi Shehu Former Director General of the ECOWAS Inter-Governmental Action Group against Money Laundering in West Africa (GIABA). Abdullahi has over three decades of vast theoretical and practical experiences on transnational organized crime. He was a Programme Expert on the UNODC Global Programmes against Corruption and Money Laundering in Vienna; Senior Anti-Corruption Policy Advisor in the UNODC Office in Nigeria. He was the pioneer Director General of GIABA from 2006 to 2014, during which he laid a solid foundation for the establishment of GIABA as a Financial Action Task Force (FATF) Style Regional Body and a specialised institution of the ECOWAS with remarkable record of programmes and projects implementation. As a professor of criminology, his main research area is anti-corruption/money laundering on which has published extensively.

Abdullahi Bello Assistant Professor, Northumbria University. Abdullahi is an Assistant Professor at Northumbria University and the Programme Leader of the MSc Forensic Accounting programme in the University. He is a fellow of the Association of Chartered Certified Accountant (FCCA, UK) and a Certified Fraud Examiner (CFE, US). He has more than 22 years' experience in law enforcement, banking, consulting and the academia in roles related to anti-money laundering, finance, intelligence analysis, forensic accounting, and financial investigation.

'De-Risking', De-Banking and Denials of Bank Services: An Over-Compliance Dilemma?

Louis de Koker and Pompeu Casanovas

Abstract This chapter considers the impact of drivers of over-compliance or so-called 'gold plating' on decisions of banks to terminate or restrict relationships with customers and counterparts. It draws on a South African study of factors that influenced overly-conservative design of anti-money laundering and counter terrorist financing measures of South African banks in a rule-based context. It considers whether the identified drivers are still relevant in a risk-based context. The chapter concludes that the broad drivers remain relevant and that regulators that wish to limit risk-informed de-banking should avoid strengthening the drivers and consider how best to neutralise them.

1 Introduction

Banks ought to comply with the law. Non-compliance holds a range of negative consequences for society, for their customers and often for the institutions themselves. Sometimes, however, banks go beyond mere compliance with the law, or act so well within the parameters of the legal requirements, that their behaviour can be called 'over-compliant' or may be labelled as 'gold plating'. In theory, acting well within the law should hold benefits. Going beyond what the law requires should be

L. de Koker (✉)
La Trobe Law School, La Trobe University, Melbourne, VIC, Australia

Department of Mercantile and Labour Law, University of the Western Cape, Belville, South Africa
e-mail: l.dekoker@latrobe.edu.au

P. Casanovas
Artificial Intelligence Research Institute, Spanish National Research Council (IIIA-CSIC), Bellaterra, Barcelona, Spain

La Trobe Law School, La Trobe University, Melbourne, VIC, Australia

Institute of Law and Technology (IDT-UAB), Universitat Autònoma de Barcelona, Bellaterra, Spain

D. Goldbarsht, L. de Koker (eds.), *Financial Crime, Law and Governance*, Ius Gentium: Comparative Perspectives on Law and Justice 116,
https://doi.org/10.1007/978-3-031-59547-9_3

viewed as an expression of good corporate citizenship. This in turn should enhance trust of its regulator and its customers. It may however also hold unintended negative consequences, for example where the additional processes are more costly and divert compliance resources from higher risk areas where they are more needed. Over-compliance can limit the ability of the bank to engage in sound business opportunities and may create additional risks.[1] Calibrating compliance responses correctly to avoid non-compliance and over-compliance is, however, challenging, especially given the rise in risk-based regulation and risk-based compliance requirements in financial services.

This chapter focuses on money laundering and terrorist and proliferation financing-related bank account closures (also known as de-banking) and related denials of banking services to customers. These decisions are essentially compliance risk decisions, often driven in part by concerns that the money laundering or terrorist or proliferation financing risk and risk management costs in these cases outweigh the benefits of doing the relevant business. De-banking is often called 'de-risking', though the latter term is best reserved for cases where risk is the primary driver of the de-banking decision. De-banking decisions are causing hardship to an increasing number of customers and countries and has attracted global regulatory attention, including a closer analysis by the Financial Action Task Force, the global standard-setting body for anti-money laundering and counter terrorist and proliferation financing (AML/CTF/CPF).[2]

'De-risking' is itself a contentious label for risk-informed de-banking decisions as it labels the action solely from the perspective of the bank that limits its own risk exposure. It does so by excluding customers and transactions it views as risky. As a result, these customers and transactions are channeled into less regulated services and often the non-transparent cash economy. This in turn increases the risk of money laundering and terrorist financing harms to society, and also increases the crime risk exposure of the parties to such transactions, where these are legitimate. Ultimately, de-risking undermines global financial policies aimed at increasing access to and usage of formal financial services.[3]

De-banking is again receiving regulatory attention. Current policy initiatives range from the FATF contemplating steps to limit unintended de-risking consequences of its standards,[4] through to national agencies such as the US Treasury,[5] the European Banking Authority,[6] and AUSTRAC (Australia)[7] adopting new strategies

[1]For example, compliance with reporting and disclosure laws is importantgood but when businesses disclose more information than they are legally required to, it can affect their relationship with customers and with regulatory and supervisory bodies. Such over-compliance increases the risk of improper disclosure and data breaches. For some examples, see Klievink et al. (2018).

[2]Financial Action Task Force (2022).

[3]Global Partnership for Financial Inclusion (2016), pp. 68–69.

[4]FATF (2022).

[5]US Department of the Treasury (2023).

[6]EBA (2022); EBA (2023).

[7]AUSTRAC (2023).

and guidance to counter unnecessary de-risking, aimed at specific customer groups or more generally. In parallel, the Financial Stability Board, in collaboration with other financial standard-setting bodies and regional and national regulators are progressing with the G20 Roadmap for Enhancing Cross-border Payments, which may address concerns about de-banking impact on correspondent banking relationships.[8]

This chapter reflects on the findings of a South African study of drivers of conservative (also called "overly compliant ") AML/CTF compliance. That study helped to raise FATF's awareness of over-compliance.[9] The chapter discusses the linkages between these drivers, de-banking and the de-risking dilemma and considers technology and especially Compliance by Design and Compliance through Design measures as potential solutions. However, a brief introduction to AML/CTF/CPF is required to provide context for the discussion of conservative compliance.

2 AML/CTF/CPF Measures

Concerns about the abuse of the financial system by drug traffickers informed the decision of the G7 plus 1 meeting in Paris in 1989 to establish a task team to advise on measures to address this problem. The task team, called the Financial Action Task Force (FATF), developed a set of forty recommendations and these were adopted by the G7 in 1990 in Houston. At that meeting the task force was given the mandate to assess member countries against the measures set out in the recommendations.[10] Since 1990, this task force developed into the global standard-setter for anti-money laundering. Its mandate also broadened. In 2001, its scope was extended to counter terrorist financing. It scope broadened again in 2012 to include support for targeted financial sanctions imposed by the UN Security Council to combat proliferation of weapons of mass destruction (proliferation financing).[11]

In April 2019, after three decades of limited term mandates, the FATF was given a permanent mandate to continue its work to combat money laundering, terrorist financing, and the financing of the proliferation of weapons of mass destruction. It does so primarily by setting global AML/CTF/CPF standards; encouraging their effective implementation; assessing its members for compliance and effectiveness of their AML/CTF/CPF measures; and strengthening the ability of FATF-style Regional Bodies to undertake similar assessments in relation to their members using the same assessment methodology employed by FATF.

The FATF standards require countries to adopt fairly uniform AML/CTF/CPF laws and create and maintain structures, such as national financial intelligence units.

[8] Financial Services Board (2020).

[9] See e.g. the citations in FATF (2013), n 37; FATF (2016), n 46.

[10] De Koker and Turkington (2016), pp. 244–247.

[11] De Koker (2024).

They also require countries to ensure that financial institutions and designated non-financial business and professions take prescribed measures to combat money laundering and terrorist financing. These include customer due diligence (CDD) measures. Given the focus of this chapter the discussion will be limited to the duties of banks. In terms of the FATF standards and related AML/CTF/CPF obligations, banks must undertake the following CDD measures:[12]

1. *Customer identification and verification*—determining who the customer is and, using reliable, independent source documents, data or information, verifying the customer's identity.
2. *Establishing beneficial ownership*—determining who is the actual controller of a client or beneficiary of a business relationship, service or transaction.
3. *Risk assessment and profiling*—understanding the purpose and intended nature of the business relationship. In essence the bank constructs a user profile of the customer and assesses the level of risk linked to that client and the services and products that the customer will use. In the course of this process the customer must be checked against applicable sanctions lists and blacklists. The bank must also determine whether the customer is a Politically Exposed Person (PEP). PEPs are people such as senior politicians, senior civil servants and their close relatives and close associates. They are distinguished as a group as they are viewed as potentially vulnerable to corruption.[13]
4. *Transaction monitoring and reporting*—monitoring the transactions of clients and detecting transactions that do not correlate with the transactional profile of the client. Unusual transactions that are detected must be investigated and, when there are grounds for deeming them suspicious, must be reported to the national financial intelligence unit.

Until 2012, FATF standards were predicated on a rule-based approach, requiring countries to stipulate the CDD measures banks had to implement This approach began to change in 2003 when the FATF allowed for CDD measures to be adjusted on the basis of assessed risk.[14] In 2012, however, the FATF adopted revised standards that embedded a mandatory risk-based approach to AML/CTF regulation and compliance.[15] The mandatory risk-based approach requires that national regulators and banks identify and assess their money laundering and terrorism financing risks. Where customers, services or products are assessed as posing a higher risk, enhanced CDD measures must be adopted. Where risks are lower, countries may allow their banks to adopt simplified CDD measures. Banks, in turn, may then elect to simplify their CDD for those customers, products and services posing a lower risk.

---

[12] FATF (2014a).

[13] FATF (2013a).

[14] FATF (2003), Rec 5.

[15] FATF (2012-2023), Rec 1. Amendments to the standards in 2020 extended a partial risk-based approach to the rule-based proliferation financing standards. For background to the 2012 developments, see Gelemerova (2009).

Proliferation financing measures were, however, excluded from the risk-based approach as they primarily support the UN Security Council's rule-based targeted financial sanctions. In 2020, however, the FATF revised its standards to require countries and regulated institutions like banks to undertake proliferation financing assessments and to adopt enhanced CDD measures where higher risks are identified.[16] Given the rule-based nature of the UN sanctions no simplification is allowed where proliferation financing risks are assessed as lower. Even low risk institutions that may benefit from a regulatory exemption from these risk assessment requirements still have to comply in full with the UN Security Council sanctions.[17]

A risk-based approach is not accompanied by regulatory provisions setting out the specific measures a regulated institution must implement to mitigate identified risks. In the AML/CTF/CPF context, for example, regulations require banks to identify and verify the identities of their customers. It is left to each bank to decide how to meet that requirement. They need to determine what would be adequate and appropriate to mitigate the relevant risks and comply with their statutory obligations to combat money laundering and terrorist financing. The FATF and some national regulators have however provided some examples of risk factors that banks can consider.[18]

The risk-based approach is viewed as an effective approach to ensure an efficient application of scarce compliance resources by focusing these resources on instances of higher risk. The approach is, however, also vulnerable to its own risks. These include the risk of failing to identify relevant risks; of assessing a risk as lower while it actually poses a higher risk; of under-designing risk control measures either by employing too few controls or not adjusting them appropriately to the level of risk, etc. This chapter focuses on the risk of overestimating risk or overdesigning risk control measures, generally referred to as "over-compliance" in the risk context.

3 Conservative and Over-Compliant Responses

Compliance generally refers to conformity with rules, i.e., following regulatory norms or demonstrating conformity with regulatory constraints.[19] As explained by Governatori, regulatory compliance is generally understood as the set of activities in

---

[16] FATF (2021); De Koker (2024).

[17] The FATF standards allow countries to exempt certain institutions in full or in part from AML/CFT obligations where risks are assessed as low. This exemption was extended in 2020 to the imposition of proliferation financing risk management measures on institutions, but in the latter case the impact of an exemption is limited as the institution still need to comply in full with UN Security Council sanctions. See FATF (2012-2023).

[18] See e.g. FATF (2012-2023), INR 10.

[19] The discussion in Part 2 is closely based on the report in de Koker and Symington (2014). The original article is more comprehensive and detailed, and readers are referred to it for further insights and nuances. The original figures were stylistically improved.

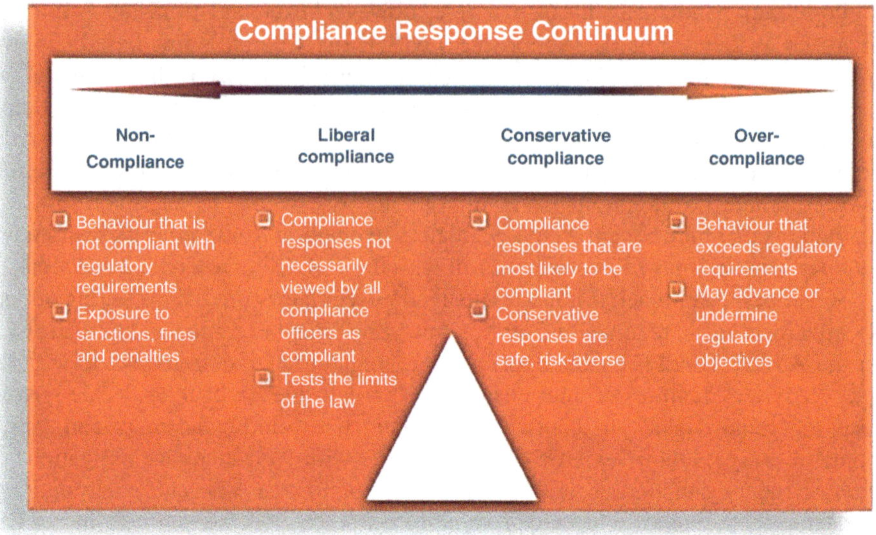

Fig. 1 Compliance Response Continuum

place in an organisation to ensure that the procedures, policies, processes and operations of the organisation comply with the normative frameworks governing the business and environment where the organisation operates.[20]

Over-compliance in a rule-based context means going well beyond what the law requires or staying very clearly well within its boundaries. See Fig. 1.[21]

The phenomenon of institutional over-compliance has been a topic of study since the 1980s, especially in relation to environmental regulations and standards.[22]

In some cases it can be adopted as a strategy, for example to signal to regulators that more stringent regulations may be adopted that would undermine competitors lacking the same capacity to comply with higher standards.[23] Wu and Wirkkala found that diverse factors may be at play, including market forces, regulatory pressure and the personal values and beliefs of senior managers regarding environmental stewardship.[24] Craswell and Calfee explored the impact of legal uncertainty on legal compliance.[25] Where penalties are large, they found that uncertain actors may wish to reduce the probability of punishment by modifying their behaviour further than the law requires.

[20]Governatori (2017), pp. 7–13.

[21]This figure was first introduced in De Koker and Symington (2014).

[22]Arora and Gangopadhyay (1995); Arora and Cason (1995); De Hart-Davis and Bozeman (2001); Gunningham et al. (2004); Gangadharan (2006); Denicoló (2008); Shimshack and Ward (2008); Wu and Wirkkala (2009).

[23]Salop and Scheffman (1983); Denicoló (2008).

[24]Wu and Wirkkala (2009), p. 401.

[25]Craswell and Calfee (1986); De Hart-Davis and Bozeman (2001), p. 476.

It has also been shown in the literature in environmental and ecological studies that 'credible enforcement significantly increases statutory over-compliance with regulations as well'.[26] However, especially in the banking sector, we should bear in mind that 'compliance is not a model of reality, but a control process exercised over the reality that unfolds'.[27]

What were, however, the factors at play in relation to over-compliance with AML/CTF obligations, especially CDD obligations? This had not been investigated before, so in 2011 a study was undertaken in South Africa to determine why banks were opting not to implement simplified due diligence measures where the law allowed them to do so. The study focused on compliance decisions that banks made in relation to a basic banking product aimed primarily at low-income individuals,[28] where regulations allowed simpler customer identity verification processes.[29]

Data for the study was collected by means of convergent interviewing of bank compliance officers using an unstructured format. The results of the semi-strucured interviews and the insights gained were discussed at two subsequent workshops with compliance and regulatory stakeholders where the findings were refined and endorsed.

In relation to the CDD measures in question the study identified 14 general drivers of conservative corporate responses by the participating institutions. These can broadly be clustered into five groups of factors, although aspects of some may resort in more than one group:[30]

1. The hard law requirement;
2. Applicable soft law;
3. Relevant business management considerations;
4. The company's own framework and reality; and
5. Supervisory conduct and relations.

4 Drivers of compliance responses

4.1 The Hard Law Requirement

Legal Uncertainty: Where the regulations were not clear, compliance officers tended to design procedures and systems that would meet the different interpretations that the regulator and the courts may give to that particular obligation, especially when the latter focus on the spirit of a law rather than the wording of a rule.[31]

---

[26] Shimshack and Ward (2008), pp. 90–105.

[27] Chorafas (2012), p. 103.

[28] De Koker and Symington (2014).

[29] De Koker (2006).

[30] This summary of the reasons and the text is drawn from the more detailed report in De Koker and Symington (2014). A number of clarifying improvements were made.

[31] Haines and Gurney (2003).

4.2 Applicable Soft Law

Concern about the Costs of Potential Changes: When they applied compliance measures, compliance officers tended to focus not only on current legal requirements but also on generally anticipated future requirements. Where South Africa was not yet compliant with the FATF standards, law reform to meet the standards was anticipated. This approach provided a measure of protection against costly changes to systems when the law would change. This may render them less attentive to current regulatory flexibility that they believe will or might be removed in future regulatory reforms.

4.3 Relevant Business Management Considerations

Conservative Approaches to Compliance Risk in the Industry: The interviewees indicated that the nature of their business and the need to protect their institutional reputation often informs a conservative compliance approach. As one bank compliance officer stated: "It is right and desirable that banks should be conservative."

Appropriate Management of Other Risks and Opportunities: Even though the law allowed them the option to simplify CDD there was also an understandable reluctance to simplify measures where compliance officers believed that simplified CDD may create alternative risks for the bank. Examples include when simplification may expose the bank to identity fraud, or where it may lead to a loss of business opportunities, for example limiting available customer information that is used to market alternative products to the customer.

Business Information Systems May Compel a More Conservative Approach: Where simplification required changed to the bank's business information systems banks were not able to respond immediately. Core changes to these systems are often expensive and may take years to be implemented in full. Simplified CDD required changes to customer enrolment forms and related changes to information systems and some banks were not able to implement such changes without significant expense and disruption.

4.4 The Company's Own Framework And Reality

Institutional Compliance Culture: A compliance culture can be defined as: 'The culture of shared values, beliefs, assumptions and behaviours existing within an organisation that characterises the organisation, especially in relation to compliance obligations'.[32] Compliance officers often hold that it is difficult, if not impossible, to

[32] Compliance Institute of South Africa (2007).

achieve corporate compliance in the absence of a general ethical corporate culture that supports compliance with legal obligations.[33] This culture is often called a 'sound compliance culture'.[34]

A number of interviewees identified a sound compliance culture as a reason for conservative compliance behaviour. According to these interviewees, the senior management embraced the need for, and fostered, a sound corporate compliance culture, often signalling that they wish their institutions to comply with the spirit and not merely the letter of the law. Where that was the case, compliance officers and business units would be reluctant to advise the adoption of a liberal compliance approach that may be technically correct and legal but might be viewed as challenging the spirit of the law.

Business Management Processes: In some cases business management processes informed conservative compliance responses, for example where it was easier and safer to adopt a uniformly high level of group-wide compliance to facilitate compliance management. In these cases, client enrolment procedures and requirements tended to be uniformly strict with little or no differentiation between types of individual clients.

Lack of Compliance Expertise: Compliance officers that lacked expertise or resources may over- or under-interpret the legal obligations of the institution. Given the support provided by the organised financial compliance profession in South Africa the risks of under-interpretation were low in banks but conservative over-interpretation was evident in some cases in advice to the management of the institution.

Foreign Compliance Imperatives: Banks that are subsidiaries of foreign banks or have important correspondent links with such banks often design elements of their compliance procedures to meet foreign compliance standards and requirements when those requirements exceed local requirements. This approach is supported by the standards of the FATF and the Basel Committee on Banking Supervision.[35] The study found evidence of such impact in foreign-owned banks in South Africa.

Foreign Compliance Examples: Domestic banks often looked to the processes implemented by international counterparts when they designed AML/CTF compliance responses. The legacy of older influences and the current international influences by compliance practices of counterparts, especially UK-based counterparts, inhibited a more flexible response to the South African regulations.

Management of Discretionary Requirements: Some legal requirements allowed banks to exercise discretion regarding appropriate customer enrolment processes to be followed in a given case. That discretion was normally exercised at a senior

[33] Regarding the relevance of a sound ethical corporate culture to corporate compliance, see Langevoort (2002), p. 104; Fiorelli (2004), pp. 578–580; Mintz (2005), p. 584. For the importance of an organizational culture to the success of a risk-based compliance approach see Black (2004), p. 51.

[34] Compliance Institute of South Africa (2007), Principle 12.

[35] See e.g. FATF (2012-2023), INR18.5.

management level and captured in operating procedures and rules as the view was that it would be too difficult to ensure compliance if customer contact staff were allowed to exercise their discretions. Those general rules tended to be more rigid and conservative than envisaged by the regulatory requirement.

Concern about Penalties and Sanctions: Management concern about institutional penalties as well as personal penalties and negative career consequences also impacted and informed a more cautious and conservative approach.

4.5 Supervisory Conduct and Relations

A Belief that the Regulator or Supervisor is Intolerant of Compliance Errors: When compliance officers experienced or viewed regulators or supervisors as intolerant of errors, they tend to react more conservatively.

Desire to Maintain a Good Relationship with Regulators and Supervisors: Compliance officers believed in some cases that a conservative approach preserved a good relationship with regulators and supervisors, providing access to informal guidance and enforcement leniency in case of compliance failures.

5 Modelling the Key Factors Impacting on Conservative Compliance

While much more research is required to understand the drivers and, importantly, how they interact with one another, the study prompted the design of an initial model of the impact of the five broad groups of factors identified above on each other and on the corporate compliance response decisions (see Fig. 2).[36]

A specific compliance response, as defined for purposes of the 2011 study, is primarily a response to a particular enforceable rule (the applicable *hard law* rule). CDD regulations were good examples of such binding, enforceable rules.

Soft law is also relevant. Soft law rules are rules that ar not enforceable in law but do have regulatory impact. Codes of conduct such as corporate governance codes and non-binding standards like the FATF standards are examples of soft law. For purposes of this analysis appropriate ethical principles are classified as soft law, although ethical principles can also be distinguished as a separate driver. Soft law can impact on compliance decisions by providing a lens through which the hard law rule is interpreted. Compliance officers, executive managers or courts may, for example, consider standards, codes and non-binding regulatory guidance when determining the spirit or purpose of a hard law rule. Corporate governance codes, for instance, guide banks and their directors to act ethically and to comply with their

[36]This figure was first introduced in De Koker and Symington (2014).

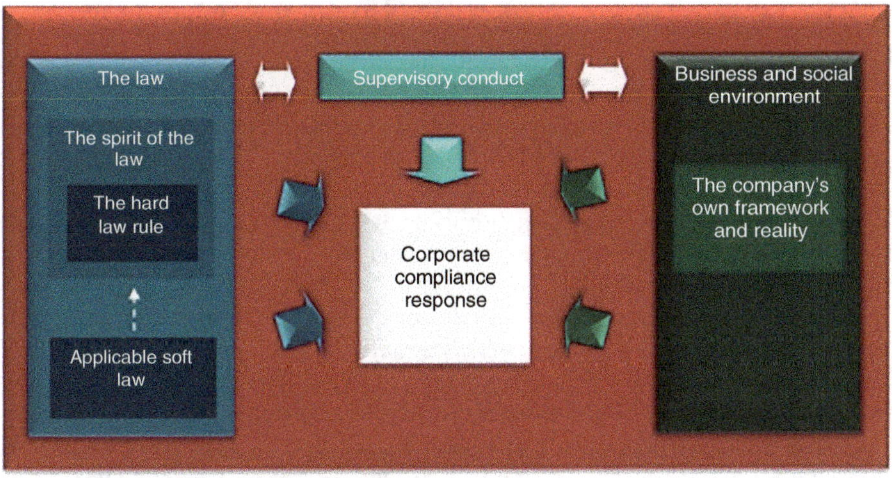

Fig. 2 Factors impacting on corporate compliance responses

legal obligations. Such principles shape corporate compliance culture and may lead companies to focus on the broader spirit, rather than the narrower language, of hard law rules.

In some cases, a soft law requirement may prompt a compliance response in its own right, even though that response is not required or enforced by the state. This may occur where the company voluntarily submits itself to compliance with that requirement, for example by signing up to an industry code.

The compliance response is also influenced by relevant *business management principles* (normal rules of commercial sustainability). These include the need to manage the business in a cost-effective manner (including managing the costs of compliance) and to manage its risks appropriately to ensure the sustainability of the business, for example protecting its reputation and continuity by avoiding crippling penalties and retaining its major business relationships and customers by maintaining trust.

The *bank's own framework and reality* includes its management's views on compliance, the company's compliance culture in general, its investment in legal and compliance capacity and resources, its financial position, etc. These factors have a significant bearing on the compliance response by the bank.

Supervisory conduct, whether actual or feared, also impacts on the compliance response. Enforcement action affects compliance by the targeted bank, but often has broader impact on compliance in the industry too. Informal signalling, such as comments in a speech by a senior supervisor, may also have impact, especially when it suggests enforcement action. Informal signalling that runs counter to action taken by the supervisor seems to have less effect, e.g., inviting banks to simplify their processes while taking harsh enforcement action when compliance failures occur.

These factors may not all be relevant or equally relevant in all cases but they do summarise and contextualise the drivers identified in the study.

6 Over-Compliance and De-Risking Denials of Services[37]

In 2014, a trend of closures of bank accounts of remittance service providers triggered global regulatory concerns.[38] An important illustration of the problem was the closure of the account of Dahabshiil, a significant cross-border remittance service provider to Somalia, by Barclays Bank in the UK. Barclays was the last large UK bank to provide services to Dahabshiil and the closure of this account threatened the continued flows of UK remittances sent by the Somalian community in the UK to family members in Somalia.[39]

The account closures of higher risk customers were not a new or unique phenomenon. It is, in fact, required by FATF standards when a financial institution finds itself unable to manage the money laundering and terrorist financing risks posed by that customer.[40] The trend of closing of accounts of small, cash-intensive businesses providing financial services to the poor was not new either.[41] However, the scale and global impact of this wave of closures caused alarm. The FATF therefore responded with a statement on 23 October 2014, expressing its concern about de-risking. It cautioned banks to implement a risk-based approach and not to engage in 'the wholesale cutting loose of entire classes of customer, without taking into account, seriously and comprehensively, their level of risk or risk mitigation measures for individual customers within a particular sector'.[42] The FATF also used the statement to deny that de-risking was solely linked to AML:[43]

> De-risking can be the result of various drivers, such as concerns about profitability, prudential requirements, anxiety after the global financial crisis, and reputational risk. It is a misconception to characterise de-risking exclusively as an anti-money laundering issue.[44]

The factors listed are however closely linked to AML/CTF, especially the costs of compliance impacting on profitability; bank liquidity and financing requirements linked to risk exposure; and reputational risk that may flow from allegations that a

---

[37] This discussion draws on the more detailed discussion in De Koker et al. (2017).

[38] See, e.g., Migration and Remittances Team (2015); Union of Arab Banks and IMF (2015); Global Standards Proportionality Working Group (2016); Collin et al. (2015); MONEYVAL Committee of Experts on the Evaluation of Anti-Money Laundering Measures and the Financing of Terrorism (2015); Durner and Shetret (2015); Scott et al. (2015); Artingstall et al. (2016); The Commonwealth (2016); Erbenová et al. (2016); Worrell et al. (2016); Alleyne et al. (2017); World Bank (2018); Woodsome et al. (2018); FATF (2022).

[39] See *Dahabshiil Transfer Services Ltd v Barclays Bank plc and Harada Ltd and another v Barclays Bank plc* [2013] EWHC 3379 (Ch); British Bankers Association (2014).

[40] FATF (2012-2023), Rec 10.

[41] Bester et al. (2008), p. 161.

[42] FATF (2014).

[43] FATF (2014).

[44] Interestingly, the 2014 statement only mentioned AML and did not specifically mention CTF or FATF's proliferation financing brief, both of which are closely linked to international political and economic sanctions. Sanctions regimes add to compliance risk concerns of banks and are often implied when the phrase AML/CTF is used.

bank allowed its systems to be abused to facilitate activities of organised crime or terror groups.

One prominent driver that has had an impact on the risk appetite of banks was the increasing size of penalties for AML/CTF-related contraventions. While million-dollar fines were imposed in serious cases in the past, the fines ballooned into the billions in 2012 when HSBC agreed to pay a then-record fine of $1.92 billion to U.S. authorities for allowing Mexican drug money to be laundered through its operations. In 2014 the record was smashed when BNP Paribas agreed to pay close on $8.9 billion in penalties because it continued to do business with countries and entities on the U.S. sanctions list.[45] Multi-million-dollar fines for AML/CTF contraventions are now standard.

Very high penalties for contravention of the AML/CTF laws combined with increased global crime, terrorism and proliferation risks globally and stricter banking standards following the global financial crisis resulted in risk averse and cost-conscious conduct by banks.[46] Higher risk customers, especially where increased compliance spending rendered the relationships unprofitable or insufficiently profitable, became primary targets of account closures.[47] Groups affected by such closures include virtual asset service providers,[48] non-profit organisations, foreign missions and diamond dealers.[49] In parallel, banks have been terminating correspondent banking relationships with other banks, where these are viewed as posing a higher risk of money laundering or financing of terrorism. These terminations have reached levels where some countries and regions of the world face a real risk of losing their access to the global financial system.[50] Despite various initial initiatives, including by the Financial Stability Board,[51] the problem still persists.

7 Conservative Compliance and the Risk-Based Approach: Perspectives on De-Risking

While the South African study was completed in an era when AML/CTF was rule-based, it is submitted that its findings are still relevant in a risk-based context.[52]

---

[45] See Collin et al. (2015), pp. 7–10.

[46] British Bankers Association (2014); Collin et al. (2015), p. 48; *E-Trans International Finance Ltd v Kiwibank Ltd* [2016] NZHC 1031 [149].

[47] De Koker and Turkington (2016), p. 262.

[48] De Koker and Goldbarsht (2022).

[49] Keatinge (2014), p. 16.

[50] Global Partnership for Financial Inclusion (2016), p. 70; D'Hulster et al. (2023).

[51] Financial Services Board (2019), p. 3. Financial Services Board (2020).

[52] Given that FATF's proliferation financing standards are still primarily rule-based, the relevance in relation to those standards continue.

Despite important differences in design, there are many similarities between the rule-based and the risk-based approach. Both consider and respond to money laundering and financing of terrorism risks. In the rule-based approach the regulator considers the risk and determines the risk mitigation measures in rules that the regulated community must implement. Risk assessments are not necessarily formally undertaken but sensible regulators consider risk-relevant information and data when they decide on the most appropriate risk mitigation measures that should be required. The risk-based approach shifts the risk assessment and risk management responsibility to the bank.

An important difference is of course that in a risk-based approach context, the detailed legal compliance response of a bank is a response to an identified and assessed risk rather than a response to a regulatory rule. A overly conservative response in this context could however be evident in risk identification (over-identifying risks), risk assessment (assessing lower risks as higher), and/or in risk mitigation (mitigating risks using excessive control measures).

In a risk-based context both the government and regulated institutions have risk assessment and risk mitigation responsibilities, and similar conservative responses may be evident in the national risk assessment and the design of the national regulatory framework.

A number of the key factors identified in the South African study are also evident in the circumstances that gave rise to de-risking account terminations by banks. For example:

Supervisory conduct drove a risk-averse compliance culture. The exceptionally large fines levied on HSBC in 2012 and on BNP Paribas in 2014 for CDD and other compliance failures impacted on the compliance risk appetite of the global banking industry. The FATF's 'naming and shaming' of jurisdictions that fail to comply adequately with its standards is also an important example of signalling that informs negative compliance and risk management responses in relation to the listed jurisdictions and their businesses. The responses can exceed the risk mitigation measures required.[53]

Supervisory conduct is also evident in the use of public statements by the FATF and regulators calling on banks not to engage in large-scale account closures. The positive impact of these statements was however limited as it was neutralised by ongoing enforcement actions globally resulting in huge fines for AML/CTF contraventions: Regulatory enforcement actions certainly speak louder here than senior supervisors in statements and speeches. The general lack of supervisory scrutiny of the reasons why services were denied to a specific client and of the quality of the data that informed that decision also signaled to banks that supervisors were actually not particularly concerned about the justification for denials of services.

The absence of a *hard law rule* requiring banks to manage ML/TF risk without unnecessarily exiting client relationships, for example through recognising a right to

[53] De Koker et al. (2023).

a bank account,[54] especially combined with the FATF soft law principle (supported by harder AML/CTF domestic rules) that banks should terminate relationships with clients where they believe they are not able to manage the risk relating to the relationship.

A lack of compliance expertise and resources, a factor relevant to the *company's own framework and reality*, may also play a role. Compliance officers have to be crime risk management experts to adopt sound risk-based compliance measures. They may lack that expertise and relevant data to inform risk-related decisions. Similarly foreign compliance imperatives and examples may be relevant where the bank foreign correspondent banks decide that particular relationships are higher risk or lie outside their risk appetite. Concerns about penalties and sanctions, including the impact of those on the careers of the compliance officers, may similarly inform conservative approaches to risk and risk assessment.

Compliance costs, related to the *business management principles* factor, emerged as an important factor in many bank decisions. The question is not whether the risk posed by the customer is unmanageable, but whether it could be managed profitably. Costs are often asserted but cost calculations in relation to individual relationships are rarely disclosed, if undertaken. Overdesigned controls can undermine the profitability of many business relationships.

Costs arguments are generally combined with concerns about reputational risk should abuse occur, i.e. the risk of negative impact that compliance with AML/CTF/CPF obligations may have on the bank's reputation, especially where these may be linked to a high-profile terrorism outrage. That risk is often raised but rarely quantified.[55] Reputational risk raises an important policy question: Have governments perhaps shifted too much responsibility to mitigate AML/CTF risk to the banks, with too little protection when they get it wrong? In *E-Trans International Finance Ltd v Kiwibank Ltd*[56] a bank's right to terminate a customer account as a result of ML/FT risks was challenged. The New Zealand High Court considered the interaction between the public policy aims relating to integrity in the financial markets, the important economic role of remittances for communities that relied on them, and the promotion of competition in the market.[57] Heath J remarked:[58]

> The problem is that those laudable policy aims conflict. The co-existence of statutory provisions designed to promote each of those public policy goals seems to have brought about unintended consequences. ... By requiring private and public business enterprises to

---

[54] De Koker et al. (2017), pp. 151–153. This was raised as a policy option in the United States too. See Office of the Comptroller of the Currency Fair Access to Financial Services," RIN 1557-AF05 (2021). This option was however not pursued in the eventual strategy. See US Department of the Treasury (2023).

[55] Analysis, when done, often focuses on short-term movements in share markets. Ferreira (2014). Fiordelis et al. (2014) found that fraud is the event type that generates the greatest reputational damage.

[56] *E-Trans International Finance Ltd v Kiwibank Ltd* [2016] 3 NZLR 241.

[57] *E-Trans International Finance Ltd v Kiwibank Ltd* [2016] 3 NZLR 241, [142-4].

[58] *E-Trans International Finance Ltd v Kiwibank Ltd* [2016] 3 NZLR 241, [145-6].

act as reporting entities under the Anti-Money Laundering Act, the public policy goal of minimising the risk of money laundering and financing of terrorism is promoted, but at the cost of reputational risk to financial institutions, such as Kiwibank.

Avoiding what may be viewed as significant compliance cost and reputational risk by refusing and terminating risky and unprofitable relationships is therefore a reasonable option for a compliance officer.[59] From a public policy perspective, however, that decision of the compliance officer holds significant negative consequences. For example, it undermines national crime combating objectives by compelling excluded customers to use cash and undermines economic development and financial inclusion goals by denying those customers access to formal banking services.[60]

The impact of these drivers may be amplified by the nature of the risk concepts and risk assessments that underpin the FATF's risk-based approach.

8 Objectivity of the FATF's Risk-Based Approach

The FATF does not define risk for purposes of its risk-based approach,[61] but states that 'risk can be seen as a function of three factors: threat, vulnerability and consequence'.[62]

ML/TF/PF risk assessment is not an exact empirical process following a scientific methodology that draws on sufficient evidence.[63] Much of the assessment is based on the judgments of the participants. The process is further complicated by challenges to quantify key elements of the risk concept. The FATF, for example, recognises the difficulty of assessing the consequences of ML/TF, accepting that

[59]See also Curry (2016): '[I]t it is not surprising that some banks have chosen to reduce their risks and shrink their exposure and international business portfolios. That choice is the result of what has been pejoratively labelled 'de-risking'. These withdrawals, particularly in regions subject to terrorism, drug trafficking, and other illicit activity, have been the subject of a good deal of publicity and, in some cases, have caused outcry both here and abroad. The process that has resulted in these decisions is better described as risk reevaluation. It's the process in which institutions review the risks they face on a continual basis and ensure they have systems in place that can identify and adequately address those risks. The actual process of regularly re-evaluating risk is a critical and expected part of the BSA/AML regulatory regime'.

[60]In the case of sanctions a further public policy risk was identified. When sanctions are lifted the reputation of entities and countries may not be immediately restored in the views of society and stakeholders. Banks may respond to continuing reputational risk by avoiding business with those who were previously-sanctioned, thereby undermining any sanctions relief that may have been granted. See Raynor (2022).

[61]De Koker (2011).

[62]FATF (2013b); El Khoury C (ed) (2023), pp 9–11.

[63]The FATF describes it as based on judgment: "As stated above, ideally a risk assessment involves making judgments about threats, vulnerabilities *and* consequences." See FATF (2013), pp. 7–8 and also De Koker and Goldbarsht (2024).

'incorporating consequence into risk assessments may not involve particularly sophisticated approaches',[64] and, in relation to TF risk, the FATF advised that 'countries need not take a scientific approach when considering consequences, and instead may want to start with the presumption that consequences of TF will be severe, (whether domestic or elsewhere) and consider whether there are any factors that would alter that conclusion'.[65] Conservative assumptions about consequences will tend to result in higher risk level assessments, even where the likelihood of an ML/TF/PF event is low. Furthermore, findings of serious and severe consequences are often linked to transactions regardless of the value involved (i.e. assessors adopt methodologies that assume that the consequences of a $100 MLT/TF/PF transaction and a $100,000 transaction are equally severe). This in turn elevates the chances that risk levels of smaller institutions and countries are assessed as higher than warranted.[66]

In 2022 the World Bank published a study by Ferwerda and Reuter.[67] They analysed 11 pre-2020 National Risk Assessments published by eight systemically important countries (Canada, Italy, Japan, the Netherlands, Singapore, Switzerland, the United Kingdom, and the United States) to assess their conceptual understanding and methodologies. The authors concluded:[68]

> Each raises serious issues regarding the risk assessment methodology. For example, most relied largely on expert opinion, which they solicited in ways that are inconsistent with the well-developed methodology for making use of expert opinion. They misinterpreted data from suspicious activity reports and failed to provide risk assessments relevant for policy makers. Only one described the methodology employed.

In a 2019 study Ferwerda and Kleemans raised six concerns regarding the use of expert opinions in these assessments:[69]

> Using expert opinions to assess money laundering risks has a number of disadvantages. First, virtually all experts asked to perform national risk assessments are part of the fight against money laundering. These experts might overestimate the risks of money laundering hoping to increase their AML budget in the future, or underestimate the money laundering risk for their own institutions eager to gain compliments for their 'good' fight against money laundering. Second, one might wonder whether these experts have sufficient objective information about money laundering activities—that by definition cannot be monitored—to correctly estimate money laundering risks, especially for sectors in which the expert does not work. Third, it is unclear how to aggregate expert opinions, particularly when experts differ in the undetermined amount of knowledge about money laundering risk. Fourth, even when all experts agree on a certain money laundering risk, one may wonder whether this is because this is a real risk or because they all read the same (e.g. FATF typology) reports or news articles. Fifth, using expert opinions can reinforce stereotypes instead of providing new

---

64 FATF (2013).

65 FATF (2019), pp. 8–9.

66 IMF/World Bank (2021).

67 Ferwerda and Reuter (2022).

68 Ferwerda and Reuter (2022), p. 5. For earlier concerns, see Gelemerova (2009) p. 51.

69 Ferwerda and Kleemans (2019), p. 46. Also see Southworth and Levi (2024).

and objective information. Finally, not all experts will always agree to inform the national risk assessment, which implies self-selection problems.

Institutional risk assessments, in turn, are informed by national risk assessments. The same subjectivity is present in institutional risk assessments and many of these assessments would also employ weak assessment methodologies with weaknesses similar to those that Reuter and Ferwerda identified in their study. Institutional assessments rely on the judgments of internal experts. The same questions raised by Ferwerda and Kleemans arise in relation to these assessments too. These participants may be impacted by some of the drivers outlined in 4.4 and assessments of institutional risk would then tend to be conservative. Where drivers such as these are present the design of risk mitigation measures will also be more conservative.

The over-compliance dilemma identified in the South African study may therefore be exarcerbated in the context of the risk-based approach. This may unduly impact on access to financial services[70] by denying services to customers whose risk levels are actually lower than assessed. Without constraints by rules, such as the right to access financial services,[71] or clear review standards for appropriate institutional ML/TF/PF risk assessments combined with supervisory reviews of the quality of institutional risk assessments and risk mitigation, the drivers of conservative responses can play a much larger role in these contexts.

Can new technologies assist to mitigate some of the de-risking risks?

9 Can New Compliance Technologies Assist in Countering De-Risking?

Technologies are transforming financial services. Digital financial services enable millions of customers to be serviced without associated with bricks- and mortar banking. Distributed ledger technologies like the blockchain that underpins bitcoin and crypto assets themselves may have a revolutionary impact on financial services.[72]

Technology is also impacting on traditional CDD and related compliance obligations. More countries are implementing biometric-based national identity systems that support digital identification and facilitate customer identification and verification, which in turn can lower AML/CTF compliance costs. Developments in regulatory technology (Regtech) and new collaborative CDD partnerships, often involving public-private partnerships) promise to transform compliance, increasing the efficiency and effectiveness of AML/CTF/CPF processes.[73]

---

[70] Bester et al. (2008); Global Partnership for Financial Inclusion (2016); FATF (2017); FATF (2022).

[71] De Koker et al. (2017), pp. 151–153.

[72] De Koker and Goldbarsht (2022).

[73] See Lyman et al. (2019), p. 1–4; De Koker et al. (2019), p. 90; Momberg and de Koker (2020), pp. 1–5.

Exciting developments are also taking place in technology-assisted compliance management, especially in relation to Compliance by Design (CbD) and AI. CbD can be defined as the relation between two sets of specifications, i.e., between the (formal) specifications of a set of regulations and the (formal) specifications of a system.[74] Thus, CbD refers to the set of formal rules that are considered in the design stage of a business or regulatory process. In the past 10 years, many formal frameworks have been proposed through a diversity of business computational languages.[75] More recently, CbD has been linked to Open Digital Rights Languages (ODRL) enabling automated business compliance checking against regulatory obligations.[76]

Can CbD assist to prevent counter the unnecessary closure of higher risk accounts? The answer unfortunately is that CbD may not provide an answer, at least not in and by itself. Clarity of the conceptual normative elements is a pre-condition of CbD, a requirement that precedes any CbD formalisation. AML/CTF is unfortunately rife with nebulous concepts. CDD is aimed at identifying suspicious transactions that may involve proceeds of crime or terrorist or proliferation financing. As has been pointed out in the literature, 'the concept of "suspicion" in itself is still vague and amorphous, proving to have a negative effect on banks to effectively identify the proceeds of crime'.[77]

To be effective in preventing over-compliance effects, the CbD formal approach should be complemented by *legal* CbD, i.e., by Compliance *through* Design (CtD). CtD aims to explicitly encompass and incorporate the social and institutional aspects that legal compliance entails—legal interpretation processes, institutionalization, the interface between modelling and coordination, and the relation between the regulated entity and citizens, consumers, and the law.[78] The more holistic CtD promises to be more useful to limit de-risking than the more formalistic CbD because it broadens and complements the CbD scope. To be successful in a risk-based approach however the CtD system needs to be informed by, and responsive to, fine-grained CDD risk data, money laundering, terrorist financing and proliferation financing data, and customer profiling data.

While risk assessment technologies are improving, much still needs to be done to improve money laundering, terrorist financing and proliferation financing risk identification and assessment systems. Much is being invested in such systems. One challenge, however, is the lack of knowledge about these activities. Our knowledge is limited to the cases of money laundering and terrorist financing that have been identified and it is generally accepted that only a small portion of these activities are correctly identified. Much of the risk may be submerged in the Rumsfeldian

[74] See Sadiq et al. (2007), pp. 149–152.

[75] Hashmi, Governatori, Lam and Wynn (2018), pp. 79–133.

[76] De Vos et al. (2019), pp. 36–51.

[77] Sinha (2014), p. 75.

[78] See Casanovas et al. (2017), pp. 33–49; Hashmi, Casanovas, and De Koker (2018), pp. 59–72; Casanovas et al. (2022), pp. 64–91.

'unknown unknowns'. Risk-based compliance systems that are designed without a broader grasp of the full risk picture, may identify mainly cases and methodologies that are similar to cases that have been identified earlier (e.g., that resemble the 'known knowns').

While CtD systems will be helpful they will, like all solutions, also breed their own problems. Coding legal rules hold its own complications[79] and coding errors may lead to expensive regulatory fines.

Given the complexity of AML/CTF/CPF, CtD applications in this context should therefore, at least at the start, have human decision makers in the loop. CtD systems may be designed to provide such humans with key information about the risks and the legal obligations to manage those risks proportionally. As appropriate data flows and the quality of CtD analysis increase, the human role may decrease.

10 Conclusion

Regulatory compliance discussions generally focus either on ensuring compliance or on the reasons for, and the impact of, failures of institutions to comply with their obligations. This chapter highlights a different problem: The risk of over-complying with the law and the negative impact of over-compliance as illustrated by the de-risking dilemma where banks have been terminating business relationships with customers and counterparts.

While technology is changing the shape of banking services it also poses intriguing possibilities of improving compliance management to prevent unnecessary de-risking. The chapter therefore also considered CbD and CtD approaches as possible solutions to the de-risking dilemma. While CbD on its own does not promise to solve the problem, CtD approaches may assist to counter de-risking-related bank account terminations and refusals. However, complex challenges await the developers of such solutions.

Regulators are clearly concerned about the levels of de-banking that is taking place. Should they wish to act more effectively to prevent ML/TF/PF risk-informed de-banking it is important to consider the drivers identified in 4.4 of this chapter. These drivers are highly relevant in the subjective, judgment-based risk assessment and risk management context of the FATF's risk-based approach.

Regulators that wish to stem de-risking should avoid strengthening any of the drivers unnecessarily, for example by making statements that would unduly inflate risk perceptions of certain types of customers or unduly inflate consequences of any criminal abuse or of minor compliance failures. Regulators should furthermore help instititions to mitigate reputational risk where, despite appropriate compliance systems, abuse occurred. Regulators can furthermore leverage the identified drivers of de-risking to address compliance-related denials of service. These drivers can be

[79] Governatori et al. (2020).

harnessed to influence the compliance decisions of banks, for example, by adopting hard law rules that recognise the rights of customers to access formal payment services. Business management and social environment factors can be leveraged by supporting collaborative CDD practices[80] that lower the costs of compliance and by providing improved risk information and data to inform institutional risk assessment and risk management of ML/TF/PF risks. Supervisory conduct can be leveraged by setting and supervising clear quality standards for institutional risk assessments and for the design and adoption of appropriate risk mitigation measures, and by reviewing the reasons way a bank denied services to a specific client or counterpart to ensure that that the reasons are sound and informed by appropriate data. A clear message that a supervisor is fair and is not trying to build a profile as the harshest policeman on the block or to create enforcement data to impress FATF mutual assessors, will also be helpful.

Acknowledgements This chapter reflects portions of text of an earlier paper on the South Africa study (De Koker and Symington (2014) in its discussion of the South African study. The chapter is based on a paper delivered at the 2018 annual conference of the German-Southeast Asian Center of Excellence for Public Policy and Good Governance (CPG), Faculty of Law, Thammasat University, in Bangkok. The authors record their appreciate to Dr. Duc Quang Ly of the CPG for his very helpful comments and editing of an earlier draft. All errors remain, however, the responsibility of the authors.

References

Alleyne T, Bouhga-Hagbe J, Dowling T, Kovtun D, Myrvoda A, Okwuokei J, Turunen J (2017) Loss of correspondent banking relationships in the Caribbean: trends, impact, and policy options. IMF, Washington DC

Arora S, Cason T (1995) Why do firms volunteer to exceed environmental regulations? Understanding participation in EPA's 33/50 program. Land Econ 72(4):413–432

Arora S, Gangopadhyay S (1995) Toward a theoretical model of voluntary over-compliance. J Econ Behav Org 28(3):289–309

Artingstall D, Dove N, Howell J, Levi M (2016) Drivers & impacts of derisking. John Howell & Co Ltd, Shamley Green

AUSTRAC (2023) Financial services for customers that financial institutions assess to be higher risk. https://www.austrac.gov.au/business/core-guidance/financial-services-customers-financial-institutions-assess-be-higher-risk

Bester H, Chamberlain D, De Koker L, Hougaard C, Short R, Smith A, Walker R (2008) Implementing FATF standards in developing countries and financial inclusion: findings and guidelines. The FIRST Initiative, Washington DC

Black J (2004) The development of risk based regulation in financial services: Canada, the UK and Australia a research report. London School of Economics and Political Science (ESRC Centre for the Analysis of Risk and Regulation), London

[80] See Lyman et al. (2019).

British Bankers Association (2014) De-risking – global impact and unintended consequences for exclusion and stability. BBA, London

Casanovas P, González-Conejero J, De Koker L (2017) Legal Compliance by Design (LCbD) and through Design (LCtD): preliminary survey. In: TERECOM-2017, Technologies for regulatory compliance proceedings of the 1st workshop on technologies for regulatory compliance, CEUR-2049, pp 33–49

Casanovas P, De Koker L, Hashmi M (2022) Law, socio-legal governance, the Internet of Things, and Industry 4.0: a middle-out/inside-out approach. J 5:64–91

Chorafas DN (2012) Basel III, The devil and global banking. Palgrave Macmillan, London

Collin M, De Koker L, Juden M, Myers J, Ramachandran V, Sharma A, Tata G (2015) Unintended consequences of anti-money laundering policies for poor countries. Centre for Global Development, Washington DC

Compliance Institute of South Africa (2007) Generally accepted compliance practice. CISA, Johannesburg

Craswell R, Calfee J (1986) Deterrence and uncertain legal standards. J Law Econ Org 2(2): 279–303

Curry TJ (2016) Remarks before the Association of Certified Anti-Money Laundering Specialists. In: 15th Annual Anti-Money Laundering and Financial Crime Conference. ACAMS, Miami. https://www.occ.gov/news-issuances/speeches/2016/pub-speech-2016-117.pdf

D'Hulster K, Morris N, Jaffer S, De Koker L (2023) The decline of correspondent banking in Pacific Island countries. Pacific Islands Forum report prepared by the World Bank https://forumsec.org/sites/default/files/2024-05/CBR%20Report_FINAL.pdf

De Hart-Davis L, Bozeman B (2001) Regulatory compliance and air quality permitting: why do firms overcomply? J Public Adm Res Theory 11(4):471–508

De Koker L (2006) Money laundering control and suppression of financing of terrorism: some thoughts on the impact of customer due diligence measures on financial exclusion. J Financ Crime 13(1):26–50

De Koker L (2011) Aligning anti-money laundering, combating of financing of terror and financial inclusion: questions to consider when FATF standards are clarified. J Financ Crime 18(4): 361–386

De Koker L (2024) The FATF's combating of financing of proliferation standards: private sector implementation challenges. In: Goldbarsht D, De Koker L (eds) Financial crime and the law: identifying and mitigating risks. Springer, Cham

De Koker L, Goldbarsht D (2022) Financial technologies and financial crime: key developments and areas for future research. In: De Koker L, Goldbarsht D (eds) Financial technology and the law: combating financial crime. Springer International Publishing, Cham, pp 303–320

De Koker L, Goldbarsht D (2024) FATF's risk-based approach: has the pendulum swung too far? In: Goldbarsht D, De Koker L (eds) Financial crime and the law: identifying and mitigating risks. Springer, Cham

De Koker L, Symington J (2014) Corporate compliance: reflections on a study of compliance responses by South African Banks. Law Context 30:228–256

De Koker L, Turkington M (2016) Transnational organised crime and the anti-money laundering regime. In: Hauck P, Peterke S (eds) International law and transnational organised crime. Oxford University Press, Oxford, pp 241–263

De Koker L, Singh S, Capal C (2017) Closure of bank accounts of remittance service providers: global challenges and community perspectives in Australia. Univ Queensl Law J 36(1):119–154

De Koker L, Morris N, Jaffer S (2019) Regulating financial services in an era of technological disruption. Law Context 36(2):90–112

De Koker L, Howell J, Morris N (2023) Economic consequences of greylisting by the Financial Action Task Force. Risks 11(5):81. https://doi.org/10.3390/risks11050081

De Vos M, Kirrane S, Padget J, Satoh K (2019) ODRL policy modelling and compliance checking. In: RuleML+RR 2019, International joint conference on rules and reasoning, proceedings, LNCS, vol 11784. Springer, pp 36–51

Denicoló V (2008) A signalling model of environmental compliance. J Econ Behav Org 68:293–303

Durner T, Shetret L (2015) Understanding bank de-risking and its effects on financial inclusion – an exploratory study. Oxfam, Oxford

EBA (2022) Opinion of the European banking authority on 'de-risking'. https://www.eba.europa.eu/sites/default/documents/files/document_library/Publications/Opinions/2022/Opinion%20on%20de-risking%20%28EBA-Op-2022-01%29/1025705/EBA%20Opinion%20and%20annexed%20report%20on%20de-risking.pdf

EBA (2023) Final report guidelines on policies and controls for the effective management of money laundering and terrorist financing (ML/TF) risks when providing access to financial services. https://www.eba.europa.eu/sites/default/documents/files/document_library/Publications/Guidelines/2023/1054144/Guidelines%20on%20MLTF%20risk%20management%20and%20access%20to%20financial%20services.pdf

El Khoury C (ed) (2023) Countering the financing of terrorism: good practices to enhance effectiveness. IMF, Washington DC. https://www.elibrary.imf.org/display/book/9798400204654/9798400204654.xml

Erbenová M, Liu Y, Kyriakos-Saad N, López-Mejía A, Gasha C, Mathias E, Norat M, Fernando F, Almeida Y (2016) The withdrawal of correspondent banking relationships: a case for policy action. IMF, Washington DC

FATF (2003) The forty recommendations. FATF, Paris. https://www.fatf-gafi.org/content/dam/fatf-gafi/recommendations/FATF%20Recommendations%202003.pdf

FATF (2012-2023) International standards on combating money laundering and the financing of terrorism & proliferation – the FATF recommendations. FATF, Paris

FATF (2013) FATF guidance: anti-money laundering and terrorist financing measures and financial inclusion. FATF, Paris. https://www.fatf-gafi.org/content/fatf-gafi/en/publications/Financialinclusionandnpoissues/Revisedguidanceonamlcftandfinancialinclusion.html

FATF (2013a) FATF guidance: politically exposed persons (recommendations 12 and 22). FATF, Paris. https://www.fatf-gafi.org/content/dam/fatf-gafi/guidance/Guidance-PEP-Rec12-22.pdf.coredownload.pdf

FATF (2013b) Guidance: national money laundering and terrorist financing risk assessment. FATF, Paris. https://www.fatf-gafi.org/en/publications/Methodsandtrends/Nationalmoneylaunderingandterroristfinancingriskassessment.html

FATF (2014) FATF clarifies risk-based approach: case-by-case, not wholesale re-risking. FATF, Paris

FATF (2014a) Guidance for a risk-based approach: the banking sector. FATF, Paris. https://www.fatf-gafi.org/content/dam/fatf-gafi/guidance/Risk-Based-Approach-Banking-Sector.pdf.coredownload.pdf

FATF (2016) Guidance for a risk-based approach: money or value transfer services. FATF, Paris. https://www.fatf-gafi.org/content/dam/fatf-gafi/guidance/Guidance-RBA-money-value-transfer-services.pdf.coredownload.pdf

FATF (2017) Guidance on AML/CFT measures and financial inclusion, with a supplement on customer due diligence. FATF, Paris. https://www.fatf-gafi.org/en/publications/Financialinclusionandnpoissues/Revisedguidanceonamlcftandfinancialinclusion.html

FATF (2019) Terrorist financing risk assessment guidance. FATF, Paris. https://www.fatf-gafi.org/en/publications/Methodsandtrends/Terrorist-financing-risk-assessment-guidance.html

FATF (2021) Guidance on proliferation financing risk assessment and mitigation. FATF, Paris. https://www.fatf-gafi.org/en/publications/Financingofproliferation/Proliferation-financing-risk-assessment-mitigation.html

FATF (2022) Mitigating the unintended consequences of the FATF standards. FATF, Paris. https://www.fatf-gafi.org/en/publications/Financialinclusionandnpoissues/Unintended-consequences-project.html

Ferreira S (2014) Measuring reputational risk in the South African Banking sector. North-West University, MCom. https://repository.nwu.ac.za/bitstream/handle/10394/17041/Ferreira_S.pdf?sequence=1&isAllowed=y

Ferwerda J, Kleemans ER (2019) Estimating money laundering risks: an application to business sectors in the Netherlands. Eur J Crim Policy Res 25:45–62. https://doi.org/10.1007/s10610-018-9391-4

Ferwerda J, Reuter P (2022) National assessments of money laundering risks: learning from eight advanced countries. NRAs. https://openknowledge.worldbank.org/server/api/core/bitstreams/b860c956-659e-5005-93c9-4f06993c37ab/content

Financial Services Board (2019) FSB action plan to assess and address the decline in correspondent banking: progress report 2019. FSB, Basel

Financial Services Board (2020) Enhancing cross-border payments: stage 3 roadmap. FSB, Basel. https://www.fsb.org/wp-content/uploads/P131020-1.pdf

Fiordelis F, Soana M-G, Schwizer P (2014) Reputational losses and operational risk in banking. Eur J Financ 20(2):105–124. https://doi.org/10.1080/1351847X.2012.684218

Gangadharan L (2006) Environmental compliance by firms in the manufacturing sector in Mexico. Ecol Econ 59(4):477–486

Gelemerova L (2009) On the frontline against money-laundering: the regulatory minefield. Crime Law Soc Chang 52(1):33–55

Global Partnership for Financial Inclusion (2016) Global standard-setting bodies and financial inclusion: the evolving landscape. CGAP, Washington DC

Global Standards Proportionality Working Group (2016) Stemming the tide of de-risking through innovative technologies and partnerships. Alliance for Financial Inclusion, Kuala Lumpur

Governatori G (2017) A short introduction to the regorous compliance by design methodology. In: TERECOM-2017, Technologies for regulatory compliance proceedings of the 1st workshop on technologies for regulatory compliance, CEUR-2049, pp 7–13

Governatori G, Barnes J, Zeleznikow J, Hashmi M, De Koker L, Poblet M, Casanovas P (2020) 'Rules as code' will let computers apply laws and regulations. but over-rigid interpretations would undermine our freedoms. The Conversation. 26 November 2020. https://theconversation.com/rules-as-code-will-let-computers-apply-laws-and-regulations-but-over-rigid-interpretations-would-undermine-our-freedoms-149992

Gunningham N, Kagan R, Thornton D (2004) Social license and environmental protection: why businesses go beyond compliance. Law Soc Inquiry 29(2):307–341

Haines F, Gurney D (2003) The shadows of the law: contemporary approaches to regulation and the problem of regulatory conflict. Law Policy 25(4):353–380

Hashmi M, Casanovas P, De Koker L (2018a) Legal compliance through design: preliminary results of a literature survey. In: TERECOM-2018, Technologies for regulatory compliance. proceedings of the 2nd workshop on technologies for regulatory compliance, CEUR-2309, pp 59–72

Hashmi M, Governatori G, Lam H-P, Wynn MT (2018b) Are we done with business process compliance: state of the art and challenges ahead. Knowl Inf Syst 57(1):79–133

IMF/World Bank (2021) A draft framework for money laundering/terrorist financing risk assessment of a remittance corridor. https://www.imf.org/-/media/Files/Research/imf-and-g20/2021/g20-methodology-for-remittance-corridor-risk-assessment.ashx

Keatinge T (2014) Uncharitable behaviour. Demos, London

Klievink B, Janssen M, Van der Voort H, Van Engelenburg S (2018) Regulatory compliance and over-compliant information sharing – changes in the B2G landscape. In: Parycek P, Glassey O, Janssen M, Scholl HJ, Tambouris E, Kalampokis E, Virkar S (eds) International conference on electronic government. Springer, Cham, pp 249–260

Langevoort D (2002) Monitoring: the behavorial economics of corporate compliance with law. Colum Bus Law Rev 71:71–118

Lyman T, De Koker L, Kerse M, Martin Maier C (2019) Beyond KYC utilities. CGAP, Washington, DC. https://www.cgap.org/sites/default/files/publications/2019_08_28_Working_Paper_Beyond_KYC_Utilities_0.pdf

Migration and Remittances Team (2015) Migration and remittances: recent developments and outlook special topic -financing for development, Migration and development brief, vol 24. World Bank, Washington DC

Mintz S (2005) Corporate governance in an international context: legal systems, financing patterns and cultural variables. Corp Gov 13(5):582–597

Momberg R, De Koker L (2020) Adopting SupTech for anti-money laundering: a diagnostic toolkit. Bankable Frontiers Associates: Regtech for Regulators Accelerator. https://bfaglobal.com/wp-content/uploads/2020/06/R2A-AML-SupTech-Toolkit-04June2020-1.pdf

MONEYVAL Committee of Experts on the Evaluation of Anti-Money Laundering Measures and the Financing of Terrorism (2015) 'De-risking' within MONEYVAL states and territories. Council of Europe, Strasbourg

Office of the Comptroller of the Currency (2021) Fair access to financial services RIN 1557-AF05. https://www.occ.gov/news-issuances/news-releases/2021/nr-occ-2021-8a.pdf

Fiorelli P (2004) Will U.S. sentencing commission amendments encourage a new ethical culture within organizations? Wake Forest Law Rev 39:565–586

Raynor B (2022) The shadow of sanctions: reputational risk, financial reintegration, and the political economy of sanctions relief. Eur J Int Rel 28(3):696–721. https://doi.org/10.1177/13540661221100540

Sadiq S, Governatori G, Naimiri K (2007) Modeling of control objectives for business process compliance. In: Alonso G, Dadam P, Rosemann M (eds) Business process management. Springer, Heidelberg, pp 149–164

Salop S, Scheffman D (1983) Raising rivals' costs. Am Econ Rev 73(3):267–271

Scott P, Schryer-Roy A-M, Murphy B, Pomfret E (2015) Hanging by a thread: the ongoing threat to Somalia's remittance lifeline. Oxfam, Oxford

Shimshack J, Ward M (2008) Enforcement and over-compliance. J Environ Econ Manag 55(1): 90–105

Sinha G (2014) To suspect or not to suspect: analysing the pressure on banks to be 'policemen'. J Bank Regul 15:75–86

Southworth R, Levi M (2024) Application of the risk-based approach (RBA) for financial crime risk management by banks. In: Goldbarsht D, de Koker L (eds) Financial crime and the law. Ius Gentium: comparative perspectives on law and justice, vol 115. Springer, Cham. https://doi.org/10.1007/978-3-031-59543-1_5

The Commonwealth (2016) Disconnecting from global finance de-risking: the impact of AML/CFT regulations in commonwealth developing countries. Commonwealth Secretariat, London

Union of Arab Banks, IMF (2015) The impact of de-risking on MENA banks. IMF, Washington

US Department of the Treasury (2023) The department of the treasury's de-risking strategy. https://home.treasury.gov/system/files/136/Treasury_AMLA_23_508.pdf

Woodsome J, Ramachandran V, Lowery C, Myers J (2018) Policy responses to de-risking: progress report on the CGD Working Group's 2015 recommendations. Centre for Global Development, Washington DC

World Bank (2018) The decline in access to correspondent banking services in emerging markets: trends, impacts, and solutions lessons learned from eight country case studies. The World Bank, Washington DC

Worrell D, Brei M, Cato L, Dixon S, Kellmann B, Walrond S (2016) De-risking in the Caribbean: the unintended consequences of international financial reform. Central Bank of Barbados, Bridgetown

Wu JJ, Wirkkala T (2009) Firms motivations for environmental over-compliance. Rev Law Econ 5(1):399–433

Louis de Koker LLB LLM (UFS) LLM (Cantab) LLD (UFS) FSALS, is a Professor and Associate Dean: Research and Industry Engagement at the La Trobe Law School (Australia), an Extraordinary Professor at the Faculty of Law of the University of the Western Cape (South Africa) and a Board member of the Financial Integrity Hub (FIH) at Macquarie Law School. From 2014 to 2019 he was the national program leader of the Law and Policy research program of the Australian government-funded Data to Decisions Cooperative Research Centre. Louis is an expert on anti-money laundering and counterterrorist and proliferation financing, and especially the relationship between financial integrity and financial inclusion policies and regulations. Louis has worked with the Consultative Group to Assist the Poor, the World Bank, the OECD, the Asian Development Bank regulators and financial service providers on the design and implementation of appropriate integrity and inclusion over the past two decades. He has advised on a range of laws and regulations and his research on integrity laws and their impact on financial inclusion has been cited in publications of various international bodies including the World Bank, IMF, the Financial Action Task Force (FATF) and the Basel Committee on Banking Supervision.

Pompeu Casanovas [h-Index: 37] is a Research Professor at the Research Institute on Artificial Intelligence of the Spanish Research Council (IIIA-CSIC), and an Adjunct Professor at La Trobe Law School and the Autonomous University of Barcelona. He has been a Key Researcher of the Australian government-funded Data to Decisions Cooperative Research Centre (2017–2019) and Research Professor at the La Trobe Law School (2017–2021). He is also Director of Advanced Research, and he has been founder and Head, of the Institute of Law and Technology at the Autonomous University of Barcelona (IDT-UAB) (2005–2020). At present, he is leading the IDT SGR 00534 (funded Research Group of Excellence, Catalan Government, 2022–2025). He has been Key or Principal Researcher in over 100 national, European, and international projects, and has authored, co-authored or edited about 30 books (in three different languages) and more than 150 scientific articles on AI, cybersecurity, regulatory models, the semantic web, and intellectual history.

Money Laundering Through Real Estate: Why, and How, New Zealand has Sought to Regulate It

Gary Hughes

Abstract New Zealand property markets have had problems with money laundering and foreign investment at times, which might have partially contributed to overheated real estate booms. Gatekeeper professions including real estate agents, lawyers and accountants were forced to address it via expanded AML regulatory measures. Challenges remain, even as neighbouring Australia begins its own journey towards regulating the sector.

1 Introduction

For a lot of people the most important and valuable possession they will come to own in a lifetime will be the house or apartment they live in. For some, the aspirational lifestyle ticket they seek may include a beach house or condominium as well. For others, real estate investments are an enticing way to grow wealth, trade up in societal levels, save for retirement, or perhaps fill a portfolio with residential rental properties or commercial real estate holdings.

In short, property investment is intrinsic to the western way of life for many ordinary citizens. Additionally, in New Zealand, Australia and Canada at least, the property sector is a very significant driver of economic prosperity. But the same sentiments are also true for criminals and those seeking to invest the profits of a lifestyle involving crime. Therein lies a regular conundrum which anti-financial crime policymakers come up against in their efforts to identify, contain and deter money laundering through real property.

This chapter seeks to explore the ways in which the proceeds of criminal endeavours may be applied into real estate markets, the concerns such laundering

G. Hughes (✉)
Barrister, Britomart Chambers, Auckland, New Zealand
e-mail: gary@garyhughes.nz

D. Goldbarsht, L. de Koker (eds.), *Financial Crime, Law and Governance*, Ius Gentium: Comparative Perspectives on Law and Justice 116,
https://doi.org/10.1007/978-3-031-59547-9_4

of money arouses, and then the attempts to build legal controls and oversight regimes to regulate the real estate sector for anti-money laundering ("AML") purposes.

In evaluating such sins and systems, this chapter primarily addresses the New Zealand experience, which has advanced rapidly as that country's anti-money laundering efforts have stepped up. To a lesser extent, key developments are noted in real estate AML controls under consideration in Western jurisdictions facing similar money laundering threats and challenges—namely, Australia and British Columbia, Canada.

The particular perspective offered comes from deep practitioner experience as a practising lawyer working across business client, regulatory enforcement and policymaker view-points on financial crime cases.

This chapter attempts to deal with those issues by focusing on New Zealand as a case study, with insights from the criminal law and the proceeds of crime recovery laws of the ways in which criminal funds have infiltrated real estate markets or investments. That reflects the author's view that the most helpful way to understand AML rules and regulatory regimes is as part of a tripartite system with (in most nations) three inter-dependent elements:

- The set of criminal laws that contain money laundering ("ML") definitions and offences;
- A framework for freezing, then potentially confiscating, assets for forfeiture under a criminal proceeds recovery ("CPR") legal regime;
- The regulatory system (part civil, part criminal) for AML controls and for countering the financing of terrorism ("CFT"), which require private sector reporting entities to help supply the information that continues to fuel the first two elements.

Dwelling on New Zealand's Anti-Money Laundering and Countering Financing of Terrorism Act 2009 ("AML/CFT Act")[1] in isolation or in advance of the other two elements can lead to a blinkered view of what AML is trying to achieve in real estate and other markets. It may miss the essential reason why regulatory compliance rules exists in the first place (risk of money laundering via property dealings) or the modern policing objective that overlays AML controls (asset seizures of tainted property).

After examining real estate risks and evidence, the particular regulatory controls imposed on reporting entities in New Zealand for AML and CFT purposes return to focus. This captured banks and financial institutions after 2013, and later evolved to real estate agents and brokers—alongside accountants, lawyers and conveyancers. A comparison with similar issues in Australia, still at the beginning of this journey to properly regulate the real estate sector for laundering threat, is made.

Brief commentary on related legislative measures to control inbound foreign property investment, and corporate or trust structures often seen in conjunction with property dealings, helps remind us that AML regulation cannot be seen in

[1] AML/CFT Act (NZ), New Zealand Parliament, public Act No 35 of 2009.

isolation. These investor and trustee controls, beneficial ownership data, and other government policy measures, all help curb abuse of the residential property market or landowner holding structures.

2 Evolution of the Money Laundering environment and Anti-Money Laundering Frameworks

These days New Zealand has a modern and comprehensive set of controls to make life difficult for those seeking to launder criminal proceeds in various parts of the economy, albeit with the usual range of strengths and weaknesses in terms of likely outcomes or effectiveness of these controls.

That has not always been the case.

Whilst New Zealand has been a member of the Financial Action Task Force ("FATF") since 1991 and its early support of multi-lateral crime prevention efforts through international advocacy led to the arrival of a basic sort of early AML statute,[2] the law in New Zealand did not keep pace with global developments. It remained misunderstood and rarely honoured by the business community, and was not updated to meet newer FATF recommendations ("FATF 2012") or expectations during later evaluation rounds.

Meanwhile, adding fuel to the international peer pressure, neighbouring Australia had in 2006 passed new Federal AML legislation.[3] New Zealand was then becoming seen as a laggard that had not progressed beyond the basics of implementing FATF standards for mostly cash-based reporting.

That led to considerable catch-up pressure (as the FATF evaluation process tends to impose upon small nations) to radically improve the regulatory regime, to equip it to deal with financial crime matters more effectively in the new century. That process had significant impact in 2008–9 as the spur to finally pass an all-embracing AML/CFT Act. That updated law was largely a response to criticisms contained in the mutual evaluation of New Zealand's legal regime publicly released in October 2009—during the same week that final reading to pass the new law was taking place in Parliament.

Given the scale of the 2009 changes and the compliance costs (falling heavily upon the banking sector initially) important policy choices had to be made about how wide coverage should go at the start. A broader 'Phase 2' coverage that would encompass real estate agents and other professionals was always contemplated at the outset as policymakers were framing the original draft AML/CFT Bill in 2008. But for various reasons the political change to bring professions under the regime did not

[2]FTR Act (NZ), public Act No 9 of 1996 - since repealed on 1 August 2019, once the full Phase II AML coverage later legislated in 2017 became operative over other professional sectors.

[3]In the shape of the Anti-Money Laundering and Counter-Terrorism Financing Act 2006 (Commonwealth).

come about until 2017, when specific Amendment reforms were hastened through. That was in response to embarrassing revelations in the Panama Papers disclosures, with New Zealand in danger of becoming branded as a tax haven due to gatekeeper and trustee abuses.

Finally then, the International Consortium of Investigative Journalists Panama exposé combined with looming revisitation of the FATF for its fourth-round evaluations by about 2019, brought about the difficult but necessary political engagements. This meant dealing with objections of professionals (lawyers, accountants, real estate, trustees/advisors) and creating compromises to get them included in a way that broadly met FATF recommendations for designated non-financial businesses and professions ("DNFBPs").[4]

In this way, like a trans-Tasman game of regulatory leapfrog, New Zealand moved ahead of Australia. It positioned itself to better protect the economy from criminal investments, and win plaudits from the international community. Australia was now left looking like the laggard. Now, some 6 years later the Attorney-General's Department of Australia's Federal Parliament looks set to emulate New Zealand's move and finally legislate to include its DNFBP sectors[5] as designated services under their counterpart legislation:

> Part 2 of this Consultation Paper proposes extending the AML/CTF regime to certain high-risk professions, including lawyers, accountants, trust and company service providers, real estate agents and dealers in precious metals and stones (also known as tranche-two entities).

Again, this consultation in the Australian context explicitly references external pressure:[6]

> Australia will undergo its next Mutual Evaluation between 2025 and 2027 and is at risk of receiving low ratings and potential grey listing if we do not undertake significant reform.

2.1 *Crimes Act: Codified Money Laundering Definitions and Offences*

Before diving into exploring the range of captured reporting entities and core compliance obligations upon those entities (including realty, licensed conveyancers, and conveyancing lawyers in New Zealand), it will help to first summarise the country's criminal ML legal structure. That lends itself to understanding the rationale and rise of New Zealand's AML regulatory laws in better context.

Primary New Zealand money laundering offences are found in the Crimes Act 1961, in terms also familiar to Australia and jurisdictions across the western world.

---

[4]See FATF Recommendations, R 22, and Glossary, for internationally understood definitions.

[5]*Modernising and Simplifying Australia's AML-CTF Law* (2023) Attorney-General's Department, p. 3.

[6]*Modernising and Simplifying Australia's AML-CTF Law*, ibid. (2023), p. 19.

The offence provisions refer to a person engaging in a "money laundering transaction", which is also separately defined. The key elements of a money laundering transaction involve a person:[7]

- dealing with, or assisting in dealing with, any property for the purpose of concealing it or enabling another person to conceal any property; and
- knowing or believing that such property is the proceeds of a criminal offence, or being reckless as to whether it is the proceeds of offending.

"Property" is widely defined in s 243(1) of the Crimes Act to cover both real property and personal property. In its breadth this matches Australian law as s 400.1 of the Criminal Code Act 1995 (Cth) makes clear:[8]

> ***property*** means real or personal property of every description, whether situated in [-New Zealand/ Australia – *as applicable*] or elsewhere and whether tangible or intangible, and includes an interest in any such real or personal property

This explicitly includes any interest in real property, which opens up the range of legal and beneficial interests in land, even if short of full ownership. It is plain that across both countries, real estate interests always have been intended to be one core type of asset class for which laundering dealings may commonly occur, and it would be surprising not to have it front and centre.

"Conceal" is defined as concealing or disguising the property and includes (without limitation) converting the property into another form and concealing or disguising the nature, source, location, disposition, or ownership of the property—or of any interest in the property. "Deal with" means to deal with the property in any manner and by any means and includes disposing of, transferring possession, or bringing the property into or out from the country.

The *mens rea* or state of mind required for money laundering is a knowledge or belief that all or part of the property is the proceeds of an offence, or being reckless as to whether the property is the proceeds of such an offence. For laundering charges, knowledge must also include some intention to conceal the property or to assist another to do so. In practice the lower threshold of 'recklessness' is very commonly included in charges and relied upon in court.

Money laundering charges carry maximum penalties of up to 7 years in jail for individuals if convicted. Corporations and other legal persons as well as natural persons can be prosecuted, in which case a court may impose a fine instead on a company.

There is also a lesser offence of *possession of property* for money laundering purposes, punishable by up to 5 years in jail.[9] To establish that offence, it must be proven that the property was the proceeds of an offence committed by another, and

[7] Elements paraphrased from s 243(2)–(4), Crimes Act 1961, public Act No 43 of 1961.

[8] Criminal Code Act 1995 (Cth), Federal legislation, No 12 of 1995.

[9] Section 243(3), Crimes Act 1961.

that the accused had the requisite knowledge or was reckless, and intended to engage in a money laundering transaction in respect of that property.

2.2 Police Financial Intelligence Materials on Real Estate Risks

The New Zealand Police Financial Intelligence Unit ("FIU") is the national body that is recipient of all AML reports. It acts as the fulcrum of the intelligence system. It operates in and amongst other Police units, including a Money Laundering Unit to focus on criminal evidence and prosecutions, several regional Asset Recovery Units, and a variety of other law enforcement agencies or regulators outside of Police to whom the FIU disseminates intelligence reports and case alerts.

The FIU produced an important report in 2015, well before New Zealand included real estate reporting entities, which highlighted money laundering drivers in property markets (Quarterly Typology Report (2015)).[10] There, the FIU noted reasons why a money cleansing scheme involving real estate may be attractive, including:

- the ultimate goal of the laundering being to integrate proceeds as real estate, to enjoy their use—just like other people, criminals enjoy having a house to live in, likely capital gains, or legitimate rental income which commercial property, flats or farms may provide—with which to mingle illicit proceeds;
- the sale of property may be used to explain the source of funds, providing a seemingly legitimate trail story;
- real estate transactions are large, allowing large sums to be laundered through one vehicle;
- beneficial ownership legal structures such as trusts, nominees or companies may be considered commonplace, and setting them up using gate keepers (lawyers, accountants, wealth advisers) unremarkable in the context of a large property investment;
- real estate is a speculative market where values may be difficult to accurately appraise—heavily turning on what a particular buyer is willing to pay, especially with atypical properties (enabling easy under/over valuing techniques);
- transactions provide access to routine financial vehicles, like mortgages, through which to mix tainted with legitimate funds;
- real estate and its investment vehicles may be seen as less conspicuous options for overseas investment, with foreign buyers not unusual;
- placement of proceeds generated by fraud into the real estate sector may be inherent in the predicate offending, or in the laundering process itself as property fraud or misrepresentation issues arise relatively frequently.

[10] Quarterly Typology report - fiu-quarterly-typology-report-Q4 of 2014–2015 Real Estate.pdf.

These local New Zealand findings are echoed in both recent FATF materials[11] and in the Cullen Commission's extensive literature survey and conclusions reached in British Columbia, Canada.[12]

The FIU conducted analysis of 47 properties subject to CPR action at that time (over the period 2009–2015) with a value of over NZ$27 m addressed in 20 court cases. Given the focus of the CPR on the wealth of motorcycle gang members during this period, the bulk of that is likely to be real estate holdings of gang members, their partners and associates or compliant third parties.

Sufficient details of the value of criminal funds directly laundered through buying properties was available from 12 of the cases to say that at least NZ$8 m in criminal proceeds had been laundered. The source of the remaining funds used for the property purchase was either not able to be proven by police, or found to come from legitimate means such as a bank mortgage.

Interesting conclusions as to methods of laundering were drawn by the FIU from this sample set. Attempts to disguise the ownership of property (e.g. placing it in the name of an associate, family member or creating a trust) was the most common laundering method and occurred in all cases the FIU analysed. The next most common method was transferring the criminal proceeds to a lawyer or estate agent by electronic transfer, followed by using tainted funds to make mortgage repayments.

Several less common loan methods were noticed, including: transferring a loan from a business borrowing into a trust which purchased the property (with the offender as a beneficiary of the trust), and transferring a loan to overseas lawyers in Australia to enable the offender to purchase a property there in his own name. With mortgage repayments being prevalent, another case study involved using property as security for mortgage applications to acquire a portfolio of investment properties, while deliberately applying for low mortgage amounts to avoid revealing the source of income, then inputting criminal proceeds disguised as rental income, to service the mortgage repayments.

Most techniques were directed at property ownership, while a minority 7 cases (15%) involved property mortgages being repaid by criminal proceeds. Given the large size of most real estate acquisitions, payment of full settlement funds in cash is less likely to be pragmatic for laundering. Interestingly, however, there was a high proportion of cash usage in repaying mortgage streams—a known methodology that banks and non-bank financiers are warned about.

Anecdotally, many real estate agents did not find it unusual to receive the deposit for a house in cash—possibly many tens of thousands of dollars—at least prior to 2019 when they became reporting entities themselves and had to ask more questions. The same might be found with a few lawyers, prior to 2018. In one significant case documented in the FIU Quarterly Typology report, some $300,000 cash was taken

[11] FATF (2022), *Guidance for a Risk-Based Approach to the Real Estate Sector.*

[12] See *Cullen Commission* B.C. Canada (2022), Chapter 15 "Vulnerabilities to Money Laundering in Real Estate", see especially pp. 773–775.

directly to a lawyer who subsequently deposited the cash into the law firm trust account via 4 separate deposits although Police noted "*this method of placing does not seem to be the norm*". The lawyer filed an STR in relation to this cash transaction, but misled in the details entered on the STR form. In that case the offender met with a lawyer to discuss purchasing a section with a view to building a house on it, both knowing the person was bankrupt and owed $1.2 m, which he was attempting to hide from the official bankruptcy assignee.

The FIU also intermittently prepare a National Risk Assessment document, setting out the most high level criminal threats affecting the country. It is seen as a key component to building an effective national response to money laundering and terrorism financing, a part of the FATF-endorsed risk-based approach. The most recent 2019 version[13] included a number of illuminating comments about the role of real estate in our illicit financing risk environment, including:

- Gatekeeper professional services such as formation of companies, trusts and charities, and including real estate, is one of the 6 highest priority national vulnerabilities.
- Channels which particularly offer laundering opportunity are real estate or legal services that offer anonymity, are widely available (including internationally), and allow movement of large values, or provide an opaque screen for illicit funds.
- Each of the 3 main predicate offences in New Zealand (drug offending, fraud and tax offending) have real estate featuring in their profiles, typically at the integration phase of ML when funds are being brought back together in shape of a valuable, clean-looking asset.
- Most assets of the biggest 5 banks are focused on lending to the domestic private sector, especially lending for residential real estate and farms—with real estate identified as vulnerable and attractive to criminal investment, the risk of high value ML in New Zealand may be more skewed towards real estate investments compared to some other jurisdictions.
- Professional persons are critical because of the specialist knowledge needed to complete a real estate transaction, where property transfers including the receipt of settlement funds are invariably facilitated by experienced law firms or conveyancers, and where Land Information New Zealand (LINZ) which administers the central land registry and transfers title online significantly limits public access to a person licensed within one of the gatekeeper professions
- Criminals may seek a client relationship with a real estate agent as either vendors or purchasers, and to buy land from, or sell to, third parties they will need introductions to counterparties, most commonly done through agents (although private advertisement of house sales is not unknown).
- Historical low rates of suspicious transaction reporting ("STR") by professional services (under the old 1996 law) indicated that general measures were not ensuring sufficient vigilance and reporting—but the Phase 2 reforms went some

[13]National Risk Assessment, of money laundering and terrorism financing, NZ Police Financial Intelligence Unit 2019.

way to addressing this vulnerability and highlighting the differing risks of ML to lawyers, conveyancers, accountants and real estate agents. FIU statistics at that stage (up to 6 June 2019) showed that since becoming reporting entities under the AML/CFT Act, it had received 137 suspicious activity reports from lawyers, 65 from real estate agents, and 14 from accountants.

2.3 Criminal (Proceeds) Recovery Act: Asset Recovery Measures

The Criminal Proceeds (Recovery) Act 2009 ("CPR Act") is a detailed legislative scheme for asset freezing and forfeiture orders over property that might represent the proceeds of crime. Like most modern international asset recovery laws, its most important break with older legal formats was to move to a non-conviction based regime. Waiting for a criminal conviction is not required for the Police to seek early restraining orders, or even a forfeiture order.

All that is required for orders to be made by the Court is identification of assets or specific criminal proceeds with proof of "significant criminal activity." That has to be demonstrated to the lower civil evidential balance of probabilities standard. Significant criminal activity means crimes that would amount to an offence imprisonable by at least 5 years, or from which property/proceeds over NZ $30,000 have been directly or indirectly obtained.

Until 2015, the AML/CFT Act also contained a definition that acted as a trigger for STRs where the underlying predicate crime was thought to be a "serious offence" engaging potential imprisonment of 5 years or more. Then, statutory amendments were made to increase the catchment of intelligence material for reporting to the Police, where that threshold of "serious offence" was removed, such that any level of offending can found a basis to make a suspicious activity report. But the threshold of 5 years' prison sentence remains in the CPR Act.

The CPR Act was passed in the same Parliamentary term in 2009 as the AML/CFT Act, and they were seen as two sides of the same dirty coin. The CPR Act's purpose statement gives clues as to why it is such a powerful weapon against organised crime:[14]

> (1) The primary purpose of this Act is to establish a regime for the forfeiture of property—
>
> (a) that has been derived directly or indirectly from significant criminal activity; or
> (b) that represents the value of a person's unlawfully derived income.

It shares the objective of deterrence and elimination of organised criminal activity with the AML/CFT Act, which speaks of "detecting and deterring" ML behaviour. At a policy level, one system generates intelligence from the reporting entity community about financial crime (and underlying criminal predicates), while the

[14] Contained in section 3, Criminal Proceeds (Recovery) Act 2009, public Act No 8 of 2009.

other system makes use of that intelligence to lead asset recovery operations that strip out the profits/benefits of such criminal activity.

Several types of orders are available: asset forfeiture orders, profit forfeiture orders and instrument forfeiture orders. Prior to forfeiture, the CPR Act provides for restraining orders to freeze assets and property, for what can be potentially a long period until court outcomes are finally determined. Freezing orders are used extensively by police, usually on a without notice court application at the outset of an intended case.

These are powerful legislative provisions, some would say draconian, and New Zealand Police asset recovery units are flexing them to maximum legal effect. Equally, there can be risk of over-reach, and evidence of disproportionate hardship in some cases, especially upon partners/spouses having interest in a home that may be seized.[15]

The most significant property seizure under this CPR Act legal artillery involved a Chinese person with Canadian residency, under suspicion due to financial fraud allegations in North America that also emanated from his home country of China. He apparently found New Zealand an attractive place for property investments, without ever setting foot here to live.[16]

Mr. Edward Gong was investigated from about 2016 being by both the Chinese Public Security Bureau (Economic Crime Investigation Department) and also the Ontario Securities Commission in Canada, where he then resided. The investigations concern an alleged large-scale fraud, linked to a pyramid financial scheme associated with the supposed sale of health supplements. It is said that the schemes gave rise to unlawful benefits exceeding NZ$200 million, of which the authorities concluded that Mr. Gong remitted some NZ$77 million obtained from the fraud to various investments in New Zealand.[17]

Once the funds were in this country, through small money remittance channels rather than mainstream banking channels, Gong used money alleged derived from the fraud to purchase property and other assets. Acting on mutual legal assistance request provisions between nations, in 2017 the Commissioner of Police initiated a CPR Act case to obtain Court orders freezing much of his New Zealand asset-base. Protracted court proceedings ultimately led to negotiations and finally in June 2021 a permanent forfeiture of NZ$70 m in assets to close a major cross border settlement—at the time, the largest single forfeiture under the CPR Act.[18]

This CPR case progressed in parallel with another enforcement proceeding based upon AML/CFT Act breaches of the foreign exchange remittance firm used by

---

[15] For instance, in the Australian context, *Pocketing the proceeds of crime*, Australian Institute of Criminology (2020), see "The case of Miss C", p. 64.

[16] Online media: https://www.nzherald.co.nz/nz/canadian-xiao-hua-gong-claims-evidence-to-freeze-70m-in-nz-coerced-in-china/TTT4PSLHRW22G5IGLTON2J7P5U/.

[17] *Commissioner of Police v Gong* [2019] NZHC 2735.

[18] https://www.police.govt.nz/news/release/pyramid-scheme-leads-nzs-largest-ever-forfeiture.

Mr. Gong.[19] In a demonstration of the degree to which the CPR and AML regimes are necessarily inter-dependent, that action against a reporting entity and its principals/compliance officer later ended up as one of New Zealand's leading case precedents now on criminal liability for AML regulatory breaches, and on structuring of transactions to avoid reporting thresholds.

The Australian Federal Police has been active also in taking out restraining orders over similar real estate portfolios that may have accrued from criminal investments or showed signs of laundering behaviour, especially with offshore owners. This is not a recent development, as evidenced by the multi-agency, multi-year Project Wickenby (Beaufighter) from 2006 onwards,[20] but stepped up in recent times including Operation Ironside (AN0M) in 2022[21] and Operation Avarus-Midas in 2023.[22]

3 Summary: Why We Need to Regulate Real Estate

This brief survey of the criminal law offences and active CPR restraints system which frequently features land and buildings seizures, ended with some recent high profile cases involving actual laundering through the property sector. These threads can be drawn together to sum up arguments for why this is a high risk field of economic activity, perhaps regulatory provisions for real estate agents and property firms engaged in relevant activities.

In summary form, key elements of real estate and property developments make them meaningful as an economic area at risk of misuse for financial crime, and hence also money laundering:

- Both legitimate persons/companies, and the criminally minded, may aspire to purchase and sell real estate—and their characteristics or motivations may from the outside appear similar.
- There is a close relationship in a property transaction between real estate agent, bank or other financier, mortgage advisor, and conveyancing lawyer—so a chain of professionals may be engaged in the same transaction. Since each of those may only have partial insight to some of the relevant information about the nature and purpose of the deal, the AML regime needs to be set up intentionally to ensure

[19] See the separate DIA/Police prosecution case, on appeal *Jiaxin Finance Ltd, Fu & Che v R* [2022] NZCA 287.

[20] Summarised in the AFP in-house publication *Platypus Magazine*, April 2013, p. 49, available at http://www5.austlii.edu.au/au/journals/AUFPPlatypus/2013/12.pdf.

[21] Online media: https://www.thomsonreuters.com/en-us/posts/investigation-fraud-and-risk/australia-money-laundering-sting/.

[22] Online media: https://www.smh.com.au/national/nsw/property-grab-afp-smashes-alleged-10-billion-chinese-money-laundering-operation-20230201-p5ch7k.html.

one or more angles would always catch such transactions for monitoring and reporting if necessary.

- Overseas buyers and customers participate, sometimes with few investment restrictions and sometimes with trust or beneficial owners designed to distance the foreign party from sight.
- The large value of land transactions, and multiple ML risks coming with it (including heavy bank retail lending) means that if laundering is taking place, the impact of that is greater.
- The crossover with opaque ownership models/vehicles, and concerns about hidden beneficial owners, is especially acute in property transactions. Notably, Australia's recent consultation on tranche two reforms expressly tied part of the rationale for reform to beneficial ownership register elements:[23]

> "Legal practitioners, accountants, conveyancers and trust and company service providers provide services that can be exploited to disguise ownership, including the individual who ultimately owns or controls the asset (known as beneficial ownership), conceal the origins and purposes of financial transactions, facilitate tax evasion and, ultimately, launder the proceeds of crime.
>
> Operating through or behind a professional adviser can provide a veneer of legitimacy to criminal activity. These practitioners can be used to create complex structures that create distance between criminals and their illicit wealth, and facilitate obscuring property ownership, providing ideal opportunities for laundering large volumes of illicit funds. The reforms proposed in this paper complement the Government's commitment to implement a beneficial ownership register for companies and other legal entities being led by Treasury."

- The involvement of both high value assets and gatekeepers can lead to professional money laundering features or at least those who facilitate such outcomes. The Australian authorities have experience with this as well, for instance in a case study identified by AUSTRAC in 2021. This involved a real estate agency firm that apparently received more than A$400,000 in proceeds of crime which were described as a loan transaction. But in fact:[24]

> "The funds were then used by the real estate agency to invest in property development. In return, the real estate agency paid the criminals a weekly 'consultancy fee', thus legitimising the proceeds of crime."

[23] *Modernising and Simplifying Australia's AML-CTF Law* (2023) Attorney-General's Department, p. 19.

[24] AUSTRAC (2021), *Australia's major banks: Money laundering and terrorism financing risk assessment*, p. 26 - https://www.austrac.gov.au/sites/default/files/2021-09/Major%20Banks%20ML_TF_Risk%20Assessment%202021.pdf.

4 The Development of Phase 2 DNFBP Regulation in New Zealand

Analysis of New Zealand's modern AML regime centres on the AML/CFT Act, but there is also a thicket of important Regulations, Gazetted Exemption Notices, Supervisor and FIU Guidance and a Code of Practice for identity verification matters. Even if it came with a very long lead time before coming into force in mid-2013, the 2009 legislation represented a major step forward in better targeted compliance steps, which can be seen as split into two phases:

- measures taken (2009–2013) for financial institutions and casinos (Phase 1); and
- extension steps from 2016 onwards for DNFBP firms, known as Phase 2 entities.

Some important and basic rules that were missing in the previous legislation included: much more formal registration of entities operating in fields subject to laundering or terrorist financing risk, clear obligations to carry out customer due diligence, or Know-Your-Customer ("KYC) measures as they are widely known) before servicing the customer, along with regular revisiting and monitoring of customer behaviour. Then there is the machinery of regulatory oversight to ensure all those private businesses subject to the AML regime have detailed written risk assessments and compliance programmes, with an array of policies and controls, assurance checks and regular external auditing and reporting—aimed to ensure obligations to understand and detect ML were being met.

In simple terms, the law aims to force each captured business to more deeply understand the nature and purpose of customer activities, the risk level they may represent, and then focus on areas of its products/services and business operations that ay generate risk of money laundering.

The ultimate goal was to design a series of rules in a compliance framework that would generate better, more frequent and systematic STRs and financial crime intelligence data to the Police. Naturally, the regulatory framework included enforcement powers to punish those entities that failed to meet the list of new elevated compliance duties.

As mentioned above, Phase 2 reforms were eventually accelerated after embarrassing revelations in the ICIJ's Panama Papers disclosures—with New Zealand in danger of becoming branded as a tax haven. It is, unfortunately, common that law reform which is complex and costly will languish until there is a crisis to be faced or an international "name and shame" deadline approaching.

The specific catalyst to move forward Phase 2 changes came in the Shewan Inquiry Report of 2016, officially titled the *Government Inquiry into Foreign Trust Disclosure Rules*.[25] This was not focused on real estate, but on foreign trust abuses and tax avoidance, although such trusts often hold property assets. Its

[25] *Report of the Government Inquiry into Foreign Trust Disclosure Rules*, John Shewan, 27 June 2016, in particular at pp. 53–55: https://www.treasury.govt.nz/publications/information-release/government-inquiry-foreign-trust-disclosure-rules.

recommendations were mainly to close loopholes around the role lawyers and accountants played in trusts, but when Government in May 2016 decided to proceed it was inevitable that real estate should also be covered.

The Shewan Inquiry and examples disclosed in Panama Papers case studies highlighted risks for legal service providers, especially around property transactions, trusts and opaque corporate structures. A particular concern was that New Zealand's renowned ease of doing business, and safe reputation, including favourable tax settings for foreign or offshore trusts, may be attracting criminal groups and agents who may seek to place and layer money for cleansing through the country.[26]

> [1.2] The Inquiry concludes that the existing foreign trust disclosure rules are inadequate. The rules are not fit for purpose in the context of preserving New Zealand's reputation as a country that cooperates with other jurisdictions to counter money laundering and aggressive tax practices.

The Government immediately adopted the Shewan recommendations, and announced intentions to accelerate Phase 2, with the amending legislation passed by July 2017. As a result, Phase 2 sectors ended up with a much shorter implementation period than Phase 1. In a staggered process, lawyers became the first professional sector cab off the rank to be captured by the AML regime, which was applied in full to law firms of all sizes if they provide any of the captured services from 1 July 2018.

Other sectors then followed at different times: accountants from 1 September 2019, real estate agents from 1 January 2019, licenced conveyancers, the TAB totalisator gaming body, and selected dealers in high-value assets later in 2019. All those groups were transitioned into the system over 2 years and now co-exist as reporting entities alongside banks, casinos and financial system players.

A Ministry of Justice discussion paper out for consultation in August 2016 identified "multiple benefits" of extending coverage to Phase 2 entities, including[27]:

- It will reduce the risk of businesses being unwittingly drawn into criminal activity.
- It will improve authorities' ability to detect and investigate serious crimes such as drug offending and tax evasion, by following the money trail that such offences generate.
- Because of its more comprehensive coverage, it will help stop the 'displacement effect' where criminals move their funds to sectors outside of regulated sectors in a bid to avoid detection.
- It will bring New Zealand into line with international best practice and help maintain public and international business confidence in New Zealand's overall financial system.

[26] Shewan Inquiry (2016), ibid., Executive Summary p. 1. The same passage also criticised then applicable light-handed rules:

> [1.4] In theory, New Zealand's existing tax disclosure and exchange of information arrangements should be sufficient to deter tax abuse, and its anti-money laundering rules should ensure that funds held by foreign trusts are from legitimate sources. However, under current law and enforcement practices the risk of detection by authorities is low. The Inquiry considers that the disclosure requirements can be justifiably described as light-handed.

[27] *Improving New Zealand's ability to tackle money laundering and terrorist financing*, Ministry of Justice consultation paper on Phase Two of the AML/CFT Act (August 2016).

New Zealand has a complicated regulatory structure involving 3 AML Supervisors, and a separate Financial Intelligence Unit housed directly within the NZ Police. The Department of Internal Affairs ("DIA") already supervised from Phase 1 casinos, non-deposit taking lenders, money changers, cash security firms, debt collection and factoring, financial leasing, payroll, safe deposit, tax pooling and non-bank credit card firms. Since 2017, it has been charged with also supervising accountants, lawyers, real estate agents, the horse racing industry TAB, and dealers in high-value goods.

The DIA is the default Supervisor and now has a much larger reporting entity catchment than its counterpart regulators at the Financial Markets Authority or Reserve Bank of New Zealand.

4.1 Regulatory Coverage Depends on Activities/Services Provided

The New Zealand regime was designed in 2009 to be an activities-based regime when it came to coverage of entities. In other words, the type of entity or label applied to it is not determinative, coverage instead turns upon whether or not any of a list of particular defined services are offered, and only to the extent those services are provided.[28]

Starting at a broad level, the coverage definitions applicable for all reporting entities are found in the interpretation section 5(1) of the AML/CFT Act—starting with listing categories of firms:

> "reporting entity -
> "(a) means
> "(i) a casino;
> "(ii) a designated non-financial business or profession;
> "(iii) a financial institution;
> "(iv) a high-value dealer;
> "(v) TAB NZ; and ..."

In addition, those core categories can be adjusted to include or exclude parties by regulations that may declare them to be in or out of scope as a reporting entity. Good use of this power during Phase 1 was the specific accelerated inclusion of some types of trust and company secretarial service providers ("TCSPs")—who might on FATF definitions be found to be within Phase 2 DNFBPs, along with casinos. That was done in 2011,[29] because of international concerns and local evidence of the misuse of trust arrangements and shell company structures, meaning at least some types of DNFBP were part of the Phase 1 rollout.

[28] AML/CFT Act 2009, see ss 5 and 6.

[29] Anti-Money Laundering and Countering Financing of Terrorism (Definitions) Regulations 2011, Reg 17: Inclusion: trust and company service providers.

Ironically, similar secretive trust concerns resurfaced in 2016 in the Shewan Inquiry Report (discussed below) which itself precipitated the adoption of all of Phase 2 coverage for other New Zealand firms.

Each of those main umbrella categories in the AML/CFT Act, such as financial institution, high-value dealer, designated non-financial business or profession, has its own separate definition and activities list. At that next level, a sweeping list of covered activities in s 5(1) elaborates further and decisively on what each type of reporting entity category means. For activities carried out by DNFBPs, definitions apply to the kind of activities that may be engaged in by any of the professional groups: lawyers, accountants, real estate agents or conveyancers.

This list can have some complexity so it is best to set it out in full:

designated non-financial business or profession means-

(a) a law firm, a conveyancing practitioner, an incorporated conveyancing firm, an accounting practice, a real estate agent, or a trust and company service provider, who, in the ordinary course of business, carries out 1 or more of the following activities:

  (i) acting as a formation agent of legal persons or legal arrangements:
  (ii) acting as, or arranging for a person to act as, a nominee director or nominee shareholder or trustee in relation to legal persons or legal arrangements:
  (iii) providing a registered office or a business address, a correspondence address, or an administrative address for a company, or a partnership, or for any other legal person or arrangement, unless the office or address is provided solely as an ancillary service to the provision of other services (being services that do not constitute an activity listed in this subparagraph or subparagraphs (i), (ii), and (iv) to (vi)):
  (iv) managing client funds (other than sums paid as fees for professional services), accounts, securities, or other assets:
  (v) providing real estate agency work (within the meaning of section 4(1) of the Real Estate Agents Act 2008) to effect a transaction (within the meaning of section 4(1) of the Real Estate Agents Act 2008):
  (vi) engaging in or giving instructions on behalf of a customer to another person for-

    (A) any conveyancing (within the meaning of section 6 of the Lawyers and Conveyancers Act 2006) to effect a transaction (within the meaning of section 4(1) of the Real Estate Agents Act 2008), namely,—

    - the sale, the purchase, or any other disposal or acquisition of a freehold estate or interest in land:
    - the grant, sale, or purchase or any other disposal or acquisition of a leasehold estate or interest in land (other than a tenancy to which the Residential Tenancies Act 1986 applies):
    - the grant, sale, or purchase or any other disposal or acquisition of a licence that is registrable under the Land Transfer Act 1952:
    - the grant, sale, or purchase or any other disposal or acquisition of an occupation right agreement within the meaning of section 5 of the Retirement Villages Act 2003:

    (B) a transaction (within the meaning of section 4(1) of the Real Estate Agents Act 2008); or
    (C) the transfer of a beneficial interest in land or other real property; or
    (D) a transaction on behalf of any person in relation to the buying, transferring, or selling of a business or legal person (for example, a company) and any other legal arrangement; or

(E) a transaction on behalf of a customer in relation to creating, operating, and managing a legal person (for example, a company) and any other legal arrangement; . . .

For the next level of clarity on what services are captured, entities must follow the cross-referenced definitions to other statutes—in particular, for our purposes, the Real Estate Agents Act 2008. That is the piece of legislation that gives the real estate industry rights, powers and legal status, and also establishes an industry disciplinary and regulatory body (the Real Estate Agents Authority) which handles ethical and related problems but does not have jurisdiction as an AML/CFT Supervisor.

The cross-reference to s 4(1) of that Real Estate Agents Act contains other relevant definitions—most notably of a "transaction" and of "land"—which are as broad as conceivably available, attempting to catch all main types of property investment activity.[30]

Beyond those statutory definitions, there will be types of situations or structure that sit at the margins, where it is unclear whether it will be treated as captured under the definition or not. To cross these deepest levels of distinction, entities need to consult Guidance issued by the DIA as Supervisor (which may be too generic), also some FAQs on its website (which may change over time) or seek their own specialist legal advice, and/or apply for a bespoke exemption if suitable.

A key point reinforcing an 'activity-based' approach is that the activities apply across DNFBP types regardless of which profession is acting. Therefore, it could be an accountant or lawyer or lay TCSP provider setting up companies and trusts, and it equally could be a lawyer, conveyancer or real estate agent in business handling conveyancing work in selling a property. Some duplication may result, but these overlaps emphasise that what matters is what is being done substantively as a regulated activity.

---

[30]Real Estate Agents Act 2008, public Act No 66 of 2008 - where

transaction means any 1 or more of the following:

(a) the sale, purchase, or other disposal or acquisition of a freehold estate or interest in land:

(b) the grant, sale, purchase, or other disposal or acquisition of a leasehold estate or interest in land (other than a tenancy to which the Residential Tenancies Act 1986 applies):

(c) the grant, sale, purchase, or other disposal or acquisition of a licence that is registrable under the Land Transfer Act 2017:

(d) the grant, sale, purchase, or other disposal or acquisition of an occupation right agreement within the meaning of the Retirement Villages Act 2003:

(e) the sale, purchase, or other disposal or acquisition of any business (either with or without any interest in land).

And **land** means:

all estates and interests, whether freehold or chattel, in real property, and includes any building and any part of a building, and any licence that is registrable under the Land Transfer Act 2017, and any occupation right agreement within the meaning of the Retirement Villages Act 2003; and, in relation to any transaction relating to land that also relates to any goods, chattels, or other property, also includes those goods or chattels and that other property.

Compare this with the present complicated but gap-ridden regulatory position of real estate in B.C., Canada, detailed in extensive terms by the Cullen Commission[31] and summarised in pithy terms as:

> Real estate licensees have a poor track record of anti–money laundering reporting and compliance. Despite progress at higher levels (industry organizations and regulators), some licensees continue to display inadequate understanding of how money laundering may occur in real estate and hold on to misplaced beliefs that impact their ability and willingness to adequately meet their anti–money laundering obligations.

Some of the listed concerns/excuses the Cullen Commission heard for non-compliance included: scepticism in the industry that STRs are of any value, or that there is evidence of actual money laundering, a persisting and misplaced perception that cash transactions is all industry needs to focus on, confusion over how to comply, concerns for client privacy and distaste for intrusive questions, and a perception that the compliance burden is unduly onerous.

Those attitudes may, anecdotally speaking, still ring true in a significant minority of New Zealand real estate agency firms, even now after almost 4 years getting used to life under the proactive and intrusive oversight of the DIA as AML/CFT Supervisor. What Australia's currently unregulated real estate sector thinks about money laundering risk is unclear but perhaps similar, if news reports interviewing the Real Estate Institute of Australia might offer any guide, for instance: "*Real estate agencies, buyers to bear costs of proposed anti-money laundering reforms, REIA warns.*"[32]

5 Details of Compliance, and Oddities of the Regulated Real Estate Position

In the build-up to January 2019, when New Zealand real estate agents would become captured, the DIA put out detailed sector compliance guidance, then updated it more than once, and also ended up adding multiple 'Frequently Asked Questions' on its website, by way of detailed granular guidance on more scenarios raised by new Phase 2 entities. Much of that concerned the intricacies of KYC rules—standard customer due diligence, and enhanced due diligence when required under the Act.

That DIA guidance described some key compliance features, being that:[33]

> Real estate agents are most likely to carry out two covered activities: real estate agency work and managing client funds.

[31] Cullen Commission of Inquiry (2022), Chapter 16 "Real Estate Professionals and Regulators", especially at pp. 810–832.

[32] Online media story: https://www.realestatebusiness.com.au/industry/25605-real-estate-agencies-buyers-to-bear-costs-of-proposed-anti-money-laundering-reforms-reia-warns.

[33] Department of Internal Affairs, December 2018, *Guideline: Real Estate Agents - Complying with the Anti-Money Laundering and Countering Financing of Terrorism Act 2009*, see pp. 11–14.

> Real estate agents are often more client-facing than other sectors and may have better oversight of their clients and transactions, which can help identify suspicious activity. For example, real estate agents will have some insight into whether a client is suspiciously under- or over-valuing a property, which may indicate the movement of illicit funds. They can also see how short a time period the client is holding onto a property, which may indicate the property is being "flipped" to disguise the origin of the funds used to purchase it.
>
> For real estate agents, the client is the person entering into an agency agreement with the real estate agent. Usually the client will be the seller of a property, although sometimes a real estate agent might be engaged by a buyer to source a property (in which case, the buyer would be the client). You do not need to conduct CDD on a party to a real estate transaction that is not your client, unless they conduct an occasional transaction with you.

The DIA and the other Supervisors are also required to put out periodic Sector Risk Assessments, risk-rating the perceived level of ML vulnerability that businesses in each sub-sector may face. The various DNFBP sectors can be seen in the left column below, with colour coding representing the current assessed inherent ML and terrorist financing risks of each, as the DIA felt it stood in 2019[34]:

Sector—Designated Non-Financial Businesses or Professions (DNFBPs) and casinos	Inherent risk of Money Laundering/ Terrorist Financing
Trust and company service providers	High
Lawyers	Medium-high
Accountants	Medium-high
Real estate agents	Medium-high
High-value dealers	Medium-high
Racing Industry Transition Agency (TAB)	Medium-high
Casinos	Medium-high
Conveyancers	Medium

Reporting Entities are expected to take guidance and cues from these specific materials describing risks in their areas of business. The AML/CFT Act (s 58) requires an entity to direct evaluate in writing at least 6 main dimensions of risk: the nature, size and complexity of its business, products/services offered, the methods by which they are delivered, and types of customer, countries, and institutions it deals with.

That risk assessment framework echoes what FATF advocates in its risk-based approach, in July 2022 re-emphasising core risks in this way:[35]

> [99] take into consideration the following areas as well as others which are deemed relevant:
>
> - Geographical risks, such as the areas of operation and those countries identified by FATF or other regional and national authorities as high-risk.
> - Customer risks including particular attention to any additional parties in a transaction and any underlying beneficial owners.
> - Transaction risks including the methods of financing and delivery channels.

[34] Department of Internal Affairs, December 2019, *Designated Non-Financial Business and Profession (DNFBPs) and Casinos: Sector Risk Assessment*, see p. 5, reproduced with permission.

[35] FATF (2022), Guidance for a Risk-Based Approach to the Real Estate Sector, p. 32.

...

[101] The risk assessment should follow an approach that considers the size of the real estate professionals' business, the financial value of the transactions involving the real estate firm, how the firm became involved in the real estate transaction, as well as the nature of the transaction itself, to include whether it is an overseas purchase or involves commercial or residential real estate.

The particular policy compromises necessary to implement New Zealand DNFBP coverage in reality, rather than academic theory, and to drive it through in short space of time, created some odd trade-offs. One challenge has been the policy choice whether to catch all buyers of property via the real estate agents, or only the vendors of property. As DIA guidance explained, ultimately it was decided that real estate agents have the seller as their primary client. Hence, although they come into contact with the lots of potential buyers (at open home events, auctions, or through sales enquiries and property marketing campaigns), they are not treated as providing a service to those persons—and so do not have AML obligations in relation to those persons.

But that left a fairly large sized hole in New Zealand's attempt to close the Phase 2 gap by regulating the real estate sector. Purchasers were left for somebody else to process for KYC purposes. That also did not comply with FATF Recommendation 22 where the relevant Interpretive Note is plain:

INTERPRETIVE NOTE TO RECOMMENDATION 22 (DNFBPS – CUSTOMER DUE DILIGENCE)

1. Real estate agents should comply with the requirements of Recommendation 10 with respect to both the purchasers and vendors of the property.

While it was never publicly acknowledged in this way, the policy trade-off has been to let the legal profession instead do the heavy lifting of due diligence on purchasers in conveyancing transactions—despite the fact that payment of a deposit for property in practice usually moves from a buyer into the real estate firm's trust account.

Separately, the timing of doing KYC has been challenging due to huge variety of situations where a contract for real estate transactions may arise. New Zealand's rule means a real estate agent must conduct due diligence on its vendor *before* entering an agency agreement with them. There is a small exception where identity details may be collected, but not yet verified until after establishing the business relationship—but only where essential not to interrupt normal business practice and certain mitigating controls are applied.

One other oddity is the uncertain position of commercial leasing under captured services definitions. Leasing itself is covered, as one of the key property rights that can be granted, entered into, sold or sub-leased. New Zealand has assumed coverage, even though FATF Standards do not technically require commercial leases to be included. But a dilemma arises in some scenarios, such as property management services over complexes like a shopping mall, where those services are not covered—unless client funds are held as part of leasing operations. This means real estate KYC onboarding takes place up to the point when a customer grants/enters a new lease, but may cease for the duration of the lease. This can lead to inconsistencies around ongoing due diligence, monitoring and potentially reportability to the FIU.

There is an inevitable chain of providers and transactions advisors: real estate agent, bank or other financier, mortgage advisor, conveyancing lawyer, sometimes an accountant or TCSP if trust structures are established. While each of those parties may hold different relevant information about the customer and the transaction, duplication of effort will be inherent in that chain of coverage. That often causes different regulated businesses to ask much the same KYC questions of increasingly irritated customers. Legal avenues to share information have been found wanting, especially with confusion over privacy concerns, compliance cost sensitivities, or unwillingness to share client data. In practice this has limited moves towards a more efficient, collaborative approach.

6 The Position of the Legal Profession in Relation to Real Estate Transactions

The **Shewan Report** and examples disclosed in Panama Papers case studies highlighted risks for legal service providers, especially around property transactions and conveyancing. These are often overlaid with a second high-risk element—trusts and opaque corporate structures. Areas of particular concern included that New Zealand's renowned ease of doing business, relatively friendly regulations towards inwards foreign investment, favourable tax settings for offshore trusts, and safe reputation as a low corruption stable jurisdiction, were attracting investment for all the wrong reasons.

From 2016, an increasing number of law enforcement operations/reports found criminal groups and agents who may have sought to place and layer money for cleansing through New Zealand—in the process, attractively bagging themselves a nice piece of land in a safe foreign country, at relatively cheap international prices.

Those core legal services—establishing trusts/companies, secretariat, transactional and trust account administration, alongside substantive real estate sale and purchase work, asset planning or tax structuring—were all intended to be captured. Full AML obligations apply to those defined limbs of activity, selected on the basis of money laundering risk. In other words, a lot of bread-and-butter legal work for firms of solicitors was seen as central to the money laundering risk. That excludes litigation, criminal defence representation of an accused (unless involving ancillary services or holding funds in trust account), and other speciality services.

Beneficial ownership is a challenging area of compliance in New Zealand, given the diverse and high proportion of trust structures used in commercial and property enterprises. A balance has been struck in the AML/CFT Act and Regulations that requires entities to verify beneficial ownership by obtaining the name and date of birth of each beneficiary of a trust or, for charitable or discretionary trusts with over

10 beneficiaries, a description of the class and types of beneficiary, plus the trust's objectives.

Many trust structures exist for benign and legitimate purposes. But the extent to which vehicles for holding assets permeate the asset base, and lawyers are well-versed in creating them, can lead to complications and extra work to meet necessary levels of enhanced due diligence. Supervisors' Guidance on beneficial ownership was issued and updated often (Joint Supervisors NZ (2012)),[36] but of necessity it is rather generalised. Without any concrete moves yet to create a beneficial ownership register, getting access to verifiable data in trust scenarios can be difficult.

Displacement of criminal funds into the legal sector was a real fear. Lawyers may have been targeted by sophisticated laundering operations precisely because they were exempt from 2013 to 2018, when ordinary businesses offering the same trust and company secretarial services were caught by the Phase 1. Criminal agents move around to avoid the greater information demands that financial businesses were compelled to make, potentially shuffling the laundering issues from one set of providers to another, until lawyers were introduced to the new regulatory net.

A particular difficulty that lawyers have which no other sectors (Phase 1 or DNFBP) face is the strong ethical duties owed to the client, including to keep client confidences and uphold legal privilege in communications. The AML regime took care to recognise that difficulty when coverage expanded to lawyers. Both legal advice and litigation privileged communications are preserved—at least, when privilege truly applies. When lawyers address the obligation to make a STR under s 40 of the AML/CFT Act, they may (and under NZ Law Society guidance must) withhold truly privileged information.

That may mean a real estate agent (who has no privileged communication obligations to the client) may report a transaction in full if identifying it as suspicious, whereas the conveyancing lawyer may not. Alternatively, the details received by the FIU by the lawyer may be much slimmer, if it is possible at all to remove/restrict privileged data from non-privileged information.

It can be especially difficult when these issues arise late in the transaction, or nearly at the time of completion of a looming real estate deal. At the best of times, closing a large property transaction can be busy, stressful, and accrue complexities—even without a dose of late red flags or unexpected twists. In recognition of the special difficulties the legal profession encounters, the recent Ministry of Justice Statutory Review of the AML/CFT Act[37] has recommended extending the time frame for lawyers to take advice and determine whether to make a STR to 5 working days (from 3 working days currently, where it will remain for other reporting entities).

[36] FMA, RBNZ, DIA—joint Supervisors "AML/CFT—Beneficial Ownership Guideline", December 2012, p. 3.

[37] MOJ Statutory Review, 6 November 2022.

7 Overseas Investment in Property also had to be Tightened

It is not reasonable to expect AML regulation to do all the heavy lifting towards creating a cleaner property market that is not inflated or distorted by criminal funds seeking a home. As a small, open trading nation, New Zealand receives a great deal of inward overseas investment, especially from Australia but in recent years also China, with whom there is a free trade agreement. Official measures put foreign investor ownership at up to 40% of the economy.[38]

New Zealand generally welcomes foreign investment, however it has seen a rush of foreign investors into property markets, particularly in Auckland. Like Vancouver, and Sydney, and other cities offering a good quality of living, Auckland had an overheated property market with consequent housing shortages and affordability problems. A variety of complex economic factors fed into that situation, but foreign investment and speculation has been a part and, while hard to quantify, some criminal funds likely played a part too.

Background checks were traditionally light, the focus being largely on other investor criteria. The Overseas Investment Office ("OIO") as a regulator attached to the Land Registry database department LINZ was ill-equipped for investigations into whether investors were fit and proper on financial crime grounds.

Accordingly, from about 2015 onwards, progressive steps were taken to tighten up these laws, especially for coastal or sensitive or residential land. The key rules in the Overseas Investment Act 2005 ("OI Act") and associated Regulations control significant business asset sales of all types, corporations, residential, farmland, agriculture and fishing quota interest, but especially property investment. The OI Act sets out a regime for regulating investments in sensitive New Zealand assets by "overseas persons" as defined.[39] Overseas investments in those assets must before being made meet certain criteria for approval or special Ministerial consent. One stated purpose is to manage certain risks, such as national security and public order risks, associated with transactions by undesirable overseas persons.

The process and tests applied to consent applications for purchasing land or assets have always had a political element, and from 2018 the Government moved to limit overseas purchases of residential land.[40] New legal tests were introduced regarding 'relevant overseas persons' and 'individuals with control', including corporate investors. This introduced 12 factors allowing deeper assessment of any past imprisonment convictions, penalties for tax evasion, corporate fines, and civil pecuniary penalties.[41] This improved OIO capacity and expertise in tracing beneficial ownership and ascertaining likely criminal connections with overseas owners or funders. The OIO cannot now say it does not have the tools to properly vet foreign buyers, although a hidden criminal history or intentions can never be ruled out.

---

[38] LINZ publication, *Changes to the Overseas Investment Act*, as at 18 February 2021.

[39] Overseas Investment Act 2005, ss 6 and 7. Public Act No 82 of 2005.

[40] Overseas Investment Act 2005, s 16 as amended.

[41] Overseas Investment (Urgent Measures) Amendment Act 2020, s 18A.

Supply-side measures in the property market have been abrupt, politically driven, and severe, but have effectively slowed overseas investors from taking advantage of booming house-price rises. The FIU's updated National Risk Assessment 2019 noted these changes as positive from its perspective:[42]

Recent amendments to the Overseas Investment Act 2005 appear to have significantly reduced the proportion of residential properties being sold to overseas buyers, with property transfers to non-New Zealand citizens (or residents) dropping by 81% in the March 2019 quarter compared with the same quarter the previous year. These controls are expected to significantly mitigate the risk of transnational laundering through New Zealand real estate.

This had improved, but certainly not corrected, the runaway property market when Covid-19 struck and much of the New Zealand economy went into damaging lockdowns. Property bubbles continued, including with impetus from central reserve bank funding pumped into a recovering economy. Much of that support money found its way into investments ranging from shares to collectibles to real estate, fuelling further bubbles. On the other hand, Covid restrictions on movement, immigration and tourism with tight border controls reduced the foreign buyers and movement of people/money during that period. Perhaps we can surmise there was less money laundering inflation than possibly occurred in past years.

8 Significantly Improved FATF Report Card, but Still more to do: And a Nod to Australia Tranche Two

By plugging many of those gaps in regulatory coverage and finally getting over the political hurdles to include professional groups (law, accounting, real estate), New Zealand achieved better results in 2021 when FATF's next evaluation came around. In particular, there were significantly more 'Largely' or 'Partially Compliant' ratings for technical compliance with the DNFBP recommendations in this Mutual Evaluation Report published in April 2021 (FATF (2012)).[43]

However, that remains a place where Australia is currently stuck, looking down the barrel of a negative set of DNFBP findings when FATF returns in 2025 for a Covid-delayed evaluation. The most obvious way forward to overcome a looming set of 'non-compliant' technical ratings will be for Australia to introduce coverage for the core professions by the time of that evaluation visit.

Even so, nothing in the world of FATF recommendations and financial crime concerns stands still for long. Further property laundering issues remained that NZ Police and the DIA were aware of, and raised during a major Statutory Review

[42] National Risk Assessment, of money laundering and terrorism financing, NZ Police Financial Intelligence Unit 2019.

[43] *MER of New Zealand* (2021), Financial Action Task Force.

process which began after the FATF review. This covered a lot of AML reform aspects, but specific to real estate noted there is more work to do[44]:

> We have identified a number of ways the Act could be strengthened to combat areas of high risk. In particular, we are concerned that illicit capital is still able to enter the real estate market despite the inclusion of law firms, conveyancers, and real estate agents in the regime between 2018 and 2019.
>
> ...
>
> ... we recommend conducting a thorough risk assessment to identify the particular ways in which real estate and the trade system are or could be exploited to ensure that any changes are appropriately risk-based.
>
> ...
>
> Recommendation 50: Agencies, particularly DIA and FIU, undertake further analysis to assess the ... ML and TF risks in the real estate sector ... and to identify the particular methods or typologies that are being used to place, layer, or integrate the proceeds of crime through real estate
>
> Recommendation 51: Following the risk assessment, consider whether any further AML/CFT controls to prevent/deter this from happening. This could include additional obligations for real estate agents and law firms (e.g., by imposing additional requirements for private sales, on selling, list and sell, measures where nominees are used for purchases, risks associated with non-finance or privately funded purchases and increasing cooperation between the parties involved).

How a country chooses to regulate its property sector for ML risk can be reasonably flexible, depending on the nuances of its own economy and how real estate agents operate in practice. It is worth taking time to figure out how to most efficiently regulate the sector, possibly with need to reduce or amend some obligations to align with local risks. But that is no reason to delay the onset of regulation forever, in light of the risk factors, as the New Zealand experience shows.

References

AML/CFT Act (NZ) - Anti-Money Laundering and Countering Financing of Terrorism Act 2009, public Act No 35 of 2009

AML-CTF Act (Aust) - Anti-Money Laundering and Counter-Terrorism Financing Act 2006 (Commonwealth of Australia), Federal legislation, No 169 of 2006

Anti-Money Laundering and Countering Financing of Terrorism (Definitions) Regulations 2011, Reg 17 (TCSPs)

AUSTRAC (2021) Australia's major banks: Money laundering and terrorism financing risk assessment. Available at: https://www.austrac.gov.au/sites/default/files/2021-09/Major%20Banks%20ML_TF_Risk%20Assessment%202021.pdf

Commissioner of Police v Gong [2019] NZHC 2735, High Court of New Zealand interim judgment, 25 October 2019

CPR Act (NZ) – Criminal Proceeds (Recovery) Act 2009, public Act No 8 of 2009

Crimes Act 1961, (section 243), public Act No 43 of 1961

Criminal Code Act 1995 (Commonwealth of Australia), Federal legislation, No 12 of 1995

[44] AML/CFT Statutory Review Report (2022) NZ Ministry of Justice, Recommendations 50 and 51, p. 11 of 256.

Cullen Commission - Final Report of the Commission of Inquiry into Money Laundering in British Columbia, Canada, the Honourable Austin F. Cullen as Commissioner, June 2022., available at: https://cullencommission.ca/files/reports/CullenCommission-FinalReport-Full.pdf

Department of Internal Affairs, December 2018, Guideline: Real Estate Agents - Complying with the Anti-Money Laundering and Countering Financing of Terrorism Act 2009. Available at: https://www.dia.govt.nz/diawebsite.nsf/Files/AML-CFT-Real-Estate-Guideline/$file/AML-CFT-Real-Estate-Guideline-Dec-2018.pdf

Department of Internal Affairs, December 2019, Designated non-financial business and profession (DNFBPs) and casinos: sector risk assessment. Available at: https://www.dia.govt.nz/diawebsite.nsf/Files/AML-CFT-December-2019/$file/DNFBPs-and-Casinos-SRA-2019-v1.0.pdf

FATF (2012, updated February 2023) International standards on combating money laundering and countering financing of terrorism and proliferation – the FATF recommendations, including glossary and interpretive notes. Financial Action Task Force, Paris. Available at: https://www.fatf-gafi.org/en/topics/fatf-recommendations.html

FATF (2021) Anti-money laundering and counter-terrorist financing measures – New Zealand, mutual evaluation report. Financial Action Task Force, April 2021. Available at: https://www.fatf-gafi.org/en/countries/detail/New-Zealand.html

FATF (2022) Guidance for a risk-based approach to the real estate sector. Financial Action Task Force. Available at: www.fatf-gafi.org/publications/documents/Guidance-RBA-Real-Estate-Sector.html

FTR Act (NZ) - Financial Transactions Reporting Act 1996, public Act No 9 of 1996, repealed on 1 August 2019

Jiaxin Finance Ltd, Fu & Che v R [2022] NZCA 287, Court of Appeal of New Zealand, 4 November 2021

Joint Supervisors NZ (FMA, RBNZ, DIA) AML/CFT – Beneficial Ownership Guideline, December 2012., available at: https://www.dia.govt.nz/Pubforms.nsf/URL/AMLCFT_BeneficialOwnershipGuideline_Dec2017.pdf/$file/AMLCFT_BeneficialOwnershipGuideline_Dec2017.pdf

LINZ (2021) Land information New Zealand (Overseas Investment Office) in-house publication. Changes to the Overseas Investment Act, February 2021

Ministry of Justice consultation (2016), Improving New Zealand's ability to tackle money laundering and terrorist financing, discussion paper on Phase Two of the AML/CFT Act

Modernising and Simplifying Australia's AML-CTF Law (2023) Attorney-General's Department consultation paper

National Risk Assessment of money laundering and terrorism financing. NZ Police Financial Intelligence Unit (2019)

Overseas Investment Act 2005, public Act No 82 of 2005

Platypus Magazine. Australian Federal Police in-house publication April 2013

Pocketing the proceeds of crime: Recommendations for legislative reform. Australian Institute of Criminology, Professors Skead, Tubex, Murray and Dr Tulich, Report to the Criminology Research Advisory Council Grant: CRG 27/16–17, July 2020

Quarterly Typology Report, NZ Police Financial Intelligence Unit (2015) fiu-quarterly-typology-report-Q4 of 2014-2015 Real Estate.pdf

REA Act (NZ) - Real Estate Agents Act 2008, public Act No 66 of 2008

Shewan Inquiry - Report of the Government Inquiry into Foreign Trust Disclosure Rules, John Shewan, 27 June 2016., available at: https://www.treasury.govt.nz/publications/information-release/government-inquiry-foreign-trust-disclosure-rules

Statutory Review (2022) NZ Ministry of Justice, Report on the Review of the AML/CFT Act 2009, Statutory Review Report under s 156A(3) of the AML/CFT Act (July 2022)

Gary Hughes Britomart Chambers, Auckland, New Zealand. Gary is a leading independent New Zealand barrister with 27 years' experience in regulatory investigations, enforcement, civil disputes, risk & compliance advice—with a focus on financial crime, competition & consumer law, fraud, corruption, privacy. Regarded as one of New Zealand's most experienced AML-CFT lawyer, he handles cases with regulators including the Serious Fraud Office, Financial Markets Authority, Commerce Commission, Privacy Commission, Police FIU and AML Supervisors. International work includes Cook Islands or Australia/AUSTRAC cases. Current Chair of the International Bar Association's AML & Sanctions Experts committee, and advisory director to the ACAMS Australasian Chapter (previously, ACAMS NZ Programme Director). Author of Thomson Reuters NZ online textbook AML/CFT Workflows—Guidance for Lawyers. Overseas expert witness to the Cullen Commission (Canada, 2021), and appointed to NZ's Ministry of Justice Statutory Review advisory group (2022–23). Admitted in NZ (1996), also dual qualified in England & Wales and NSW, Australia.

Environmental Crime and Money Laundering in Australia

Benjamin Scott

Abstract Environmental crime, driven by profit motives, leads to the accumulation of illicit gains. Despite the original intention of the global anti-money laundering and counter-terrorism financing (AML/CTF) framework after the September 11 attacks, its application in addressing environmental crime presents a logical progression for nations confronting transnational and organized environmental offenses. This chapter explores the international and Australian perspectives on comprehending and investigating environmental crime, and how these intersect with AML/CTF practices. It provides a broad overview of Australia's risk profile as both a source and destination for the proceeds of environmental crime. Furthermore, it focuses on recent instances of waste trafficking and water-related crime in Australia. These two categories of environmental crime have garnered law enforcement attention and public scrutiny within the country.

1 Introduction

Australia's natural environment is under increasing pressure. Drought, flooding, loss of native vegetation and biodiversity and water scarcity have impacted upon Australian communities in recent years. In some cases, formal enquiries and reporting have highlighted human causes and regulatory failures that have contributed to these environmental harms. With this comes pressure on governments to enforce effectively and consistently the laws that protect the Australian environment. This pressure is applied domestically, in the form of community concerns, and internationally, through the initiatives of international organisations of which Australia is a member state.

B. Scott (✉)
Sydney, NSW, Australia

Macquarie Law School, Macquarie University, Sydney, Australia
e-mail: benjamin.scott7@students.mq.edu.au

D. Goldbarsht, L. de Koker (eds.), *Financial Crime, Law and Governance*, Ius Gentium: Comparative Perspectives on Law and Justice 116,
https://doi.org/10.1007/978-3-031-59547-9_5

Recent work by the Financial Action Task Force (FATF) has explored the link between environmental and financial crime and provided guidance to FATF member states on identifying, analysing and disrupting the illicit international and domestic financial flows it generates.[1] FATF has also identified three key challenges for member states: inadequate legal frameworks; limited understanding of money laundering risks relating to environmental crime, and a lack of cooperation between specialist environmental agencies and law enforcement.[2] All of these challenges are present in Australia, and are discussed in more detail later in the chapter.

This chapter examines how environmental crime is understood and investigated internationally and in Australia, and how this intersects with AML/CTF practice. It provides a general overview of Australia's risk profile as source and destination country for the proceeds of environmental crime. It then focuses on recent Australian cases of waste trafficking and water crime, two environmental crime types which have been the subject of law enforcement action and public attention in Australia. These cases help to identify challenges in applying financial crime methods to environmental offending, and opportunities to improve the way this is done. The main opportunity identified here is the development of a national environmental crime risk assessment which would help drive a coordinated approach to investigation and intelligence activities by Commonwealth and state governments.

2 Environmental Crime: Background and International Context

Environmental crime is 'typically defined on a continuum ranging from strict legal definitions through to broader harm perspectives.'[3] A narrow legal definition encompasses harms to the environment that are defined as unlawful and subject to criminal penalties.[4] Green criminology seeks to widen the definition of environmental crime to include acts that are ecologically and socially harmful but may not be strictly illegal.[5] This analysis focuses on law enforcement and intelligence processes that are intended to mitigate and manage the risk of criminal activity. Therefore for present purposes, environmental crime is considered to be activity which breaches state or federal laws that prohibit harming or destroying the natural environment.[6]

The United Nations estimates that the annual market value of environmental crime is of a similar order of magnitude to that generated by human trafficking and the drug trade.[7] A 2018 study concluded that the proceeds of environmental crime

[1] Financial Action Task Force (2021).

[2] Ibid.

[3] White (2018).

[4] Bricknell (2010).

[5] White (2018).

[6] Pain (2018).

[7] United Nations Environment Program (2016).

were the largest single source of income for non-state armed groups and terrorist organisations.[8] FATF observes that there are limitations in the regulation and enforcement of environmental crime which inhibit the effectiveness of national responses and international collaboration. Environmental crime offences are often narrowly drafted and do not address the range of environmental crime activity in a given jurisdiction. Penalties are often too low to address the environmental harm caused by the offence, failing to have a deterrent effect or attract a consistent focus from law enforcement agencies and governments. Where charges are laid, there is a tendency for courts to apply penalties at the low end of the range and use prison sentences as a last resort. This leads to a perception among criminals that environmental crime is a 'low-risk, high reward' undertaking.[9]

Environmental crime enforcement and anti-money laundering have developed on separate tracks until fairly recently. In the 1980s and 1990s, while the international AML/CTF framework under FATF was being established, the criminal aspects of environmental problems were not a priority for governments. From the 1990s to the mid-2010s, accelerating globalisation drove an expansion in the trade of illicit commodities, including wildlife and forestry products. The end of this period saw international organisations starting to build the capability to disrupt and investigate environmental crime in response. From around 2014, international organisations became increasingly aware of the links between environmental crime and transnational organised crime. Governments began to use law enforcement strategies against environmental crime and collaborate on cross-border investigations with some success, particularly against illegal wildlife trafficking.[10]

In 2020, FATF released its report on money laundering and the illegal wildlife trade, building on previous studies by international organisations and the private sector. The report expressed concern at the limited use of financial intelligence and investigations to combat illegal wildlife trafficking (IWT). It identified opportunities for jurisdictions to use existing AML frameworks to combat IWT. These included assessing their money laundering risk in relation to IWT; co-ordinating intelligence-sharing between government FIUs, financial investigators and environmental agencies; increasing cooperation with foreign countries in IWT investigations; and sharing IWT-related typologies with the private sector.[11]

FATF's 2021 report on money laundering and environmental crime focused on waste trafficking, illegal logging and illegal mining. It summarised existing knowledge about money laundering relating to these crime types, identified gaps in countries' frameworks for mitigating and managing money laundering relating to environmental crime, and made recommendations on how to strengthen these. The report emphasised that countries could be linked to illicit financial flows from environmental crime as a source, transit or destination country, meaning that even

[8] Global Initiative Against Transnational Organised Crime (2018).

[9] Financial Action Task Force (2021).

[10] Global Initiative Against Transnational Organised Crime (2022).

[11] Financial Action Task Force (2021).

countries without natural resources or domestic environmental crime needed to assess relevant money laundering risks.

The report also highlighted how countries can combat environmental crime through the adoption of FATF measures and the use of their existing AML/CTF reporting framework. Law enforcement agencies need to have sufficient powers to identify and confiscate criminal assets across all crime types, including environmental crime. Illicit financial flows from environmental crime often move through complex corporate structures established by lawyers and accountants. Ensuring that private sector entities are aware of their reporting obligations helps mitigate this risk. Criminal groups use existing methods such as trade-based money laundering (TBML) to launder the proceeds of environmental crime. This means that methods used to detect and investigate TBML can be effective in environmental crime enforcement. In an Italian case study highlighted by FATF, a tax audit of a scrap metal company identified irregularities in invoices and other documentation. Further investigation and analysis of Suspicious Transaction Reports (STRs) identified a scheme to launder the proceeds of the company's waste trafficking by moving funds abroad disguised as trade transactions.[12]

3 Australia's Money Laundering and Financial Crime Framework

Australia has a national framework for regulating reporting entities and investigating, prosecuting and producing intelligence on financial crime. Both state and federal criminal law enforcement agencies can investigate and prosecute money laundering offences. Australia is a member state of FATF and the Asia-Pacific Group (APG).

Australia's national legislative regime for AML/CTF regulation, the *Anti-Money Laundering and Counter-Terrorism Financing Act 2006* (Cth) ('the AML/CTF Act') is modelled on FATF principles. It imposes obligations on reporting entities to maintain a risk-based AML/CTF program, and prescribes obligations to report threshold transactions and suspicious matters, and to understand a customer's business and risk profile.[13]

Commonwealth money laundering offences are captured under section 400 of the *Criminal Code Act*.[14] Sections 400.3 to 400.8 of the Code make it an offence to deal with money or property which is proceeds of crime or is intended to be an instrument of crime. Sections 400.9(1) and (1A) apply to any dealing with money or property where it is reasonable to suspect it is proceeds of an indictable offence. The money laundering offences are tiered with reference to the amount involved. There are equivalent offences in the criminal codes of Australian states. Commonwealth law

[12]Financial Action Task Force (2021).

[13]De Koker and Goldbarsht (2024).

[14]1995 (Cth).

does not define specific predicate offence types, and in theory, any indictable offence producing proceeds of crime can be a predicate offence for money laundering.[15]

Australia's financial crime regulator and Financial Intelligence Unit, the Australian Transaction Reports and Analysis Centre (AUSTRAC), is responsible for monitoring and enforcing AML/CTF compliance by Australian reporting entities, and for collecting, analysing and disseminating financial intelligence collected from those entities to law enforcement and intelligence agencies. Other Commonwealth agencies also play an important role in financial crime investigation and enforcement. The Australian Federal Police conducts most of the money laundering investigations under Commonwealth law. The Australian Criminal Intelligence Commission (ACIC) is responsible for making intelligence assessments of the Australian serious and organised crime threat environment.

The Australian Tax Office (ATO) is responsible for the enforcement of Australia's taxation laws. The ATO leads the Serious Financial Crime Task Force (SFCTF), which is a joint agency task force set up in 2015. The SFCTF includes members from the AFP, AUSTRAC and ASIC. The SFCTF was formed to combat the most serious and complex areas of financial crime, with its current priorities including offshore tax evasion, cybercrime, phoenixing and fraud against COVID-19 stimulus measures. The SFCTF does not currently list environmental crime as a priority area.[16]

Corruption by public officials in Australia is primarily dealt with by dedicated anti-corruption bodies at the state level. These include New South Wales Independent Commission against Corruption (ICAC) and the Victorian Independent Broad-based Anti-Corruption Commission. A federal anti-corruption commission was established in 2023, with responsibility for detecting and investigating serious and systemic corruption at the Commonwealth level.[17]

Australia has been the subject of a FATF Mutual Evaluation Report (MER) in 2015. The MER observed that Australia had a mature financial intelligence capability and effectively disseminated financial intelligence to law enforcement agencies but was less effective at translating financial intelligence into prosecution outcomes. Improvements were also needed in how Australia defined the objectives and measured the effectiveness of AML/CTF activities. FATF identified the exclusion of Designated Non-Financial Business Providers (DNFPBs) as a vulnerability in Australia's financial compliance and intelligence coverage which needed to be addressed. With respect to the prosecution of money laundering, FATF observed that Australian law enforcement placed a higher priority on the prosecution of predicate offences such as fraud and drug supply than the investigation of money laundering as a standalone offence.[18]

---

[15] Commonwealth Director of Public Prosecutions (2017).

[16] Australian Tax Office (2023).

[17] National Anti-Corruption Commission (2023).

[18] Financial Action Task Force (2015).

4 Environmental Crime Risk in Australia

Australia is the world's twelfth-largest economy, with a relatively stable legal and financial system which makes it an attractive destination for illicit financial flows, including those from environmental crime. Australia is also "one of the most resource- and carbon-intensive OECD economies," and "remains highly reliant on the extraction of natural capital". As the world's driest continent, it is unusually vulnerable to the impacts of climate change for a highly developed country.[19] Australia is exposed to environmental crime and related money laundering risks both as a potential destination and transit country for transnational illicit flows and as a source country for laundering of the proceeds from domestic environmental crime activity.

This can be illustrated by examining FATF's current areas of priority: illegal logging, wildlife trafficking, waste trafficking and illegal env. Forestry operations are conducted in all states and territories, but there is little evidence of large-scale forestry crime taking place in Australia in the sense that FATF has defined it.[20] In 2010, the Australian Institute of Criminology (AIC) described forestry crime as "the least frequently perpetrated category of environmental crime in Australia."[21] The same is true for illegal mining in the sense of criminal mining operations conducted without government approval. Australia's mining industry is heavily regulated and dominated by large corporations that interact closely with their regulators. In some cases, these corporations have operated outside the terms of their approvals,[22] but this is not generally treated as a matter for law enforcement investigation or prosecution.

However, Australia's regional neighbours, particularly Papua New Guinea (PNG) and Indonesia, are some of the world's highest-risk jurisdictions for forestry crime and illegal logging. Australia is exposed to this risk as a wealthy trading partner and importer of timber products from these jurisdictions. PNG's 2017 national money laundering risk assessment highlighted illegal logging and fishing as the environmental crimes producing the largest amount of criminal proceeds, most of these funds were laundered offshore. It also identified Australia as Papua New Guinea's second-largest export market, and observed that the value of international payments from PNG to Australia greatly exceed the value of imported goods and services in the period reviewed.[23] These factors suggest that Australia is likely to be a destination country both for illegally harvested timber products, and for the proceeds of illegal logging in PNG.

---

[19] Organisation for Economic Co-operation and Development (2019).

[20] FATF defines illegal mining as mining activity that is undertaken without state permission, or with state permission obtained through corruption.

[21] Bricknell (2010).

[22] See for example the case study in Sect. 7 of this chapter concerning the Acland Coal company's Queensland operations.

[23] Financial Analysis and Supervision Unit (2017).

Illegal logging enabled by government corruption is a major problem for Indonesia; analysis by Chatham House estimated that between eight and seventy-seven percent of Indonesia's 2018 exports of wood-based products were illegally produced.[24] Indonesia is an important source of imported timber for Australia, with exports of timber products to Australia valued at over USD $300 million per year in the period 2013–2017.[25] Australia took steps to address exports of illegally logged timber in 2012, passing the *Illegal Logging Prohibition Act 2012* (Cth). This imposed obligations on Australian timber importers to conduct due diligence over the origin of imported timber, and created an indictable offence of knowingly, intentionally or recklessly importing illegally logged timber, punishable by up to 5 years' imprisonment.[26]

It is likely that Australia receives illicit financial flows and exported materials from illegal logging in PNG and Indonesia, due to the prevalence of illegal logging in these two countries and Australia's trade relationship with them. Australia's law enforcement agencies and AUSTRAC have strong relationships with Indonesia and PNG, and the importation offences under the *Illegal Logging Prohibition Act* could serve as predicate offences for money laundering charges. There are opportunities for Australia to collaborate with these jurisdictions to share intelligence and identify wealth sourced from illegal logging. This could lead to confiscation action and criminal prosecution. Australia's most effective role in combating illegal logging in the Asia-Pacific region is likely to be as a partner for these two jurisdictions. Rose (2017) has advocated for the sharing of financial intelligence between Indonesia and Australia and the use of civil confiscation to seize the proceeds of illegal logging in Australia.[27]

Compared with illegal logging, illegal waste trafficking and wildlife trafficking have a more established domestic presence, and are more likely to generate domestic proceeds for laundering. Reptiles are the main target of Australian wildlife traffickers, with some reptiles fetching 28 times their domestic price on the international market.[28] Wildlife trafficking leaves a relatively clear financial trail compared with some environmental crimes, requiring payments for transport, couriers and the trafficked animals. This provides opportunities for multi-agency and public-private partnerships to generate intelligence leads and assist investigations. In 2020–2021, AUSTRAC conducted a project through its Fintel Alliance partnership with the Department of Agriculture, Water and the Environment (DAWE) to target the illicit trade in native reptiles. Financial intelligence from this project led to the establishment of four wildlife trafficking investigations and contributed to an AUSTRAC financial crime guide on stopping illegal wildlife trafficking.[29]

[24] Chatham House (2023).

[25] Department of Agriculture and Water Resources (2018).

[26] *Illegal Logging Prohibition Act 2012* (Cth), ss. 8–9.

[27] Rose (2017).

[28] Australian Transaction Reports and Analysis Centre (AUSTRAC) (2020).

[29] AUSTRAC (2021).

Illegal waste trafficking is discussed in the following section of this chapter. There is no comprehensive data on waste offences at the national level. Owing to limitations in the identification and detection of waste crimes in Australia, it would be speculative to estimate the scale of illegal waste trafficking. However there is enough evidence to identify it as a significant domestic threat. There are examples of New South Wales enforcement cases related to illegal waste dumping. Events in Victoria in 2018–2019 identified a case of syndicated waste trafficking which spanned four states, continued over a 6-year period and contributed to two major urban fires in Melbourne.[30]

Another way of understanding environmental crime threats in Australia is to link them to the harms to which they contribute and consider the impact of those harms on the Australian environment. The Australian State of the Environment report, an independent report commissioned by the Commonwealth government, is a useful tool for doing this. The most recent report, released in 2021, provides a summary of the overall condition of the Australian environment across twelve themes which include air quality, biodiversity, climate, inland water, land and extreme events.[31]

The vulnerability of Australia's water systems is a recurring theme in the report. The report points to the negative impact of agricultural water extraction and climate change on groundwater levels, aquatic ecosystems and wetlands. It draws attention to shortcomings in water system management in the Murray-Darling Basin and to the exclusion of indigenous people from water entitlements and conversations about future use. The report evidences scientific foundations for community and political concerns about water theft and over-extraction in the Murray-Darling system.

In a similar way, the report emphasises the impact of environmental harms linked to illegal waste trafficking and dumping. While air quality in Australia is considered good, the report indicates that it is declining in cities as a result of pollution and bushfires. Two of the major air pollution events listed in the report were chemical waste fires linked to a Victorian dumping syndicate (see Sect. 5 of this chapter). The report also notes the direct impact of illegally dumped waste on soils, water, biota and habitats.

The State of the Environment report is a useful resource for understanding the impact of different environmental harms on Australia. This kind of information could be combined with law enforcement intelligence and economic analysis to form the basis of a national risk assessment for environmental crime. As discussed in Sect. 6, this would encompass both domestic crime, where Australia is a source country for proceeds of environmental crime, and transnational crime like illegal logging, where Australia is primarily a destination country. It would provide the basis for a national enforcement strategy that would incorporate international collaboration like that envisaged by Rose along with national initiatives to target high-priority domestic environmental crimes.

---

[30]This case is discussed in more detail in Sect. 5 of this chapter, and is summarised at Environmental Protection Authority Victoria (2021).

[31]Cresswell et al. (2021).

5 Australian Cases and Enforcement: Water and Waste Crimes

In Australia, the majority of enforcement against environmental crime is undertaken at the state level, where the state government anti-corruption bodies, state police, local councils and environmental agencies operate. The Commonwealth government is responsible for environmental enforcement where areas of national significance are involved, and also has responsibility for matters relating to international trade.[32]

The following section examines Australia's domestic exposure to two important environmental crime types, illegal waste trafficking and dumping and water-related crime, through analysis of enforcement cases. As documented in FATF's 2021 report, waste trafficking is attractive to criminal groups because enforcement activity is often limited, profits are high and penalties are low compared with more traditional criminal activity. Its financial flows are not well understood, but are more often domestic rather than transnational. Waste trafficking therefore provides a useful focal point for understanding how Australia is currently addressing a domestic environmental crime problem. Water-related crime has not been the subject of FATF analysis. However arguably Australia has a unique opportunity to lead on the investigation and disruption of this crime type, given the public and political attention it has received in recent years, and the vulnerability of Australia's water resources.

5.1 *Waste Trafficking and Illegal Waste Dumping*

In New South Wales, the Environmental Protection Agency (NSW EPA) is responsible for enforcing the state's primary environmental protection legislation, the *Protection of the Environment Operations Act 1997* (NSW) (POEO Act). Local councils are also responsible for enforcing provisions of the POEO Act that relate to their waste disposal obligations. The New South Wales Land and Environment Court is the specialist court which deals with New South Wales civil and criminal court relating to the POEO Act and other environmental legislation.

In New South Wales, the environmental regulator brought a series of criminal prosecutions against Hanna, a waste disposal business operator, for illegal dumping. No money laundering or other financial crime-related charges were laid, but the cases were notable for the escalating seriousness of the sanctions applied to his repeated waste offending, culminating in a custodial sentence in 2019.

[32] Areas of national significance are set out in the *Environment Protection and Biodiversity Conservation Act 1999* (Cth) and include World Heritage Sites, wetlands of international importance and endangered species.

In the 2014 case,[33] Hanna was found guilty of illegally transporting and dumping building waste on vacant private land and in a public park. The judge imposed a monetary penalty of over AUD $200,000. Partly as a result of Hanna's repeated offending, the New South Wales Parliament incorporated the option of a custodial sentence for waste offending in the legislation. In 2018, Hanna again appeared before the New South Wales Land and Environment Court.[34] The offences took place in 2015 and 2016. Hanna arranged for the dumping of building waste on four private properties. In each case, the waste included more than ten tonnes of extremely hazardous asbestos waste. Hanna misled the owners of the property to believe that the material being dumped was clean topsoil. This time the court had the option of imposing a custodial sentence, and sentenced Hanna to a 3-year prison term.

The Hanna cases did not involve substantial profit, and no money laundering charges were laid. However, the cases demonstrate a clear shift in enforcement approach by the authorities and the court from treating illegal waste dumping as a quasi-civil matter to be dealt with by fines, to a serious criminal matter. In the 2019 case, the court found that Hanna's offending was part of planned, organised criminal activity, and that a prison sentence was warranted in order to achieve the purposes of retribution, deterrence and protection of society.

"Hanna's case can be read as a gradual move up the pyramid of enforcement in response to sustained repeat offending by regulators, courts and the legislature."[35] It demonstrates that courts are prepared to treat illegal waste dumping as a serious crime deserving of a custodial sentence, sending a signal to law enforcement and environmental agencies that such investigations are worth resourcing and pursuing.

This is also important from the perspective of money laundering enforcement. In money laundering prosecutions, it is often challenging to prove the accused's level of knowledge that they are dealing with the proceeds of crime. As judges criminalise waste dumping offences and address intent and motivation in their judgments, that may make it easier to prove the elements of money laundering, especially if financial evidence has been collected as part of a parallel investigation.

Because state agencies regulate the dumping of waste, corruption is an enabler for illegal waste dumping, as it is for other environmental offences. In a 2018 investigation, operation Scania, the New South Wales Independent Commission Against Corruption (ICAC) found that an officer of the Western Sydney Regional Illegal Dumping Squad (RIDS) acted corruptly by accepting cash payments and mobile phones in exchange for failing to investigate the unlawful disposal of waste. The RIDS officer was part of a compliance squad that investigated incidents of illegal dumping on behalf of a group of councils. The officer accepted the bribes in exchange for failing to investigate an associate's illegal dumping of asbestos-contaminated waste on property he leased. The RIDS officer also assisted another

[33] *Bankstown City Council v Hanna* [2014] NSWLEC 152.

[34] *Environment Protection Authority v Dib Hanna Abdallah Hanna* [2018] NSWLEC 80.

[35] Crofts (2015).

associate who was illegally operating a skip bin business to avoid detection and enforcement action.[36]

One of the associates engaging in illegal dumping earned $107 K in a 3-month period for these activities, and the RIDS officer received multiple payments in exchange for his corrupt facilitation of waste dumping. The RIDS officer and his associates were subsequently convicted of bribery and corruption offences.[37]

FATF analysis indicates that financial flows for illegal waste dumping are more regional and domestic in nature compared to financial flows for other types of environmental crime.[38] The ICAC and the Hanna prosecutions provide evidence of a domestic market for illicit waste dumping in western Sydney, driven by intensive construction activity. Operation Scania showed how this illicit market encouraged entrepreneurial corruption by the RIDS officer. The extent of this kind of activity is not clear, but given the risk of public harm and potential for illicit profits there are obvious benefits to proactive monitoring and detection. While Scania and the Hanna prosecutions offer relatively small-scale, localised case studies in illegal waste disposal, an ongoing Victorian case involves alleged criminality on a scale that affected the national chemical waste market and has caused long-term environmental damage.

A huge environmental fire in Footscray, Melbourne in 2018 led to the discovery of a rural property near the town of Kaniva in western Victoria which had been used as a dumping site for a vast quantity of chemical and industrial waste, including asbestos and toxic liquids. The Victorian EPA has commenced prosecution of the operator of the site for multiple illegal waste offences.[39]

It is alleged that the site operator operated a network of sites including leased warehouses and the Kaniva property which were used to store waste. The owner took delivery of hazardous waste from multiple waste disposal businesses at a reduced price. The waste was then transported to one of the sites, sometimes from interstate, and stored there. The scale of the waste operation was so large that it distorted the legitimate market for solvent waste nationwide, resulting in an unexplained drop in processing volumes across four states in the period 2014–2015.[40]

The Kaniva case is remarkable for the scale and environmental impact of the alleged offending. The Victorian EPA's remediation of the Kaniva site has taken over 3 years.[41] The 2021 State of the Environment report listed ten major events affecting air quality since 2016; two of them were factory fires connected to the operator of the Kaniva site.[42]

---

[36] Independent Commission Against Corruption (2017).

[37] Hamilton-Irvine (2020).

[38] Financial Action Task Force (2021).

[39] Environmental Protection Authority Victoria (2021).

[40] Latimer (2019).

[41] Environmental Protection Authority Victoria (2023).

[42] Cresswell et al. (2021).

5.2 *Water Theft and Fraud*

To date, FATF has not examined water theft and other water-related crimes. However in Australia's drought-affected climate, access to water is an area of great political sensitivity and in recent years the authorities that regulate water have become more proactive about enforcement.

The use of water from the Murray-Darling Basic for large-scale irrigation began in the nineteenth century and accelerated after the Second World War. It has become essential to agriculture, placing extreme stress on the Murray-Darling Basin's resources. In recognition of this, the Commonwealth Government passed the *Water Act*[43] in 2007. The Water Act aimed to protect the water resources of the Murray-Darling Basin by involving all of the Basin States in the collective regulation and restoration of its ecosystem. The *Water Act* established a Commonwealth body, the Murray-Darling Basin Authority, which is responsible for creating and administering the Basin Plan to enable the integrated management of Basin water. The Basin Plan established and enforced sustainable limits on the quantities of water that could be extracted from the Basin and created offences relating to the unauthorised taking of water.[44]

In 2017, an ABC Four Corners documentary, 'Pumped,' raised concerns about the compliance of major irrigators in the Murray-Darling Basin with the Basin Plan. The documentary alleged that in New South Wales, Basin water resources were not being properly regulated, that water was being taken unlawfully on a large scale and that New South Wales environmental regulators were not taking enforcement action in part due to regulatory capture by irrigators.[45]

Following the broadcast of Pumped, enquiries and prosecutions took place in New South Wales, Queensland and at the Commonwealth level. In 2018, the South Australian government established a Royal Commission to enquire into the effectiveness and sustainability of the Water Act and Basin Plan. A key aspect of the Royal Commission was to determine the impact of illegal water-taking and other forms of non-compliance, the adequacy of enforcement powers under the Act and the extent of enforcement proceedings by state authorities responsible for compliance by individual water users.

The Royal Commission's final report was released in 2019. A section of the report was devoted to compliance and enforcement of water resource laws by the Basin States. The Commissioner found that, despite variation in penalties for unauthorised water take between states, the state legislation was adequately equipped with penalties to deal with unlawful behaviour.

However the Commission found that enforcement and prosecution for water theft fell short of public expectations, largely due to a lack of metering and monitoring of water take, and the limited operational capacity of regulatory authorities to

[43] *2007* (Cth).

[44] Murray-Darling Basin Royal Commission (2019).

[45] Australian Broadcasting Corporation (2017).

investigate offending. This contributed to a perception that states were unwilling to take necessary enforcement action and undermined public confidence in the effectiveness of the Murray-Darling Basin Authority and state environmental crime regulators.[46]

The final report pointed to positive developments in New South Wales and Queensland, particularly the establishment of the New South Wales Natural Resource Access Regulator (NRAR) to enforce water laws, and prosecutions in Queensland. The report noted that in addition to prosecutions, improvements were needed to metering, monitoring and availability of information to the public. In the period since Pumped went to air, there have been additional prosecutions under water laws in New South Wales and Queensland.

In 2023, two prosecutions of New South Wales cotton farmers resulted in convictions and fines being imposed.[47] In one of these, New South Wales irrigator Henry Payson Pty Ltd. ('Payson') was convicted of taking water from a regulated water source while a meter was not working properly and related offences and fined approximately AUD $350,000.[48] The prosecution alleged that in 2016, Payson, through its director Barnes, knowingly took water from a metered water source on its property, Binneguy Station, while the meter was not working. The court found that Payson had taken approximately 1.8 times the water that was metered during the offending period. The main aggravating factor was Payson's level of knowledge of the meter under-recording. The court accepted evidence from a former employee of Payson that Barnes had repositioned a valve and sensor on the dam pump to ensure that the under-reporting continued. The court found that the offending was partly motivated by financial gain because Payson planned produce a larger cotton crop the following year, and was relying on the meter continuing to produce inaccurate data.

Defrauding of government water initiatives offers potentially greater opportunities for quantifying and pursuing proceeds of crime, and investigating related money laundering. This can be seen in the 2018 prosecution of two executives from Queensland cotton farming company Norman Farming for fraud offences. Police alleged that John Norman and Stephen Evans defrauded the Commonwealth government of approximately AUD $20 million dollars in funding allocated for water efficiency projects under Queensland's Healthy Headwaters scheme. Under the scheme, funding provided was required to relate to water storage, distribution or in-field systems. Allegedly, invoices for general farming work were modified to meet the requirements of the scheme and used in applications for funding.[49]

In 2019, Queensland Police and the Queensland Crime and Corruption Commission (CCC) obtained a court order to force Norman to pay the Queensland public

---

[46] Murray-Darling Basin Royal Commission (2019).

[47] *WaterNSW v Harris (No 3)* [2020] NSWLEC 18, and *Grant Barnes, Chief Regulatory Officer, Natural Resources Access Regulator v Henry Payson Pty Ltd* [2023] NSWLEC 5.

[48] *Grant Barnes, Chief Regulatory Officer, Natural Resources Access Regulator v Henry Payson Pty Ltd* [2023] NSWLEC 5.

[49] Brewster (2018).

trustee $15.7 million, after finding out that Norman Farming had sold its cotton farm to a Canadian company for AUD $100 million. The AUD $15.7 million represented Norman's share in the farm.[50]

The Norman case is a milestone in Australian environmental crime enforcement because of the seriousness of the charges and the willingness of the police to mount a complex covert investigation and use asset confiscation powers normally reserved for organised crime investigations. This may be because fraud is a familiar category of financial crime whose elements are well understood by investigators, as opposed to offences under environmental legislation. The evidentiary trail created by invoices, transactions and business records would have helped to quantify the financial benefit resulting from the alleged fraud, and the harm caused. There is also a single identifiable victim, the Commonwealth Government, which has suffered loss. All of these factors increase the likelihood of successful civil confiscation action and help prosecutors prove the elements of the fraud offences.

In the Payson case, the offences were detrimental to the environment, and to public confidence in the administration of environmental water in New South Wales. However it was difficult to define the harm caused and the financial benefit obtained, despite the large quantities of water taken in these cases. While environmental damage to the Murray-Darling Basin is readily apparent, attributing this damage directly to individual or corporate actors is less straightforward. This does not undermine the importance of criminal prosecutions for environmental offences, but authorities may benefit from identifying opportunities to prosecute fraud as an environmental crime as well, particularly in the heavily regulated water and waste sectors.

6 Challenges and Opportunities

FATF has identified challenges countries face in identifying and disrupting environmental crimes and related illicit financial flows.[51] These include:

- Legal frameworks which do not address the full range of environmental criminality and money laundering within countries;
- Limited understanding within countries of their exposure to money laundering risks from environmental crime; and
- Limited cooperation between traditional law enforcement agencies and their partners and the specialised agencies and bodies responsible for investigating environmental crime.

Australian states have introduced more severe penalty regimes for some environmental crime types, and applied these through prosecutions and convictions. The

[50] Carson (2019).

[51] Financial Action Task Force (2021).

waste and water crime prosecutions discussed in the previous section are examples of this. Penalties for wildlife trafficking and illegal logging offences are also severe,[52] and include an option for custodial sentences for serious offences.

However, there is also evidence supporting the AIC's observation that "incidents of environmental harm are still treated somewhat leniently in Australia."[53] In 2023, the New Acland Coal company (NAC) entered into an Enforceable Undertaking with the Queensland Department of Environment and Science over the unauthorised excavation of a coal pit. Pursuant to the undertaking, NAC agreed to pay $2 million to rehabilitate part of the site as a koala habitat. The allegedly unauthorised mining activity has been described as 'the most profitable environmental crime in Queensland history,' although NAC disputes claims their activity was illegal.[54] Certainly the EU was a favourable outcome for NAC, as it enabled the company to avoid criminal sanctions and retrospectively validate their excavation activity at a low cost. The example illustrates how the decisions of environmental authorities are just as important as the existence of strong penalties in determining how environmental crimes are treated.

Lenient treatment of predicate offending in turn limits opportunities to instigate money laundering prosecutions. As discussed previously, money laundering involves dealing with money or property which is the instrument or proceeds of an indictable offence. If higher-level, indictable environmental crime offences are seldom used, and lower-level charges or EUs are preferred, there is a low likelihood of successful money laundering charges relating to environmental crime.

In addition, the way courts interpret money laundering makes it difficult to ground money laundering charges in environmental predicate offences. Commonwealth prosecution guidance indicates that money laundering charges may be appropriate when the predicate offence does not properly reflect the seriousness of the conduct.[55] Courts have criticised the laying of money laundering charges when the accused was simply using funds obtained through criminal activity, with no attempt to hide the source or change the nature of the funds.[56] That is consistent with the objective of using money laundering prosecutions to disrupt serious organised crime.

However, financial deception and concealment elements are unlikely to be identified in the majority of environmental crime cases prosecuted in Australia today. In many cases of serious environmental crime, the offending takes place through unauthorised activity conducted as part of the normal course of business, and proceeds are not realised until well after the offending has taken place. One

[52] See for example *Environment Protection and Biodiversity Conservation Act 1999* (Cth), s. 303DD(1) relating to exporting a regulated native specimen and *Illegal Logging Prohibition Act 2012* (Cth), ss. 8–9 relating to importation of illegally logged timber.

[53] Bricknell (2010).

[54] Hope (2022).

[55] Commonwealth Director of Public Prosecutions (2017).

[56] Thorn v The Queen [2009] NSWCCA 294.

exception to this might be complex frauds against governmental programs of the type allegedly identified in the Norman case. Another would be illegal wildlife trafficking, where payments for smuggled wildlife may coincide with the predicate offending and generate cash proceeds which need to be integrated into the financial system.[57]

In theory, the Australian legal framework enables both prosecutions for indictable environmental crimes, and the use of these crimes as predicate offences for money laundering. However money laundering charges will not be universally appropriate or effective wherever serious environmental crime is prosecuted. This highlights the importance of the next point, which is understanding Australia's environmental crime risks and typologies.

In some areas of Australian environmental crime enforcement, authorities have shown persistence and dedication in targeting serious offenders. Assessed at a national level, though, enforcement activity is reactive and fragmented. For example, the increased enforcement activity around water crime at the state level appears largely driven by adverse media coverage and public concern, and is inconsistent across Australian jurisdictions. The State of the Environment reporting provides an overview of the condition of the Australian environment and the key emerging issues facing Australia.[58] What Australia lacks at present is an assessment of the risk of environmental crimes and related money laundering to Australia based on the incidence, impact and economic scale of criminal activity.

The AIC's 2010 report[59] called for a comprehensive analysis of trends in Australian environmental offending and criminal methodologies. The AIC report highlighted the importance to Australian environmental regulators and enforcement agencies of understanding:

- The prevalence of different types of offending and the impact of regulatory and policy initiatives on this;
- The costs and impact of different types of environmental crime; and
- Regulatory best practice and enforcement processes that have led to improved outcomes.

FATF's 2021 report[60] also highlights the importance of risk assessment. Its first priority action for countries is that they holistically consider the money laundering threats posed by environmental crimes within their national financial crime risk assessments. This should encompass assessment of the country's risk as a source, transit and destination country for proceeds of environmental crime, and include dialogue with environmental regulators and non-government stakeholders that may not be reporting entities.

[57] See R v Kennedy [2019] NSWCCA 242, where a former professional rugby league footballer was convicted of attempting to export regulated native specimens and dealing with proceeds of crime.

[58] Cresswell et al. (2021).

[59] Bricknell (2010).

[60] Financial Action Task Force (2021).

The AIC's recommendations and FATF's are distinct but connected, and Australia would benefit from both. It is necessary to understand the nature of serious environmental offending in Australia in order to assess related money laundering risk, just as it is necessary to understand Australian illicit drug markets in order to understand how drug proceeds are laundered. The ACIC and AIC, two closely-connected Commonwealth agencies, would be well-placed to collaborate on a holistic assessment of environmental crime risk in Australia.[61] AUSTRAC, as Australia's financial crime regulator and liaison point with FATF, would be responsible for incorporating money laundering risks from environmental crime into the national financial crime risk assessment.

In the absence of these assessments, it is likely that the priority areas identified by FATF—illegal logging, illegal mining, waste trafficking and wildlife crime—will flow into national AML/CTF intelligence collection and enforcement priorities. This would represent some progress, but also a missed opportunity to build a picture of environmental crime and related laundering that is specific to Australia. The case studies and typologies in the FATF report focus on countries in Africa, South America and Asia with resource-intensive economies and limited government resources. Where developed European countries appear, it is usually as partners in the investigation and disruption of transnational organised environmental crime originating outside their borders. Australia certainly has a role to play as a regional partner in disrupting illicit cross-border financial flows and trade activity that relates to crimes like illegal logging and mining. However this should not come at the expense of assessing and targeting domestic environmental crime threats. That is why adoption of FATF priorities is no substitute for assessing Australia's specific risks.

The development of an Australian environmental crime risk assessment is an opportunity to engage stakeholders from outside the traditional coalition of law enforcement and their established private sector partners. Environmental agencies, NGOs and broader industry all have relevant expertise. Importantly, there is an opportunity to seek insights from indigenous groups affected by environmental crime. Indigenous communities are some of the most affected by environmental harms, but are not generally consulted by the enforcement and compliance arms of government. Indigenous knowledge of biodiversity and the environment is recognised in Commonwealth law,[62] and is essential to the State of the Environment reports, which recognise the unique perspectives of First Nations communities on the environment. It should also inform Australia's understanding of environmental crime.

---

[61] Although the AIC is an independent entity, the Chief Executive Officer of the ACIC is also the Director of the AIC.

[62] Two of the objects of the *Environment Protection and Biodiversity Conservation Act* 1999 (Cth) are to recognise the role of indigenous people in conserving Australia's biodiversity (s.3(1)(f)) and to promote the use of indigenous peoples' knowledge of biodiversity (s.3(1)(g)).

Developing Australia-specific risk assessments would be complex, involving multiple stakeholders and the collection of information from disparate sources, but the benefits would be considerable. They would provide an intelligence resource that would enable the prioritisation of government responses to international and domestic environmental crime, and the targeted use of AML/CTF capabilities where money laundering risk was identified.

Another challenge recognised by FATF is the limited collaboration between traditional law enforcement and financial intelligence agencies and the environmental agencies that have primary responsibility for investigating environmental crime. This challenge is exacerbated by Australia's federal structure, which means that a single environmental crime type may be the responsibility of multiple state agencies across Australia. Collaboration is likely to deliver benefits in three main areas: detection of predicate offending and illicit flows; parallel investigation of financial crime alongside environmental offences; and referral of matters to partner agencies with specific jurisdiction over them.

We can see some of these factors at play in the Kaniva case discussed earlier. In this case, a waste dumping syndicate operated at scale in the period 2012–2018, collecting waste from four states and storing it at the Kaniva site and nine urban warehouses. Information from multiple sources pointed to a potential environmental crime issue. At the national level, data on hazardous waste collection indicated that legitimately collected solvent waste volumes dropped inexplicably from 2012 onwards across four states.[63] At the local level, Victoria Police referred the site operator to the Victorian environmental regulator in 2016 after conducting an inspection and identifying open drums containing potentially hazardous chemicals.[64] They made a second referral in 2017 while conducting an illegal firearms investigation.[65] In hindsight, this case seems ideally suited to a joint task force arrangement involving police, financial investigators and environmental regulators. There would also be a role for federal law enforcement given the interstate waste trafficking involved. Collaboration of this type is likely to result to earlier detection and better enforcement outcomes, potentially mitigating some of the environmental damage caused by long-term offending.

The importance of collaboration goes beyond law enforcement agencies and environmental regulators. Anti-corruption bodies also have a role to play. Environmental crime is heavily dependent on corruption because of the role of governments in regulating activity involving environmental damage. Australia has dedicated anti-corruption bodies in several states and will have a national anti-corruption commission from 2023. Anti-corruption bodies have broad authority to investigate corruption issues that go beyond criminal acts.

The New South Wales ICAC can investigate corrupt conduct that could constitute a criminal offence, a disciplinary offence or grounds for dismissal of a public

[63] Latimer (2019).

[64] Vedelago and Ilanbey (2019).

[65] Vedelago et al. (2019).

official.[66] The National Anti-Corruption Commission has the power to investigate a range of corrupt conduct including any conduct of a public official involving a breach of public trust and any conduct that could adversely affect the honest or impartial exercise of a public official's powers.[67] As the Australian public becomes more sensitive to issues of environmental harm, there is a risk that sophisticated environmental criminals will seek to influence public officials so that they can achieve economic ends that are environmentally harmful. Financial analysis can identify transactional and business links between the subjects of environmental crime investigation and public officials, so that these can be promptly referred to the appropriate bodies.

7 Conclusion

Over the last decade, the Australian approach to environmental crime enforcement has shifted. Penalties have increased, agencies have devoted greater resources to investigation and prosecution, and courts have begun to impose serious financial penalties and even prison sentences. There are still examples of serious environmental breaches which go unpunished or are treated leniently. As Australia's environmental situation becomes more critical, the lenient approach is unlikely to meet public expectations. Law enforcement has a range of tools to combat money laundering and financial crime, and it is logical to expand the use of these tools to combat environmental crime as well. FATF's recent work will motivate state and federal agencies to focus on the link between environmental crime and money laundering, which can only be beneficial.

However it would be unfortunate if Australian governments were to rely exclusively on the environmental crime types highlighted by FATF instead of independently assessing Australia's risks. Wildlife trafficking, illegal mining, illegal logging and waste disposal are all serious environmental harms, but not all of them are directly applicable to Australia. Indeed, much of FATF's guidance seems more suited to developing countries with abundant natural resources, weak central government and low prosperity levels. Australia is more likely to be a destination country for the proceeds of resource crimes in these countries, rather than a source of illicit flows. Therefore Australia can play an important regional role in helping identify and potentially repatriate the proceeds of environmental crime that are laundered into Australia. Papua New Guinea and Indonesia would be obvious regional partners for this type of collaborative work.

---

[66] See *Independent Commission Against Corruption Act 1988* (NSW), ss. 12A (Serious corrupt conduct and systemic corrupt conduct), 7 (Corrupt conduct) and 8 (General nature of corrupt conduct).

[67] See *National Anti-Corruption Commission Act 2022* (Cth), ss. 3 (Objects of this Act) and 8 (Meaning of corrupt conduct).

Within Australia, the first priority should be first to understand environmental crime risk more holistically, rather than importing FATF priorities. Australia would benefit from an environmental crime risk assessment. Such a risk assessment would seek to identify the incidence of different types of environmental crime, and their impact on the Australian environment.

This would highlight environmental crime types which affect Australia but have not been the subject of FATF analysis. The most obvious of these is water crime. Australia's drought-affected landscape, large-scale agricultural cultivation and reliance on irrigation mean that water theft and fraud can generate great profits and cause great harm. There is potential for corruption due to the role of governments in regulating water entitlements and permits, and the complexities of water entitlement trading create risks of market manipulation. Arguably this combination of factors makes water crime a long-term strategic environmental crime threat for Australia. An Australian environmental crime risk assessment would enable identification of these types of threats, and prioritisation based on the level of environmental harm, the scale of criminal activity and other factors.

Using financial crime enforcement methods against environmental crime will require the involvement of stakeholders outside traditional law enforcement and existing public-private partnerships with reporting entities. State and federal environmental enforcement agencies within government have experience in investigating and prosecuting serious environmental offences which can assist with understanding environmental crime indicators and typologies. Because of the community interest in environmental protection, non-government organisations (NGOs) have also developed expertise in investigating environmental harms. Enforcement and intelligence partnerships should draw on this expertise. Broadening public-private partnerships in this way may create tensions between stakeholders with different perspectives on environmental harms, but the pooling of knowledge will also deliver benefits.

The tools of financial crime enforcement—money laundering prosecutions, civil confiscation, public-private partnerships—are powerful, but deploying them effectively is not always straightforward. Translating financial intelligence on money laundering into prosecutions and convictions is a known challenge for Australian law enforcement, and this challenge will persist whether the predicate offending is drug supply or environmental crime. However understanding financial flows linked to environmental crime has benefits beyond improving prosecution and confiscation statistics. Identifying customers and industries linked to environmental crime concerns helps financial institutions manage their risk. Australian state and territory governments can use intelligence about emerging environmental crime risks to drive legislative and policy change and allocate compliance resources. Ultimately, the public interest is served by persistent, visible efforts to stop the flow of profits from environmental crime into and within Australia.

References

Australian Broadcasting Corporation (2017) Pumped. Available via Four Corners. https://www.abc.net.au/news/2017-07-24/pumped/8727826. Accessed 21 Dec 2023

Australian Tax Office (2023). Serious financial crime task force. https://www.ato.gov.au/General/The-fight-against-tax-crime/Our-focus/Serious-Financial-Crime-Taskforce/#Seriousfinancialcrime. Accessed 21 Dec 2023

Australian Transaction Reports and Analysis Centre (2020). Financial Crime Guide - stopping the illegal trafficking of Australian wildlife. Available via AUSTRAC website. https://www.austrac.gov.au/sites/default/files/2020-10/AUSTRAC_IWT%20Guide_October%202020.pdf. Accessed 21 Dec 2023

Australian Transaction Reports and Analysis Centre (2021). Fintel alliance extract – 2020-2021 AUSTRAC annual report. Available via AUSTRAC website. https://www.austrac.gov.au/sites/default/files/2021-11/FintelAlliance_PerformanceReport20-21_v5_Web.pdf. Accessed 21 Dec 2023

Brewster K (2018) Queensland cotton farmer charged with $20m Murray-Darling plan fraud (28 August). https://www.theguardian.com/australia-news/2018/aug/28/queensland-cotton-farmer-charged-with-20m-murray-darling-plan. Accessed 21 Dec 2023

Bricknell (2010) Environmental crime in Australia, AIC Research and Public Policy series no. 109. Available via Australian Institute of Criminology. https://www.aic.gov.au/publications/rpp/rpp109. Accessed 21 Dec 2023

Carson V (2019) Water 'fraudster' tapped for $16m after sale of farm for $100m (25 January). https://www.couriermail.com.au/news/queensland/water-fraudster-tapped-for-16m-after-sale-of-farm-for-100m/news-story/12421f7da97ae23020c8f8e987830bb5. Accessed 21 Dec 2023

Chatham House (2023) Indonesia – Forest policy and governance. Available via Forest Governance and Legality. https://forestgovernance.chathamhouse.org/countries/indonesia. Accessed 21 Dec 2023

Commonwealth Director of Public Prosecutions (2017) Money laundering – guidance for charging offences under Division 400 of the Code

Cresswell ID, Janke T, Johnston EL (2021) Overview: Australia State of the Environment 2021. https://soe.dcceew.gov.au/. Accessed 21 Dec 2023

Crofts P (2015) Communicating the Culpability of Illegal Dumping: Bankstown v Hanna (2014). AUJ Environ Law 3:57–76

Department of Agriculture and Water Resources (2018) Country-specific guideline for Indonesia. https://www.agriculture.gov.au/sites/default/files/sitecollectiondocuments/forestry/australias-forest-policies/illegal-logging/indonesia-country-specific-guideline.pdf. Accessed 21 Dec 2023

De Koker L, Goldbarsht D (2024) FATF's risk-based approach: has the pendulum swung too far?. In: Goldbarsht D, De Koker L (eds) Financial crime and the law. Ius Gentium: Comparative perspectives on law and justice, vol 115. Springer, Cham. https://doi.org/10.1007/978-3-031-59543-1_10

Environmental Protection Authority Victoria (2021) EPA's role and enforcement action. https://www.epa.vic.gov.au/for-community/incidents/illegal-dump-site-south-of-kaniva/epas-role-and-enforcement-action. Accessed 21 Dec 2023

Environmental Protection Authority Victoria (2023) Lemon Springs update 24 April 2023. https://www.epa.vic.gov.au/about-epa/news-media-and-updates/media-releases-and-news/lemon-springs-april-update. Accessed 21 Dec 2023

Financial Action Task Force (2021) Money laundering from environmental crimes. https://www.fatf-gafi.org/publications/methodsandtrends/documents/money-laundering-environmental-crime.html. Accessed 21 Dec 2023

Financial Action Task Force and Asia-Pacific Group (2015) Anti-money laundering and counter-terrorist financing measures - Australia, Fourth Round Mutual Evaluation Report. www.fatf-gafi.org/topics/mutualevaluations/documents/mer-australia-2015.html Accessed 21 Dec 2023

Financial Analysis and Supervision Unit (2017) Papua New Guinea money laundering and terrorism financing national risk assessment. https://www.bankpng.gov.pg/wp-content/uploads/2019/04/Money-Laundering-and-Financing-of-Terrorism-National-Risk-Assessment-4.pdf. Accessed 21 Dec 2023

Global Initiative Against Transnational Organised Crime (2018) The World Atlas of Illicit Flows. https://globalinitiative.net/wp-content/uploads/2018/09/Atlas-Illicit-Flows-Second-Edition-EN-WEB.pdf. Accessed 21 Dec 2023

Global Initiative Against Transnational Organised Crime (2022) An analytic review of past responses to environmental crime and programming recommendations. https://globalinitiative.net/analysis/responses-environmental-crime/. Accessed 21 Dec 2023

Hamilton-Irvine G (2020) Nosir Kabite and Craig Izzard: Sentence for bribe and asbestos dumping (August 1). https://www.dailytelegraph.com.au/newslocal/blacktown-advocate/nosir-kabite-and-craig-izzard-sentence-for-bribe-and-asbestos-dumping/news-story/69c4d192a1f654e2f4d30eebad1da319

Hope Z (2022). Unearthed: while dispute dragged, mining company kept chasing pay dirt (August 26). https://www.brisbanetimes.com.au/national/queensland/unearthed-while-dispute-dragged-mining-company-kept-chasing-pay-dirt-20220817-p5bana.html

Independent Commission Against Corruption (2017) Investigation into the conduct of a regional illegal dumping squad officer and others (Operation Scania). https://www.icac.nsw.gov.au/ArticleDocuments/322/Investigation-into-the-conduct-of-a-regional-illegal-dumping-squad-officer-and-others_Operation-Scania.pdf.aspx. Accessed 21 Dec 2023

Latimer G (2019) Hazardous waste in Australia 2019. Available via Department of Climate Change, Energy, the Environment and Water website. https://www.dcceew.gov.au/sites/default/files/documents/hazardous-waste-australia-2019.pdf. Accessed 21 Dec 2023

Murray-Darling Basin Royal Commission (2019) Murray-Darling Basin Royal Commission Report. Accessed via Department for Environment and Water, South Australia website. https://cdn.environment.sa.gov.au/environment/docs/murray-darling-basin-royal-commission-report.pdf. Accessed 21 Dec 2023

National Anti-Corruption Commission (2023) Overview of the NACC. https://www.nacc.gov.au/about-nacc/overview. Accessed 22 Dec 2023

Organisation for Economic Co-operation and Development (2019) OECD environmental performance reviews – Australia 2019. https://read.oecd-ilibrary.org/environment/oecd-environmental-performance-reviews-australia-2019_9789264310452-en#page1. Accessed 21 Dec 2023

Pain N (2018) Encouraging restorative justice in environmental crime. Newc Law Rev 2:29–52

Rose G (2017) Australian law to combat illegal logging in Indonesia: a gossamer chain for transnational enforcement of environmental law. Rev Eur Comp Int Environ Law 26(2): 128–138

United Nations Environment Program (2016) The rise of environmental crime: a growing threat to natural resources, peace, development and security. https://www.unep.org/resources/report/rise-environmental-crime-growing-threat-natural-resources-peace-development-and. Accessed 21 Dec 2023

Vedelago C, Ilanbey S (2019) Authorities failed to act on potential toxic waste disaster two years ago (March 19). https://www.theage.com.au/national/victoria/authorities-failed-to-act-on-potential-toxic-waste-disaster-two-years-ago-20190315-p514lp.html

Vedelago C, Ilanbey S, Houston C (2019) The man who made a toxic waste disaster (December 22). https://www.theage.com.au/national/victoria/the-man-who-made-a-toxic-waste-disaster-20191205-p53h1x.html

White R (2018) Ecocide and the crimes of the powerful. U Tas Law Rev 13:96–117

Benjamin Scott has worked in financial crime intelligence and compliance roles in banking and government. He spent 8 years as a financial intelligence analyst at an Australian state law enforcement agency, working on joint investigations into transnational organised crime. He has degrees in history and law. His research on intelligence practice and anti-money laundering compliance has been published in academic journals including the Journal of Financial Crime and the Journal of Money Laundering Control. Benjamin's research interests include intelligence methodology, financial crime law and the history of organised crime.

Giving Shape to Finance and the City of London: Permissive Regulation and Minimalist Governance

Alex Simpson, Corina Sheerin, and Vince Hurley

> What was happening [. . .] was that the reward mechanisms got out of control. It became crazy. You had these pot-headed guys running round and they were all focused on making money because that is what their incentives were. And they lost sight of the impact of what they were doing. [. . .] They just got out of control, [. . .] people were trading [and] asset stripping companies, making vast amount of money along the way, and saying, 'That's alright, it is what I was targeted to do – to make lots of money'. But at look what they did (Former CEO of UK Bank: citied in Simpson 2021, p. 104).

1 Introduction

To walk through the close streets and narrow alleys of the City of London is to step into another world. A world ostensibly *in* London, but certainly not *of* London. This is a space defined by finance; it is a cathedral to the power of capital, competition and, above all, pure market ideology. Almost everything that operates within this space does so for the purposes of enshrining competitive market exchange. Yet, in the decades subsequent to the 2008 financial crisis, we have only seen how this market ideology often runs unchecked and is too often stalked by, what Susan Strange (1997) so emphatically referred to as, *casino capitalism*. For Strange (1997), the important distinction between the gambling of casinos and that of finance is, at least in the context of the former, there is a level of voluntary engagement.

A. Simpson (✉) · V. Hurley
Department of Security Studies and Criminology, Macquaire University, Macquaire Park, NSW, Australia
e-mail: alex.simpson@mq.edu.au

C. Sheerin
School of Business, National College of Ireland, Dublin, Ireland

D. Goldbarsht, L. de Koker (eds.), *Financial Crime, Law and Governance*, Ius Gentium: Comparative Perspectives on Law and Justice 116,
https://doi.org/10.1007/978-3-031-59547-9_6

However, in the context of finance, and as the crisis of 2008 laid so bare, we are all woven into the tapestry of risk as involuntary participants, ensnared and unable to escape. Of less interest here is whether any specific crime was committed during this time. After all, as Tombs and Canning (2021) remind us, crime is little more than a state labelling process. Of more importance is the systemic harm the cascaded out of decades of permissive regulation, corporate greed and endemic cultures of risk and aggression with little concern for any social impact not reflected on the profit and loss sheet. The true legacy of the Great Financial Crisis is that it enshrined the truism that, as the Joseph Rowntree Foundation (2011) highlighted, it was the poorest and most vulnerable in our society who paid the highest price, whilst contributing the least to its origins and development. And so it continues, all aspects of finance punish those most marginalised across society (Baeckström 2022).

Examining the profound ethical issues around the nature of social responsibility and financial efficacy, this chapter attempt at giving shape and form to how the financial markets are *created*, *sustained* and *managed* through a system of governance and permissive control. After all, as Foucault (2010) reminds us, finance and the ideological force of market competition has no *natural essence*, rather it must be *realised* and *sustained* as a *coherent idea* within the imaginations and cultural practices of individuals and institutions alike. So much of finance, both its deep roots embedded within the City of London and the legitimised harms that seep out across society are presented as 'natural', 'inevitable' and even an example of functioning competition (Shaxson 2018; Simpson 2021; Stiglitz 2013). Yet, what this chapter reveals, is how the *coherent idea* of finance is rooted in permissive regulatory governance with limited controls beyond that which protect the integrity of the market itself.

The City of London may be an ideological construction, containing all the promise of market efficiency and perfect movement. Contra to the idealism of a *neo*liberal market order, where people, capital and products are transferred 'seamlessly' across the globe, the City of London retains the local and human-scale setting in which financial markets operate as a coalescence of the spatial, material, technological and, above all, social. Fundamentally, the City is a governed entity, one which is given shape and form by the possibilities afforded to it by governments, regulatory bodies and a global word order that runs through the channels of financial optimism. Framed in this context, the City of London occupies two registers—one 'real' and embedded in space and another 'regulatory' that functions to establish a frictionless system of market exchange. Here, the City of London is a tightly bounded spatial parameter at sits at the heart of London (though, crucially, it is not itself a London Borough). Totalling 1.22 square miles, this City stretches from the Thames at Victoria Embankment, clockwise up through Fleet Street, the Barbican in the north, then to Liverpool Street in the northeast and back down to the Tower of London. This City is an island; what the late Tony Benn (Hansard 2000) called, an off-shore island moored on the river Thames. As an offshore island, the City retains a strong attachment to physical locality and, within its tight topography of institutional, technological and spatial importance, reaches back to its past to continue to produce and enact a coherent system of financial exchange (Simpson 2021). St

Paul's Cathedral stands as the marker, separating Westminster and the centre of government to the west from the finance centre to the east. Pass the corridor of (albeit former) newspaper officer on Fleet Street and you arrive at the Bank of England building, with its high columns standing as the separating barrier between the world of politics from the world of finance. If you want to find the home of the principal regulator, the Financial Conduct Authority, then you need to track further east still, to the new Olympic development of Strathfield—away from both the City and its tributary, Canary Wharf. Yet, it is important to understand how, to return to Foucault, the origins of finance within the City has no natural essence. Rather, the City as a financial hub needs to be framed as a system of governance; one which emerged out of the shape of Empire, and which continues to shape a post-colonial landscape of control (see Shaxson 2018; Simpson 2021). In other words, the presence of the City of London is no historical accident, but it is the consequence of active planning, decision making and regulation, in the loosest possible sense, that brought its present form into existence.

The enduring presence of the City of London as an autonomous socio-economic entity to be defended as a point of national pride is one of the more perverse outcomes of late-capitalism[1] (Rötheli 2010). Strip back the hubris and cut through the numbers of largely private wealth being generated, then what are we left with? Perhaps, as John Lanchester suggest, little more than the practices of a robber baron's castle. For all the "art and colour and life and music, with the most beautiful tapestries, and the highest standard of living", it is important to retain the vison of how the City, like the robber baron's castle, "glitters so brightly precisely because it devastates the landscape in which it sits. Its glory comes that the cost of the desolate it causes" (Lanchester 2015). How then did we get to this place? A financial system that is predicated on extractivism just as much as any mining industry, but where the true harms and cost of the industry remain hidden in plain sight? The way in which we, as a society, have become co-opted by the controlling interest of finance helps explain why our banks, and the industry at large, are too big to fail and the bankers too powerful to jail. Fighting for the preservation of profits, the production of social harms become almost an expected consequence and embedded part of financial cultural practice. The City is, in almost every sense, a disconnected arena. This chapter evaluates the role played by governance and regulation, principally birth and legacy of the Euromarket, that has contributed to an arena controlled by what can be, at best, characterised as 'permissive' and, at worse, 'harmful'. After all, as the former CEO who opens this chapter highlights, it is the regulatory environment and reward mechanisms that gives shape and form to the 'permissive' environment that gives shape and meaning to concepts of risk, ethics and harm in the context of finance.

[1] See Jameson (1991) and Carroll and Jarvis (2022).

2 A Terrible Waste of a Good Crisis

Writing in response to the first rumblings of financial discontent in 2008, the Guardian's economics editor, Larry Elliot (2008), noted that what we are bearing witness to is like the "cut-off point between 'an Edwardian summer' of prosperity and tranquillity and the trench warfare of the credit crunch". This was a moment when the speculative over-exposure to sub-prime mortgages became real; when banks and financial firms realised that the assumptions and risk models underpinning their trades was, quite simply, wrong. The key moments of the financial crisis are well documented (see Elliot 2008; Foster and Magdoff 2009; Inman 2012), but they key message is the way it sent shards of financial debris were shed around the globe and the enduring legacy was the costs of failure were seen by successive governments to be far greater than the cost of propping up a choking industry (Dinerstein et al. 2014; French and Leyshon 2010). 'Too big to fail' quickly became the caption of the day and reflected broader public anger. The UK government effectively functioned as a public guarantor to the City's reckless gambling, first by pumping in £566 billion, roughly 90 percent of Treasury assets at the time (National Audit Office 2011), then by turning a 'banking crisis' into a 'national debt crisis' that needed to be repaid through a logic of austerity. The events of 2008 proved the City of London to be detached, unaccountable and, ultimately, elevated above the social landscape in which it sits.

As Jamie Peck (2010a, p. 9) noted soon after, for all the 2008 financial crisis was meant to be the "Berlin Wall moment" for finance and neoliberalism, it proved to be just the opposite. Crises, economic or otherwise, are defined by change; signalling the demise of past unsustainable conditions before recalibrating towards a more socially profitable equilibrium (French and Leyshon 2010). Under these conditions, 2008 was a crisis of stasis. More of the same. The 'change' that many were expected at the time never came; rather the financial crisis has precipitated a doubling down on the ideological maxim of financial market liberalisation. No wonder why French and Leyshon (2010) called it a *terrible waste of a good crisis*. The preceding economic and political failures that stemmed from a permissive landscape which placed far too much trust in 'more market' and relied far too heavily in the 'security' of innovation was, in short, 'let off'. If the events of 2008 were are Deleuzian *event*, then it only functioned as a moment to bury bad practice behind. While the discourses of crisis that were once so prevalent in the media and in the public consciousness appear to be receding, we, as a society, continue to live in its aftermath (Dinerstein et al. 2014). Far from being over, the effects of crisis continue to have a profound impact in relation to issues of inequality and social justice throughout society today. The sobering realisation is that the immediate for change has not spelt the end of the neoliberal maxim of more market; rather, the logic of the finance plays an ever-increasing role in the structural organisation of our daily lives (Hall 2017; Revington and August 2020; Souleles 2019). This era of aggressive financialisation has, arguably, been accelerated as powerful financial elites successfully obscured their own responsibility for the crisis whilst introducing a restraining force of impossibility and inevitability of the power of capital (Dinerstein et al. 2014). The outcome is a society that, in the Polanyian sense, begins to be run as an adjunct to financial values rather than the other way round. Nowhere is this more true that within the hubs of global finance.

Whereas previous crises had given birth to a new imagination—shaped in the image of previous failures to create a new future—we have since been stuck with 'more of the same'. Yet, going back to the failures of the first wave of economic liberalism and the subsequent crash in the 1930s, we can see how crisis gave way to a new consensus of, what Ruggie (1982) would later call, *embedded liberalism*. Enshrined by the 1944 Bretton Woods agreement, there was a concerted effort on the part of the forty-four allied nations, including the United Kingdom, United States, Canada, Australia, Japan and Western European countries, to eradicate the speculative trading of financial liberalism (Kindleberger 1996). As far as the powers of the day saw the problem, the ability of investors to rapidly flood a market with capital before retracting it just as quickly without penalty had fuelled a destructive cycle of speculation that led to the boom-and-bust era of 1920s and 1930s (Helleiner 2017; Kindleberger 1996). The Bretton Woods agreement was an attempt to put the shackles of regulation on the City and to build a financial era that would clip the wings of British-backed financialisation and, in turn, the City of London. Market liberalism of the Nineteenth Century established and artificial phenomenon of the self-regulated market that endorsed a *disembedded* financial order, meaning, for Polanyi (2001 [1944], p. 60), "no less than the running of society as an adjunct to the market" and reversing standard social/market relations. The drive towards *embeddedness* captures the disconnection and order of priority inherent to pre-1914 British-backed market liberalism, an order which culminated in subordinating issues of social concern to market and financial interest. This led to, as Keynes summarises, the world of finance becoming more concerned with "forecasting the next shift of market sentiment' than with the long term yield of capital assets—an endpoint that is little more than the 'by-product of the activities of a casino" (Keynes 2008 [1936], p. 316). Yet again, the analogy of the casino invoking a spirit of recklessness and speculation that creates ripples of harm far beyond those individuals and corporations immediately engaged in the practice.

3 The Euromarket and the Birth of 'New Financialisation'

The regulatory restrictions of the Bretton Woods agreement created a very different City of London. Tight capital mobility controls that choked off the free and loose flow of capital previously flooding the City's channels. With strict limits on the amount of capital that could move across country borders at any one time, the speculative practices of finance were severely curtailed (Helleiner 2017). The idea was that the City would be forced to turn its investment capacity to supporting UK society as opposed to extracting and repatriating wealth from it—embedded liberalism in practice (Shaxson 2018). While it is fair to say that the Bretton Woods agreement was not an unqualified success, with the onset and escalation of the Cold War presenting major obstacles, the important thing to hold on to here is the scale of ambition. Throughout the 1950s and 1960s, the heyday of the Bretton Woods agreement, international cooperation and agreement actively sought to create a landscape that restrained capital mobility (Helleiner 2017; Simpson 2021). With this in mind, a pertinent question arises: how did we go from a global economic order of tight regulatory control and restricted financial speculation to the hyper-accelerated and globalised financial markets of today? It is important to understand the ways in which the City, backed by successive governments, set about to systematically work around the capital mobility restrictions and, in doing so, reassert what it saw as the 'right' for capital liberalism in terms of movement and exchange.

Arguably, the most important and far-reaching of the slow reassertions of financial liberalisation came in the form of the *Euromarket*. Beginning in the 1960s, the Euromarket was, in essence, a 'spatial slippage' that created a whole new market located within the City of London, thus restoring its prevalent position and the centre of global financial trade, yet which fell beyond the regulatory remit of both the United Kingdom and the Bretton Woods protocols (Simpson 2021). Not to be confused with the European Single Market, the Euromarket is a term for when a currency is held or traded outside its country of issue—the US dollar held or traded outside of the USA, sterling held or traded outside of the UK, yen held and traded outside of Japan (Helleiner 1994; Kynaston 2002). With City banks severely restricted by capital controls, the by shifting the currency of trading from sterling to, primarily, US dollars, the City created its own fictional space beyond the clutches of regulation. By trading in US dollars, both the Bank of England and the British government deemed that such transactions were beyond UK regulatory control; yet, since trading was located within the UK, no other authority was able to regulate it either (Helleiner 2017). As Kynaston (2002) notes in his history of the City of London, the result was the creation of a stateless financial market that operated within the City of London but, crucially, beyond the control of state regulations. In short, the Euromarket not only reaffirmed the global dominance of the City of London but marked the starting point of a wave of political changes which reasserted the dominance of markets in the organisation of society.

The scale of growth and importance of the Euromarket to the development City of London and modern finance is hard to overstate (Scott and Quaglia 2020; Simpson 2021, p. 19). The practice would mark herald a new emergence of financialisation, with the City of London one of the biggest players, that reflects a stateless, wild-west 'ideal' of aggressive deregulation designed to support offshore investment vehicles and multinational corporations. While, as Shaxson (2018) explains, the precise start of the Euromarket is unknown, its earliest presence can be traced to 1955, when the Bank of England first became aware of the Midland Bank (now part of HSBC) switching its deposit holdings from sterling to US dollars to circumnavigate currency restrictions. By 1960, however, this practice would become a \$1 billion industry and would later balloon to \$114.5 billion of holdings by the end of the 1970s as American banks flocked to the City to avoid the restrictive Federal Reserve rules (Burn 1999; Shaxson 2018). In the subsequent decade, the Euromarket would become formalised, most notably with the opening up of the London Stock Exchange to foreign investment firms in 1986, known as the Big Bang. However, Nicholas Shaxson (2018, p. 89) argues that it was its predecessor, the Euromarkets, that was the much Bigger Bang. It was, after all, the Euromarkets that transformed the very nature of international finance and, like a 'slow motion nuclear explosion', marked the first steps for the neoliberal free market ideology that remains dominant today (Shaxson 2018, p. 59).

Whilst it is possible to paint a picture in which the development of the Euromarket stands as a marker of financial 'freedom', with the financial markets—like water—finding an inevitable pathway through the restrictions of regulation and control. However, the substantive point lies in the way the emergence and success of the Euromarket as more to do with active inaction on the part of US and UK governments and the subsequent move to incorporate this fictionalised trading zone, removed from the cumbrance of place or control, within the fabric of the City as a march of so called market 'progress' (Simpson 2021). As Helleiner (1994) explains, the Euromarket emerged at a time when the rest of Britain was stuck in post-war stasis; sterling was a currency in turmoil and its empire was crumbling, confirmed by the international humiliation of the Suez crisis. The Euromarket provided the UK government with a pathway that could restore London's international position as a leader in financial market activity and boost Britain's deteriorating economic position. In other words, at crucial junctures the UK and the USA governments chose not to utilise their authority to curtail the development of the Euromarket, thus reconstructing the London-New York financial axis that was so prevalent prior to Bretton Woods. Helleiner (1994) takes a step further by arguing that, through the 1970s and 1980s, Westminster and Washington policymakers were actively promoting the Euromarket as a way of preserving a more liberal international financial system in the face of growing external restraints. Quite simply, contemporary finance grew out of a double shift of market innovation and a state/regulatory axis characterised by decisive inactivity that continues to shape how states actively promote and enshrine a regulatory environment free from the cumbrance of controls.

The extraordinary development within the Euromarket was a fully functioning market exchange that had no physical embodiment in an exchange building, nor was it rooted within a geographically defined jurisdiction of regulatory rules and regulations. It was a 'space' fully created out of imagination. It is a system that, whilst supposedly draws from the 'natural', is no less born of an ontology fiction than the other of modernity's great institutions (Cetina 1994). The lens of 'fictions' help shine a light on the 'double speak' that underscores financial markets, being, as they are, simultaneously material and immaterial, solid and fluid, abstract and real (Simpson 2019, 2021). Through the advent of the Euromarket, two fictions came into being with world-shaping effect. First is the supposedly 'natural' state of capital mobility to flow unencumbered by friction in and out of international borders, with the second creating an imaginary in which finance is removed from the restrictions of politics and is establishes as an autonomous order of knowledge in need of protecting (Simpson 2021). Here, we can begin to see the, what Chopra (2003, p. 421) calls, the 'validating consensus' of financial capitalism take root; a strong discourse, in Goffman's (1961) sense of the term, that draws its power from politics of control but is expressed as a naturalising discourse of inevitability or efficiency. As an unquestionable orthodoxy, the political economy of financialisation operates as constant and objective truth without contestation. This, in turn, as both Bourdieu (1998, 2001) and Foucault (2010) have argued, has led to the embedding of the interests of capital mobility, a complicit precarious arrangements that produce insecurity and a structural belief in the 'free trade faith' that sanctifies the power of markets in the name of economic efficiency, the elimination of administrative or political barriers capable of inconveniencing the owners of capital and the preaching of the requirement of economic freedom.

The Euromarkets functioned to 'remove' the City of London from regulatory controls of the UK. This sleight of hand had the purpose, as we know by now, to evade capital restrictions but it also had the effect of disestablishing the City from the rest of the UK. Together, these fictions of financial activity establish the City of London as no longer of London, nor of the UK. From this moment onwards it had effectively become a carefully constructed and protected autonomous 'off-shore island'. Yet, at the same time, the development of the Euromarkets created a new strong discourse in which its central tenets of deregulated trade and speculative freedoms become woven into a new coherent idea of financial 'order', which has come to dictate perceptions of economic and political practices (Bourdieu 1998; Chopra 2003). Multi-national institutions such as the European Union, the IMF, the World Bank and the Organisation for Economic Cooperation and Development (OECD) set out the rules that oblige its members to open up their economies and liberalise capital flows across borders—establishing a distinctly global and uninhibited market order. Moreover, regulatory systems set up in the wake of the Euromarket have all been designed to promote financial 'freedoms' in a manner that priorities freedom over risk (Tsingou 2010). Turning the attention of this chapter towards the regulatory environment, it is possible to observe how the ideological basis of the Euromarket has become embedded at within the institutional arrangement of finance—as well as the City of London—that, in Foucault's (1980) terms, imposes its legitimate power of distinction on to the social world.

4 Permissive Regulation and the City of London

One of the central conceit of financialisation as a political project, as Strange (2000) highlights, is the way in which the organisation of the market should dictate social and political decisions, while the state should voluntarily reduce its role of influence. While there is always a certain about of 'rolling-back' of state apparatus, the shape of regulation is almost always enacted through state-led policy frameworks, establishing a layer of 'ideological choice' over inevitability (Larner 2000; Peck 2010b). In other words, the role of the state within the project of financialisation, as Larner (2000) explains, defaults to the building of national and multi-national institutions that reassert the fundamental tenets of 'free' market governance. To focus on the regulatory agencies that govern and give structure to the City of London is to reflect on the aims and objectives of the macro political and economic environment (Kassim et al. 2020). Straddling both the political and economic sphere, Tsingou (2010) argues that the regulatory framework surrounding finance serves to highlight the ideologies, policy agendas and political position of an ideological order, yet shrouded in an a-political framework of technocratic governance.

Reflecting on the regulatory landscape active around 2008, we can see the macro and micro frameworks of permissiveness that created the financial instability that continues to dominate the industry today. At the heart of this are the Basel frameworks. Issued by the Bank for International Settlements (BIS), Basel II was set up in in 2004 and acts as the main formal regulatory tool for the global financial market. Its three-pillared framework stipulated the minimum capital requirement to be held by banks in a global economy, a supervisory review programme to equip national regulators in a dispute as well as a codified framework of market discipline (BIS 2004). While the framework sought to facilitate greater transparency and security in an increasingly global market, its effect was to place private finance preferences at the forefront of regulatory control (Pauly 2011; Tsingou 2010). Far from acting as an external check of market practice, Basel II fostered a 'pro-cyclical' financial environment that encouraged banks to imprudently expand during booms, encouraging the over-production of unstable and risky financial innovations to the detriment of regulatory standards (Pauly 2011; Porter 2010). In other words, while increasingly complex financial innovations were seen to promote greater capital mobility and growth, in actuality, employing such levels of financial innovation came at the cost of usability and gave a false sense of security while the economy was over-heating. By encouraging spurious financial innovation, the terms of Basel II facilitated a market of risk that failed to foresee the resulting negative costs following their collapse in 2008. After the global financial crisis, it was clear that a far more robust and complex regulatory structure was needed within global financial markets to avoid the catastrophic events of 2008 recurring. The response was Basel III, an international regulatory accord that introduced a comprehensive set of reforms which expanded the scope of financial regulation in relation to funding and liquidity risk requirements as well as rules governing the definition and calculation of capital requirements.

During the crisis it became apparent very quickly that banks were not holding sufficient liquid assets to meet their obligations, which when coupled with decreasing prices of certain financial products like mortgage-backed securities (MBS) a perfect storm of vulnerability and substantial losses in the system took place (Mishkin 2011). Thus, Basel III reforms included a range of enhanced international bank rules including minimum capital requirements and liquidity measures. Under Basel III, all banks were required to hold additional reserves beyond that specified in Basel II, thus ensuring that in times of economic crisis financial institutions were independently stable with no need for government intervention (Le et al. 2023). Regarding liquidity, a range of measures was introduced including the Liquidity Coverage ratio (LCR). The LCR required all banks to hold high quality liquid assets such that they could meet their obligations in times of stress and crisis for a period lasting 30 days (Schmitz 2013). In addition, the Net Stable Funding ratio (NSFR) was introduced in most domains post 2019. This regulation required that in the longer-term banks have a stable funding model relative to their on- and off-balance sheet activities, thus ensuring they can absorb financial shocks (BIS 2022). Along-side a range of tools to monitor bank liquidity more broadly and beyond LCR and NSFR were implemented. Stress tests and scenario analysis as part of risk management banks strategies are now seen as standard requirements, thus ensuring that a comprehensive and transparent understanding of the banks financial position is always available (BIS 2022). Within the City, the implementation of Basel III has been steady but slow, with concerns expressed regarding the complexity of the new regulatory framework, the influence of fintech and emerging cryptocurrencies (Amadxarif et al. 2019; Greenwood et al. 2017; Ramlall 2018). Moreover, the post Brexit landscape has only lead to weakened political relations between the EU and the City, with ongoing debates regarding the continental 'rules-based' approach to regulation versus the UK's 'judgement-based' response (Whyte 2012). The desire for the City (and the UK more broadly) to circumvent regulatory control was, after all, a driving political force behind the Brexit decision, with the creation of 'Singapore-on-Thames' style of low-friction financial movement.

Acting under the Basel frameworks are the national regulatory agencies, which, for the City of London, are the 'twin peaks' approach of the Prudential Regulation Authority (PRA) and the Financial Conduct Authority (FCA). The bodies replaced the Financial Services Authority (FSA) in 2013. the importance of the FSA to the New Economy lies in the way in which, like Basel II, it was complicit in facilitating rather than limiting market practice with grave social and economic costs. Established in 2001 to unite the nine disparate regulatory bodies under one single institution, the general duties of the FSA as set out by the Financial Services and Market Act 2000 were to promote market confidence, increase financial stability, protect consumers and reduce financial crime. Together, these duties placed the FSA as both judge and jury of the financial system and the companies working within it. Just like the macro regime of Basel II, the FSA presided over one of the most sustained booms in the history of the financial services industry as well as its near total collapse in 2008. The organising principle of the FSA was to create an open and free economic space that encouraged the launch of new financial products as well as removing any regulatory barriers that would damage the UK's competitiveness (Augar 2009; Shaxson 2018). In short, the ideological basis of the FSA was a fundamental belief that the role of the financial regulator was to promote a conciliatory rather than adversarial relationship between the regulators and partners (Fooks 2003). This led to a market which failed to take account for the social and economic costs of their action, focusing instead on their overarching objective; profit maximisation.

The central policy framework of the FSA was termed by the then chief executive, John Tiner, as the 'principles approach'. In essence, principles based regulation upheld a system whereby the firms and their management were seen to be responsible for identifying and controlling risk, not the regulators. As Tiner (2006) states, the principles approach is "about outcomes or ends ... [allowing] firms to decide how best to achieve required outcomes and, as such, it allows a much greater alignment of regulation with good business practice". By placing emphasis on the ends, as opposed to the means, the FSA created an environment which increased the scope in which firms can act (i.e. enabling a diverse and competitive economic landscape with few restrictions), while the priority of the firm is simply to meet its business objectives. What emerged from the FSA's principles based guidance was a culture which heavily rewarded private gain with a reduced sense of accountability. As the Turner Review (2009) outlined in its response to the regulatory failures that preceded the financial crisis, waves of financial innovations, encouraged under the regulatory terms of the FSA, focused on repackaging and securitising debt as a way of 'creating value'. In placing their faith in these financial innovations, the FSA believed they were creating a diverse economic environment which measured and managed much of the involved risk (The Turner Review 2009). However, when the crisis broke it was apparent that the diversification of risk, encouraged by the FSA's principles approach, had not been achieved. Instead, deep seated vulnerabilities of highly leveraged balance sheets, fragile funding structures and the rapid creation of high-risk, poor-quality assets were sharply exposed (EIU 2012).

Since its inception in 2013, the FCA has set out to take a tougher stance on acts that, in Calavita and Pontell's (1994) terms, threaten the integrity of the market mechanism such as the successive PPI, Libor and Forex scandals. For example, in 2014 the FCA collected nearly £1.5bn in fines. Of this, £1.1bn came from five banks for manipulating the currency rates on the foreign exchange (FX) markets by putting "their Banks' interests ahead of those of their clients, other market participants and the wider UK financial system" (FCA 2014). In 2015, Barclays was fined a record £284 m by the FCA for similar breaches of conduct on the FX markets (FCA 2015). These figures represent a remarkable increase on the FSA who recorded just over £200 m in fines in 2012 and £66 m in 2011, while in 2007, the year the crisis broke, the figure was just £5 m (National Archives 2007, 2011, 2012). However, the role of the FCA is not without critique. For example, the financial services consumer panel, an independent entity representing financial services consumers highlighted that while the FCA is supporting a more robust regulatory environment, for consumers there is a lack of transparency given that firms are protected from being identified as having breached the rules and standards unless there has been an enforcement action undertaken. For consumers, there is no real way to identify financial institutions who may be serial offenders. It conversely disadvantages those banks and entities who are compliant and fosters a perception of "all firms are the same" (Financial Services Consumer Panel 2018, p. 2).

Other concerns include post-pandemic debt management in the consumer and SME markets and the role of the regulator in same. Chiu et al. (2021) argue that the UK regulators in facilitating banks making local '*tailored arrangements*' during the Covid period has put in jeopardy wider financial welfare goals for the economy in the longer term. The authors cite the need for increased attention by both the FCA and the PRA concerning debt management of the SME sector as well as consumers and the need for support from these entities as they navigate the 'hazards of post-pandemic indebtedness'. More recently issues such as the global pandemic and the emergence of big data, data analytics and financial technology has brought sharply to the fore the need for an agile regulatory environment. To date, regulatory bodies including the UK, lag behind the rapidly evolving financial ecosystems—this is despite the FCA being represented as one of the most innovative "open, creative, proactive, transformational" regulators in the world (Friend 2021, p. 8). Going forward and in the wake of the 2008 crisis, regulators face increased scrutiny and issues such as artificial intelligence algorithms, cryptocurrency regulation as well as algorithmic trading and its market impact all warrant innovative and complex consideration (Buckley et al. 2020). Once again, it appears that the 'principles based approach', as espoused by the FSA, continues to hold sway with regulatory control largely handing responsibly of governance over to the financial bodies they are supposed to regulate. What we see from the surrounding regulatory frameworks are how the structural and governmental control of regulation serves to promote specific forms of practice; a system of finance engineered around structured risk, external harms and punishing only acts that threaten the integrity of the market, not the harms of the market. The result is a form of market action in which broader social concerns go unrepresented. Created and established under the auspices of the dominant political and economic environment, these institutions give structure and form to the field of finance by defining how markets work and to what end.

5 Conclusion: Enshrining 'Casino Capitalism'

In this chapter, we have sought to undertake a critical evaluation of the regulatory landscape that surrounds the City of London, examining both its origins as well as recent developments to shed crucial light on the governance structures that give finance both shape and form. Crucially, as we argue, the ideological basis of Euromarket and the 'wild west' it came to represent has, in the subsequent decades, become enshrined within the regulatory structures, giving meaning to the institutional arrangement of finance within the City we recognise today. However, this shape and form was designed to promote financial 'freedoms' in a manner that priorities freedom over risk, with the outcome being a largely permissive regulatory environment and encouraged to diversify and expand according to the principles of the market—rather than the needs of society (Tsingou 2010). It is important to recognise, however, the core social function of finance; to provide safeguards for depositions as well as manage the associated risks of investments to expand and diversify the economy (Rethel and Sinclair 2012). Yet, under a permissive regulatory environment with limited socially embedded safeguards, the financial institutions that underpin the City of London are encouraged to engage in ever-reckless games of risk in the ceaseless quest for profit, growth and market share (Stiglitz 2010).

The outcome is, one the one hand, the casino capitalism the Susan Strange (1997) forewarned. Arguably of greater impact, we increasingly see a disconnected finance system, encapsulated by a City of London that makes objects out of you and me. Not *of* the City, we become pawns for financial extraction. We are the *social* on to whom the risk is placed, whilst financial firms hoover up the profits. Yet, this distinct separation is far from new. Writing in response to the economic turmoil of the 1930s, Keynes (2008 [1936], pp. 315–316) lamented:

> It is of the nature of organised investment markets, under the influence of purchasers largely ignorant of what they are buying and of speculators who are more concerned with forecasting the next shift of market sentiment than with a reasonable estimate of the future yield of capital assets, that, when disillusion falls upon an over-optimistic and over-bought market, it should fall with sudden and even catastrophic force.

Purchasers do not know (or care) what they are buying; speculators focus more on the projected numbers mapped out on a changing computer screen than the lives such calculative cartographies erase. Keynes likens these characteristics to the "by-product of the activities of a casino" (Keynes 2008 [1936], p. 316). The enduring message in these sentiments is a disconnection and separation of speculation from the social which, as ill-defined as it is, underpins all things financial and which is structured and guided by a permissive regulatory environment focused more on enshrining a 'frictionless' market experience than protected core social values. The importance of regulatory governance here lies in the way that it produces knowledge structures, systems of expected behaviour and incentive measures (Foucault 1980). Here, again, we can link the regulatory system with the quote the opened this chapter. Regulation is not just a restrained designed to say 'no', it is a productive language that gives shape and form to a financial landscape with its embedded truths of ethics, governance and control. It is within this environment that individuals are recruited, socialised and structured in the ideology of action to unwittingly reproduce, through a competitive struggle of domination, the homologous effects of the field (Bourdieu 1991). Crucially, it is within the autonomous framework of action that markets are enacted and brought to life, producing a structural rule of profit that exists over and above basic issues of social wellbeing.

The lure of short-term profits in the run up to the financial crisis and its continuing aftermath have, as Rethel and Sinclair (2012) argue, distracted key financial institutions from fulfilling their core social and economic function. Rather than promoting securitisation, finance is shaped by a focus on hedging increasingly large investments in ever move diverse products and opportunities with varying degrees of risk. For example, as Stiglitz (2010) outlines, during all of the preceding 'go-go years of growth', the financial services industry did not come up with one good mortgage product. Nowhere was there a product that managed the risk of homeownership, based on lower transaction costs and stable interest rates. Instead, the finance sector became embroiled in high-risk, short term productivity with negative social outcomes rather than long-term financial innovations that would actually be beneficial for society. These innovations were shrouded with the promises of containing and managing risk through the repackaging and passing on of debt in the form of credit default swaps but, in reality, these products only served to proliferate risk through hiding bad lending and gambling on defaults (Stiglitz 2010). These actions are not an isolated case of a few rogue individuals failing to act in accordance to the 'social principles of the market'. Rather, they represent an endemic case of market capture which has conflated the core objectives and interests of profitability with social productivity. And here is the endless casino of finance that we, as its objects, are trapped within—a system shaped by, rather than protected from, regulatory governance and control.

References

Amadxarif Z, Brookes J, Garbarino N et al (2019) The language of rules: textual complexity in banking reforms: Bank of England staff working paper, No. 834. Bank of England, London

Augar P (2009) Reckless: the rise and fall of the city. Random House, London

Baeckström Y (2022) Gender and finance: addressing inequality in the financial services industry. Routledge, Abingdon

BIS (2004) International convergence of capital measurement and capital standards: a revised framework. Bank for International Settlements, Basel

BIS (2022) Basel Committee on Banking Supervision: evaluation of the impact and efficacy of the Basel III reforms. Bank for International Settlements, Basel

Bourdieu P (1991) Language and symbolic power. Harvard University Press, Cambridge

Bourdieu P (1998) The essence of neoliberalism [Online]. Le Monde Diplomatique [English Edition]

Bourdieu P (2001) Firing back: against the tyranny of the market 2. The New Press, New York

Buckley RP, Arner DW, Zetzsche DA et al (2020) The road to RegTech: the (astonishing) example of the European Union. J Bank Regul 21:26–36

Burn G (1999) The state, the city and the Euromarkets. Rev Int Polit Econ 6:225–261

Calavita K, Pontell H (1994) The state and white collar crime: saving the savings and loans. Law Soc Rev 28:297–324

Carroll T, Jarvis D (2022) Understanding the state in relation to late capitalism: a response to "new" state capitalism contributions. Antipode 54(6):1715–1737. https://doi.org/10.1111/anti.12846

Cetina KK (1994) Primitive classification and postmodernity: towards a sociological notion of fiction. Theory Cult Soc 11:1–22

Chiu IHY, Kokkinis A, Miglionico A (2021) Addressing the challenges of post-pandemic debt management in the consumer and SME sectors: a proposal for the roles of UK financial regulators. J Bank Regul:1–19

Chopra R (2003) Neoliberalism as doxa: Bourdieu's theory of the state and the contemporary Indian discourse on globalisation and liberalisation. Cult Stud 17:419–444

Dinerstein A, Schwartz G, Taylor G (2014) Sociological imagination as social critique: interrogating the 'global economic crisis'. Sociology 48:859–868

EIU (2012) UK regulations: financial regulation in the United Kingdom. Economist Intelligence Unit, London

Elliot L (2008) Credit crisis - how it all began. The Guardian

FCA (2014) FCA fines five banks £1.1 billion for FX failings and announces industry-wide remediation programme. Available at: http://www.fca.org.uk/news/fca-fines-five-banks-for-fx-failings. Accessed 21 Dec 2023

FCA (2015) Fines. London: financial conduct authority [Online] Available at: https://web.archive.org/web/20150629120437/http://www.fca.org.uk/firms/being-regulated/enforcement/fines. [Accessed 03 06 2023]

Financial Services Consumer Panel. (2018) FCA mission: approach to supervision. Available at: https://www.fs-cp.org.uk/sites/default/files/fscp_response_approach_to_supervision.docx__0.pdf. Accessed 21 Dec 2023

Fooks G (2003) In the valley of the blind the one-eyed man is king. In: Tombs S, Whyte D (eds) Unmasking the crimes of the powerful. Peter Lang Publishing, New York, pp 105–227

Foster J, Magdoff F (2009) The great financial crisis: causes and consequences. Monthly Review Press, New York

Foucault M (1980) Power/knowledge: selected interviews and other writings. The Harvester Press, Brighton

Foucault M (2010) The birth of biopolitics: lectures at the College de France, 1978–79. Palgrave Macmillan, Basingstoke

French S, Leyshon A (2010) "These F@#king Guys": the terrible waste of a good crisis. Environ Plan 42:2549–2559

Friend A. (2021) The financial conduct authority's innovation journey: moving forward in the face of uncertainty. Available at: https://regulationinnovation.org/wp-content/uploads/2021/03/The-FCAs-Innovation-Journey-Moving-Forward-in-the-Face-of-Uncertainty-AIR-Final-2.pdf. Accessed 21 Dec 2023

Goffman E (1961) Asylums: essays on the social situation of mental patients and other inmates. Anchor Books, Garden City

Greenwood R, Hanson SG, Stein JC et al (2017) Strengthening and streamlining bank capital regulation. Brook Pap Econ Act 2017:479–544

Hall S (2017) Global finance: places, spaces and people. Sage, London

Hansard (2000) Statement of compatability with the European Convention on Human Rights

Helleiner E (1994) States and the reemergence of global finance: from Bretton Woods to the 1990s. Cornell University Press, Ithaca

Helleiner E (2017) The evolution of the international monetary and financial system. In: Ravenhill J (ed) Global political economy, 5th edn. Oxford University Press, Oxford, pp 199–224

Inman P (2012) The financial crisis. Guardian Books, London

Jameson F (1991) Postmodernism, or, the cultural logic of late capitalism. Duke University Press, Durham

Joseph Rountary Foundation (2011) How people in poverty experienced recent global economic crises. Joseph Rountary Foundation, York

Kassim H, James S, Warren T, Hargreaves Heap S (2020) Preferences, preference formation and position taking in a eurozone out: lessons from the United Kingdom. Polit Stud Rev 18:525–541

Keynes JM (2008 [1936]) The general theory of employment, interest and money. Classic House Books, New York

Kindleberger CP (1996) Manias, panics and crashes: a history of financial crises. John Wiley, New York

Kynaston D (2002) The city of London volume IV: a club no more 1945–2000. Pimlico, London

Lanchester J (2015) How to speak money. Faber & Faber, London

Larner W (2000) Neo-liberalism: policy, ideology, governmentality. Stud Political Econ 63:5–25

Le TNL, Nasir MA, Huynh TLD (2023) Capital requirements and banks performance under Basel-III: a comparative analysis of Australian and British Banks. Q Rev Econ Finance 87:146–157

Mishkin FS (2011) Over the cliff: from the subprime to the global financial crisis. J Econ Perspect 25:49–70

National Archives (2007) FSA Fines Table 2007

National Archives (2011) FSA Fines Table 2011

National Archives (2012) FSA Fines Table 2012

National Audit Office (2011) The comptroller and auditor general's report on accounts to the house of commons. HM Treasury, London

Pauly L (2011) The political economy of the financial crisis. In: Ravenhill J (ed) Global political economy. Oxford University Press, Oxford, pp 215–272

Peck J (2010a) Constructions of neoliberal reason. Oxford University Press, Oxford

Peck J (2010b) Constructions of neoliberalism. Oxford University Press, Oxford
Polanyi K (2001 [1944]) The great transformation. Beacon Press, Boston
Porter T (2010) Risk models and transnational governance in the global financial crisis. In: Helleiner E, Pagliari S, Zimmermann H (eds) Global finance in crisis: the politics of international regulatory change. Routledge, London, pp 56–73
Ramlall I (2018) Challenges of financial stability: the road ahead. Tools Tech Financ Stab Anal 5: 115–117
Rethel L, Sinclair T (2012) The problem with banks. Zed Books, London
Revington N, August M (2020) Making a market for itself: the emergent financialization of student housing in Canada. Environ Plan A 52:856–877
Rötheli T (2010) Causes of the financial crisis: risk misperception, policy mistakes, and banks' bounded rationality. J Socio-Econ 39:119–126
Ruggie J (1982) International regimes, transactions and change: embedded liberalism in the postwar economic order. Int Org 36:379–413
Schmitz SW (2013) The impact of the liquidity coverage ratio (LCR) on the implementation of monetary policy. Econ Notes 42:135–170
Scott J, Quaglia L (2020) The UK and multi-level financial regulation: from post-crisis reform to Brexit. Oxford University Press, Oxford
Shaxson N (2018) The finance curse: how global finance is making us all poorer. The Bodley Head, London
Simpson A (2019) Establishing a disciplining financial disposition in the city of london: resilience, speed and intelligence. Sociology 53:1061–1076
Simpson A (2021) Harm production and the moral dislocation of finance in the city of London: an ethnography. Bingley, Emerald
Souleles D (2019) The distribution of ignorance on financial markets. Econ Soc 48:510–531
Stiglitz J (2010) Freefall: free markets and the sinking of the global economy. Penguin Books, London
Stiglitz J (2013) The price of inequality. Penguin Books, London
Strange S (1997) Casino capitalism. Manchester University Press, Manchester
Strange S (2000) A short history of neoliberalism: twenty years of elite economics and emerging opportunities for structural change. In: Beller W, Bullard N, Malhotra K (eds) Global finance: new thinking on regulating speculative capital markets. Zed Books, London, pp 27–35
The Turner Review (2009) A regulatory response to the global banking crisis. FSA, London
Tiner J (2006) Principles based regulation: the EU in context
Tombs S, Canning V (2021) From social harm to zemiology. Routledge, London
Tsingou E (2010) Regulatory reaction to the global credit crisis. In: Helleiner E, Pagliari S, Zimmermann H (eds) Global finance in crisis: the politics of international regulatory change. Routledge, London, pp 21–36
Whyte P (2012) Britain, Europe and the City of London: can the triangle be managed? Centre for European Reform, p 20

Alex Simpson Informed by the cultural theory of Bourdieu, Foucault and Derrida, Alex's research draws predominantly on ethnographic research methods to examine fundamental questions of *power* and *inequality*. This has led to a critical focus on the 'performative rituals' of elite social groups, the maintenance and development of financial landscapes and distinct masculinist identities that sustain neoliberal 'traits' of competition aggression and risk seeking. Alex undertook his PhD with the support of an ESRC studentship at the University of York, completing in 2015. Since, his work has been published in leading international journals, including *Sociology*, *Cities*, *Sociological Review*, *Gender, Work & Organization* and *Ethnography*. In 2021, his research monograph, titled *Harm Production and the Moral Dislocation of Finance,* was published by Emerald. Currently, he has an edited book in production (*Gendering Place and Affect*, Bristol University Press) and is undertaking research on erasure and incorporation of the Barangaroo financial district in Sydney.

Corina Sheerin is a lecturer in finance at the National College of Ireland (NCI), Dublin. Corina is a Chartered Financial Analyst (CFA) and lectures primarily in the areas of mathematics in finance and contemporary issues in finance. Her research agenda is underpinned by a feminist stance and is multidisciplinary in nature. Situated at the nexus of gender, work, and organisations, Corina has published widely in a range of ABS peer-reviewed journals, including Critical Perspectives in Accounting, Human Resource Development International, and Gender, Work, and Organization. Corina's work has been recognised internationally, having been awarded the Monica Lee Award for Outstanding Research in 2021 from the Academy of Human Resource Development, the Emerald Best Paper Award, and a Highly Commended Award in 2019 for both the Journal of European Training and Development and Gender in Management: An International Journal. Her current research is focused on issues of gender and space, gender performativity, and gendered organisations.

Vince Hurley is one of Australia leading policing and criminological academics specialising on the contemporary role of the police and policing. His PhD examined the impact of financialisation on policing practice in the UK, from 2010–2020. In doing so, he drew on the theoretical work of Foucault, O'Malley and Freud. Before joining the Department of Security Studies and Criminology at Macquarie University Vince spent 29 years as an operational police officer in the New South Wales Police Force achieving the rank of Detective Superintendent. As an experienced industry practitioner, he draws on the pragmatic role of the police and policing to academic theory.

Enhancing Integrity in the Implementation of FATF Recommendations: Robust Governance Frameworks to Combat Financial Crime in an Age of Intergovernmental Rulemaking

Doron Goldbarsht and Hannah Harris

Abstract In this chapter, we discuss the main governance challenges posed by the Financial Action Task Force (FATF) recommendations for addressing money laundering and terrorist financing. The key task for states is to find a balance between meeting international demands and upholding strong domestic laws. The chapter focuses on the potential role for an integrity branch of government in upholding robust processes and procedures, in light of the increasing power of intergovernmental organisations such as the FATF. The chapter engages with arguments in support of an integrity branch of government in Australia and expands these arguments on the basis that such a branch may enhance the integrity and legitimacy of laws that adopt and adapt the FATF recommendations. It is argued that the FATF example is illustrative of a broader trend towards intergovernmental rulemaking, which holds significant potential to streamline legal approaches to global challenges such as financial crime. However, this intergovernmental model and the focus on consistency and conformity across jurisdictions should not be allowed to erode domestic sovereignty and the legitimacy of domestic legal processes in the development and implementation of law and policy frameworks. As such, the chapter weighs the merits and limitations of establishing an integrity branch in response to increasing intergovernmental power. It draws on the FATF example to demonstrate how an integrity branch may have impacted the law-making process in Australia, in the context of implementing the FATF recommendations and legislating to combat financial crime. The chapter furnishes an initial framework for invigorating existing institutions to champion integrity, reinforce legitimacy, and preserve the foundational tenets of good governance.

D. Goldbarsht (✉) · H. Harris
Macquarie University, Macquarie Park, NSW, Australia
e-mail: doron.goldbarsht@mq.edu.au

D. Goldbarsht, L. de Koker (eds.), *Financial Crime, Law and Governance*, Ius Gentium: Comparative Perspectives on Law and Justice 116,
https://doi.org/10.1007/978-3-031-59547-9_7

1 Introduction

This chapter articulates the core governance challenges presented by the Financial Action Task Force (FATF) recommendations to combat money laundering and terrorist financing. Essentially, states must implement the recommendations in a way that balances responsiveness to international pressure with the maintenance of robust domestic legislative processes. This imperative exists in almost all areas of governance today, driven by increasing pressures to align domestic law and policy with global norms. However, the need is particularly acute in the context of financial crime, where the dominant intergovernmental rulemaking body (the FATF) has a unique and powerful influence over domestic law and policy.[1] Furthermore, a lack of transparency and legitimacy in domestic legislative processes can have dangerous implications for core rights and freedoms. Scholarship has shown that increases in executive power and legislative infringement on individual rights and freedoms are more likely in contexts where the protection of national security or market stability can be used to justify action.[2] Financial crime—in particular, money laundering and terrorist financing—is intimately connected with the stability of domestic markets and national security concerns, both of which amplify the necessity of strong domestic processes and controls to protect sovereignty and align legislative change with the realities of the domestic operating environment. Considering this challenging context, the chapter explores the potential role for an integrity branch of government in upholding robust processes and procedures to balance the increasing power of intergovernmental organisations such as the FATF.

The chapter introduces the challenges presented by intergovernmental rulemaking and the FATF in the context of the doctrine of separation of powers and the related risk of overreach by the executive branch of government. It then engages with arguments in support of an integrity branch of government in Australia and expands these arguments on the basis that such a branch may enhance the integrity and legitimacy of laws that respond to the FATF recommendations. It is argued that the FATF example is illustrative of a broader trend towards intergovernmental rulemaking, which holds significant potential to streamline domestic legal approaches to prevent and punish harmful conduct perpetrated across borders. Such conduct walks the gambit from money laundering, terrorist financing, and other forms of financial crime to disparate areas of transnational concern, including environmental protection, supply chain governance, and the enforcement of robust systems of taxation.

While the intergovernmental model, including the focus on consistency and conformity across jurisdictions, has practical and normative value,[3] it should not be allowed to erode domestic sovereignty and the legitimacy of domestic legal processes. As such, the chapter draws on the FATF example to demonstrate how a

[1] Goldbarsht and Harris (2022).

[2] See, for example, Cozzolino (2019); Draghici (2009).

[3] Esty (2006).

more robust integrity branch, aware of and responsive to the challenge of intergovernmental rulemaking, could have positively impacted the development of Australia's anti-money laundering (AML) and counter-terrorist financing (CTF) frameworks. It is suggested that an empowered integrity branch, alive to the influence of intergovernmental bodies such as the FATF, may have brought increased transparency and accountability to the implementation of the FATF recommendations. In particular, the integrity branch could have drawn attention to the overreach by the executive branch of government in agreeing to the FATF recommendations, thus protecting the core principle of separation of powers. In practice, absent the empowerment of the integrity branch, the actions of the executive in Australia (in joining the FATF and promoting domestic alignment with the FATF mandate) have empowered an intergovernmental body to exert pressure for domestic legislative change, despite disagreement within the legislature regarding the appropriateness of implementing such laws. Examples of this overstep have been provided in other scholarship and will be further elaborated below.

Given the potential of an integrity branch to support transparency, accountability, and robust legislative processes in a transnational world, the chapter concludes with actionable recommendations aimed at fortifying the Australian institutional landscape. The chapter does not claim to provide an exhaustive roadmap for establishing an integrity branch that is robust to the challenges of intergovernmental rulemaking. Rather, it aspires to contribute to the crucial ongoing discourse surrounding the establishment of an integrity branch, demonstrating its value in the context of intergovernmental rulemaking and international efforts to combat financial crime. Further, the chapter presents opportunities to invigorate existing institutions (the Ombudsman, the Auditor General, and the National Anti-Corruption Commission) to champion integrity, reinforce legitimacy, and preserve the foundational tenets of representative and responsive government within the Australian legislative context.

2 The Separation of Powers and the Challenge of Intergovernmental Rulemaking

Maintaining the separation of powers and securing integrity in government decision-making are essential components of good government. These imperatives are made even more vital in response to evolutions in the nature and scope of governmental decision-making in the modern age—including, but not limited to, the increasing rulemaking power of intergovernmental organisations and the transnationalisation of global issues.

Montesquieu, the French judge and political philosopher, emphasised the fundamental need for the separation of powers: 'There would be an end of every thing were the same man, or the same body, whether of the nobles or of the people to exercise those three powers that of enacting laws, that of executing the public resolutions, and that of judging the crimes or differences of individuals.'[4] The separation of powers doctrine has been the 'cornerstone on which the governance of the Western legal world is based in its constant dialectic of democracy and capitalism'.[5]

Theoretically, the separation of powers calls for a tripartite division of functions, where the parliament makes laws, the executive administers them, and the judiciary decides whether the laws have been correctly interpreted and applied.[6] Since power is not centralised in a single institution but distributed across the three branches of government, each branch can check the functioning of the other two branches.[7] However, this division overlooks the unjustified concentration of power in any one branch of government, which can hinder the ability of another branch to act as a counterbalance, as well as undermine the ability of an independent judiciary to conclusively resolve legal disputes about government power.[8]

In Australia, the concerning concentration of power occurs with the executive branch. Although the constitutional basis for judicial independence and review of legislative actions is well accepted, the basis for judicial review of executive actions is disputed, leaving ultimate decision-making power with the executive.[9] An unclear theoretical basis for the particular institutional form of the separation of powers in Australia,[10] together with an ambiguous manifestation and application of the doctrine, creates tensions.[11] This has resulted in a situation in which the executive branch is often empowered beyond the constraints of parliament or the judiciary.[12] This creates opportunities for transnational rulemaking to penetrate domestic law and policy to an unprecedented degree, as demonstrated by the FATF example.

Existing scholarship by Goldbarsht and Harris has demonstrated the influence of the FATF on Australian law and policy, facilitated through the executive branch. They use the example of the FATF review process, facilitated through Mutual Evaluation Reports (MERs), to show that the FATF was able to shape not only legislative drafting in Australia, but also enforcement practices—despite domestic criticism of, and resistance to, FATF recommendations by the legislative branch.[13] This example demonstrates the influence of the executive branch in securing compliance with international norms. In fact, the article asserts that:

[4]Montesquieu (1777), vol 1, pp. 221–237.

[5]Lordi (2009), p. 939.

[6]Lordi (2009), p. 939.

[7]Goldbarsht and Harris (2022).

[8]McMillan (2010), p. 423.

[9]McMillan (2010), p. 423. Kerr and Williams argue that the importance of *Plaintiff S157/2002 v Commonwealth* (2003) 211 CLR 476 is that it expresses the constitutional basis for judicial review of executive action: Kerr and Williams (2003). See also *Ruddock v Vadarlis* (2001) 110 FCR 491.

[10]Kerr and Williams (2003), p. 225.

[11]Gelber (2006), p. 439.

[12]Goldbarsht and Harris (2022), p. 536.

[13]Goldbarsht and De Koker (2024); Goldbarsht and Harris (2022), p. 547.

> the approach taken by the FATF means that domestic legislative initiatives to address money laundering and terrorist financing are shaped by the executive branch, with the legislature playing a subsidiary role at best. Indeed, this process of norm development reduces domestic parliaments to rubber-stamping pre-ordained laws that mimic the standards set by the FATF.[14]

Furthermore, several scholars have raised concerns about the transparency and accountability of the FATF rulemaking process, recommending revisions to the current approach at the intergovernmental level.[15] Such concerns further emphasise the need to preserve domestic legislative autonomy in the context of potentially illegitimate and arbitrary intergovernmental rulemaking.

Certainly, the risk of transnational actors overstepping into the domestic sphere through an unchecked executive branch, thus undermining democratic processes and legitimacy, is not limited to the FATF. With over 300 intergovernmental organisations in existence today,[16] and a legitimate need for transnational collaboration on global issues,[17] the protection of domestic processes, the rule of law, and the separation of powers is crucial for States to survive and thrive in a globalised world. This reality provides impetus to engage further with the proposal of establishing an integrity branch to 'strengthen the doctrine of separation of powers and bolster Australia's engagement with transnational governance'.[18] In their article on the subject, Goldbarsht and Harris acknowledge that 'this proposal is novel and requires further research to ensure its effective implementation'.[19] The present chapter responds to that call for further research.

[14] Goldbarsht and Harris (2022), p. 552.

[15] de Koker (2022): this commentary suggests that the FATF should consider the adoption of a Regulatory Impact Assessment approach to increase transparency and legitimacy in FATF rulemaking. See also Goldbarsht (2017), p. 136; Goldbarsht (2020), p. 213; Ghoshray (2015), p. 533.

[16] National Geographic Education Resource Library (n.d.).

[17] See generally Slaughter (2005). It is generally well established that issues such as human rights, environmental protection, and supply chain governance all require transnational collaboration between governments and other stakeholders. Slaughter highlights the valuable contributions to this collaborative effort made by intergovernmental organisations and the cooperation between bureaucrats from diverse jurisdictions. However, her book does not detail the risks and challenges that this form of cooperation can create for government legitimacy or protecting the rule of law and the democratic process.

[18] Goldbarsht and Harris (2022), p. 529.

[19] Goldbarsht and Harris (2022), p. 529.

3 Securing 'Integrity' in the Era of Global Administrative Law

The separation of powers doctrine and the three branches of government were conceptualised and developed in a world very different from the one in which we now live. In the past, closed nation-states focused on governing people within their own territory. This model was successful because governance issues and the demands of citizens could be directly resolved by one of the three branches.[20]

The current legal-economic landscape presents new challenges for these nation-states and their three branches.[21] Recently, major changes in the legal and economic arenas compel us to consider how these changes may have influenced the doctrine of separation of powers. The changes include globalisation, the development of new technologies that increase accessibility for consumers, financial deregulation, the emergence of law without a state, and the decentralisation or dispersion of state activities.[22] Among them, the most relevant for the purposes of this discussion is the emergence of law without a state, either in private law (*lex mercatoria*) or in public law (global administrative law).[23]

Global administrative law has emanated either from the regulation of functions that escape state control or from solving issues that necessitate global coordination—for example, environmental protection and refugee protection are increasingly regulated through a network of international treaties and global norms. This has led to the establishment of global regulatory bodies, known also as global decision-making bodies.[24] These bodies are responsible for standard-setting and decision-making in their respective fields.[25] They often take the form of intergovernmental organisations, 'defined as organizations with at least three state parties, a permanent headquarters or secretariat, as well as regular meetings and budgets'.[26] Unlike their domestic counterparts, which presuppose a shared sense of natural justice or procedural fairness in administrative decision-making,[27] these bodies make decisions in a dynamic and flexible manner.[28] Their decisions impact the rights of individuals, states and other actors and organisational groups, without the traditional accountability measures that are inherent in domestic decision-making.[29]

---

[20] Lordi (2009), p. 940.

[21] Lordi (2009), p. 940.

[22] Lordi (2009), p. 943.

[23] Lordi (2009), p. 943.

[24] Kingsbury et al. (2005), p. 16. See also Tripathi (2011), p. 356.

[25] Mitchell and Farnik (2009), p. 238.

[26] Eilstrup-Sangiovanni (2020), p. 342.

[27] See, for example, *Haoucher v Minister for Immigration and Ethnic Affairs* (1990) 169 CLR 648, 653 (Deane J).

[28] Kingsbury et al. (2005), pp. 15–17.

[29] Kinchin (2014), p. 1.

We have already introduced the FATF, the global money-laundering and terrorist-financing watchdog that serves as an example of a powerful intergovernmental rule maker. In the Australian context, when the executive is engaging with the FATF, its actions can proceed largely unchecked and may, in certain circumstances, encroach into the territory of the legislature—particularly when seeking to gain compliance with the FATF's recommendations.[30] Other intergovernmental bodies of relevance here include the World Trade Organization, which has been subject to substantial criticism for infringing on state sovereignty in the context of global trade,[31] and the International Monetary Fund, which has a fraught history of interference with government economic policy in the developing world.[32] Other international groupings, such as the International Organization of Securities Commissions and the Egmont Group of Financial Intelligence Units, have less scope for direct impact on domestic law and policy because of their limited coercive power, but they do have the potential to shape the normative persuasions of their domestic representatives, who in turn have authority to shape policy and enforcement strategy in their given areas of bureaucratic influence.

Thus, ensuring the integrity of domestic government processes and decision-making in a globalised age is perhaps one of the most pressing legal challenges of the twenty-first century. Taking the establishment of an integrity branch as the starting point for securing the separation of powers and maintaining democratic processes in the development of domestic law and policy, this chapter presents two possibilities: first, the establishment of a new constitutionally enshrined integrity branch within Australia's governmental structure; and, second, the strengthening of the existing tripartite integrity institutions (the Ombudsman, the Auditor-General and the National Anti-Corruption Commission) through legislative drafting and amendments that protect and extend the autonomy and efficacy of these institutions in light of the governance challenges of the twenty-first century.

4 Integrity as a Concept

Before introducing the two possible avenues for establishing an integrity branch, it is valuable to briefly expand on the concept of integrity and its value as a check on undue influence and the erosion of the separation of powers in modern government. In any stable state, there is a generally accepted view on how governance should operate in practice. Integrity is central to effective and equitable governance.[33] Therefore, the role of the integrity branch should be to ensure that this concept is realised, so that the 'performance of governmental functions is uncorrupted, not

[30] Kinchin (2014), p. 1.

[31] Gonzalez Arreaza (2017), p. 266; Capeloto (2017).

[32] Lee (2003); Lowenfeld (2002); Delonis (2004).

[33] Huberts (2018); Menzel (2005).

merely in a narrow sense that government officials do not take bribes, but in a broad sense, of observing proper practice'.[34]

The integrity branch—or the integrity agencies (the terms are used interchangeably in this chapter)—is concerned with ensuring that each institution of the government exercises the powers conferred on it in the expected manner, and solely for the purpose for which those powers were conferred. This concept of integrity connotes an 'unimpaired or uncorrupted state of affairs',[35] focused on institutional integrity rather than personal integrity—notwithstanding that ensuring the personal integrity of public officials will undoubtedly support institutional integrity. In fact, if the integrity branch functions correctly, it should support personal integrity by establishing structures and processes that also incentivise and reward integrity on an individual level. This could be understood as the integrity branch creating a culture of integrity in government.

In this sense, institutional integrity goes beyond matters of legality. However, it is not broad enough to encompass any misuse of power. Beyond issues of legality, the integrity of a governmental institution is determined by two additional considerations: first, the maintenance of fidelity to the public purposes for which the institution was created; and, second, the application of the public values, including procedural values such as accountability and transparency, to which the institution is expected to adhere.[36]

5 Options for Integrity

One of the key issues for the effective operation of integrity agencies is understanding where they 'fit' within the broader structures of government. The placement of the integrity branch relative to other branches of government is fundamental to ensuring that it is adequately empowered and possesses the necessary independence to do its job and uphold public trust, as well as ensuring adequate accountability.[37] This gives rise to another logical question: Should the integrity branch be a separate branch of the government, or should integrity functions be performed by an existing statutory body? This section deliberates on where integrity institutions best fit in the existing framework of government in Australia. It summarises the existing literature and argues for independence of the integrity branch from the executive, to ensure that relevant integrity agencies can effectively check the misuse of power and processes that may occur through interaction between the executive branch and intergovernmental bodies such as the FATF.

[34] Spigelman (2004), p. 725.

[35] Spigelman (2004), p. 725.

[36] Spigelman (2004), p. 726.

[37] Brown (2018), pp. 17–18; Solomon (2012), p. 32.

Australian supporters of the integrity branch hold varying and sometimes unclear views on where integrity agencies should be situated and to whom they should be accountable. Spigelman describes the main institutions as 'the three recognised branches of government, including the parliament, the head of state, various executive agencies and the superior courts', through which the fourth branch does its work.[38] Equally vaguely, Solomon describes integrity agencies as 'not a separate, distinct branch', but incorporated within the existing three conventional branches, which 'collectively constitute the integrity branch of government'. Thus, 'there would be no advantage in trying to remove those functions and send them off to a fourth'.[39]

Opponents of this conception of the fourth branch understandably seek more clarity, albeit in divergent directions. Gummow rejects Spigelman's proposition that the fourth branch idea might provide 'broader context' to inform administrative and constitutional law. Rather, he finds that it offers 'little utility and some occasion for confusion'.[40] For Gummow, an integrity branch requires no separate recognition because this function is meant to be fulfilled by the existing third branch, the judiciary. In his view, potential functions of the integrity branch already fall within the authority of the existing branches. The executive branch administers administrative law, which stipulates the administrative remedies for failures and breaches of governmental bodies, while the High Court is the peak arbiter of questions of public integrity and decides whether government officials are acting within the scope of their power.[41] Underpinning this suggestion that the judiciary is the supreme custodian of integrity is the assertion of constitutional hierarchy and concern about the idea that agencies within the integrity system can be politically or constitutionally comparable to the judiciary—particularly in a manner in which they could intrude on judicial power or, worse, be immune from the judiciary's supervision.[42]

Other scholars argue that integrity agencies cannot have any formal determinative role in administrative law, or in any other area of law. So, while these agencies may be subject to judicial oversight, they cannot exercise judicial power or function simply as a junior limb of the judicial branch. They do not exercise legislative power, nor is it intended that they do so. Hence, a different answer is provided by Callinan and Aroney, who regard the absence of any 'constitutionally established fourth arm of government, distinct from the legislature, the Executive and the Judiciary' as implying that, by its very nature, an integrity agency is intended to be 'part of the Executive'.[43] Other academics have described as simply 'unrealistic' the idea that an integrity or accountability branch not be subordinate to executive government.[44]

[38] Spigelman (2004), p. 75.

[39] Spigelman (2004), p. 75.

[40] Gummow (2012), p. 19.

[41] Gummow (2012), p. 19.

[42] Brown (2018), p. 18; Martin (2014).

[43] Callinan and Aroney (2013), p. 25.

[44] Prasser (2012), p. 31.

There are two problems with this suggestion of a subordinated integrity branch. First, the courts themselves cannot be regarded as the backbone of the modern public integrity system directing these agencies. Unlike other bodies charged with policing integrity among executive officials, the judiciary is reactive, not proactive, with minimal 'own motion' jurisdiction to initiate the review of misuses of power, thereby lacking any central feature of proper accountability.[45] Second, the raison d'être of integrity agencies is to act independently of the executive to ensure its integrity at all levels. This rationale has in fact informed the entire justification for our analysis of the integrity branch as a mechanism through which to secure accountability not only in domestic governmental processes, but also in the interaction between domestic representatives of state and intergovernmental organisations such as the FATF. To describe integrity agencies as simply constituent agencies of the executive cannot be correct, as this would prohibit them from achieving their primary function. Callinan and Aroney recognise this and assert that integrity agencies are different from their executive counterparts. As 'auxiliary precautions' to the constitutional system supporting the government maintaining control over itself, they go beyond the 'distinct roles played by the fundamental institutions of Parliament, the Executive and the Courts'.[46] In reality, most are 'creatures of statute, enacted by the Parliament and responsible to the Parliament or to one of its committees', rather than to the executive government.[47] From this perspective, the practical position of the integrity branch within the Australian government is established through the legislature, subordinate to the executive, and largely ungoverned by the judiciary.

The above debate provides some helpful guidance on the positioning of the integrity branch relative to other branches of government. However, another question then arises as to whether integrity agencies can be seen to exercise a form of governmental power, recognisably different from that exercised by the existing three branches. A negative answer might not prevent justification for an additional branch, but a positive answer would seem to end the argument as to whether a fourth branch is needed. Ultimately, this helps determine whether integrity agencies should remain part of the executive—not simply because their independence is more flexible, but because they do not exercise any unique kind of power.[48]

For the purposes of this discussion, the definition of 'power' can be understood as 'the capacity or ability to direct or influence the behaviour of others or the course of events'.[49] In the realm of political science and constitutional law, the nature of the power being exercised by a public official or body is determined by four factors: (1) the body exercising the power; (2) the laws or conventions authorising or describing what they purport to do; (3) the purposes and functions actually or

[45] Callinan and Aroney (2013), pp. 23–24.

[46] Callinan and Aroney (2013), p. 23.

[47] Callinan and Aroney (2013), pp. 23–24.

[48] Brown (2018), p. 25.

[49] Oxford dictionary of English (2010), 'power' (def 2).

purportedly served by the body; and (4) the actual or intended effects of these functions. In ascertaining what is the nature of the power of integrity agencies, it cannot be said to be legislative or judicial. Integrity agencies exercise a considerable amount of executive power, akin to other policy agencies and investigative bodies.[50]

While it makes sense to view integrity power as being partly diffused and exercised by the three branches, the existence, position and needs of core integrity agencies confirm that their powers also have their own unique institutional sources. The reality is that integrity agencies do not and cannot subsist as part of the executive if they are to do their job independently and without any influence, even though the bulk of their power is executive by nature. Nor do they sit as part of the judiciary, despite their comparability and close relationships. While an integrity agency might exist as an offshoot of parliament, and is certainly subject to parliamentary as well as judicial oversight, it does not exercise legislative power or carry out administrative tasks relating directly to the making or the quality of legislation (or of public policy). Hence, functional and operational independence from the day-to-day politics of the parliament is a prerequisite. By analysing power this way, the purpose and the justification for recognising the integrity branch become clear.

Consequently, the pertinent question becomes not what is possible, but rather what steps must be taken 'to better define, enable, interpret and regulate' the power of this branch.[51]

Against such ambiguity, two proposals emerge for achieving integrity, based on where integrity agencies best fit and their intended functions. The *first option* is amending the Australian Constitution to establish a fourth branch of government, known as the integrity branch. The *second option* is to empower existing integrity bodies, including the Ombudsman (a statutory body, which sits within the executive), to safeguard integrity and fortify their position as custodians and protectors of the rule of law. While the possibility of constitutional change should be acknowledged, it is the position of the authors that this course of action is likely unfeasible, and certainly will not address the challenge of intergovernmental encroachment on domestic legislative processes in the timely manner necessary to secure the continued legitimacy of domestic law and policy in a globalised world. Therefore, this option will only be addressed in passing, before focusing on the potential for existing integrity bodies to be empowered to safeguard the rule of law from both national and international threats.

5.1 Constitutional Change

According to Ackerman, the credible construction of a separate integrity branch should be a top priority for drafters of modern constitutions, suggesting that there is a

---

[50] Brown (2018), p. 32.

[51] Brown (2018), p. 33.

need for a constitutionally empowered fourth branch of government.[52] Further, he suggests that the new branch should be armed with powers and incentives to engage in ongoing oversight. Members of the integrity branch should be guaranteed very high salaries that are protected against legislative reduction. They should be guaranteed career paths that permit them to avoid serving later under officials whose probity they are charged with investigating. The Constitution should also guarantee the branch a minimum budget of a certain percentage of total government revenues, as politicians may otherwise respond to the threat of exposure by reducing the agency to a token number of highly paid employees.[53] Clearly, Ackerman's focus was for the integrity branch to be a constitutionally empowered fourth branch of government. While this may be a viable option for relatively new and emerging constitutional democracies, it is less feasible in the well-established Australian constitutional context.

As Williams, Brennan and Lynch assert, the mechanism for altering the text of the Constitution in Australia reflects its federal and democratic characteristics.[54] In Part VIII of the Constitution, section 128 stipulates the requirements for constitutional reform. In addition to passage by an absolute majority of both houses of the federal parliament, or passage by one house twice, the reform must be submitted to each state and territory elector qualified to vote. This component of constitutional reform is facilitated through referendum, as set out in the Referendum (Machinery Provisions) Act 1984 (Cth).[55] Including the most recent referendum in 1999, 44 proposals for constitutional change have been put to Australian electors, but only eight have been successful.[56] The last successful referendum was held in 1977, when the Constitution was amended in a number of ways—including through the imposition of a mandatory retirement age of 70 years for judges of the High Court and other federal courts.[57] Otherwise, the text of the Constitution has remained almost the same as it was in 1901.[58]

Various theories have been presented to explain this low success rate, although the exact reasons remain unclear. Perhaps the most compelling arguments include the nature of the proposals put to the people, and the complexity of securing popular opinion in support of change when the details of the reform are often complex or difficult to convey to the public at large—especially given that Australians have a relatively low level of constitutional literacy. To the first point, given that referendums can only be initiated by the federal parliament, most proposals (24 of 44) have sought to grant the Commonwealth additional power. Such proposals have almost

[52] Ackerman (2000), p. 694.

[53] Ackerman (2000), p. 694.

[54] Williams et al. (2018), p. 1408.

[55] Referendum (Machinery Provisions) Act 1984 (Cth), s 45.

[56] Australian Electoral Commission (2011).

[57] Williams et al. (2018), p. 1409.

[58] Williams et al. (2018), p. 1409; see also Kildea and Williams (2010).

always been rejected, with only three succeeding.[59] To the second point, surveys of the Australian public show a worrying lack of knowledge about the Constitution and government. The 1994 report on citizenship by the Civics Expert Group found that only one in five people had some understanding of what the Constitution contained.[60] Educational problems are exacerbated during referendum campaigns. A lack of knowledge, or the existence of false knowledge, on the part of the voter can translate into a misunderstanding of the proposals or an unwillingness to consider change. This can be leveraged by those opposed to constitutional change. For example, in the 1999 referendum, the 'No' campaign relied on the simple argument 'Don't know?—Vote "NO"'.[61]

Finally, there is the high public cost of referendum campaigns. This is difficult to justify except in the most exceptional circumstances, considering the low success rate of referendums in securing constitutional change. In 1999, the proposal for a republic model put to vote was supported by a $24.5 million government-funded advertising campaign and a 71-page pamphlet that was sent to every voter, accompanied by widespread media coverage. Yet most Australians had little understanding of what a republic would mean, or how the proposed model would have worked.[62]

For all the reasons discussed above, constitutional change is not easily achieved. Integrity is an inherently complex concept that is heavily debated—and often misunderstood—by academics. A referendum to amend the Constitution and create an integrity branch of government is unlikely to be met with large-scale support. Consequently, this chapter will focus on the more feasible potential of empowering existing integrity institutions to achieve enhanced governmental integrity in the age of intergovernmental rulemaking.

The discussion to come will focus on empowering the Commonwealth Ombudsman, noting that the Auditor-General and the National Anti-Corruption Commission are also likely to play vital roles in the construction of an integrity branch in Australia. The focus on the Ombudsman is due to its well-established history as a bastion of integrity—being one of the oldest integrity mechanisms in Australia's governmental framework—and its broad mandate, which extends beyond the use of public funds (Auditor-General) or allegations of corrupt conduct (Anti-Corruption Commission). The National Anti-Corruption Commission is also a recent creation; time is needed to assess its capacity and effectiveness.

It is envisioned that the following analysis of the Ombudsman as a core integrity agency, and the recommendations made to enhance its capacity in light of the governance challenges presented by intergovernmental rulemaking, will have some translatable value in the context of enhancing the roles of the Auditor-General and the Anti-Corruption Commission. These agencies will certainly need to be leveraged to achieve the appropriate balance between international responsiveness

[59] Williams et al. (2018), p. 1409.

[60] Williams et al. (2018), p. 1411.

[61] Williams et al. (2018), pp. 1411–1412; Australian Electoral Commission (1999).

[62] Williams et al. (2018), pp. 1411–1412.

and the integrity of domestic legal processes. As already highlighted, the imperative to combat financial crime in a coordinated manner across jurisdictions—combined with the nexus between money laundering, terrorist financing, and national security—amplifies the need for robust protections for domestic processes. Thus, we encourage further research on how other integrity agencies (including the Auditor-General and the National Anti-Corruption Commission) can be strengthened and adapted to respond to this emergent challenge.

5.2 *Leveraging Existing Agencies: Empowering the Commonwealth Ombudsman*

The ombudsman has its origins in Sweden, where it was first established in 1809, and has since spread around the globe.[63] An Ombudsman is:

> an office provided for by the constitution or by action of the legislature or parliament and headed by an independent high level public official who is responsible to the legislature or parliament, who receives complaints from aggrieved persons against Government agencies, officials, and employees, or who acts on his own motion, and who has the power to investigate, recommend corrective action, and issue reports.[64]

As this definition demonstrates, the scope of the Ombudsman role is broad and far-reaching. According to the International Ombudsman Institute, the role of ombudsman institutions is:

> to protect the people against violation of rights, abuse of powers, unfair decisions and maladministration. They play an increasingly important role in improving public administration while making the government's actions more open and its administration more accountable to the public.[65]

Based on this explanation alone, the Ombudsman seems to have significant potential for enhancing the transparency and legitimacy of government decision-making, particularly in the context of executive overreach and the incursion of intergovernmental rulemaking into domestic legislative processes. This potential seems all the more significant considering the global scope of the ombudsman role. 'Today, ombudsman institutions are present in more than 140 countries in various forms and models.'[66] Therefore, if this agency could be leveraged to assist with the challenges identified so far in this chapter, the impact could extend beyond Australia to more than 140 jurisdictions around the globe, many of which are likely also struggling to adapt to the new global order.

---

[63] Field (2018).

[64] Resolution of the International Bar Association (1974), quoted in Senate Standing Committee on Finance and Public Administration (1991).

[65] International Ombudsman Institute (n.d.).

[66] Glušac (2021).

The first Australian ombudsman office was established by statute in Western Australia in 1971. Other jurisdictions soon followed: South Australia in 1972, Victoria in 1973, Queensland in 1974, New South Wales in 1975, the Commonwealth in 1976, the Northern Territory in 1977, Tasmania in 1978, and, finally, the Australian Capital Territory in 1983. Today, there is legislation establishing ombudsman offices at the federal level and in every state and territory.[67]

The statutory models of the ombudsman offices are largely the same in each Australian jurisdiction. The Office of the Commonwealth Ombudsman is created by the Ombudsman Act 1976 (Cth). The Ombudsman is appointed by the Governor-General for a term of up to 7 years and can be removed by a resolution of both houses of parliament.[68]

The core functions of the Commonwealth Ombudsman comprise investigating, either on the receipt of a complaint or on its own motion, action that relates to a matter of administration by a department or a prescribed authority.[69] The concept of administrative action is defined broadly to include a decision, act, recommendation, proposal to act, or refusal or failure to act.[70] Simply put, the Ombudsman can investigate complaints about actions and decisions of Australian government agencies to determine whether they are wrong, unjust, unlawful, discriminatory or just plain unfair. The Ombudsman also seeks remedies for those affected by administrative deficiency and acts to improve public administration generally.[71]

In the public sector, the jurisdiction of the Ombudsman extends to the Australian Public Service, the Australian Federal Police, and most executive and statutory authorities that have been constituted for a public purpose.[72] The jurisdiction of each state ombudsman extends to central government agencies and local authorities. Allegations of police misconduct are handled in each state by other bodies—for example, in New South Wales, the Law Enforcement Conduct Commission handles police complaints.[73] There is also a specific provision in each state statute excluding the ombudsman's jurisdiction in relation to action taken by a person acting as a legal adviser.

With a few exceptions, the Commonwealth Ombudsman is unable to investigate actions taken by a minister, court or tribunal, as well as actions related to the employment of individuals within the Australian Public Service.[74] Further, the Commonwealth Ombudsman can decline to investigate a complaint if the

[67] Ombudsman Act 1976 (Cth); Ombudsman Act 1989 (ACT); Ombudsman Act 1974 (NSW); Ombudsman Act (NT); Ombudsman Act 2001 (Qld); Ombudsman Act 1972 (SA); Ombudsman Act 1978 (Tas); Parliamentary Commissioner Act 1971 (WA).

[68] Ombudsman Act 1976 (Cth), ss 21, 28.

[69] Ombudsman Act 1976 (Cth), s 5. See Commonwealth Ombudsman (n.d.-a).

[70] McMillan (2005).

[71] Commonwealth Ombudsman (n.d.-b).

[72] Ombudsman Act 1976 (Cth), s 5.

[73] Creyke et al. (2019), p. 234.

[74] Ombudsman Act 1976 (Cth), s 5.

complainant does not have sufficient interest in the matter,[75] if there is an alternative method for administrative or judicial review of the complaint, if the complaint was not first raised with the agency to which it relates, or if investigation is unnecessary or unjustified having regard to all the circumstances.[76]

In addition to the Commonwealth and state ombudsman offices, there are also ombudsman offices for particular industries, including the Telecommunications Industry Ombudsman, the Australian Financial Complaints Authority, and the Energy & Water Ombudsman NSW. Industry ombudsmen are created and regulated in different ways,[77] reflecting the evolution of the ombudsman role in response to a neo-liberal trend in government since the 1990s and the increasing overlap between the public and private spheres.[78] For the purposes of our analysis—assessing the potential for the Commonwealth Ombudsman to act as a core agency of an integrity branch and enhance transparency in cases of executive overreach resulting from efforts to implement intergovernmental rulemaking—it is valuable to note also the existence of other sector-specific ombudsmen that operate in a variety of jurisdictions around the globe. For example, Reif explores the impactful role of human rights ombudsmen, 'found throughout Central and Eastern Europe and Latin America, in much of Western Europe and in some countries in Africa and Asia'.[79] She notes that these ombudsmen act as powerful intermediaries between international legal norms and the domestic legislative frameworks that implement them.[80] Furthermore, Pacific ombudsman have a robust track record for promoting legislative and administrative decision-making in line with human rights obligations and global norms.[81] Both of these examples illustrate that the expansion of the Commonwealth Ombudsman mandate in Australia, to account for international norms and the unique challenges of intergovernmental rulemaking, is not beyond the scope of existing Ombudsman institutions viewed from a global perspective. The success of the ombudsman agency in diverse jurisdictional contexts presents positive potential for this body to play a central role in enhancing Australia's integrity branch.

5.2.1 Shortcomings of the Commonwealth Ombudsman: A Toothless Tiger

Over the past decades, the ombudsman model has firmly taken root in Australia, handling complaints against every tier of government—national, state and territory,

[75] Note that the website of the Commonwealth Ombudsman states that '[a]nyone can make a complaint to the Ombudsman': Commonwealth Ombudsman (n.d.-b).

[76] Ombudsman Act 1976 (Cth), ss 6, 6A.

[77] Ombudsman Act 1976 (Cth), ss 6, 6A.

[78] Stuhmcke (2016).

[79] Reif (2017), p. 605.

[80] Reif (2017), p. 615.

[81] Taumoepeau (2019).

and local.[82] A key mark of stability of the ombudsman offices is that all were established in the 1970s or early 1980s and still exist in the same form with the same core roles, although more functions have been added. Stuhmcke notes that these non-traditional functions are a product of the changing political context in which ombudsmen operate, flagging a need to be cautious about such expansion to protect the subtle balance of independence and integrity on which these offices rely.[83] For instance, besides safeguarding the community in its dealings with the Australian government, the Commonwealth Ombudsman discharges the separately titled roles of Postal Industry Ombudsman, Overseas Students Ombudsman, and Private Health Insurance Ombudsman, as well as handling complaints relating to Defence and to providers of loans to vocational education and training students.[84] Additionally, the Commonwealth Ombudsman supervises the work of the Fair Work Building Industry Inspectorate and receives whistleblower complaints under the Public Interest Disclosure Act 2013 (Cth). The state and territory ombudsmen also exercise multiple functions. For example, the Western Australian Ombudsman is also the Energy and Water Ombudsman and reviews family and domestic violence fatalities.[85] While the expansion of the ombudsman role demonstrates its continued position of authority in Australian governance, the office is not without limitations. The following paragraphs will discuss these shortcomings, using the Commonwealth Ombudsman as an example.

First, as noted above, the Commonwealth Ombudsman considers that complaints are often best handled by the agencies concerned.[86] This is partly because the complaints are more often about procedural justice than about the substantive correctness of decisions.[87] The prevalent issues raised include delay, unexplained reasons, misleading advice, lost paperwork, and discourtesy. Seldom will the remedy for such a grievance be the reversal of a decision by a determinative decree or a declaratory, mandatory or injunctive order of the kind granted in judicial review. The more appropriate remedy is often simply an explanation or an apology. Such remedies do not find a place in rule of law theory or the doctrine of separation of powers; nevertheless, their importance should not be overlooked in evaluating how to civilise a system of government and standardise its accountability and responsibility to the public.[88]

Second, the Commonwealth Ombudsman relies on recommendation, persuasion and publicity to effect change.[89] It cannot injunct an agency, command action, or award compensation for defective administration. The Ombudsman does not make

[82] del Villar (2003).

[83] Stuhmcke (2016).

[84] Commonwealth Ombudsman (n.d.-b).

[85] Creyke et al. (2019), p. 229.

[86] Commonwealth Ombudsman (n.d.-b).

[87] Howieson (2002).

[88] McMillan (2005).

[89] Ombudsman Act 1976 (Cth), ss 12(3), 15, 16.

fresh administrative decisions; rather, it considers the way a decision has been made by the agency concerned and makes recommendations on how the decision or process can be enhanced.[90] Because it does not have determinative powers to alter a decision, the Ombudsman can conclude an investigation only by reporting to the agency and recommending that further action of some kind be taken.[91] If the Ombudsman is of the opinion that the agency has not taken appropriate action with respect to a report or recommendation, it can then report to the prime minister and to parliament.[92] Because of this, some scholars have argued that the Commonwealth Ombudsman cannot be truly effective in safeguarding integrity, since it lacks determinative powers to set aside or vary an administrative decision or to award compensation. This has led to it being labelled a 'toothless tiger'.[93] Absent determinative powers, the Ombudsman's influence rests on two capacities: to make recommendations and to publish reports.[94] The reality is that the Ombudsman 'must use a combination of techniques—from adverse publicity to cajoling and persuasion—to convince government departments of the correctness of its advised course of action'.[95]

There is no denying that the absence of determinative powers inhibits the ability of the Commonwealth Ombudsman to provide relief as easily or assuredly as can a court or tribunal. Recognising this, the Ombudsman will often suggest to a complainant that an issue in dispute can be addressed more appropriately in a judicial or tribunal review. Often, it will decline to investigate on that basis.[96] However, this limitation of authority is not necessarily a weakness. As noted by Stuhmcke and Tran, the lack of enforceability of ombudsman recommendations has not prevented targeted agencies from accepting recommendations for systemic administrative improvements: 'Indeed, the majority of the recommendations made by the Ombudsman are accepted by agencies.'[97] The authors argue that '[d]eterminative, as opposed to recommendatory, powers could in fact diminish the co-operative relationship which exists between government agencies and the ombudsman and which is an important feature in effectiveness of the office'.[98]

The third limitation is jurisdictional and concerns the significant restrictions on what the Commonwealth Ombudsman can investigate. Notable exclusions include ministerial actions and decisions, the conduct of security intelligence bodies such as the Australian Security Intelligence Organisation, and employment action in the

[90] McMillan (2005).

[91] Ombudsman Act 1976 (Cth), ss 12, 15.

[92] Ombudsman Act 1976 (Cth), ss 16, 17.

[93] Creyke et al. (2019), p. 244.

[94] Pearce (1998).

[95] Stuhmcke and Tran (2007).

[96] Ombudsman Act 1976 (Cth), s 6(3).

[97] Stuhmcke and Tran (2007).

[98] Stuhmcke and Tran (2007).

Australian Public Service.[99] Further, the Ombudsman states that it will not normally investigate a complaint unless it raises a serious matter and contains sufficient information.[100]

Finally, the fourth limitation is practical and common across any government institution: whether sufficient resources and capacity are available for the Ombudsman to conduct its mandate effectively and, relatedly, whether the structure of the office is appropriate to ensure a balance of efficiency, effectiveness, and much-needed independence. This limitation can be categorised as falling under attempts to conform with the six categories established by the Venice Principles on the Protection and Promotion of the Ombudsman[101] and discussed by Glušac.[102] These categories comprise (1) establishment, status and institutional model; (2) appointment and terms of office; (3) immunity and security of tenure; (4) mandate and powers; (5) independence; and (6) reporting. Of particular importance are the recommendations to ensure that remuneration demonstrates the high institutional standing of the office, that the term of the office is longer than the mandate of the appointing body, and that adequate and independent budgetary resources are secured to the office, along with sufficient staff members and legal immunity for them. Each of these components of budget, remuneration, tenure and immunity must be secured and enshrined to ensure the independent functioning of the Ombudsman and to protect it from perceptions and risks of co-optation. While the Commonwealth Ombudsman has addressed most of these issues, budgeting and remuneration are ongoing considerations to be reviewed in light of its expanding mandate and workload.

Given these limitations, it is clear that the Commonwealth Ombudsman can only ever supplement, and not displace, the function of the judiciary in reviewing executive action or administrative decision-making.[103] Yet, as scholars argue, the effectiveness of such judicial review ‘rests partly on a blend of faith and assumption’.[104] This is because we have scant empirical data or scientific understanding as to what happens after a court reaches a finding that an executive action or government decision is invalid. There is no published record revealing the ultimate outcome of such decisions and there is no procedure for reporting what has occurred. Nor is any official responsible for monitoring the outcome of a court decision to ensure that it is properly implemented or that its principles are applied in comparable cases considered by the agency.[105] Given this reality, the Ombudsman may have one advantage over the formal judicial branch when reviewing executive action or

---

[99] Ombudsman Act 1976 (Cth), s 5(2).

[100] Commonwealth Ombudsman (n.d.-b).

[101] Venice Principles on the Protection and Promotion of the Ombudsman, adopted by the Venice Commission at its 118th Plenary Session, 15–16 March 2019.

[102] Glušac (2021).

[103] McMillan (2005).

[104] McMillan (2005); Creyke and McMillan (2002).

[105] McMillan (2005), p. 9.

administrative decision-making. That advantage is transparency, stemming from the cooperative dynamic that can be fostered between the Ombudsman and the branches of government it seeks to hold accountable, even in (and arguably because of) the absence of enforcement and remedial powers.

Another strength of the Ombudsman over the more traditional judicial review mechanism is its capacity to directly address rule of law issues. Two empirical studies undertaken by scholars reveal a high level of support among executive officers for court and tribunal review of executive action and administrative decision-making, as well as a high rate of implementation of court decisions in individual cases and across the board.[106] However, these studies also reveal a lack of institutional support for ensuring that judicial review fulfils the role of upholding the rule of law.[107] The Commonwealth Ombudsman model is more familiar with this issue. It is conventional for the office to define its role as 'one concerned as much with systemic problems in public administration as with transitory malfunctions in administrative decision-making'.[108] The Ombudsman routinely follows through and examines whether recommendations have been implemented and promises have been honoured. Particularly through own motion investigations and publications on decision-making,[109] the Ombudsman has both a functional and an educative role in improving public administration, including legal compliance. Furthermore, as noted above, the Ombudsman has a good track record of compliance by the agencies that it reviews and critiques, even on issues as politically volatile as immigration and child detention.[110]

5.2.2 Recommendations

Having considered its limitations, we can turn now to recommendations as to how the Commonwealth Ombudsman can contribute more effectively to the goal of government integrity in an age of intergovernmental rulemaking. Some guidance can be taken from existing discourse around the key criteria important for all ombudsmen offices, as explored by the Productivity Commission in its 2014 report on Access to Justice Arrangements.[111]

First, the Commonwealth Ombudsman must be independent. It must be established either by legislation or as an incorporated or accredited body, so that it is independent of the organisations being investigated. The Ombudsman should not

[106] Creyke and McMillan (2002).

[107] Creyke and McMillan (2002).

[108] McMillan (2005).

[109] See, for example, Commonwealth Ombudsman (1999); Ombudsman New South Wales (2017b); Ombudsman New South Wales (2017a); Queensland Ombudsman (2003); Victorian Ombudsman (2007); Western Australian Ombudsman (2003).

[110] Stuhmcke and Tran (2007).

[111] Productivity Commission (2014), vol 1, pp. 326–329.

be subject to direction, must be able to select its own staff, and must not be—or be perceived as—an advocate for a special interest group, agency or company.

Second, the jurisdiction of the Ombudsman should be clearly stipulated in the legislation or instrument that establishes it. It should decide on its own whether a matter falls within its jurisdiction, subject only to a contrary ruling of a court.[112]

Third, there should be focus on the accessibility of the Ombudsman. A person must be able to approach the office directly. It must be for the Ombudsman to determine whether or not to investigate a complaint. There must be no charge to a complainant for the Ombudsman's investigation,[113] as is already the case.[114] Moreover, a person who complains to the Ombudsman in good faith must be protected against civil proceedings.[115]

Fourth, the procedure that governs the investigative work of the Commonwealth Ombudsman must embody a commitment to the fundamental requirements of procedural fairness. The complainant, the organisation or agency complained about, and any person adversely impacted by a decision or recommendation of the Ombudsman, or investigated by it, should be given an opportunity to respond before the investigation is concluded. The actions of the Ombudsman and staff must not give rise to apprehensions of bias or prejudgment. The Ombudsman must provide reasons for any decision, finding or recommendation to both the complainant and the organisation that is the subject of the complaint.[116]

Finally, there should be an emphasis on the Commonwealth Ombudsman's accountability. The Ombudsman must be required to publish an annual report of its work and it must be responsible to the parliament.[117]

Besides ensuring that these overarching principles are protected and realised in practice, there should be a review of the kinds of remedies that the Commonwealth Ombudsman can provide to complainants, especially when the complaint relates to actions of the executive. It may be that the remedies available could be extended without encroaching on the jurisdiction of the judicial branch.

The rule of law is especially concerned with legal compliance by the executive—which, ostensibly, is an issue that can be resolved only by a court through judicial review.[118] Studies of judicial review cases undertaken by scholars demonstrate that two of the legal grounds most likely to be argued by applicants and accepted by courts in such instances are failure to take a relevant consideration into account and breach of natural justice.[119] While these are clearly legal errors that can invalidate a

[112]Productivity Commission (2014), vol 1, pp. 326–329.

[113]Productivity Commission (2014), vol 1, pp. 326–329.

[114]Commonwealth Ombudsman (n.d.-b).

[115]Ombudsman Act 1976 (Cth), s 37.

[116]Productivity Commission (2014), vol 1, pp. 326–329.

[117]Australian and New Zealand Ombudsman Association (2010).

[118]McMillan (2005).

[119]Creyke and McMillan (2004). In the almost 300 cases analysed in this study, failure to consider relevant matters was argued in 48.3% and upheld in 35.3% of cases; breach of natural justice was

decision, they are also administrative shortcomings that are not unlike the errors that are routinely the focus of investigation by the Commonwealth Ombudsman.[120] In this way, expanding available remedies for the Ombudsman would not usurp any functions of the judiciary.

Furthermore, in addition to deciding on its own jurisdiction (subject only to the contrary ruling of the court),[121] carve-outs—such as actions taken by ministers—should be reviewed and consideration should be given to whether such actions should really be beyond the scope of the Commonwealth Ombudsman's jurisdiction. It is noteworthy that the Ombudsman in some jurisdictions already has scope to review the actions of ministers, providing a precedent for this expansion.[122]

Finally, there is the subject of the Ombudsman's scope and capacity to consider issues of transnational concern, such as the creeping impact of intergovernmental rulemaking into domestic policy, legislative processes, and law enforcement. Here, the first step is for the Ombudsman to be aware of and responsive to such risk and its impact on the separation of powers and the accountability of the executive to parliament and of both to the judiciary. This task of expanding the perspective of integrity institutions such as the Ombudsman should also be undertaken in respect of those other integrity agencies mentioned earlier, the Auditor-General and the National Anti-Corruption Commission. Furthermore, the effectiveness of each of these bodies as a component of an emerging and strengthening integrity branch will be reliant on their ability to see each other; to understand that their roles may be related and, in some cases, overlapping; and to understand how each can contribute to and strengthen the work of the other. This will take time and concerted effort. It may also require ongoing research and empirical insight to detect as yet unaddressed limitations or unexplored avenues for collaboration that will further enhance the integrity of government.

Recognising the role of the Ombudsman as a key institution comprising an integrity branch of government is but the first step in a journey to enhance government integrity in Australia. Some more concrete steps that could be taken to improve the Ombudsman's responsiveness to the challenge of intergovernmental rulemaking would be to include a review of legislative changes and treaty commitments in response to intergovernmental pressure as part of the office's annual reporting. This would act to increase transparency around the influence of transnational actors on domestic law and policy, an initial step towards protecting the rule of law from undue influence by the executive in its pursuit of transnational objectives.

argued in 38.5% and upheld in 34.2% of cases. The more common ground was error of law (including misinterpretation of legislation), which was argued in 49.3% and upheld in 42.3% of cases.

[120] McMillan (2005).

[121] McMillan (2005).

[122] Taumoepeau (2019).

6 Conclusion

This chapter has demonstrated the increasingly pressing challenge of balancing international responsiveness with domestic integrity and due process in an age of intergovernmental rule-making. Using the example of the FATF and the implementation of FATF recommendations on money laundering and terrorist financing in Australia, the chapter has illustrated the weaknesses of the current separation of power framework, where the executive branch of government can overstep into the legislative role. In response, the chapter presents two proposals for enhancing integrity: amending the Constitution to establish a fourth branch of government, or empowering the Commonwealth Ombudsman and other existing integrity bodies to better responded to the evolving challenges of intergovernmental rulemaking. As a concept, integrity does not replace more traditional legal concepts, such as the rule of law and the separation of powers, in defining the fundamentals of the system of law and government. On the other hand, concepts such as integrity present renewed ways of looking at the structure of the government and its various agencies, acting as a reminder of the need for conventional concepts to be reconsidered from time to time to take account of other changes in society and governance.[123]

Given the increasing power of intergovernmental organisations, illustrated above in the context of financial crime and the FATF, a reimagining of the mechanisms and structures that protect integrity in Australian government is warranted. While enshrining an integrity branch within the Constitution may be impractical, there are ways that the tripartite institutions of the Ombudsman, the Auditor-General and the National Anti-Corruption Commission may be adapted and enhanced to protect integrity and preserve the separation of powers and rule of law principles in Australian government.

By reviewing the institutional standing, scope and powers of the Commonwealth Ombudsman, it may be possible to balance more effectively the power of the executive in Australia, thus also mitigating the risk of intergovernmental rulemaking shaping domestic law and policy without democratic process. These steps may also increase the transparency of decision-making, which will in turn enhance the legitimacy of government decisions and the laws that implement them—an important bulwark against public apathy and distrust, which weaken democratic institutions. It is essential that the integrity institutions of the Ombudsman, the Auditor-General and the Anti-Corruption Commission have sufficient scope and resources to explore the impact of intergovernmental rulemaking and policy—focusing on the actions of the executive in facilitating the translation of such rulemaking into domestic law. Traditionally, these integrity institutions have been inward looking, but—as has been demonstrated—domestic policy is often shaped by organisations outside of the state. The need to maintain integrity in and sovereignty over the legislative process when translating global norms and commitments into domestic law is a vital and increasingly important imperative. When global norms relate to

[123] McMillan (2005).

issues such as financial crime, money laundering, and terrorist financing (as in the case of the FATF recommendations), the need for transparency and integrity in domestic implementation is further amplified. This is because such issues impact directly on the sovereignty of nation-states through their impact on national security and the resilience of the domestic economy. Such issues should not be left open to the whims of intergovernmental organisations, especially those whose rulemaking power has been questioned based on a lack of transparency and an absence of clear procedural standards and processes.[124]

References

Ackerman B (2000) The new separation of powers. Harv Law Rev 113(3):633–729

Australian and New Zealand Ombudsman Association (2010) Essential criteria for describing a body as an ombudsman. Policy Statement, 18 May 2010

Australian Electoral Commission (1999) Yes/No referendum '99: your official referendum pamphlet

Australian Electoral Commission (2011) Referendums overview. https://www.aec.gov.au/Elections/referendums/Referendums_Overview.htm. Accessed 23 Dec 2023

Brown AJ (2018) The fourth, integrity branch of government: resolving a contested idea. Presidential Address, International Political Science Association World Congress, July 2018. https://auspsa.org.au/wp-content/uploads/2020/09/Brown-A-J-2018-Fourth-Integrity-Branch-of-Government-APSA-Presidential-Paper.pdf. Accessed 23 Dec 2023

Callinan I, Aroney N (2013) Review of the Crime and Misconduct Act and related matters: report of the Independent Advisory Panel. Queensland Government, 28 March 2013. https://documents.parliament.qld.gov.au/tableOffice/TabledPapers/2013/5413T2447.pdf. Accessed 23 Dec 2023

Capeloto T (2017) The WTO is inappropriately usurping American sovereignty. Wiley Law, 14 July 2017. https://www.wiley.law/article-The-WTO-Is-Inappropriately-Usurping-American-Sovereignty. Accessed 23 Dec 2023

Commonwealth Ombudsman (1999) A good practice guide for effective complaint handling, 2nd edn

Commonwealth Ombudsman (n.d.-a) Australian government agency complaints. https://www.ombudsman.gov.au/complaints/australian-government-agency-complaints. Accessed 23 Dec 2023

Commonwealth Ombudsman (n.d.-b) Frequently asked questions. https://www.ombudsman.gov.au/publications-and-news-pages/publication-pages/faqs/frequently-asked-questions. Accessed 23 Dec 2023

Cozzolino A (2019) Reconfiguring the state: executive powers, emergency legislation, and neoliberalization in Italy. Globalizations 16(3):336–352

Creyke R, McMillan J (2002) Executive perceptions of administrative law: an empirical study. Aust J Adm Law 9(4):163–190

Creyke R, McMillan J (2004) Judicial review outcomes: an empirical study. Aust J Adm Law 11: 82–100

Creyke R et al (2019) Control of government action: texts, cases and commentary, 5th edn. LexisNexis, Chatswood

de Koker L (2022) Editorial: regulatory impact assessment: towards a better approach for the FATF. J Money Laund Control 25(2):265–267

[124] de Koker (2022); Goldbarsht (2017); Ghoshray (2015).

del Villar K (2003) Who guards the guardians? Recent developments concerning the jurisdiction and accountability of ombudsman. AIAL Forum 36:25–53

Delonis RP (2004) International financial standards and codes: mandatory regulation without representation. NYU J Int Law Pol 36:563–630

Draghici C (2009) Trading justice for security? UN anti-terrorism, due process rights, and the role of the judiciary. Centre on Human Rights in Conflict, Policy Paper No 2. https://openaccess.city.ac.uk/id/eprint/5250/1/. Accessed 23 Dec 2023

Eilstrup-Sangiovanni M (2020) Death of international organizations. The organizational ecology of intergovernmental organizations, 1815–2015. Rev Int Organ 15:339–370

Esty D (2006) Good governance at the supranational scale: globalizing administrative law. Yale Law J 115:1490–1562

Field C (2018) The ombudsman in the 21st century. UW Aust Law Rev 43(1):118–123

Gelber K (2006) High Court review 2005: the manifestation of separation of powers in Australia. Aust J Polit Sci 41(3):437–453

Ghoshray S (2015) Compliance convergence in FATF rulemaking: the conflict between agency capture and soft law. NYU Law Rev 59(3):521–546

Glušac L (2021) A critical appraisal of the Venice Principles on the Protection and Promotion of the Ombudsman: an equivalent to the Paris Principles? Hum Rights Law Rev 21(1):22–53

Goldbarsht D (2017) Who's the legislator anyway? How the FATF's global norms reshape Australian counter terrorist financing laws. Fed Law Rev 45(1):127–151

Goldbarsht D (2020) Global counter-terrorist financing and soft law. Edward Elgar Publishing, Cheltenham

Goldbarsht D, De Koker L (2024) Global standard-setting on financial crime–navigating challenges. In: Goldbarsht D, De Koker L (eds.), Financial crime, law and governance, Ius Gentium: Comparative Perspectives on Law and Justice. Springer, Cham.

Goldbarsht D, Harris H (2022) Check the balance: is the doctrine of separation of powers sufficient in the context of intergovernmental organisations? A case study of Australia's AML/CTF financing framework. Fed Law Rev 50(4):527–557

Gonzalez Arreaza A (2017) Natural resource sovereignty and economic development in the WTO in light of the recent case law involving raw materials and rare earths. RECIEL 26(3):266–275

Gummow WMC (2012) A fourth branch of government? AIALF 70:19–25

Howieson J (2002) The justice of court-connected mediation. VCAT Med Newsl 6:24

Huberts LWJC (2018) Integrity: what it is and why it is important. Public Integr 20(4):1–15

International Ombudsman Institute (n.d.) About the IOI. https://www.theioi.org/the-i-o-i. Accessed 23 Dec 2023

Kerr D, Williams G (2003) Review of executive action and the rule of law under the Australian Constitution. PLR 14(3):219–233

Kildea P, Williams G (2010) Reworking Australia's referendum machinery. Altern Law J 35(1): 22–25

Kinchin N (2014) Accountability in the global space: plurality, complexity and UNHCR. Dissertation, University of New South Wales

Kingsbury B, Krisch N, Stewart RB (2005) The emergence of global administrative law. LCP 68(3&4):15–62

Lee CH (2003) To thine own self be true: IMF conditionality and erosion of economic sovereignty in the Asian financial crisis. U Pa J Int Law 24(4):875–884

Lordi A (2009) Globalized world and separation of powers: a new role for the independent administrative authorities. Duq Law Rev 47(4):939–946

Lowenfeld AF (2002) The international monetary system and the erosion of sovereignty: essay in honor of Cynthia Lichtenstein. BC Int Comp Law Rev 25(2):257–272

Martin W (2014) Forewarned and four-armed: administrative law values and the fourth arm of government. ALJ 88:106–124

McMillan J (2005) The ombudsman and the rule of law. AIALF 44:1–16

McMillan J (2010) Re-thinking the separation of powers. Fed Law Rev 38(3):423–443

Menzel DC (2005) State of the art of empirical research on ethics and integrity in governance. In: Frederickson HG, Ghere RK (eds) Ethics in public management. Routledge, London
Mitchell AD, Farnik J (2009) Global administrative law: can it bring global governance to account? Fed Law Rev 37(2):237–261
Montesquieu (1777) The spirit of the laws. (trans: Nugent T). J Nourse, London
National Geographic Education Resource Library (n.d.) International organization. https://education.nationalgeographic.org/resource/international-organization. Accessed 23 Dec 2023
Ombudsman New South Wales (2017a) Effective complaint handling guidelines, 3rd edn
Ombudsman New South Wales (2017b) Good conduct and administrative practice: guidelines for state and local government, 3rd edn
Oxford dictionary of English (2010) 3rd edn. Oxford University Press, Oxford
Pearce D (1998) The Commonwealth ombudsman: the right office in the wrong place. In: Creyke R, McMillan J (eds) The Kerr vision of administrative law: at the twenty-five year mark. Centre for International and Public Law, Canberra
Prasser S (2012) Australian integrity agencies in critical perspective. PSJ 33(1):21–35
Productivity Commission (2014) Access to justice arrangements. Report No 72
Queensland Ombudsman (2003) An easy guide to good administrative decision-making
Reif L (2017) The UN Guiding Principles on Business and Human Rights and Networked Governance: improving the role of human rights ombudsman institutions as national remedies. Hum Rights Law Rev 17(4):603–632
Senate Standing Committee on Finance and Public Administration (1991) Review of the Office of Commonwealth Ombudsman. Parliament of the Commonwealth of Australia
Slaughter A-M (2005) A new world order. Princeton University Press, Princeton
Solomon D (2012) What is the integrity branch? AIAL Forum 70:26–32
Spigelman JJ (2004) The integrity branch of government. ALJ 78(11):724–737
Stuhmcke A (2016) Australian ombudsmen: a call to take care. Fed Law Rev 44(3):531–556
Stuhmcke A, Tran A (2007) The Commonwealth ombudsman: an integrity branch of government? Altern Law J 32(4):233–236
Taumoepeau A (2019) The ombudsman and good governance: Tonga's experience. Asia Pac J Public Adm 41(3):33–41
Tripathi R (2011) Concept of global administrative law: an overview. India Q 67(4):355–372
Victorian Ombudsman (2007) Good practice guide
Western Australian Ombudsman (2003) The ombudsman's guidelines for conducting administrative investigations
Williams G, Brennan S, Lynch A (2018) Blackshield and Williams: Australian constitutional law and theory. Federation Press, Annandale

Doron Goldbarsht LLB, LLM (HUJI), PhD (UNSW), is the Director of the Financial Integrity Hub (FIH) and an Associate Professor at Macquarie Law School, where he teaches banking and financial crime. He is an authority on anti-money laundering and counter-terrorist financing (AML/CTF) regulations, with expertise in the related fields of compliance and financial innovation, with over 20 years of experience in the field. His recent books *Financial Crime and the Law: Identifying and Mitigating Risks* (Springer 2024, co-edited), *Financial Crime, Law and Governance: Navigating Challenges in Diverse Contexts* (Springer 2024, co-edited), *Financial Technology and the Law: Combating Financial Crime* (Springer, 2022 co-edited), and *Global Counter-Terrorist Financing and Soft Law: Multi-Layered Approaches* (Edward Elgar, 2020), as well as journal and chapter publications, focus on international AML/CTF standards and the mechanisms for their effective implementation and compliance at the national level.

Hannah Harris is a scholar, Senior Lecturer at Macquarie Law School and a Research Fellow with the Financial Integrity Hub (FIH). Her research area is transnational law and corporate regulation. Her current work analyses legal responses to transnational challenges, including illegal logging and forest degradation, modern slavery, foreign bribery and financial crime. She is also engaged in research that seeks to understand the interaction between law and technology, focusing on the challenges and opportunities presented by Artificial Intelligence for policing, law enforcement, and regulatory compliance. Dr. Harris' research is concerned with development of optimal regulatory incentives and sanctions, as well as optimal internal governance practices within key organisations and institutions that shape the way the law is practiced and experienced by stakeholders and regulatory targets.

To Report or Not to Report? An Analysis of the Relationship Between Defence Against Terrorism Financing Suspicious Activity Reports and Fraud in the United Kingdom

Nicholas Ryder

Abstract To tackle terrorism financing, the United Kingdom has implemented the global mechanisms introduced by the United Nations and the Financial Action Task Force. The ensuing legislative provisions have forced terrorism financiers to adapt their funding mechanisms and move away from their traditional funding sources. Consequently, terrorists can obtain funding by committing fraud, often without detection. While efforts have been made to identify new typologies and adapt relevant legislation, the link between fraud and terrorism financing is misunderstood. This chapter provides a novel investigation and identifies a new terrorism financing fraud typology which will assist in improving our understanding of how terrorists raise and use money. Furthermore, it will also shed a new light on the inadequacies of the United Kingdom's counter-fraud and counter-terrorism financing reporting mechanisms. In doing so, it will highlight the deficiencies in the use of financial intelligence and the exchange of information from the submission of defence against terrorism financing suspicious activity reports.

1 Introduction

Terrorism financiers have been able to obtain access to a wide range of funding avenues, yet it was not until the al Qaeda terrorist attacks in the United States of America (US) in September 2001 (9/11) that the international community responded by implementing the Financial War on Terrorism. This consisted of five counter-terrorism financing (CTF) mechanisms: criminalisation; confiscation and/or forfeiture; an asset freezing regime; a designated terrorism sanctions scheme; and the use of financial intelligence gathered by the submission of defence against terrorism

N. Ryder (✉)
School of Law and Politics, Cardiff University, Cardiff, UK
e-mail: RyderN@cardiff.ac.uk

D. Goldbarsht, L. de Koker (eds.), *Financial Crime, Law and Governance*, Ius Gentium: Comparative Perspectives on Law and Justice 116,
https://doi.org/10.1007/978-3-031-59547-9_8

financing suspicious activity reports (DATF SARs).[1] As a result of these CTF measures terrorists have moved away from their traditional funding mechanisms and this chapter presents evidence that fraud has become one of the most frequently used methods to finance their activities.[2] DATF SARs contain financial and other information that has been submitted to a Financial Intelligence Unit (FIU) by the regulated sector indicating that a customer's financial activity is suspicious.[3] Therefore, DATF SARs provide the FIU with an opportunity to identify and analyse emerging financial crime typologies across a broad spectrum of financial activity. Thus, allowing them to anticipate and counteract emerging financial crime typologies. To assist in the identification of terrorism financing and thus prevent and combat terrorism, international bodies such as the Financial Action Task Force (FATF) established and now regularly use typologies.[4] A typology focuses on the way terrorists obtain and use funds and refers to the various techniques used to finance terrorism. The FATF adds that the 'these typologies provide a contemporary snapshot of the ways in which terrorists raise, move and use funds'.[5]

Typologies in the United Kingdom (UK) have identified different types of fraudulent activity, the victims and offenders. For example, typologies by the Financial Conduct Authority (FCA),[6] the National Fraud Authority[7] and the Home Office[8] have focused on the identification of the victims and the offenders of fraud.[9] Therefore, these typologies have been unable to identify how terrorists have obtained funds, that is, they do not pinpoint the link between terrorism financing and fraud. For instance, the Home Office acknowledged that fraud is associated with other types of crime, but it does not refer to terrorism financing. However, academic literature in the UK has identified a brevity of terrorism financing fraud typologies. For example, Perri and Brody focus on the similarities between the funding models of organised criminal gangs and terrorists.[10] The authors identify a brief typology, which includes mortgage fraud, non-profit organisations (NPO) fraud, identity fraud, insurance fraud and immigration fraud.[11] Freeman offers an interesting, but rather generic typology, which focuses on state sponsorship, illegal activities, legal activities and popular support funding mechanisms.[12] Irwin et al. identify typologies for money laundering and terrorism financing, but largely focused on the three stages of

[1] Ryder (2015), pp. 30–62.

[2] Financial Action Task Force (2009a), p. 18 and Financial Action Task Force (2021), pp. 8–19.

[3] Proceeds of Crime Act 2002, schedule 9.

[4] Financial Action Task Force (2009b).

[5] Ibid, p. 5.

[6] Harvey et al. (2014), pp. 36–45.

[7] The National Fraud Authority (2009).

[8] Home Office (n.d.).

[9] Button et al. (2014) and Levi (2008).

[10] Perri and Brody (2011).

[11] Ibid, pp. 53–56.

[12] Freeman (2011).

money laundering, not on the link between terrorism financing and fraud.[13] Vittori divided terrorism financing into a typology of seven broad categories including lone wolf, state sponsored, franchise, bundles, support, shell state and transnational corporations.[14] Finally, Wood et al. refers to a terrorism financing fraud typology that is divided into three parts: fraud against individuals, fraud against the state and fraud against the private sector.[15] Collectively, these typologies are narrow and their contribution to knowledge is limited. The need for a terrorism financing fraud typology was discussed by the Fraud Review who noted that 'particular concern was expressed [by HM Government] that the linkages of some types of fraud with . . . terrorist funding were being *missed* [author's emphasis]'.[16] Thus, the importance of a detailed comprehensive study of the association between terrorism financing and fraud cannot be emphasised enough due to the limited literature on the subject. This article fills this gap by identifying a terrorism financing fraud typology on how terrorists are financed rather than those typologies that have focused on identifying the victims and offenders of fraud. What is more, the literature has only provided a cursory glance towards the association between terrorism financing and fraud. The use of this new typology will assist in improving our understanding of how terrorists raise and use money and so enable shedding a new light on the current UK counter-fraud and CTF reporting mechanisms.[17] In doing so, the chapter will highlight the deficiencies in the operation of DATF SARs and will make recommendations aimed at addressing these shortcomings. Therefore, the chapter has three objectives. Firstly, it seeks to identify an authoritative typology. Secondly, the chapter determines the suitability of the reporting obligations to counter the threat presented by this typology. Finally, this chapter makes a series of novel recommendations to policymakers to reduce the risks presented by fraud.

2 The Terrorism Financing Fraud Typology

Terrorists have traditionally relied on two forms of financial support—state sponsorship and private individuals.[18] Terrorism financiers are also able to acquire funding via a multitude of, yet non exhaustive list of sources, including the proceeds of drug trafficking,[19] kidnapping for ransom,[20] counterfeit currencies,[21] oil

[13] Irwin et al. (2012).

[14] Vittori (2011), p. 7.

[15] Wood et al. (2021), pp. 29–38.

[16] Attorney General's Office (2006), p. 74 and 134.

[17] Hereinafter 'reporting obligations'.

[18] Chase (2004) and Acharya (2009).

[19] Federal Research Division Library of Congress 2002).

[20] Financial Action Task Force (2015a), p. 18.

[21] Financial Action Task Force (2013a).

refining,[22] natural resources,[23] piracy,[24] cryptocurrencies,[25] Hawala,[26] private donations[27] and extortion.[28] As the Financial War on Terrorism has been able to limit some of the funding avenues terrorism financiers have turned towards alternative sources, such as fraud.[29] This part of the chapter provides a comprehensive terrorism financing fraud typology.

2.1 Passport Fraud

The first part of the typology is passport fraud which international terrorists have used to facilitate acts of terrorism.[30] The al Qaeda Encyclopaedia of the Afghani Jihad 'provided explicit instructions for the procurement and handling of fraudulent passports'.[31] As part of the planning stage for 9/11, al Qaeda officials played a crucial role in 'facilitating travel for its operatives'.[32] In fact, al Qaeda had a passport office located at the Kandahar airport.[33] Similarly, the Islamic State of Iraq and the Levant (ISIL) have been able to 'print legitimate-looking Syrian passports ... since taking over the city of Deir ez-Zour, home to a passport office with boxes of blank passports'.[34] This was confirmed by the then French Interior Minister who said, 'ISIL have acquired blank passports and has now set up a real fake document industry'.[35] In fact, German investigators estimated that ISIL holds approximately 11,000 blank Syrian passports,[36] which can be purchased for between $250 and $2000.[37] It has been suggested that one of the ISIL terrorists involved in the Paris terrorist attack (2015) entered Europe with one of these Syrian passports.[38] The UK has experienced similar problems with passport fraud and terrorism financing. For example, between 2005 and 2006, 'an estimated 10,000 British passports were

[22] Financial Action Task Force (2015a), p. 5.
[23] Ibid, pp. 39–42.
[24] Financial Action Task Force (2011).
[25] Financial Action Task Force (2019).
[26] Financial Action Task Force (2013b).
[27] Financial Action Task Force (2015b).
[28] Ibid.
[29] C Michaelsen (2010).
[30] Financial Action Task Force (2018a), p. 21.
[31] Unknown author (n.d.), pp. 24–25.
[32] National Commission on Terrorist Attacks (2004), p. 97.
[33] Ibid, pp. 177–178.
[34] ABC News (2015).
[35] ABC News (2016).
[36] Aljazeera (2017).
[37] Hawramy et al. (2015).
[38] BBC News (2016).

issued after fraudulent applications ... [and] al-Qaida have successfully faked applications'.[39] Furthermore, there have been criminal convictions for passport fraud associated with terrorism financing in both the US and UK.[40]

2.2 Immigration Fraud

Fraudulently obtained passports have enabled terrorists to illegally enter a country under the premise as a non-immigrant visa holder. The only documented al Qaeda sleeper agent in the US, Iyman Faris, entered the country on a student visa and passport that belonged to another person.[41] Ibrahim Elgabrowny, the al Qaeda messenger during the 1993 World Trade Centre attack, was convicted for using false immigration documents.[42] Similarly, Ahmad Ajaj was convicted of immigration fraud,[43] as was his travelling companion, Ramzi Yousef,[44] who was the architect of the 1993 World Trade Centre Bombing and the formulating of the Bojinka terrorist plot.[45] Other immigration fraud terrorism financing convictions include Mahmoud Youssef Kourani,[46] Khalid Abu Al-Dahab,[47] Mohamad Youssef Hammoud,[48] Khalid Abu Al-Dahab,[49] Enrique Marquez Jr.[50] and Naif Abdulaziz M. Afallaj.[51]

---

[39] Sturcke (2007).

[40] This includes Ahmed Ressam, Shivam Patel, Sajmir Alimehmeti, Amine Mezbar, Slimane Khalfaoui, Tarek Ben Habib Maaroufi, Dhiren Barot, Salah Abdeslam, Hedi Ben Youseff Boudhiba and Jabed Hussain.

[41] *United States of America v. Iyman Faris*, 'Complaint to Revoke Naturalization' (March 20 2017), available at https://www.justice.gov/opa/press-release/file/949946/download

[42] *Elgabrowny v. U.S.*, S5 S7 93 Cr. 181 (MBM) 01 Civ. 162, `169, "175," 176, 222, 596, 1988; 00 Civ. 7981 (S.D.N.Y. Oct. 21, 2003).

[43] Bernstein (1994).

[44] Reeve (1999). Other immigration fraud convictions include Mahmoud Youssef Kourani, Khalid Abu Al-Dahab, Mohamad Youssef Hammoud, Khalid Abu Al-Dahab, Enrique Marquez Jr. and Naif Abdulaziz M. Afallaj.

[45] Ramzi Yousef was convicted of his role in the 1993 terrorist attack and the Bojinka terrorist plan and was sentenced to two life sentences and an additional 240 years.

[46] *United States v. Mahmoud Youssef Kourani* (2006) Case number 03CR81030-1.

[47] National Commission on Terrorist Attacks (2004), p. 52.

[48] United States Immigration and Customs Enforcement (2011).

[49] United States Department of Justice (2017a).

[50] United States Department of Justice (2017b).

[51] United States Department of Justice (2019).

2.3 Identity Fraud

Identity fraud enables terrorists who have entered a country using a fraudulently obtained passport and mislead authorities on their immigration status to acquire documents which allow them to avoid no fly lists, detection by intelligence agencies, gain employment, obtain a driver's licence, access bank accounts and credit cards.[52] The Federal Bureau of Investigation (FBI) described identity fraud as the 'key catalyst fuelling many terrorism financing methods'.[53] The 9/11 Commission concluded that 'all but one of the [19] hijackers acquired [by fraud] some form of identification'.[54] They added that terrorists frequently use evasive methods 'such as altered and counterfeit visas, supportive travel agencies, immigration and identity fraud'.[55] Writing in 2005, Kane and Wall concluded that out of 100 US terrorist indictments, 54% related to identity fraud.[56] Consequently, there have been numerous convictions for terrorism financing involving identify fraud in the US and UK.[57]

2.4 Financial Fraud

Once terrorists have illegally entered a country, they will seek to fraudulently obtain finance via a loan from a financial institution and/or credit provider. For example, the terrorist attacks in San Bernardino (2015);[58] Paris (2015);[59] the offices of Charlie Hebdo and Jewish Supermarket (2015) were all financed by fraudulently obtained consumer loans using forged documents.[60] The use of financial fraud in the UK to fund acts of terrorism was illustrated following the convictions of Brahim Benmerzouga and Baghdad Meziane.[61] The ability of terrorism financiers to obtain access to finance in the UK is exacerbated by convenient credit, 'credit that is granted ... with little or no reference to the credit worthiness of the debtor'.[62]

[52] Federal Bureau of Investigation (2003).

[53] Federal Bureau of Investigation (2002).

[54] National Commission on Terrorist Attacks (2004), p. 390.

[55] Ibid, p 384.

[56] Kane and Wall (2005), p. 9.

[57] Examples include Colleen LaRose and Jamie Paulin Ramirez, Barry Walter Bujol Jr., Ali Charah Damache, Abderrahman Bouanane, Amer Sinan Alhaggai, Ardit Ferizi, Younes Tsouli and Ciaran Maxwell.

[58] Whitcomb and McAllister (2015). Related fraud convictions in the US include Nader Elhuzayel, Khalid Ouazzani, Khalid Awan, Yahya Farooq Mohammad and Zoobia Shahnaz.

[59] European Commission (2017), p. 42.

[60] Europol (n.d.).

[61] *R. (on the application of Benmerzouga) v Secretary of State for the Home Department* [2009] EWHC 3599 (Admin), [2009] 11 WLUK 603.

[62] Thomas and Ryder (2011).

Examples of convenient credit which terrorism financiers have exploited include commercial cash loans, non-commercial cash loans, credit tied to the purchase of goods and pay-day lenders.[63] Therefore, terrorism financiers with good credit ratings are ideally positioned to defraud credit institutions.[64]

2.5 *Online Fraud*

Terrorism financiers have also used Internet fraud to funds acts of terrorism. In 2009, FBI announced that it had successfully secured 47 convictions for phishing and identify theft offences that could have been "an attempt by a terrorist group to raise funding for an operation".[65] Furthermore, it has been reported that ISIL has been using online romance fraud or 'Tinder terror' schemes which have involved the victims sharing intimate pictures, only to be faced with demands for money when they are blackmailed.[66] Terrorists have used fraudulent e-mail and websites to gain finances and personal information.[67] In 2015, an ISIL hacker, Ardit Ferizi stole personal information relating to 1300 employees of the US government and threatened to post the names on Twitter. Following his extradition from Malaysia to the US, Ferizi pleaded guilty and was sentenced to 20 years in prison.[68] In August 2020 it was alleged that ISIL used a fake website to sell fake personal protective equipment during the global pandemic.[69] Online payment facilities have also been exploited by terrorist financiers. For example, Younis Tsouli committed fraud to fund 180 websites to promote al Qaeda propaganda videos.[70]

2.6 *Public Funding and Grant Fraud*

Terrorism financiers have been able to exploit public funding and government grants during the Covid-19 global pandemic. The FATF stated that 'as aid responses to COVID-19 increase, governments should emphasise the importance of implementing the risk-based approach when mitigating the risk of funds being

[63] See for example the 'Birmingham rucksack bomb plot' as discussed in Anderson (2013), p. 26.

[64] It has been suggested that securities fraud and market manipulation could be used for the purposes of terrorism financing, but there are no reported cases. See Financial Action Task Force (2009a), pp. 50–54.

[65] Federal Bureau of Investigation (2009).

[66] Flannagan (2022)

[67] Hinnen (2004).

[68] United States Department of Justice (2016).

[69] Herridge (2020).

[70] Jacobson, 2010.

diverted to support terrorists and terrorist groups'.[71] Indeed, the US Department of Treasury emphasised the importance of 'simultaneously seeking to mitigate the potential for this assistance [public funding/grant assistance] to be diverted or misused by terrorists'.[72] As part of the UKs response to the Covid-19 pandemic, the Coronavirus Job Retention Scheme (CJRS) allowed employers to instruct employees to stop working and apply for a grant from HM Revenue and Customs (HMRC) to cover 80% of the employers' wages.[73] The CJRS was used by 1.3 million employers, protected 11.7 million jobs and the total amount claimed was £70 billion.[74] The HM Treasury Select Committee noted that the there was a 'very real risk of fraudulent claims for support'.[75] This was confirmed by the Chief Executive of HMRC, Jim Harra who stated that the CJRS fraud rate was between 5% and 10%, 'our planning assumption is between £1.75 billion and £3.5 billion'.[76] The National Audit Office reported that the amount of fraud associated with the CJRS has increased to £4.5 billion, with HMRC estimating is totalled £6.3 billion'.[77] It has been suggested that organised criminal gangs defrauded the CJRS (£630 million),[78] and that terrorism financiers have also exploited the scheme. For example, in January 2022 Tarek Namouz was convicted of terrorism financing offences and sentenced to 12 years imprisonment after transferring £25,000 from the CJRS to ISIL sympathises in Syria.[79]

2.7 *Benefit Fraud*

Terrorism financiers have exploited state welfare systems. This part of the typology has been referred to in the ISIL manual 'How to Survive in the West', which contains a part entitled 'Easy money ideas'. The manual stated that 'if you can claim extra benefits from a government, then do so'.[80] In the US, both Muhanad Badawi and Guled Omar were convicted for conspiring to provide material support to ISIL by committing benefit fraud.[81] The FATF,[82] the Norwegian Defence Research

[71] Financial Action Task Force (2020a), p. 10.
[72] United States Department of Treasury (2020).
[73] HM Government (2020a).
[74] HM Government (2020b).
[75] House of Commons Treasury Committee (2020), p. 20.
[76] Public Accounts Committee (2020).
[77] National Audit Office (2022), p. 4.
[78] Omoigui (2022).
[79] Jolly and Sinmaz (2023).
[80] Unknown author (2015) as cited in Vidino et al. (2020), p. 24.
[81] United States Justice Department (2016a, b).
[82] Financial Action Task Force (2015a), p. 26.

Establishment,[83] and the Danish Security and Intelligence Service have all concluded that benefit fraud is strongly associated with foreign terrorist fighters.[84] A clear link between benefit fraud and terrorism financing has been also established in Sweden,[85] France,[86] Germany,[87] Belgium,[88] the UK[89] and Denmark.[90]

2.8 *Student Loan Fraud*

Terrorists have been able to secure funds by student loan fraud, which has been described as the perfect mechanism for terrorists to exploit.[91] An example of terrorists using student loan fraud was Hamza Naj Ahmed, Hanad Mustafe Musse and Guled Ali Omar.[92] The Stockholm suicide bomber, Abdelwahab al-Abdaly, received $119,000 from the Swedish National Board for Student Aid.[93] Whilst in the UK, Yahya Rashid used his student loan to fund travel for himself and his associates to Turkey.[94] Furthermore, Salman Abedi used his student maintenance grant and student loans to finance the terrorist attack in Manchester Arena 2017.[95]

2.9 *Non-Profit Organisation Fraud*

NPO fraud is a frequently used financing mechanism for terrorist groups including al Qaeda,[96] the Liberation of Tamil Eelam,[97] ISIL[98] and al-Shabaab.[99] The association between this part of the typology and terrorism financing is illustrated by the

[83] Norwegian Defence Research Establishment (2015), p. 23.
[84] BBC News (2012).
[85] Swedish Companies Registration (2019), p. 26.
[86] Chazan (2017), Sage (2017) and Maremont and Pop (2016).
[87] European Commission (2017), p. 48.
[88] Gardham (2016).
[89] United Nations Office on Drugs and Crime (n.d.), p. 13.
[90] Bilefsky (2017).
[91] Financial Action Task Force (2015a), p. 18.
[92] United States Department of Justice (2015a).
[93] The Local (2013).
[94] *R v. Yahya Rashid* [2016] EWCA Crim 568; [2016] 1 WLR 3156.
[95] Mendick (2017).
[96] Financial Action Task Force (2014).
[97] Ibid. Goldbarsht (2024).
[98] Financial Action Task Force (2014), p. 18.
[99] Masters (2013).

designation of 40 charities as terrorist supporters by the US Treasury Department.[100] Charities that were designated included the Global Relief Foundation,[101] Benevolence International Foundation,[102] the Islamic American Relief Agency,[103] Tamils Rehabilitation Organization[104] and the Holy Land Foundation.[105] The link between NPO fraud and terrorism financing was illustrated in the UK following the convictions of Irfan Naseer and Irffan Khalid,[106] Mohammed and Shafiq Ali,[107]Adeel Ul-Haq,[108] Syed Hoque and Mashoud Miah.[109] Furthermore, the Charities Commission concluded that Anatolia People's Cultural Centre was being used to promote the actions of the proscribed terrorist group 'Revolutionary Peoples' Liberation Party Front.[110]

2.10 *Tax Fraud*

The frequency of tax fraud to fund acts of terrorism is illustrated by successful prosecutions in the US including Mohammed and Chawki Hammoud,[111] Pedrouz Sedaghaty and Soliman Hamd Al-Buthe,[112] Emadeddin Muntasser, Muhammed Mubayyid and Samir al-Monla,[113] Johnathan Paul Jimenez,[114] Michael Todd Wolfe,[115] Hossein Lahiji and Najmeh Vahid Dasterjerdi[116] and Houcine Becher Ghoul.[117] Terrorism financiers in Europe have used tax fraud to fund acts of terrorism.[118] For example, Europol provided three examples.[119] Firstly, in Sweden and Denmark a tax fraud scheme worth £8.5 million was believed to have funded

[100]US Treasury Department (2006), p. 5.
[101]United States Treasury Department (2002).
[102]United States Treasury Department (2022).
[103]United States Treasury Department (2004).
[104]United States Treasury Department (2014).
[105]United States Department of Justice (2009).
[106]Young (2013).
[107]HM Government (2015), p. 94.
[108]The Charity Commission (2016).
[109]The Charity Commission (2017).
[110]The Charity Commission (2018).
[111]United States Immigration and Customs Enforcement (2011).
[112]*United States v. Mubayyid*, 658 F.3d 35 (first Cir. 2011).
[113]United States Department of Justice (2008).
[114]Federal Bureau of Investigation (2013).
[115]United States Department of Justice (2015b).
[116]United States Department of Justice (2013).
[117]Federal Bureau of Investigation (2018).
[118]Europol (2017), p. 12.
[119]European Parliament (2018).

al-Qaida. Secondly, law enforcement agencies (LEAs) in Germany disrupted a £54 million VAT fraud scheme for terrorists. Finally, information found in Pakistan led investigators to a criminal network based in Italy that stole £0.9 billion through VAT fraud on CO2 certificates.[120] Tax fraud was an essential funding avenue for terrorists in the UK.[121] The Ulster Volunteer Force (£1.5 million), the Ulster Defence Association (£1.5 million) and the Irish Republication Army (£28.5 million) have consistently exploited loopholes relating to tax exemption status.[122] In 2015, Thomas Murphy, who is regarded as a key domestic terrorism financier, was convicted of tax fraud.[123] Al Qaeda and ISIL have secured funding via tax fraud in the UK. For example, in March 2019 it was reported that UK taxpayer money had been used to fund the London terrorist attacks in July 2005.[124] The Times reported that 'a network [of terrorists] mounted VAT and frauds ... and netted an estimated £8 billion in public money'.[125] The report suggests that one percent of this figure (£80 million) was funnelled to al Qaeda representatives in Pakistan and Afghanistan.[126]

2.11 *Counterfeiting*

Counterfeiting is an attractive funding mechanism for terrorists due to limited entry barriers, the demand from consumers for counterfeited goods, the low priority given to counterfeiting by LEAs and that counterfeiting is a cash only business.[127] Terrorists have gained finance from counterfeit cigarettes,[128] branded clothes,[129] medicines,[130] personal protective equipment[131] and tax stamps.[132] The FBI concluded that the 1993 terrorist attack on the World Trade Centre was partly financed by sale of counterfeit goods.[133] Terrorist financing counterfeiting related convictions in the US include Gale Nettles,[134] Imad Hammoud[135] and Saifullah Anjum

[120] Ibid.

[121] Horgan and Taylor (1999, 2003).

[122] Silke (1998).

[123] *Director of Public Prosecutions v. Murphy* [2017] IECA 6.

[124] Williams (2019).

[125] Harper (2019).

[126] Williams (2019).

[127] Sullivan et al. (2014), p. 360.

[128] United States Department of State (2017).

[129] Intellectual Property Office (2020).

[130] Cannon (2015), p. 343.

[131] Herridge (2020).

[132] Sullivan et al. (2014).

[133] Federal Bureau of Investigation (n.d.).

[134] *United States v. Nettles*, 400 F. Supp. 2d 1084, (N.D. Ill. November 2005).

[135] *United States v. Imad Mohamad-Musbah Hammoud,* et al., (E.D. Mich. March 2006).

Ranjha.[136] Counterfeiting was used to partly finance the terrorist attacks in Mumbai 2008 and one of the terrorists was provided with 'high quality fake Indian currency notes'.[137] In January 2021, the senior leader of the terrorist group Laskkar-e-Taiba, Zakiur Rehman Lakhvi, was sentenced to 15 years imprisonment for financing the terrorist attack.[138]

2.12 Insurance Fraud

Insurance fraud is another mechanism used by terrorists. In 2005 members of the US terrorist group, Jamaat Ul Fuqra, were convicted of insurance fraud.[139] In December 2007, three terrorism financiers were convicted in Germany of attempting to raise funds for al Qaeda through life insurance fraud estimated at €4 million.[140] Some of these fraudulent schemes used by terrorism financiers are referred to as 'crash for cash' and often involve fraudsters deliberately crashing into vehicles of innocent motorists or submitting false claims for accidents. Crash for cash schemes are one of the most popular motor insurance frauds and other examples include 'fronting, failing to declare changes in circumstance, failing to declare modifications, vehicle dumping, ghost broking, phantom hire, flash for cash and slam on'.[141] It has been suggested by the Insurance Fraud Bureau that such schemes cost UK based insurers approximately £340 million per year.[142] The Association of British Insurers estimated that the average insurance fraud in the UK exceeds £12,000 and that over 1300 insurance frauds are committed every day.[143] The FATF highlighted several instances of terrorism financiers in Spain where terrorism financiers committed frauds by faking traffic accidents and hiring bogus policies.[144]

---

[136] Office of the United States Attorney's (2008).

[137] Financial Action Task Force (2015a), p. 35.

[138] BBC News (2021).

[139] Kane and Wall (2005), p. 9.

[140] OLG Düsseldorf (2009).

[141] RAC (n.d.).

[142] Association of British Insurers (n.d.).

[143] Association of British Insurers (2019).

[144] Financial Action Task Force (2015a), p. 16.

2.13 *Mortgage Fraud*

Mortgage fraud has been associated with terrorism financing in the US, as illustrated by the convictions of Ahmad Jebril[145] and Nemr Ali Rahal.[146] The FATF were able to provide a number of instances where mortgage fraud was used by terrorism financiers in Belgium[147] and Spain.[148] There are no reported instances for mortgage fraud and terrorism funding in the UK.[149] The Association of Chief Police Officers reported that there was no evidence of mortgage fraud directly funding acts of terrorism, but that mortgage fraud could be used to fund safe houses.[150] Indeed, the FATF stated that as a result of an investigation by the UK FIU, terrorism financiers have engaged in mortgage fraud.[151]

2.14 *Trade Based Terrorism Financing*

The final part of the typology is trade based terrorism financing (TBTF) which involves terrorists and the physical movement of goods through the international trade system.[152] The FATF warned that TBTF 'schemes are attractive in moving value, offered the same opportunities to terrorist financiers'.[153] TBTF has been defined as 'disguising the movement of value through the use of trade transactions in an attempt to finance terrorism, whether from legitimate and illegitimate sources'.[154] The international trade system is subjected to a wide range of risks and vulnerabilities that are exploited by terrorism financiers.[155] Examples of how terrorism financers have abused the international trade system include multiple invoicing of good and services, over the under shipment of good and services and falsely described good and services.[156] The FATF stated that 'suspected terrorists

[145] Perri and Brody (2011), p. 44.

[146] *USA v. Nemr Ali Rahal* (2006) Case No. 05-CR-80476.

[147] Financial Action Task Force (2007), p. 9.

[148] Ibid, pp. 22–24.

[149] Mortgage Strategy (2008).

[150] BBC News (2008).

[151] Financial Action Task Force (2014), p. 30.

[152] Financial Action Task Force (2006), pp. 3–6.

[153] Financial Action Task Force (2020b), p. 32.

[154] Ibid, p 2.

[155] United States Department of Treasury (2011).

[156] Financial Action Task Force (2006), p. 12.

used the false invoicing technique to facilitate the transfer of funds to terrorists',[157] a funding technique used by Hezbollah[158] and the Taliban.[159]

This part of the chapter has identified a terrorism financing 'dossier' or 'black book' of frauds. Fraud has become a common, easy and can be classified as the funding mechanism of choice for disparate terrorist entities. It has become an integral part of the planning stage of terrorist incidences, and it is a threat to national security. It is interesting to note that HM Government (HMG) has only categorised fraud as a threat to national security in February 2023, giving it the same status as terrorism.[160] This decision to categorise fraud as a national security threat is to be welcomed, yet it is surprising that it has taken several decades for the threat to be acknowledged given its strong association with domestic terrorist groups.[161] Additionally, fraud has been added to the Strategic Policing Requirement which means that police forces are required to treat the threat presented by fraud as a top priority in conjunction with serious and organised crime, cyber-attacks, civil emergencies, and child sexual abuse.[162] Nonetheless, it is not in doubt is that fraud continues to be used to fund and support terrorists. Therefore, in light of this, the second part of the chapter determines whether the reporting obligations are able to address this typology.

3 Defence Against Terrorism Financing Suspicious Activity Reports

One of the most important mechanisms to tackle terrorism financing are DATF SARs.[163] The FATF stated that 'effective information-sharing is the cornerstone of a well-functioning' reporting regime.[164] The exchange of information between the regulated sector and the FIU via a DATF SAR has been described as 'critical' and 'crucial' in the fight against terrorism financing.[165] In order to facilitate the use of financial intelligence and the related exchange of information the international anti-money laundering/counter-terrorism financing (AML/CTF) provisions and the FATF Recommendations provide a template for countries to follow.[166] Each version

157 Ibid, p. 34.

158 Unknown author (2016), p. 5.

159 United States Treasury Department (2003), p. 16.

160 Hymas (2023).

161 Silke (1998).

162 Home Office (2023).

163 Kaiafa-Gbandi (2019).

164 Financial Action Task Force (2017), p. 2.

165 Ibid.

166 See United Nations Convention against Illicit Traffic in Narcotic Drugs and Psychotropic Substances (adopted 20 December 1988, entered into force 11 November 1990) 1582 UNTS

of the Recommendations has been implemented in the European Union through a series of Money Laundering Directives.[167] The Recommendations require countries to criminalise money laundering and terrorism financing, the adoption of a risk based approach as well as implementing measures to enable the confiscation of the proceeds of crime.[168] Of relevance here, is the gathering and exchange of financial intelligence through Recommendations requiring the identification of those who enter into financial transactions,[169] including those who operate through legal entities and other arrangements,[170] as well as the submission of DATF SARs to the FIU.[171] The Recommendations provide that FIUs, LEAs and supervisor authorities must 'have effective mechanisms in place which enable them to cooperate ... coordinate and exchange information ... with each other concerning ... [preventing] money laundering [and] terrorist financing'.[172] Furthermore, LEAs must be able to pursue parallel investigations into terrorist financing, money laundering and associated predicate offences.[173] Additionally, the Organisation for Economic Co-operation and Development, as the international standard-setter for international taxation and international tax evasion, has also promoted the exchange of information as a crucial tool in combatting tax evasion.[174] The OCED requires countries to enact both international cooperation mechanisms and an effective framework for domestic inter-agency cooperation as part of its Ten Global Principles in Fighting Tax Crimes.[175] The value of sharing intelligence has been demonstrated by recent trends towards expanding information sharing initiatives between LEAs and the private sector for AML/CTF purposes in a number of countries, including the UK, the US, Singapore, the Netherlands, Thailand, Bahrain and Canada.[176]

In the UK, SARs, which are submitted to the National Crime Agency (NCA) by reporting entities for money laundering by virtue of the Proceeds of Crime Act 2002

95, United Nations Convention against Transnational Organized Crime (adopted 15 November 2000, entered into force 29 September 2003) 2225 UNTS 209, United Nations Convention against Corruption (adopted 31 October 2003, entered into force 14 December 2005) 2349 UNTS 41 and United Nations Security Council (UNSC) Res 1373 (28 September 2001) UN Doc S/RES/1373.

[167] See Directive (EU) 2018/1673 of the European Parliament and of the Council of 23 October 2018 on Combating Money Laundering by Criminal Law [2018] OJ L 284/22; Directive (EU) 2018/843 of the European Parliament and of the Council of 30 May 2018 Amending Directive (EU) 2015/849 on the Prevention of the Use of the Financial System for the Purposes of Money Laundering or Terrorist Financing, and Amending Directives 2009/138/EC and 2013/36/EU [2018] OJ L 156/43.

[168] Financial Action Task Force (2022).

[169] Ibid.

[170] Financial Action Task Force (2022).

[171] Ibid.

[172] Financial Action Task Force (2022).

[173] Ibid.

[174] Organisation for Economic Co-operation and Development (n.d.).

[175] Organisation for Economic Co-operation and Development (2021).

[176] Law Commission (2018), p. 170.

(POCA) and the Terrorism Act 2000 (TACT) for suspected instances of terrorism financing. If a member of the regulated sector suspects that it is being used for the purposes of money laundering, it is required to notify its Money Laundering Reporting Officer, who will complete a SAR and file it with the NCA, who determines if further action is to be taken. For the purposes of terrorism financing, a similar reporting requirement was imposed by the Anti-terrorism, Crime and Security Act 2001.[177] The current complicated manual-driven SARs system is considered deficient by the FATF.[178] The UK SARs regime has been criticised with regards to resource allocation and the clarity of the law. In 2018, the FATF identified the 'UK FIU suffers from a lack of available resources',[179] in terms of both personnel, technology, and 'analytical capability'.[180] SARs are under-utilised by LEAs, and LEAs continue to have poor management information on how the reports are used.[181] Notwithstanding these criticisms, though, the existence of these reporting requirements has created a fear factor across the regulated sector, which in turn has prompted a significant increase in the number of SARs submitted to the NCA.[182] For instance, 1995 and 2002 the number of submitted SARs increased from 5000 to 60,000,[183] and the trend remained upwards in subsequent years. In January 2023, the NCA reported it had received 901,255 SARs, an increase of 21% from 2021.[184] Only 358 DATF SARs were submitted to the NCA.[185] These increases are directly attributable to the threat of civil financial penalties by regulators such as the FCA.[186] For example, Deutsche Bank AG was fined by the FCA £163 million for failing to maintain adequate AML controls,[187] HSBC Plc was fined £63.9 million for a series of deficiencies in its AML monitoring and reporting system,[188] Santander UK was fined £107.7 million for repeated AML failures,[189] Al Rayan Bank PLC[190] and Guaranty Trust Bank (UK) Limited.[191] Furthermore, in 2021 NatWest Bank Plc was the first UK bank to be convicted for of failing to comply with the AML reporting obligations under the Money Laundering Regulations.[192] The Law

[177] Terrorism Act 2000, s 21A.

[178] Financial Action Task Force (2018a), p. 39.

[179] Ibid, para 6.

[180] Financial Action Task Force (2018b).

[181] KPMG (2003), p. 14.

[182] Sarker (2006).

[183] KPMG (2003).

[184] National Crime Agency (2023), p. 4.

[185] Ibid.

[186] Leong (2006), p. 142.

[187] Financial Conduct Authority (2017).

[188] Financial Conduct Authority (2021a).

[189] Financial Conduct Authority (2012).

[190] Financial Conduct Authority (2023a).

[191] Financial Conduct Authority (2023b).

[192] Financial Conduct Authority (2021b).

Commission linked the high numbers of SARs to three connected causes, a low threshold for reporting based on suspicion,[193] defensive reporting due to criminal liability for failing to report[194] and the concept of suspicion remaining poorly defined.[195] In *R v Da Silva*,[196] Longmore LJ held that 'it [suspicion] seems to us that the essential element of the word suspect and its affiliates, in this context, is that the defendant must think that there is a possibility, which is more than fanciful, that the relevant facts exist. A vague feeling of unease would not suffice'.[197] *Da Silva* has been upheld, most notably by *K Ltd v National Westminster Bank plc*[198] and *Shah v HSBC Private Bank (UK) Ltd.*[199] Despite the problems associated with the interpretation, the Law Commission recommended against amending POCA 2002 or TACT 2000 to define the suspicion.[200]

Furthermore, the regulated sector has also complained about the increase in compliance costs.[201] Estimates of these compliance costs vary. In 2004, UK Finance (then the British Bankers Association) claimed that its members spent £250 million each year to comply with the regulations,[202] while the previous year KPMG had estimated annual costs at nearer to £90 million.[203] Either way, such costs appear to rise significantly each year. Respondents to a KPMG survey felt that their compliance costs had increased by 61 per cent over the previous year. In 2007, average costs again increased by a reported 58 per cent; and there were further 45 per cent and 53 per cent increases in 2010 and 2014, respectively.[204] The House of Lords European Committee noted that 'individual institutions are dedicating very large sums of money to fulfilling their statutory obligations ... as much as £36 million a year from one bank'.[205] Research has suggested that AML costs in the UK are higher than those in other European countries, including Germany, France and Italy.[206] UK Finance estimated that its members are dedicating £5 billion a year in order to comply with these reporting obligations.[207] In June 2021, LexisNexis Risk Solutions reported that annual compliance costs in the UK was £28.7 billion.[208]

---

[193] Law Commission (2018), para. 5.11.

[194] Ibid, para 5.12.

[195] Law Commission (2018), para 5.13.

[196] [2007] 1 WLR 303.

[197] Ibid.

[198] [2006] EWCA Civ 1039.

[199] *Shah* v *HSBC Private Bank (UK) Ltd* [2012] EWHC 1283.

[200] Law Commission (2019), p. 100.

[201] Home Office (2004a), pp. 19–20.

[202] Ibid.

[203] KPMG (2003), pp. 46–47.

[204] KPMG (2014).

[205] House of Lords European Union Committee (2009).

[206] Yeandle et al. (2005).

[207] Home Office and HM Treasury (2016), para. 2.1.

[208] LexisNexis Risk Solutions (2021)

It is against this background that the primary statutory obligation for reporting instances of fraud is contained in POCA 2002.[209] It is a criminal offence to fail to disclose via a DATF SAR where there is knowledge, suspicion, or reasonable grounds to know or suspect, that a person is laundering the proceeds of criminal conduct. Successful fraud is defined as money laundering for the purpose of this Act.[210] However, there is no legal obligation to report an unsuccessful or attempted fraud because they do not give rise to any legal criminal proceedings and therefore fall outside the scope of the submission of a DATF SAR. Ultimately, the decision whether or not an investigation will be conducted lies with the police. The Home Office has advised that the police should only investigate where there are good grounds to believe that a criminal offence has been committed.[211] The chapter presents evidence that questions the appropriateness of the reporting obligations by examining three terrorist attacks—London (July 7 2005), the Manchester Arena (May 22 2017) and the London Bridge (June 3 2017).

3.1 London July 72,005

In July 2005, four suicide bombers killed 52 people and injured over 770 others after detonating four improvised explosive devices on the London Underground near Aldgate, Edgware Road, Russel Square stations and Tavistock Square.[212] The financing of this terrorist attack and its association with fraud was in 1995, when HMRC connected several suspected frauds with Shahzad Tanweer, one of the July 2005 terrorists, yet this information was not disclosed to the FIU or the Security and Intelligence Service (SIS).[213] The group linked to Tanweer gained approximately £8 billion VAT and benefit frauds, of which it sent '1% of its gains, or £80 million to al-Qaeda'.[214] HMRC officials 'were prevented from sharing intelligence with SIS due to its desire to keep tax records confidential'.[215] Interestingly, the Anti-terrorism, Crime and Security Act 2001 permits the disclosure of information held by HMRC and provides that 'no obligation of secrecy ... prevents the voluntary disclosure of information ... to assist any criminal investigation ... the section *allows* [author's emphasis] for disclosure to the intelligence services ... in support of their

[209] Proceeds of Crime Act 2002, s 330.

[210] It is important to note that the Proceeds of Crime Act 2002 applies to serious crime, which includes fraud.

[211] Home Office (2004b).

[212] Intelligence and Service Committee (2006).

[213] It has been suggested that HMRC became aware of the tax fraud scheme as early as 1995. See Harper and Macaskill (2019).

[214] Williams (2019).

[215] Ibid.

functions'.[216] However, the ability of HMRC to disclose information is restricted by the Commissioners for Revenue and Customs Act 2005, which provides that information must not be disclosed to anyone unless the person making the disclosure has the authority to do so.[217] This applies to HMRC providing information to government departments, LEAs, FIUs and other public bodies. This restriction does not apply if the disclosure is 'made for the purposes of a criminal investigation or criminal proceedings relating to a matter in respect of which the Revenue and Customs have functions'.[218] HMRC's duty of confidentiality is also 'subject to any other enactment permitting disclosure',[219] and many legal gateways have been enacted to provide for the exchange of information between HMRC and LEAs. The Counter Terrorism Act 2008 provides that 'a person may disclose information to any of the intelligence services for the purposes of the exercise by that service of any of its functions'.[220] Additionally, the Money Laundering Regulations provide that HMRC as a 'supervisory authority which, in the course of carrying out any of its supervisory functions or otherwise, knows or suspects, or has reasonable grounds for knowing or suspecting, that a person is or has engaged in money laundering or terrorist financing *must* [author's emphasis] as soon as practicable inform the NCA'.[221] Between 2021 and 2022 the HMRC Economic Crime Supervision 'continued to submit SARs to the NCA in line with its regulatory obligations in respect of SARs that are relevant to the supervisory'.[222] They added that it:

> 'has also worked to increase its interactions and close working with the NCA . . . in relation to SAR submissions and has worked with [the FIU] . . . to look at when reporting is relevant and required to ensure the best use of intelligence sharing within the Regulations . . . to ensure that intelligence . . . is not duplicated, creating potential resourcing impacts for any party in the process'.[223]

HMRC, in its capacity as a statutory supervisory authority under the Money Laundering Regulations, has potentially breached Regulation 46(5) by not submitting a DATF SAR to the NCA. However, it is unlikely that HMRC will be subjected to a civil penalty for breaching the Money Laundering Regulations because they are imposed by statutory supervisory authorities on the regulated sector, not on statutory supervisory authorities. Furthermore, HMRC will not be exposed to any disciplinary action by the Office for Professional Body AML Supervising which supervises professional body supervisors in the legal and accountancy sectors.[224] Additionally,

[216] Anti-terrorism, Crime and Security Act 2001, s 19.

[217] Commissioners for Revenue and Customs Act 2005, s 18(1).

[218] Commissioners for Revenue and Customs Act 2005, s 18(2)(d).

[219] Commissioners for Revenue and Customs Act 2005, s 18(3).

[220] Counter Terrorism Act 2008, s 18(1).

[221] The Money Laundering, Terrorist Financing and Transfer of Funds (Information on the Payer) Regulations 2017, SI 2017/692, regulation 46(5).

[222] HM Revenue and Customs (2022).

[223] Ibid.

[224] Financial Conduct Authority (2018).

HMRC also has a 'duty to co-operate' and 'disclosure' under the Money Laundering Regulations,[225] which provide that 'co-operation may include the sharing of information which the supervisory authority is not prevented from disclosing'.[226] The decision by HMRC not to disclose the information, despite several mechanisms facilitating the exchange of information is problematic. The difficulty is not with the legislation or guidance, but the restrictive interpretation of 'taxpayer confidentiality'. HMRC practice is not in line with national, regional, and international legal instruments, thus illustrating that the reporting obligations are not suitable to address the typology.

3.2 Manchester Arena May 222,017

On May 222,017, Salman Abedi detonated an improvised explosive device in the Manchester Arena, killing 22 people and injuring over 800 others (Manchester Arena Inquiry, 2022). In order to commit this terrorist attack, Salman Abedi fraudulently used student loans and his maintenance grant.[227] Abedi received £7000 from the Student Loans Company after securing a place on a degree at Salford University in October 2015. An investigation by the European Commission estimated that Abedi had received up to $18,000 in student loans and other benefit payments.[228] The Student Loan Company paid £1000 in to Abedi's account at the start of January 2017 and a further £2258 at the end of that month. The money from the student loan was withdrawn in regular amounts of up to £300.[229] It is interesting to note that Abedi continued to receive funds from the Student Loan Company even though he had stopped attending classes at Salford University.[230] The Money Laundering Regulations do not apply to higher education institutions (HEIs), and they are under no legal obligation to report any suspicions of fraud or terrorism financing to the NCA.[231] The obligations only apply to the regulated sector.[232] As such, HEIs would not fall within this definition. Could HEIs be regarded as a High-Value Dealer for the reporting obligations to apply? The term is defined as 'a firm or sole trader who by way of business trades in goods ... when the trader makes or receives, in respect of any transaction, a payment or payments in cash of at least 10,000 euros in

[225] The Money Laundering, Terrorist Financing and Transfer of Funds (Information on the Payer) Regulations 2017, SI 2017/692, Rgulation 50 and 52.

[226] Ibid, Regulation 50(3).

[227] Mendick (2017).

[228] European Commission (2017), p. 48.

[229] Stubley (2020).

[230] European Commission (2017).

[231] Ryder et al. (2022).

[232] The Money Laundering, Terrorist Financing Transfer of Funds (Information on the Payer) Regulations 2017, SI 2017/692, Regulation 8(2).

total'.[233] A survey of the application of the reporting obligations to the HEIs noted that only 2 out of 110 respondents considered themselves to be high value dealers.[234] Therefore, the uncertainty surrounding the application of the reporting obligations to HEI illustrates further weaknesses in the use of DATF SARs highlighted by the typology.

3.3 *London Bridge June 32,017*

One June 32,017, Khuram Butt, Rachid Redouane and Youssef Zaghba used a van to knockdown several pedestrians on London Bridge before continuing their terrorist attack on foot (Intelligence and Security Committee, 2018). In total, eight people were killed and 48 were injured. The terrorist attacks in London in June 2017, illustrates deficiencies in the use of DATF SARs and the reporting obligations.[235] Here, one of the terrorists, Khuram Butt, was investigated and arrested on suspicion of falsely reporting fraudulent activity (£3300),[236] on three bank accounts in October 2016.[237] It was alleged that Butt had been making 'unauthorised withdrawals from his accounts, with Santander, and then pocketing the refunds'.[238] Indeed, in preparation for the terrorist attack, Butt emptied his two other bank accounts (Nationwide and Lloyds) and had successfully applied for two loans (totalling £14,000).[239] After his arrest, Butt was granted bail and the fraud charges were eventually dropped due to insufficient evidence.[240] The Intelligence and Services Committee (ISC) stated that 'during Butt's arrest ... counter-terrorism police had discovered files that it considered "may be successfully used in a prosecution under the Terrorism Act"; however ... the issue was not explored further'.[241] The ISC noted that 'in July 2016, there was a potential disruption opportunity presented by Butt's suspected engagement in bank fraud, and counter terrorist police arrested Butt in October 2016. However, by June 2017 it was decided that no further action (against Butt) could be taken, due to a lack of evidence'.[242] Similarly, Anderson noted that "while under investigation by MI5, Khuram Butt was arrested for fraud in October 2016 and granted bail. He had not yet been told by 3 June 2017, the date of the attack that on

[233] Ibid, Regulation 14.

[234] Ryder et al. (2022).

[235] Anderson (2017), p. 1.

[236] White (2019).

[237] Intelligence and Security Committee (2018), p. 85.

[238] London Bridge Inquests (2019).

[239] Ibid, pp. 42, 43, 66 and 67.

[240] London Bridge Inquests (2019), p. 41.

[241] Ibid.

[242] Intelligence and Security Committee (2018), p. 85.

1 June the decision had been taken not to prosecute him'.[243] Here, Santander was under no legal obligation to submit a DATF SAR to the NCA.[244] Therefore, the reporting obligations, are unable to prevent the terrorism financing threat as identified by the typology. Clearly, the reporting obligations are unsatisfactory.

4 Conclusions and Recommendations

The spate of terrorist attacks before the Covid-19 pandemic had two common themes: low capability weapons and micro financing. How these terrorist attacks are financed is a question that is extremely difficult to answer. However, what we have learned is that some of these terrorist attacks have been financed by fraud and this research has identified a terrorism financing dossier, a black book or fraud typology. Frequently used methods within Europe are benefit fraud (Belgium, Finland, Norway, Sweden, Denmark and the UK), credit card/personal loan/bank fraud (US and the UK) and NPO fraud (US, UK and Spain) and tax fraud (US, UK and Spain). It is difficult to determine which fraud within the typology is the most frequently used, which frauds are on the decline or one which are becoming more popular. What is not in doubt is that fraud continues to be used to fund support terrorist groups. The UK's policy towards terrorism financing has been described as the best in the world,[245] yet it is broken, and it has been hindered by a number of missed opportunities. Despite the plethora of reporting obligations, there is a clear disparity between reporting fraud and terrorism financing. Critically, this chapter has identified a number of loopholes that have been exploited by terrorism financiers, the loopholes have not been closed. The reporting obligations are mistakenly treated in isolation.

This chapter reaches a number of important conclusions. Firstly, the existing fraud typologies are victim centric and only a minority have focused on the association between terrorism financing and fraud. The typologies have formulated their findings and conclusions on a few limited secondary sources. This chapter adds to this literature by providing a more detailed and authoritative typology that is based on decided cases from multiple jurisdictions. Secondly, the ability of terrorism financiers to attract funding from fraud, has been identified by HMG and there have been several attempts to improve the reporting requirements.[246] For example, the Fraud Review, recommended that businesses and individuals could report fraud to the National Fraud Reporting Centre (NFRC).[247] This recommendation resulted in the creation of the National Fraud Intelligence Bureau (NFIB), an agency

[243] Anderson (2017), p. 17.

[244] Goldstraw-White and Gill (2021).

[245] Financial Action Task Force (2018b).

[246] Attorney General's Office (2006), p. 74.

[247] Ibid.

dedicated to analysing and assessing fraud with the aid of analysts from both LEAs and the private sector.[248] The NFIB was managed by the City of London Police as part of its role as the National Lead Force for fraud and was funded by the Home Office. The NFRC 'became established as Action Fraud run by the City of London Police'.[249] These measures have been described as 'an impressive list of strategic aims: tackling the key threats of fraud that pose the greatest harm to the UK'.[250] However, the Home Affairs Select Committee concluded that:

> 'Action Fraud has irretrievably lost the confidence of the public, and reasonable expectations from victims are not being met. It is sensible to have a centralised reporting facility for fraud, but this must not simply become a way to divert and fob off victims of crime. Most importantly, it must be accompanied by a proper system to investigate crimes and respond to victims, or it will become irrelevant'.[251]

Subsequently, Action Fraud was abolished following a 2019 investigation by *The Times* which illustrated how the organisation's staff were trained to mislead victims of fraud that their cases were being investigated.[252] The Times reported that fewer than two percent of reports submitted resulted in an arrest and fewer than one percent of police officers were assigned to fraud investigations. Consequently, the Home Office commissioned a review of how fraud is policed in the UK by Sir Craig Mackey, which agreed with the findings of *The Times* and concluded that the police are not adequately prepared to tackle fraud.[253] As a result, HMG announced in July 2021 that Action Fraud was to be abolished and placed within the NCA in 2024.[254] However, the decision to place fraud within the NCA is questionable because it has been described as 'incompetent' and 'negligent'.[255] It has also been criticised for failing to investigate reports relating to banks forged signatures in court action to repossess properties and[256] it 'does not have dedicated fraud investigation teams but will allocate resources to investigate complex frauds on a case-by-case basis'.[257] Fraud is not a police priority, many victims do not report fraud. So even when reports are taken, little is done with them. As a result, 'fraud is massively underreported'.[258] In July 2021, HM Government published its 'Beating Crime Plan' which outlined how it intended to tackle fraud.[259] Here, HMG noted 'the threat post by fraud to our economy and the public is one we are determined to address, working with the public

---

248 Attorney General's Office (2006), p. 10.

249 Palmer (2018), p. 46.

250 Rider (2009).

251 Home Affairs Select Committee (2018), para. 50.

252 Morgan-Bentley (2021).

253 Mackey and Savil (2020).

254 HM Government (2021), p. 2.

255 Syal (2014).

256 HM Inspectorate of Constabulary and Fire and Rescue Services (2019a).

257 HM Inspectorate of Constabulary and Fire and Rescue Services (2019b).

258 Attorney General's Office (2006), p. 2.

259 HM Government (2021), p. 2.

and industry to prevent the crime and by disrupting, pursuing and brining to justice the most harmful'.[260] In March 2023, HM Government published its Fraud Strategy 'Stopping Scams and Protecting the Public',[261] which contains a number 'key actions' aimed at addressing the threat presented by fraud. This includes, *inter alia*, creating a National Fraud Squad, replacing Action Fraud, appointing an Anti-Fraud Champion, providing more support and reimbursing the victims of fraud. The Fraud Strategy repeats the findings of previous HM Government publications and recognises the threat presented by fraud and terrorism but fails to make *any* specific recommendations aimed at addressing the threat presenting by the terrorism financing typology. Thirdly, there are inherent flaws in the UK's ability to obtain and exchange information to detect fraud and terrorism financing. In light of this assessment, the following recommendations for reform are put forward. Firstly, the reporting of fraud should become mandatory placing it on the same legislative footing as money laundering and terrorist financing.[262] Therefore, to reduce the risks presented by the typology and close the loopholes, the Fraud Act 2006 could be amended to include a failure to disclose offence based on money laundering and terrorism financing.[263] The offence would be committed under the Fraud Act 2006 for failing to report a suspected fraud where a person 'receives information in the course of a business in the regulated sector ... thereby knows or suspects or has reasonable grounds for knowing or suspecting that another person is engaged in fraud' and 'fails to disclose a nominated officer, or person authorised for by the Director of NCA, the information on which his knowledge or suspicion is based as soon as is practicable after the information comes to him'. These amendments would provide clarity and certainty regarding the nature and extent of the reporting obligations. There are advantages to adopting this approach will lead to an enhanced understanding of fraud, and it will result in better intelligence for the policing fraud. Furthermore, this amendment could address the faults in reporting of fraud as illustrated by the three terrorist attacks above. However, if the reporting of fraud does become mandatory, it will lead to an increased administrative and financial burden on reporting entities. HM Treasury announced that it would provide an £18 million (2022–2023) with an additional £12 million (2023–2024) to tackle money laundering and fraud.[264] This funding is further supported by the Economic Crime Levy,[265] which is expected to contribute £100 million per year.[266] The impact of the Economic Crime Levy is debatable, because it contains no specific reference towards tackling fraud. Furthermore, the benefits of the additional funding on tackling fraud

---

[260] Ibid, p. 3.

[261] HM Government (2023)

[262] This approach has been adopted in South Africa, the Republic of Ireland and Scotland.

[263] See Proceeds of Crime Act 2002, s 330 and Terrorism Act 2000, s 19.

[264] HM Treasury (2021), p. 99.

[265] Economic Crime (Anti-Money Laundering) Levy Regulations 2022, SI 2022/26.

[266] The Economic Crime Levey is paid by reporting entitles who are subjected to the AML/CTF reporting obligations. See HM Revenue & Customs (2021).

has been questioned by Spotlight on Corruption who asserted that HMG only spends 0.042% of GDP, or £852 million, on tackling financial crime.[267] The All-Party Parliamentary Groups on Fair Business and Anti-Corruption and Responsible Tax concluded, 'LEAs are outspent and outgunned by criminals and the corrupt'.[268] Indeed, the House of Commons Treasury Committee noted, 'spending on economic crime needs to be sufficient to meet the challenge'.[269] HMG responded and stated 'we recognise the need for increased spending to tackle economic crime ... [we] have developed a sustainable funding model [totalling £400 million] that demonstrates our commitment to tackling economic crime'.[270] However, the amount of money equates to 0.2% of the extent of fraud of £190 billion.[271] In order to address this criticism, there are a number of mechanisms that could be introduced to soften the financial burden on reporting entities. Firstly, HM Treasury and the Home Office could resource and equip LEAs to tackle fraud by providing an additional £300 million. Secondly, the additional funding could form part of a cross-governmental Economic Crime Fighting Fund. Thirdly, a proportion of the financial crime penalties received by the FCA should be redistributed towards supporting the additional costs of mandatory reporting of fraud.[272]

References

ABC News (2015) US Intel: ISIS may have passport printing machine, blank passports (December 10), available at https://abcnews.go.com/International/us-intel-isis-passport-printing-machine-blank-passports/story?id=35700681

ABC News (2016) ISIS has whole fake passport 'industry'. Official Says (January 25), available at https://abcnews.go.com/International/isis-fake-passport-industry-official/story?id=36505984

Acharya A (2009) Targeting terrorist financing – international cooperation and new regimes. Routledge, London

Aljazeera (2017) ISIL holds 11,100 blank Syrian passports: report. (September 10), available at https://www.aljazeera.com/news/2017/9/10/isil-holds-11100-blank-syrian-passports-report

All Parliamentary Group on Anti-Corruption & Responsible Tax (2009) Economic Crime Manifesto. All Parliamentary Group on Anti-Corruption & Responsible Tax, London

Anderson D (2013) Independent Reviewer: The Terrorism Acts in 2012 Report of the Independent Reviewer on the Operation of the terrorism Act 2000 and Part I of the Terrorism Act 2006. HM Government, London

Anderson D (2017) Attacks in London and Manchester March–June 2017 independent assessment of MI5 and police. HM Government, London

[267] Spotlight on Corruption (2022).

[268] All Parliamentary Group on Anti-Corruption & Responsible Tax (2009), p. 10.

[269] House of Commons Treasury Committee (2022), p. 71.

[270] House of Commons Treasury Committee (2021), pp. 5–6.

[271] National Crime Agency (n.d.).

[272] There is precedent for HM Treasury diverting funds from financial penalties received by the FCA. See HM Government (2016).

Association of British Insurers (2019) Detected insurance frauds in 2018 (August 28), available at https://www.abi.org.uk/news/news-articles/2019/08/detected-insurance-frauds-in-2018/

Association of British Insurers (n.d.) Fraud, Available at https://www.abi.org.uk/products-and-issues/topics-and-issues/fraud/#:~:text=In%202016%2C%20insurers%20detected%20125%2C000,across%20every%20type%20of%20insurance

Attorney General's Office (2006) Fraud review – final report. Attorney General's Office, London

BBC News (2008) Mortgage fraud is funding crime (March 5), available at http://news.bbc.co.uk/1/hi/business/7279043.stm

BBC News (2012) Four guilty of Danish plot over Muhammad cartoons (June 4), available at https://www.bbc.co.uk/news/world-europe-18321160

BBC News (2016) Paris attacks: Who were the attackers? (April 27), available at https://www.bbc.co.uk/news/world-europe-34832512

BBC News (2021) Zakiur Rehman Lakhvi, suspected Mumbai attack leader, jailed in Pakistan (January 8), available at https://www.bbc.co.uk/news/world-asia-55545519

Bernstein R (1994) Trade center bombers get prison terms of 240 years (May 25), available at https://www.nytimes.com/1994/05/25/nyregion/trade-center-bombers-get-prison-terms-of-240-years.html

Bilefsky D (2017) Danes fighting for ISIS were paid welfare benefits. Government Says (February 21), available at https://www.nytimes.com/2017/02/21/world/europe/danes-fighting-for-isis-were-paid-welfare-benefits-government-says.html

Button M, Lewis C, Tapley J (2014) Not a victimless crime: the impact of fraud on individual victims and their families. Secur J 27(1):36–54

Cannon D (2015) War through pharmaceuticals: how terrorist organizations are turning to counterfeit medicine to fund their illicit activity. Case West Reverse J Int Law 47:343–375

Chase A (2004) Legal mechanisms of the international community and the United States concerning state sponsored terrorism. Va J Int Law 45:41–138

Chazan D (2017) French jihadists regularly received welfare payments after joining Isil. Police reveal (October 26), available at https://www.telegraph.co.uk/news/2017/10/26/french-jihadists-regularly-received-welfare-payments-joining/

European Commission (2017) Study on an EU initiative for a restriction on payments in cash. European Commission, Brussels

European Parliament (2018) Special committee on financial crimes, tax evasion and tax avoidance Ordinary meeting - TAX3 PUBLIC HEARING Special committee on financial crimes, tax evasion and tax avoidance Special Committee on Terrorism Joint meeting – the use of tax frauds – including VAT or carousel fraud - to finance terrorism (June 28), available at https://multimedia.europarl.europa.eu/en/special-committee-on-financial-crimes-tax-evasion-and-tax-avoidance-ordinary-meeting-tax3-public-hea_20180628-0900-COMMITTEE-TAX3_vd

Europol (2017) European Union terrorism situation and trend report 2016. Europol, The Hague

Europol (n.d.) Forgery or administrative documents and trafficking therein, available at https://www.europol.europa.eu/crime-areas-and-trends/crime-areas/forgery-of-administrative-documents-and-trafficking-therein

Federal Bureau of Investigation (2002) Dennis M. Lormel Chief, Terrorist Financial Review Group, FBI, Before the Senate Judiciary Committee, Subcommittee on Technology, Terrorism, and Government Information (July 9), available at https://archives.fbi.gov/archives/news/testimony/the-fbis-support-of-the-identity-theft-penalty-enhancement-act

Federal Bureau of Investigation (2003) John S. Pistole, Assistant Director, Counterterrorism Division, FBI, Testimony Before the House Select Committee On Homeland Security (October 1), available at https://archives.fbi.gov/archives/news/testimony/fraudulent-identification-documents-and-the-implications-for-homeland-security

Federal Bureau of Investigation (2009) FBI—Operation 'Phish Phry' (October 7), available at FBI—Operation 'Phish Phry'

Federal Bureau of Investigation (2013) Man Sentenced to 10 Years in Federal Prison for Lying in Terrorism Investigation and False Claim Conspiracy (April 19), available at https://archives.fbi.

gov/archives/tampa/press-releases/2013/man-sentenced-to-10-years-in-federal-prison-for-lying-in-terrorism-investigation-and-false-claim-conspiracy

Federal Bureau of Investigation (2018) North Carolina man sentenced for immigration fraud and tax charges (August 8), available at https://www.justice.gov/usao-ednc/pr/north-carolina-man-sentenced-immigration-fraud-and-tax-charges

Federal Bureau of Investigation (n.d.) Famous cases by category, World Trade Center Bombing 1993, FBI 100 - First Strike - Global Terror in America. Federal Bureau of Investigation, Washington DC

Federal Research Division Library of Congress (2002) A global overview of narcotics-funded terrorist and other extremist groups. Library of Congress, Washington DC

Financial Action Task Force (2006) Trade based money laundering. Financial Action Task Force, Paris

Financial Action Task Force (2007) Money laundering and terrorist financing through the real estate sector. Financial Action Task Force, Paris

Financial Action Task Force (2009a) Money laundering and terrorist financing in the securities sector. Financial Action Task Force, Paris

Financial Action Task Force (2009b) Terrorist financing. Financial Action Task Force, Paris

Financial Action Task Force (2011) Organised Maritime Piracy and Related Kidnapping for Ransom. Financial Action Task Force, Paris

Financial Action Task Force (2013a) Money laundering and terrorist financing related to counterfeiting of currency. Financial Action Task Force, Paris

Financial Action Task Force (2013b) The role of Hawala and other similar service providers in money laundering and terrorist financing. Financial Action Task Force, Paris

Financial Action Task Force (2014) Risk of terrorist abuse in non-profit organisations. Financial Action Task Force, Paris

Financial Action Task Force (2015a) Emerging terrorist financing risk. Financial Action Task Force, Paris

Financial Action Task Force (2015b) Financing of the terrorist organisation Islamic State in Iraq and the Levant. Financial Action Task Force, Paris

Financial Action Task Force (2017) Private sector information sharing. Financial Action Task Force, Paris

Financial Action Task Force (2018a) Anti-money laundering and counter-terrorist financing measures United Kingdom Mutual Evaluation Report. Financial Action Task Force, Paris

Financial Action Task Force (2018b) Financing of recruitment for terrorist purposes. Financial Action Task Force, Paris

Financial Action Task Force (2019) Virtual assets and virtual asset service providers. Financial Action Task Force, Paris

Financial Action Task Force (2020a) COVID-19-related money laundering and terrorist financing risks and policy responses may. Financial Action Task Force, Paris

Financial Action Task Force (2020b) Trade-based money laundering trends and developments. Financial Action Task Force, Paris

Financial Action Task Force (2021) Ethnically or racially motivated terrorism financing. Financial Action Task Force, Paris

Financial Action Task Force (2022) International standards on combating money laundering and the financing of terrorism & proliferation. Financial Action Task Force, Paris

Financial Conduct Authority (2012) FCA fines Santander UK £107.7 million for repeated anti-money laundering failures (December 9), available from FCA fines Santander UK £107.7 million for repeated anti-money laundering failures | FCA

Financial Conduct Authority (2017) FCA fines Deutsche Bank £163 million for serious anti-money laundering controls failings (January 1), available from https://www.fca.org.uk/news/press-releases/fca-fines-deutsche-bank-163-million-anti-money-laundering-controls-failure

Financial Conduct Authority (2018) Office for professional body anti-money laundering supervision (OPBAS) (January 23), available from Office for Professional Body Anti-Money Laundering Supervision (OPBAS) | FCA

Financial Conduct Authority (2021a) FCA fines HSBC Bank plc £63.9 million for deficient transaction monitoring controls (December 17), available from https://www.fca.org.uk/news/press-releases/fca-fines-hsbc-bank-plc-deficient-transaction-monitoring-controls

Financial Conduct Authority (2021b) NatWest fined £264.8 million for anti-money laundering failures(December 13), available from https://www.fca.org.uk/news/press-releases/natwest-fined-264.8million-anti-money-laundering-failures#:~:text=NatWest%20failed%20to%20comply%20with,money%20laundering%20and%20terrorist%20financing

Financial Conduct Authority (2023a) FCA fines Guaranty Trust Bank (UK) Limited £7.6 million for further failures in its anti-money laundering systems and controls (January 10), available from FCA fines Guaranty Trust Bank (UK) Limited £7.6 million for further failures in its anti-money laundering systems and controls | FCA

Financial Conduct Authority (2023b) FCA penalises Al Rayan Bank PLC for anti-money laundering failures (January 11), available from FCA penalises Al Rayan Bank PLC for anti-money laundering failures | FCA

Flannagan J (2022) ISIS fund terror with Tinder love scams, (November 14), available at Isis funds terror with 'Tinder' love scams (thetimes.co.uk)

Freeman M (2011) The sources of terrorist financing: theory and typology. Stud Conflict Terrorism 34(6):461–475

Gardham D (2016) The 'man in the hat' spills terror gang's secrets (December 7), available from https://www.nbcnews.com/storyline/brussels-attacks/man-hat-spills-terror-gang-s-secrets-n693046

Goldbarsht D (2024) Dancing in the dark: terrorist financing via the dark web. In: Goldbarsht D, de Koker L (eds) Financial crime and the law: identifying and mitigating risks. Springer. Chapter 7

Goldstraw-White J, Gill M (2021) The mandatory reporting of fraud: finding solutions and sharing best practice. Fraud Advisory Panel, London

Harper T (2019) Taxman kept quiet while £8bn fraud helped fund Osama bin Laden (March 30), available at https://www.thetimes.co.uk/article/taxman-kept-quiet-while-8bn-fraud-helped-fund-bin-laden-gmvj0b7gs

Harper T, Macaskill M (2019) Glaswegian in £300m Fraud Linked to Bin Laden (April 14), available from https://www.thetimes.co.uk/article/glaswegian-in-300m-fraud-linked-to-bin-laden-x707d09pk?region=global

Harvey S, Kerr J, Keeble J, Nicholls C (2014) Understanding victims of financial crime A qualitative study with people affected by investment fraud. Financial Conduct Authority, London

Hawramy F, Greenwood P, Dominic M, Kingsley P (2015) How easy is it to buy a fake Syrian passport? (November 17), available at https://www.theguardian.com/world/2015/nov/17/how-easy-is-it-to-buy-fake-syrian-passport

Herridge C (2020) ISIS accused of selling fake PPE online to finance terrorism (August 13), available at https://www.cbsnews.com/news/isis-accused-of-selling-fake-ppe-online-to-finance-terrorism/

Hinnen T (2004) The cyber-front in the war on terrorism: Curbing terrorist use of the internet. Colum Sci Technol Law Rev 12:105

HM Government (2015) UK national risk assessment of money laundering and terrorist financing. HM Government, London

HM Government (2016) LIBOR fines to be used to support military charities and Royal Voluntary Service (July 12), available from LIBOR fines to be used to support military charities and Royal Voluntary Service - GOV.UK (www.gov.uk)

HM Government (2020a) HMRC Coronavirus (COVID-19) statistics, available from HMRC coronavirus (COVID-19) statistics - GOV.UK (www.gov.uk)

HM Government (2020b) The Chancellor Rishi Sunak provides an updated statement on coronavirus (March 20), available from The Chancellor Rishi Sunak provides an updated statement on coronavirus. - GOV.UK (www.gov.uk)

HM Government (2021) Beating crime plan – fewer victims, peaceful neighbourhoods, safe country. HM Government, London

HM Government (2023) Fraud review – stopping scams and protecting the public. HM Government, London

HM Inspectorate of Constabulary and Fire and Rescue Services (2019a) Fraud: time to choose an inspection of the police response to fraud. HM Inspectorate of Constabulary and Fire and Rescue Services, London

HM Inspectorate of Constabulary and Fire and Rescue Services (2019b) National Crime Agency inspection: an inspection of the national crime agency's relationship with regional organised crime units. HM Inspectorate of Constabulary and Fire and Rescue Services, London

HM Revenue & Customs (2021) Policy paper – Economic Crime (Anti-Money Laundering) Levy (October 27), available from https://www.gov.uk/government/publications/economic-crime-anti-money-laundering-levy/economic-crime-anti-money-laundering-levy

HM Revenue and Customs (2022) Corporate report – HMRC economic crime supervision annual assessment report: 1 April 2021 to 31 March 2022 (October 6), available from HMRC economic crime supervision annual assessment report: 1 April 2021 to 31 March 2022 - GOV.UK (www.gov.uk)

HM Treasury (2021) Autumn budget and spending review 2021: a stronger economy for the British People. HM Treasury, London

Home Affairs Select Committee (2018) Policing for the future report. Home Affairs Select Committee, London

Home Office (2004a) Home office circular 47/2004 priorities for the investigation of fraud cases. Home Office, London

Home Office (2004b) Report on the operation in 2004 of the Terrorism Act 2000. Home Office, London

Home Office (2023) The strategic policing requirement. Home Office, London

Home Office (n.d.) The scale and nature of fraud: a review of the evidence. Home Office, London

Home Office and HM Treasury (2016) Action plan for anti-money laundering and counter-terrorist finance. Home Office and HM Treasury, London

Horgan M, Taylor M (1999) Playing the 'Green Card' - financing the provisional IRA: Part 1. Terror Polit Viol 11(2):1–38

Horgan J, Taylor M (2003) Playing the 'green card' – financing the provisional IRA: part 2. Terror Polit Viol 15(2):1–60

House of Commons Treasury Committee (2020) Economic impact of coronavirus: Gaps in support. House of Commons Treasury Committee, London

House of Commons Treasury Committee (2021) Economic crime: responses to the Committee's Eleventh Report Eighth Special Report of Session 2021–22 Ordered by the House of Commons. House of Commons Treasury Committee, London

House of Commons Treasury Committee (2022) Economic Crime. House of Commons Treasury Committee, London

House of Lords European Union Committee (2009) Money laundering and the financing of terrorism. House of Lords, London

Hymas C (2023) Fraud set to be upgraded as a threat to national security (February 4), available from Fraud set to be upgraded as a threat to national security (telegraph.co.uk)

Intellectual Property Office (2020) IPO counterfeit good research (September 2), available at https://www.gov.uk/government/publications/ipo-counterfeit-goods-research/ipo-counterfeit-goods-research

Intelligence and Security Committee (2006) Report into the London Terrorist Attacks on 7 July 2005. Intelligence and Security Committee, London

Intelligence and Security Committee (2018) The 2017 attacks: what needs to change? Westminster, Manchester Arena, London Bridge, Finsbury Park, Parsons Green. Intelligence and Security Committee, London

Irwin A, Choo K, Liu L (2012) An analysis of money laundering and terrorism financing typologies. J Money Laund Control 15(1):85–111

Jacobson M (2010) Terrorist financing and the Internet. Stud Conflict Terrorism 33(4):353–363

Jolly J, Sinmaz E (2023) UK barber jailed after sending Islamic State thousands of pounds from Covid grants (January 5), available from UK barber jailed after sending Islamic State thousands of pounds from Covid grants | UK news | The Guardian

Kaiafa-Gbandi M (2019) Information exchange for the purpose of crime control: the EU paradigm for controlling terrorism – challenges of an "open" system for collecting and exchanging personal data European. Crim Law Rev 9(2):141

Kane J, Wall A (2005) Identifying the links between white-collar crime and terrorism. United States Department of Justice, Washington DC

KPMG (2003) Money laundering: review of the reporting system. KPMG, London

KPMG (2014) Global anti-money laundering survey. KPMG, London

Law Commission (2018) Anti-money laundering: the SARs regime consultation paper. Law Commission, London

Law Commission (2019) Anti-money laundering: the SARs regime. Law Commission, London

Leong A (2006) Chasing dirty money: domestic and international measures against money laundering. J Money Laund Control 10(2):140–156

Levi M (2008) Organized frauds and organising frauds: unpacking the research on networks and organisation. Criminol Crim Just 8:389–419

LexisNexis Risk Solutions (2021) Cutting the costs of AML compliance. LexisNexis Risk Solutions, London

London Bridge Inquests (2019) Inquests concerning the attackers Day 6A (July 9), available from https://londonbridgeinquests.independent.gov.uk/wp-content/uploads/2019/07/LBI-Day-6A.pdf

Mackey C, Savil J (2020) Fraud: a review of the national 'lead force' responsibilities of the City of London Police and the effectiveness of investigations in the UK. City of London, London

Maremont M, Pop V (2016) Terrorist suspects in Europe got welfare benefits while plotting attacks (August 4), available from https://www.wsj.com/articles/terrorist-suspects-in-europe-got-welfare-benefits-while-plotting-attacks-1470350251

Masters J (2013) Al-shabab (September 23), available from www.cfr.org/somalia/al-shabab/p18650

Mendick R (2017) Exclusive: Manchester suicide bomber used student loan and benefits to fund terror plot (May 27), available at https://www.telegraph.co.uk/news/2017/05/26/exclusive-manchester-suicide-bomber-used-student-loan-benefits/

Michaelsen C (2010) The Security Council's Al Qaeda and Taliban Sanctions Regime: "essential tool" or increasing liability for the UN's counterterrorism efforts? Stud Confl Terror 33(5): 448–463

Morgan-Bentley M (2021) Action fraud scrapped after time expose (July 28), available from https://www.thetimes.co.uk/article/fraud-line-scrapped-after-times-expose-n2tlkbmrv

Mortgage Strategy (2008) Mortgage fraud is funding terrorism (May 14), available at https://www.mortgagestrategy.co.uk/news/mortgage-expo-2008-mortgage-fraud-is-funding-terrorism/

National Audit Office (2022) Delivery of employment support schemes in response to the Covid-19 pandemic. National Audit Office, London

National Commission on Terrorist Attacks (2004) The 9/11 Commission report--final report of the National Commission on Terrorist Attacks upon the United States. Norton & Company, Washington DC

National Crime Agency (2023) SARs Annual Report 2022. National Crime Agency, London

National Crime Agency (n.d.) Fraud, available at https://www.nationalcrimeagency.gov.uk/what-we-do/crime-threats/fraud-and-economic-crime

Norwegian Defence Research Establishment (2015) The financing of jihadi terrorist cells in Europe. Kjeller, Norwegian Defence Research Establishment

Office of the United States Attorney's (2008) Money remitter pleads guilty to money laundering conspiracy and concealing terrorist financing (August 22), available at https://www.justice.gov/archive/usao/md/news/archive/MoneyRemitterPleadsGuiltytoMoneyLaunderingConspiracyandConcealingTerroristFinancing.html

OLG Düsseldorf, Urteil vom 5. Dezember 2007 – III/IV 10/05 – nicht veröffentlicht (ie not published) and BGH (Bundesgerichtshof): BGH, Urteil vom 14. August 2009 - 3 StR 552/08

Omoigui N (2022) Furlough fraud cost HMRC £100m (August 22), available from HR Magazine - Furlough fraud cost HMRC £100 million

Organisation for Economic Co-operation and Development (2021) Ten global principles in fighting tax crime. Organisation for Economic Co-operation and Development, Paris

Organisation for Economic Co-operation and Development (n.d.) Who we are, available from https://www.oecd.org/about

Palmer A (2018) Countering economic crime: a comparative analysis. Routledge, London

Perri F, Brody R (2011) The dark triad: organized crime, terror and fraud. J Money Laund Control 14(1):44–59

Public Accounts Committee (2020) Oral evidence tackling the tax gap, HC 650 (7 September), Qs 11–13, available from Unrevised (parliament.uk)

RAC (n.d.) Car insurance scams and fraud, available at https://www.rac.co.uk/drive/advice/legal/car-insurance-scams-and-frauds/

Reeve S (1999) The New Jackals: Ramzi Yousef, Osama Bin Laden and the future of terrorism. Northeastern University Press, Boston

Rider BA (2009) Bold step? Company Lawyer 30(1):1

Ryder N (2015) The Financial War on Terror: a review of counter-terrorist financing strategies since 2001. Routledge, London

Ryder N, Bourton S, Hillman H, Hall D (2022) Higher education institutions and money laundering. Wales Fraud Forum Annual Conference, Cardiff

Sage A (2017) ISIS recruits got benefit cheques from France (October 27), available at https://www.thetimes.co.uk/article/isis-recruits-got-benefit-cheques-from-france-rf288kmbl

Sarker R (2006) Anti-money laundering requirements: too much pain for too little gain. Company Lawyer 27(8):250–251

Silke A (1998) In defense of the realm: financing loyalist terrorism in Northern Ireland—part one: extortion and blackmail. Stud Conflict Terrorism 21(4):331–361

Spotlight on Corruption (2022) Government spend equivalent of just 0.042% of GDP on fighting economic crime – new analysis (January 24) available from PRESS RELEASE: Government Spends Equivalent of Just 0.042% Of GDP on Fighting Economic Crime - New Analysis - Spotlight on Corruption (spotlightcorruption.org)

Stubley P (2020) Hashem Abedi Trial: benefits claimed by Manchester Bomber's family were used in terror plot jury hears. The Independent (February 10), available from https://www.independent.co.uk/news/uk/crime/manchester-arena-bombing-benefits-family-samia-abedi-hashem-trial-a9327816.html

Sturcke J (2007) Al-Qaida gets fake papers as Home Office issues 10,000 passports to fraudsters (March 20), available at https://www.theguardian.com/uk/2007/mar/20/terrorism.alqaida

Sullivan B, Chermaka S, Wilson J, Freilich J (2014) The nexus between terrorism and product counterfeiting in the United States. Global Crime 15(3–4):357–378

Swedish Companies Registration (2019) National risk assessment of money laundering and terrorist financing in Sweden. Swedish Companies Registration Office, Uppsala

Syal R (2014) Judge Criticises National Crime Agency over Collapse of Fraud Trial (December 2), available from https://www.theguardian.com/law/2014/dec/02/judge-criticises-national-crime-agency-fraud-trial

The Charity Commission (2016) Charity Commission today welcomes conviction of individual for terrorist offences (February 10), available at https://www.gov.uk/government/news/charity-commission-today-welcomes-conviction-of-individual-for-terrorist-offences

The Charity Commission (2017) Regulator publishes reports of cases involving individuals convicted of terrorism offences (October 16), available at https://www.gov.uk/government/news/regulator-publishes-reports-of-cases-involving-individuals-convicted-of-terrorism-offences

The Charity Commission (2018) Decision – Anatolia People's Cultural Centre (March 1), available at https://www.gov.uk/government/publications/charity-inquiry-anatolia-peoples-cultural-centre/anatolia-peoples-cultural-centre

The Local (2013) Suicide bomber lived off Swedish student aid (February 18), available at https://www.thelocal.se/20130218/46250

The National Fraud Authority (2009) Fraud typologies and victims of fraud literature review. National Fraud Authority, London

Thomas R, Ryder N (2011) Convenient credit and consumer protection – a critical review of the responses of labour and coalition government. J Soc Welf Fam Law 33(1):85–95

United Nations Office on Drugs and Crime (n.d.) Training manual for law enforcement agencies. United Nations Office on Drugs and Crime, New York

United States Department of Justice (2008) Former Officers of a Muslim Charity, Care International, Inc., Convicted (January 11), available at https://www.justice.gov/archive/opa/pr/2008/January/08_nsd_021.html

United States Department of Justice (2009) Federal judge hands down sentences in Holy Land Foundation Case (May 27), available at https://www.justice.gov/opa/pr/federal-judge-hands-downs-sentences-holy-land-foundation-case

United States Department of Justice (2013) Texas couple sentenced to prison for conspiracy to defraud the U.S. and to engage in money laundering (November 27), available at https://www.justice.gov/usao-or/pr/texas-couple-sentenced-prison-conspiracy-defraud-us-and-engage-money-laundering

United States Department of Justice (2015a) Texas man sentenced to 82 months in prison for attempting to travel to Syria to join ISIL (June 5), available at https://www.justice.gov/opa/pr/texas-man-sentenced-82-months-prison-attempting-travel-syria-join-isil

United States Department of Justice (2015b) Seven Minnesota men indicted for conspiracy to provide material support to the Islamic State of Iraq and the Levant (May 19), available at https://www.justice.gov/usao-mn/pr/seven-minnesota-men-indicted-conspiracyto-provide-material-support-islamic-state-iraq-and

United States Department of Justice (2016) ISIL-linked Kosovo hacker sentences to 20 years in prison (September 23), available at Office of Public Affairs | ISIL-Linked Kosovo Hacker Sentenced to 20 Years in Prison | United States Department of Justice

United States Department of Justice (2017a) Enrique Marquez Jr. agrees to plead guilty to plotting violent attacks and buying firearms for shooter in San Bernardino terrorist attack (February 14), available at https://www.justice.gov/usao-cdca/pr/enrique-marquez-jr-agrees-plead-guilty-plotting-violent-attacks-and-buying-firearms

United States Department of Justice (2017b) Justice Department Secures the Denaturalization of a Senior Jihadist Operative Who Was Convicted of Terrorism in Egypt (April 20), available at https://www.justice.gov/opa/pr/justice-department-secures-denaturalization-senior-jihadist-operative-who-was-convicted

United States Department of Justice (2019) Saudi citizen sentenced to more than 12 years in prison for concealing attendance at al Qaeda training camp and visa fraud (October 3), available at https://www.justice.gov/opa/pr/saudi-citizen-sentenced-more-12-years-prison-concealing-attendance-al-qaeda-training-camp-and

United States Department of State (2017) The global illicit trade in tobacco: a threat to national security. United States Department of State, Washington DC

United States Department of Treasury (2011) Treasury identifies Lebanese Canadian Bank Sal as a "Primary Money Laundering Concern" (February 2), available at https://www.treasury.gov/press-center/press-releases/Pages/tg1057.aspx

United States Department of Treasury (2020) Treasury underscores commitment to global flow of humanitarian aims in face of Covid-19 pandemic (April 9), available from Treasury Underscores Commitment to Global Flow of Humanitarian Aid in Face of COVID-19 Pandemic | U.-S. Department of the Treasury

United States Immigration and Customs Enforcement (2011) Mohamad Youssef Hammoud sentenced to 30 years in terrorism financing case (January 27), available at https://www.ice.gov/news/releases/mohamad-youssef-hammoud-sentenced-30-years-terrorism-financing-case

United States Justice Department (2016a) Nine twin cities men sentenced for providing material support to ISIL (November 16), available at https://www.justice.gov/usao-mn/pr/nine-twin-cities-men-sentenced-providing-material-support-isil

United States Justice Department (2016b) Two orange county men convicted of conspiring to join ISIL; they also engaged in fraud to finance one's trip to Syria (June 21), available at https://www.justice.gov/usao-cdca/pr/two-orange-county-men-convicted-conspiring-join-isil-they-also-engaged-fraud-finance

United States Treasury Department (2002) Treasury department statement regarding the designation of the global relief foundation (18 October), available at https://www.treasury.gov/press-center/press-releases/Pages/po3553.aspx

United States Treasury Department (2003) 2003 money laundering strategy. United States Treasury Department, Washington DC

United States Treasury Department (2004) Treasury designates Global Network, Senior Officials of the IARA for Supporting bin Laden, Others (October 13), available at https://www.treasury.gov/press-center/press-releases/Pages/js2025.aspx

United States Treasury Department (2014) Treasury designates three key supporters of terrorists in Syria and Iraq (August 6), available at www.treasury.gov/press-center/press-releases/Pages/jl2605.aspx

United States Treasury Department (2022) Treasury designates Benevolence International Foundation and Related Entitles as Financiers of Terrorism (19 November), available at https://www.treasury.gov/press-center/press-releases/Pages/po3632.aspx

Unknown Author (2015) How to survive in the west: a Mujahid guide. Unknown Publisher

Unknown Author (2016) Trade-based money laundering: overview and policy issues. Congressional Library Research, Washington DC

Unknown Author (n.d.) Encyclopaedia of the Afghani Jihad. Unknown Publisher

US Treasury Department Office of Terrorism and Financial Intelligence (2006) US Department of Treasury fact sheet. US Department of Treasury, Washington DC

Vidino L, Lewis L, Mines A (2020) Dollars for Daesh analyzing the finances of American ISIS supporters. George Washington University, Washington DC

Vittori J (2011) Terrorist financing and resourcing. Palgrave Macmillan, London

Whitcomb D, McAllister E (2015) California shooters borrowed £28,000 before attack: source (December 9), available at https://www.reuters.com/article/us-california-shooting-account-idUSKBN0TR27P20151209

White M (2019) London bridge attack: MI5 accused of "damning list" of failures (June 28), available from https://news.sky.com/story/london-bridge-attack-mi5-accused-of-damning-list-of-failures-11750204

Williams S (2019) £80m of British taxpayers' money 'funnelled to al-Qaeda' in decades-long scam (March 31), available at https://www.telegraph.co.uk/news/2019/03/31/80m-british-taxpayers-money-funnelled-al-qaeda-decades-long/

Wood H, Keatinge T, Ditcham K, Janjeva A (2021) The silent threat: the impact of fraud on UK National Security. RUSI, London

Yeandle M, Mainelli M, Berendt A, Healy B (2005) Anti-money laundering requirements: costs, benefits and perceptions. Corporation of London, London

Young N (2013) Charity Commission condemns 'abhorrent' abuse of Muslim Aid by terror plotters (February 22), available at https://www.civilsociety.co.uk/news/charity-commission-condemns%2D%2Dabhorrent%2D%2Dabuse-of-muslim-aid-by-terror-plotters.html#sthash.C8yr4aEf.dpuf

Nicholas Ryder, with an international reputation for excellence in policy-oriented research in financial crime, Nic has played advisory roles both nationally (Home Office, Law Commission, the Nationwide, Transparency International) and internationally (NATO, United Nations and Cepol, Europol). Professor Ryder research has attracted funding from InnovateUK, Economic and Social Research Council the City of London Police Force and RUSI. Professor Ryder is the editor of the Law of Financial Crime Series and is the co-editor in chief of the Journal of Economic Criminology. Collectively, he has published 5 monographs, edited books and over 50 articles in internationally recognised journals including Legal Studies, the Cambridge Law Journal, the Journal of Business Law and the Criminal Law Review. Professor Ryder has also contributed towards two REF Impact Case Studies in 2014 and 2021.

Terror on the Blockchain: The Emergent Crypto-Crime-Terror Nexus

Ariel Burgess, Rhianna Hamilton, and Christian Leuprecht

Abstract Inadequate oversight and an inchoate appreciation are giving terrorist groups ready access to transboundary financial transfers by means of virtual currency. This chapter counters the prevailing approach that treats cryptocurrency-enabled crimes, such as terrorism, as monolithic. This chapter demonstrates that terrorist groups are using cryptocurrency and decentralized finance to fundraise and transfer funds in conjunction with the traditional financial system. Since actual case studies are few and data limited, this chapter is a proof of concept: it compares terrorist financing schemes by the Al-Qassam Brigades and Al Qaeda that used virtual assets. The comparison of virtual assets being used finds that standards developed and recommended by the Financial Action Task Force (FATF) are wholly inadequate to contain the proliferation of decentralized finance technology and centralized virtual assets as drivers of the global Illicit International Political Economy (IIPE). FATF recommendations are not sufficiently nuanced, nor are they effective at detecting, disrupting and deterring he nexus of crypto, crime and terror. To make matters worse, FATF members are falling short on implementing even FATF's inadequate standards. The chapter concludes that FATF needs to: clarify inclusion criteria under the current definition of virtual assets; broaden regulations, improve interagency collaboration, and formulate more nuanced recommendations

Open Access funding was made possible by the Human-Centric Cybersecurity Partnership, funded by the Social Sciences and Humanities Research Council of Canada, grant #895-2021-1007.

A. Burgess
Royal Military College of Canada, Kingston, ON, Canada

R. Hamilton
The University of Adelaide, Adelaide, Australia

C. Leuprecht (✉)
Royal Military College of Canada, Kingston, ON, Canada

Queen's University, Kingston, ON, Canada
e-mail: christian.leuprecht@rmc.ca

D. Goldbarsht, L. de Koker (eds.), *Financial Crime, Law and Governance*, Ius Gentium: Comparative Perspectives on Law and Justice 116,
https://doi.org/10.1007/978-3-031-59547-9_9

that are sensitive to crypto-enabled crimes across different criminal activities and criminogenic factors.

1 Introduction

As cases are prosecuted, and crypto wallets included on many sanctions' lists, new and more data is becoming available.

Virtual currencies have broad application in criminal contexts.

Terrorist groups raise money through myriad illicit networks, from state sponsors, transnational crime, and occupying territory to exercising the trappings of a crypto state, such as taxation.[1] This chapter focuses on the way terrorist organizations solicit donations through fraudulent charities which then use front companies to transmit and hide transactions.[2] Initially, scholars and policymakers were not overly concerned with crypto in terrorism.[3] Then the United Nations' Counter-Terrorism Committee Executive Directorate estimated that crypto and other digital assets financed 5 percent of terrorist attacks. That estimate has since risen to 20 percent. Terrorist groups have been shifting to cryptocurrency-based financing, in part because cryptocurrencies have increased viability in complementary and adjacent markets that terrorists frequent, including the darknet.[4] Yet, the co-optation of cryptocurrency by terrorist groups has received little scholarly attention compared to other crypto-enabled crimes.[5]

Virtual currency, and specifically Decentralized Finance (DeFi), are emerging as the new frontier in terrorist financing. According to congressional testimony by the U.S. Department of Homeland Security, "cryptocurrency has some appealing attributes that have already been exploited by terrorists, and we anticipate violent extremists will continue to use this tool to facilitate their terrorist activities, especially as the technology becomes easier to access and more wide-spread in use in general commerce and the commercial sector."[6] Enabling attributes include anonymity, decentralization, global reach, speed, non-repudiation, ease of use, low cost of use, the ability to upgrade anonymity and security, and the ability to move networks to new venues, taking advantage of the uneven development of cryptocurrency regulation between different countries.[7]

---

[1] Goldbarsht (2020), p. 32.

[2] Leuprecht et al. (2019).

[3] Shukla (2022).

[4] Dion-Schwarz et al. (2019); Goldbarsht (2024).

[5] OECD (2022).

[6] 117th United States Congress (2021).

[7] Brill and Keene (2014); Wang and Zhu (2021).

DeFi technology operates on peer-to-peer networks with more anonymity than crypto coins such as Bitcoin.[8] Crypto offers an alternative financial system of transboundary pseudonymous transactions for terrorists. DeFi harnesses the benefits of crypto while expanding anonymity. Compared to the traditional financial system, cryptocurrency is under-regulated and under-enforced: crypto coins are subject to far fewer counter-terrorist financing (CTF)[9] and anti-money laundering (AML) requirements than fiat currencies.[10] Alongside traditional mechanisms such wire transfers and cash, the virtual financial ecosystem is rapidly emerging as a key transnational funding mechanism for terrorism. Al-Qaeda, Jam'at al Tawhid wa'al-Jihad, and al-Nusrah Front have all received crypto through social media.[11] Their networks then laundered funds through layered transactions using crypto.[12]

DeFi makes accessible financial services such as borrowing, trading, and investing, without relying on banks or brokerages. DeFi is an extension of the traditional financial system insofar as it provides open source, interoperable smart contracts that exist on the blockchain, most often Ethereum. However, any form of DeFi that supports script or coding can develop DeFi protocols throughout their platforms. Examples of DeFi include non-fungible tokens (NFTs), altcoins such as Monero, and tokens.[13] Whereas banks are required to track and verify the identity of clients and their transactions, DeFi exchanges are only subject to these requirements when they are classified as Virtual Asset Service Providers (VASPs); but for jurisdictions to identify DeFi exchanges and classify them as such is proving difficult.[14] That makes DeFi vulnerable to being leveraged by terrorist groups to solicit and receive donations, use social media to share wallets IDs, and promptly move funds through exchanges or mixers. The result is a complex web that makes transactions nearly untraceable. DeFi thus heightens the risk of terrorist financing.[15]

Since the introduction of Bitcoin in 2009, cryptocurrency has gained in popularity as an alternative financial system. It has proven popular with illicit actors, especially transnational criminal networks. Cryptocurrency is premised on open access, decentralized finance independent of traditional political and economic institutions such as banks or federal reserves. Instead, cryptocurrency (also referred to as crypto or virtual currency) transactions are recorded on a public ledger accessible on the blockchain. Theoretically devoid of central authority, Bitcoin ushered in an alternative financial system. Other virtual currencies emerged alongside technological advances and social responses. Crypto has experienced numerous crashes, coins

[8] Hamilton and Leuprecht (2023).

[9] Siripurapu and Berman (2023).

[10] Leuprecht et al. (2019).

[11] United States Department of Justice (2020); Leuprecht (2020).

[12] United States v. 155 Virtual Currency Assets (2021); United States Department of Justice (2020).

[13] OECD (2022), p. 10.

[14] Ibid, p. 55; FATF (2023a), p. 29.

[15] Ibid.

have collapsed, many because of fraud allegations. Still, crypto has grown into a multibillion-dollar industry.

Concerns about a putative nexus between crime and terrorism are well known.[16] Yet, concerns about the role of virtual currency in terrorism previously seemed farfetched given the public ledger of the blockchain. Now, not only have terrorist groups begun leveraging cryptocurrency as a financing tool, but they are also integrating DeFi technology. DeFi and crypto markets overlap: many crypto coins are decentralized, non-custodial, community driven, and operate on distributed ledger technology (DLT).[17] However, this is not a given; many forms of cryptocurrency, such as coins that are backed by central banks as well as stablecoins, are centralized and operate with a degree of oversight. Mainstream coins such as Bitcoin are centralized and not DeFi. In fact, relative to total crypto assets, DeFi markets are small. Still, DeFi is quickly becoming integral, not only to the crypto-crime nexus, but especially to the crypto-terror nexus.

The chapter is driven by recommendations made by the Financial Action Task Force (FATF) to evaluate the current regulatory environment of cryptocurrency and DeFi. FATF has a mandate to develop a global CTF regime, in collaboration with committees of the European Union (EU) and United Nations (UN).[18] State jurisdictions and national financial intelligence units are then responsible for implementing the regime. Organizations such as FATF, the EU, and the UN have mandates to combat financial crime, particularly money laundering. Due to pressure to mobilize counter-terrorism efforts expeditiously post-9/11, CTF rules were grafted onto pre-existing regulations and legislation that had originally been developed as AML protocols. The resulting regulatory standard has effectively resulted in the same instrument being used to contain two types of crimes that are quite different in character.[19] But just how effective FATF's recommendations and regulations in compliant jurisdictions really are is up for debate.[20]

This research has three objectives: (1) To ascertain the conditions under which terrorist groups use cryptocurrency and/or DeFi to fund their activities. (2) To draw on the Al-Qaeda Joint Campaign and the Al-Qassam Brigades Campaign case studies to inform our understanding of cryptocurrency-enabled crime in the illicit international political economy (IIPE). (3) For findings to inform regulatory recommendations for domestic actors and FATF. The chapter's two case studies, review of the literature, and overview of the novel terrorism dataset on which it draws point to an emerging crypto-crime-terror nexus: terrorist organizations are using cryptocurrency to raise funds through criminal ventures. Under-regulation makes crypto and DeFi an attractive option for criminals and terrorists alike. This inference from our data and literature review leads us to conclude that current FATF standards

[16] Leuprecht et al. (2019).

[17] OECD (2022), p. 9.

[18] Leuprecht et al. (2019).

[19] Phillips (2004); Winer and Roule (2002).

[20] King et al. (2018).

on terrorist financing are inadequate given the scale of risk posed by virtual currencies and DeFi in financing terrorist groups, their activities, and attacks. FATF needs to include DeFi in updated guidance for Virtual Assets and Virtual Asset Providers (VASPs) to make the technology and degree of central authority verifiable. Unless standards are adapted, or new standards developed, that account for software, DeFi technologies will remain vulnerable to exploitation by bad actors.[21] To be sure, this will vary by blockchain, technology and jurisdiction. For FATF to offer no clear, specific, guidance on DeFi regulations amounts to a failure, and abdication of its mandate.

The chapter is organized accordingly. First, a section on materials and methods outlines the role of FATF in curtailing terrorist financing, reviews the literature, and introduces key methods and terms. Second, the chapter reviews the relationship between cryptocurrency and terrorist financing. Third, case studies of the Al-Qassam Brigades and Al Qaeda illustrate the role of cryptocurrency and DeFi in terrorist fundraising. The chapter concludes by assessing the relationship between virtual currency, DeFi, and financing terrorism.

Literature relevant to the role of cryptocurrency as a terrorist financing tool is limited, and public legal documents and data are scarce. This is true to an even greater extent for DeFi, which is almost entirely unaccounted for in the literature and policy discussions of crypto and crypto-enabled crime. This information failure is sanguine. First, cryptocurrency operates with minimal government oversight. As a result, information on crypto is not readily available at the same rate as government information on other types of financial transactions that underpin the economy. Research can thus play an outsized role in ascertaining the value and risk of cryptocurrency. Second, terrorist financing has significant implications: from harms to destruction of infrastructure and radicalization. Third, cryptocurrency is already being used at a scale to enable other crimes. Yet, FATF's recommendations do not differentiate among crypto nuances in enabling and perpetrating different crimes.[22]

2 Materials and Methods

2.1 Key Terms

This section reviews concepts that are key to understanding how cryptocurrency is leveraged to finance terrorism: Bitcoin, decentralized coins, centralized coins, fiat currency, altcoins, distributed ledger technology, decentralized finance (DeFi), crypto bridges, crypto mixers, and cryptocurrency exchanges.

[21] FATF (2023a), p. 29.

[22] Hamilton and Leuprecht (2023).

Bitcoin was the first cryptocurrency to market. It is created through a process called "mining", which requires solving a complex mathematical problem with an easily verifiable solution. Each Bitcoin has its own solution, and once the solution is found it is added to the blockchain, ensuring it cannot be "mined" again. This process is expensive and resource-intensive, requiring a lot of time, expensive computer hardware, and a lot of electricity.[23] Bitcoin is a fiduciary currency: once it is mined, it has no intrinsic value other than in exchange. Although the market price fluctuates regularly, the value of Bitcoin relative to fiat currencies is high.

Most cryptocurrencies are *decentralized coins,* including Bitcoin. Decentralized coins facilitate peer-to-peer transactions with limited oversight from a central authority such as a bank or government.[24] These currencies exist as a means of circumventing power structures inherent to centralized coin systems.

Decentralized finance is a sector of the financial system that was built on principles of being open source, near anonymous, financially inclusive, and separate from central authority. DeFi takes place on the blockchain, for example the Ethereum Blockchain. DeFi technology often does not require verification of identity, which makes crimes that involve DeFi coins or exchanges difficult to trace.[25] These transactions have some form of peer-to-peer transaction and often use smart contrast and self-executing codes to manage the blockchain.[26]

Centralized coins are owned or operated by a central authority with oversight. Unlike decentralized coins, centralized coin transactions must go through and operate within a central exchange monitored by an authority.[27]

Centralized coins include *fiat currencies*: monies that are created and regulated by a sovereign nation state (i.e., the US dollar). Fiat currencies can be converted into other fiat currencies, where their relative value is determined on foreign exchange markets.[28]

In a non-digital context, *altcoins* refer to currencies other than a given fiat currency. In cryptocurrency circles, the term altcoin encompasses all cryptocurrencies other than Bitcoin. Most altcoins use blockchain technology like that of Bitcoin and aim to improve on and complement Bitcoin features.[29]Altcoins are frequently used in conjunction with Bitcoin and fiat currencies to enable virtual money-laundering.[30]

Financial institutions use ledgers to ensure that the same money is not spent twice. In centralized networks, each institution tracks transactions of individual account holders on an internal ledger. Transactions between financial institutions

[23] Velde (2013).

[24] Clements (2022), p. 4.

[25] Kirimhan (2023), p. 1; Trozze et al. (2023), p. 1.

[26] United States Department of the Treasury (2023).

[27] Clements (2022), p. 6.

[28] Georgiou (2020), p. 121.

[29] Ciaian et al. (2018), p. 2.

[30] Jenkins et al. (2023).

are then validated by a central ledger. *Distributed ledger technology*, commonly referred to as blockchains, serves the same purpose in cryptocurrency networks. Blockchains are maintained by the cryptocurrency network and members can verify and validate each transaction. Once a consensus is achieved among the network, a transaction can be added to the blockchain. These ledgers are publicly available, permanent, and cannot be altered.[31]

Crypto bridges allow users to exchange cryptocurrency coins and assets between different blockchains, a process known as "chain hopping". Bridges are beneficial to criminals because they lack ID verification requirements and allow assets to be easily converted to other blockchains, allowing a large amount of liquidity to flow. These bridges often take place on blockchains smaller in scale with lower security testing and regulatory obligations. Beyond their risks to investors and users and involvement in crime, bridges are particularly susceptible to being hacked and losing funds. Bridge hacks surpassed $USD 1 billion in the first quarter of 2023. Bridges are targeted by criminals for their liquidity and high volume of throughflow.[32]

Crypto mixers allow individuals to warp the value of cryptocurrency assets and redistribute them. This process makes it more difficult to trace the movement of funds across public blockchains.[33]

Cryptocurrency exchanges function much like traditional currency exchanges. They provide opportunities for users to exchange crypto assets for other cryptocurrencies or for fiat currencies. These exchanges can be centralized in structure, or peer-to-peer. While some exchanges operate legally, other cryptocurrency exchanges specialize in cryptocurrency originating from or providing funding to illicit activities.[34]

2.2 *Illicit International Political Economy*

This chapter draws on recent work on money and crypto laundering, especially its role in the Illicit International Political Economy (IIPE). IIPE gauges political and economic variables of illicit transnational trade. As in the legal economy, distinct trends manifest across networks, geography, and flows of goods in IIPE, which focuses on globalization, financial flows, and the role of the state.[35] Past research on IIPE has focused on the role of digital currency;[36] the intersection between licit and illicit markets and policy;[37] and cross-border cooperation.[38] This chapter expands

[31] Haksar and Bouveret (2018).

[32] Annison (2023).

[33] Chainalysis (2022a).

[34] Chainalysis (2022b).

[35] Andreas (2004).

[36] Leuprecht et al. (2022); Jenkins et al. (2023).

[37] Legrand and Leuprecht (2021), p. 567.

[38] Leuprecht et al. (2021), p. 360.

this work by analyzing the use of virtual currency by terrorist groups, specifically the growing role of DeFi within the broader IIPE.

2.3 Literature Review

This chapter makes three contributions to the literature. First, it contributes to the research on cryptocurrency, DeFi, and terrorist financing. Second, it presents a proof-of-concept argument that terrorist organizations are actively integrating DeFi into their financing networks. It raises the issue of DeFi in the financial regulation of cryptocurrencies. Implications of this gap are the third contribution of the chapter. It contributes new data to scholarship on cryptocurrency and terrorist financing by drawing on case studies of crypto and DeFi in terrorist financing networks and identifying trends within these cases while situating them in the context of the crypto-crime nexus. In addition, this chapter contributes to novel research in the field of IIPE, notably crypto laundering and the role of DeFi within the IIPE.

Notwithstanding extant literature on terrorist financing in the traditional financial system, research on cryptocurrency and terrorist financing is still relatively new, and there is a significant gap in the literature on DeFi in general, and its use for criminal purposes in particular. Extant literature that discusses crypto terrorist financing is generally restricted to theory, with little supporting evidence. That scholarship has significant limitations. A large subset is specific to Bitcoin rather than cryptocurrency broadly, and discussion of terrorist entities is often restricted to the Middle East; right-wing extremism and other forms of terrorism are generally absent. The research that has been conducted flags cryptocurrency as an alternative financial system that is attractive to terrorists for the same reason it is popular with criminals: anonymity, decentralization, and globalized reach.[39] Cryptocurrency transactions are also irreversible and low-cost.[40] As a high-value commodity, it can be used to create venture capital, which matters to terrorist organizations that operate in regions that have weak financial infrastructure or domestic instability.[41] While plenty of crypto regulation has been developed in recent years, much of it has been achieved through adjustments to existing legal or regulatory frameworks developed for traditional financial systems. Some scholars have argued that the unique attributes of cryptocurrencies such as Bitcoin are not adequately covered by these existing frameworks, making it difficult to devise effective regulation.[42]

---

[39] Wang and Zhu (2021); Brill and Keene (2014); Dyntu and Dykyj (2021).

[40] Brill and Keene (2014).

[41] Baron et al. (2015).

[42] Fletcher et al. (2021), p. 13.

2.4 Methodology

This research is based on data on transnational crypto laundering and crypto-funded terrorist financing that was distilled from a larger original dataset on prosecutions of cases of transnational terrorist financing. The chapter analyzes observations in the context of the existing literature, synthesizes findings and identifies priority areas for future research and policy.

The dataset is comprised largely of terrorist financing prosecutions in rule-of-law jurisdictions: the United States, Canada, and Europe. The scope of transnational terrorist financing activities is thus limited to information collected and which the prosecution has opted to disclose. A funnelling effect thus limits the evidence presented in legal contexts and publicly available. These limitations are exacerbated by the pseudonymity and highly adaptable nature of cryptocurrencies used in terrorist financing contexts, which is compounded by cryptocurrency regulation and monitoring practices across global jurisdictions.

Notwithstanding evidentiary limitations, the chapter still makes an important contribution to advancing the understanding of the relationship between cryptocurrency and terrorism. The use of cryptocurrency in terrorist financing networks is postulated widely in the literature, but actual evidence is scant—in part, at least, due to a dearth in prosecutions of related offences. Hardly any literature exists on the intersection of terrorist financing and DeFi. The cases reviewed in this chapter are part of a dataset of 43 other cases of transnational terrorist financing. However, the two cases in this chapter are so different from the other cases that they warrant a discreet analysis. The coding instrument is comprised of variables such as investor identity and location, recipient identity and location, financial intermediary identification and location, banks, type of currency, value transferred, value raised, etc. Other legal documents, news sources, blogs, corporate reporting, and informal interviews are used to triangulate results and expand the number of data points.

3 FATF's Counterterrorism Recommendations

Countering terrorism became a priority for FATF after the terrorist attacks of 9/11 in 2001 in New York City, and was re-prioritized following 2015 when attacks around the world were attributed to the Islamic State (IS) and Al Quaeda.[43] FATF sets the global standard of CTF, AML, and counter-proliferation financing recommendations at the international and domestic levels and requires relevant risk assessments. It does not develop or implement regulations, and it does not formally define risks or set risk assessment standards. Rather, it develops standards and provides specific recommendations to inform the development of regulation by individual jurisdictions. FATF has published relevant reports on terrorist financing for decades,[44] but

[43] FATF (2021a).

[44] See FATF (2019, 2021a, b, 2023a).

with little attention to virtual currencies. Instead, FATF's recommendations are focused on traditional forms of terrorist financing, particularly in the Middle East and West Africa. A recent report on risk factors associated with Right Wing Extremism and terrorism is the exception. It observes that a recent decline in credit card access has incentivized some terrorist groups to use virtual assets, most notably Bitcoin.[45] These reports highlight the role of cash, foreign currencies, NGO's, recruitment, and risk assessment; virtual assets are conspicuously absent.

As the international watchdog for terrorist financing, proliferation financing, and money-laundering activities, FATF sets international standards in CTF, counter-proliferation financing, and AML regulation.[46] These standards are applicable to banks and other financial institutions, not individual behaviour. This can present a challenge in CTF and AML regulation, as these crimes are perpetrated by actors who fall outside of the scope of FATF standards. FATF is funded by 39 member countries and observed by over 20 organizations, including the United Nations. As both a policy diffusion body, FATF standards and mandates hold sway. Jurisdictions are expected to develop regulations in accordance with FATF recommendations and mandates. Jurisdictions with strategic deficiencies are placed on one of two lists.[47] The Black List is comprised of jurisdictions with serious strategic deficiencies. Other jurisdictions have been called upon to apply enhanced due diligence and, in some cases, apply countermeasures to reduce international risks stemming from illicit financial activities within blacklisted regions. Those on the Grey List have strategic deficiencies that they have committed to resolve and are under increased monitoring.[48]

FATF has been the most proactive international body in identifying and responding to the risks cryptocurrency poses as a terrorist financing tool. In 2018, it amended mandatory recommendation 15 by explicitly stating that it applied to financial activities involving cryptocurrency, and ensured cryptocurrencies were identified as subject to other mandatory recommendations by adding the terms "virtual asset" and "virtual asset service providers" to its definitions.[49] Virtual asset service providers (VASPs) are subject to the most stringent oversight—all jurisdictions of the FATF must establish VASP licencing or registration requirements, in addition to being subject to the same obligations as other financial intermediaries. These obligations include conducting customer due diligence and monitoring, recordkeeping, submissions of suspicious transaction reports, and screening of transactions and customers. VASPs are required to obtain, hold, and transmit originator and beneficiary information immediately when conducting virtual asset transactions. However, VASPs are only subject to oversight when they are

[45] FATF (2021a), p. 24.

[46] FATF (2023b).

[47] FATF has suspended membership of the Russian Federation, effective February 24, 2023. See FATF (2023c).

[48] FATF (2023d).

[49] Wagman (2022), pp. 93–94.

licenced and registered, and registration or licencing is not a requirement in many jurisdictions.[50] Virtual asset (VA) transfers over 1000 Euros trigger FATF cross-border customer due diligence requirements. This threshold is relatively low. FATF features a single report published in 2020 on virtual assets and terrorist financing, entitled *Virtual Assets Red Flag Indicators of Money Laundering and Terrorist Financing*. While the combined outputs of FATF's recommendations and requirements are a good step forward, implementation and enforcement vary widely across FATF jurisdictions,[51] which significantly limits the practical impact of these regulations. It is also hard to assess the success of these regulations. Although cryptocurrency has been identified as a means of terrorist financing, evaluating the extent of its use in terrorism financing is a challenge due to the difficulty in prosecuting crypto terrorist financing cases.

4 Cryptocurrency and Terrorist Financing

4.1 Overview: Cryptocurrency and Terrorist Financing

Terrorist financing refers the process by which terrorists accumulate funds. Often the funds used to finance terrorism originate from legitimate sources, but enable illicit activities.[52] Terrorist financing networks often appear "remarkably ordinary", with small amounts being moved through legitimate channels such as bank transfers, cash, and other money services providers.[53] Those involved in terrorist financing networks may be guilty of additional crimes such as offshore tax evasion and international money laundering, depending on how funds are reported and transported across borders. Terrorists also use illicit means of generating resources, ranging from petty theft and money laundering to kidnapping and extortion.[54] Terrorist financing is consequential, contributing to geopolitical risks, regional instability, impaired economic development, and instability of financial markets in affected regions.[55]

The introduction of cryptocurrencies has caused an evolution in terrorist resourcing models, resulting in cases that differ from traditional terrorist financing schemes. Cryptocurrency transactions and assets cannot be frozen and are difficult to confiscate because they exist virtually. Compared to traditional financing

[50]FATF (2021b), p. 41.

[51]FATF (2021b), pp. 10–13.

[52]Leuprecht et al. (2019), p. 293.

[53]Normark and Ranstorp (2015), p. 8.

[54]Leuprecht et al. (2019), p. 296.

[55]International Monetary Fund (2023).

mechanisms, that complicates disruption.[56] Crypto also lends itself to terrorist financing because of its anonymity, security, ease of movement, and untethered nature, and the uneven regulatory practices which exist between different countries make it especially attractive.[57] In particular, USDT, Bitcoin, and decentralized finance have gained in popularity among terrorist groups in recent years.[58]

Dozens of terrorist financing campaigns utilizing cryptocurrencies were identified in 2022,[59] and one analysis suggested that there may be a significant long-run link between Bitcoin transactions and terrorist financing.[60] However, much of the scholarship on crypto-enabled terrorist financing highlights the ways crypto lends itself to terrorist resourcing networks, and research on the extent and impact cryptocurrency has had on terrorist financing is limited. How does the use of cryptocurrency change the dynamics of terrorist financing models and establish how terrorist agents accrue and use cryptocurrencies? That will help gauge crypto's broader impact on the IIPE. This is all the more important given the significant risks terrorist financing poses to international security and economic stability within affected countries.

4.2 Cryptocurrency Case Study Case Study: Al-Qaeda Joint Campaign

From late 2018 until mid-2020, Al-Qaeda, Al-Nusra Front (ANF), Hay-at Tahrir Al-Sham (HTS), and other affiliated terrorist groups conducted a fundraising campaign using Bitcoin. The period of solicitation began via a Telegram group, where Bitcoin donations to an address serving as a repository were specifically requested by the group administrator. All donations sent to this repository were later moved to a central hub via a cluster of Bitcoin addresses. This hub was used to collect and redistribute funds for the remainder of the campaign. Multiple charities and businesses affiliated with terrorist activities also posted virtual currency exchange deposits to their respective Telegram and Twitter channels for the purpose of contributing to the fundraising effort. Donations made via PayPal, MoneyGram, and Western Union were also encouraged by these affiliates. Funds raised by these organizations were linked to the financing network via clusters of Bitcoin addresses and deposits made to the central hub. Specifically, Leave an Impact Before Departure, Al Ikwah, Malhama Tactical, Reminders from Syria, and Al Sadaqah were implicated as affiliated organizations. Al Ikwah was associated with a total of 15 Bitcoin addresses, four of which were posted to Facebook and eleven of which were posted to Telegram. Malhama Tactical posted two Bitcoin addresses on Twitter

[56] Krishnan (2020).

[57] Brill and Keene (2014); Wang and Zhu (2021).

[58] TRM (2023), pp. 14–15.

[59] Ibid p. 14.

[60] Majumder et al. (2019), p. 137.

which were connected to a cluster of 23 Bitcoin addresses used to distribute funds throughout the network. Two virtual currency exchanges were used to transfer money collected by the financing network and launder it through mixing services.[61]

An undercover agent was able to contact an administrator of the Reminders from Syria Telegram channel, asking to donate Bitcoin. The administrator provided a Bitcoin address that was later clustered with two others, in addition to his own personal Bitcoin wallet. Along with ongoing social media presence, this was used to generate donations and made it possible to identify some actors in this network. However, other actors could only be identified via Bitcoin addresses. A number of these addresses originated in Idlib, Syria.[62] This was also the location of the central hub, which was hosted by a publicly registered cryptocurrency exchange known as BitcoinTransfer.[63] The use of both Telegram and BitcoinTransfer in this case is consistent with law enforcement records indicating a history of use by Al-Qaeda. Millions of dollars were generated through this network. Some of the funds were used in gift card exchanges and to purchase online Bitcoin gaming vouchers in a manner consistent with money laundering.[64] The Bitcoin Terror Takedown Team composed of FBI, IRS-CI Cyber Crimes, and HSI agents detected and investigated this case.[65] In total, 155 virtual currency assets were implicated. The assets were civilly prosecuted in U.S. District Court.[66]

5 DeFi and Terrorism

5.1 *Overview of DeFi*

The ascent of DeFi is cause for concern from law enforcement and counterterrorism agencies. In the United States, the Office of Foreign Assets Control (OFAC) sanctioned crypto mixer Tornado Cash for enabling sanctions evasions using cryptocurrency. Almost half of the funds, (49.6 percent) originated with "Defi protocols".[67] Tornado Cash is an example of a smart contract-based mixer, similar to other mixers and bridges. Their code runs without central oversight; so, when a mixer such as Tornado Cash is sanctioned, it continues to run, which places a significant onus on VASP's to be vigilant against platforms that may interact with the mixer. This creates regulatory complications. DeFi technology that continues to run independent of sanctions and human oversight can be used by terrorist groups to

[61] United States of America v. 155 Virtual Currency Assets (2020).

[62] Ibid.

[63] Chainalysis Team (2020).

[64] United States of America v. 155 Virtual Currency Assets (2020).

[65] United States Department of Justice (2020).

[66] United States of America v. 155 Virtual Currency Assets (2020).

[67] Chainalysis (2023) OFAC.

facilitate financing. For example, a group can crowdsource donations to a DeFi coin and easily distort the source of those funds using mixers or bridges. Taking particular care to engage only with smart contract services allows for simple distortion of funds with no identification or transaction transparency required.

While there is growing risk associated with truly decentralized DeFi technology, many DeFi services have a centralized authority that performs some blockchain management. For example, many forms of DeFi use the Ethereum blockchain which has a small group overseeing the blockchain. This means that in some cases DeFi entities are susceptible to the AML, KYC, and CTF measures put in place for their parent organizations and are simply not meeting their obligations. The U.S Department of the Treasury has identified DeFi services being used in terrorist financing, among other crimes. Specifically, DeFi services are being selected to launder illicit funds using mixers, bridges, and coins with a perceived lack of oversight. Although noncompliance is pegged as an overarching issue, there is little proof to this effect.[68]

5.2 *DeFi Case Study: Al-Qassam Brigades Campaign*

From 2019 until mid-2020, the Al-Qassam Brigades perpetrated a three-stage fundraising campaign via social media platforms and websites affiliated with the military wing of the terrorist organization Hamas. In the first stage, donations were solicited via Twitter and other social media platforms as requesting for Bitcoin deposits. These deposits were made to a single address hosted at the US Bitcoin Exchange. In the second stage, the Al-Qassam Brigades maintained the request for donations to be sent to a single address, however this address was hosted within Al-Qassam Brigade controlled infrastructure. In the final stage, the Al-Qassam Brigades developed and deployed technology that generated a new Bitcoin address for every individual donation made. In total, 53 virtual currency accounts, 127 virtual currency properties, 5 accounts held at traditional financial institutions, and three websites were implicated. At least 12 virtual currency exchanges were used, in addition to 26 financial intermediaries. The locations of most actors involved in this network were not identified, although one individual was identified via an email address, and another was identified by name through association with an unregistered money service business involved in the financing network. The origin of some Bitcoin addresses could also be traced to Turkey and the Palestinian Territories. The money service business (MSB) converted the Bitcoin donations received into centralized currencies and assets such as gift cards. Wire transfers of U. S dollars were also converted to altcoins and Bitcoin by this money service business.[69] In this case, altcoins included Ethereum, XRP, and EOS. The use of altcoins in this case is consistent with virtual money laundering.[70] Amounts totaled

[68]United States Department of the Treasury (2023).

[69]United States of America v. 53 Virtual Currency Accounts (2020).

[70]Leuprecht et al. (2022).

approximately $168,200,812 USD, 13,987.1543833 Bitcoin, 11,824 Ether, 188,043 EO, and 1,080,609 XRP. In USD, the value of these combined currencies totals approximately $558,383,568.

Using third-party anti-money laundering software, investigators disrupted the network and initiated legal proceedings. Agents from the Federal Bureau of Investigations (FBI), the Internal Revenue Service's Criminal Investigations (IRS-CI) Cyber Crime Unit, and Homeland Security Investigations (HSI) collaborated as part of the Bitcoin Terror Takedown Team.[71] The case was brought against the virtual currency accounts, virtual currency properties, financial institution accounts, and websites in U.S civil court.[72]

6 Implications and Recommendations

6.1 DeFi Regulation

While FATF requirements related to VASPs and virtual assets may technically apply to DeFi, the nature of DeFi makes them irrelevant. The majority of FATF requirements and recommendations hinge on the collection of identifying information from parties engaging in virtual asset transactions.[73] DeFi operates, at least hypothetically, without central oversight.[74] The collection of identifying information is, therefore, impossible, and FATF recommendations, if they have been implemented at all, are nugatory. The pseudonymous nature of cryptocurrencies makes them attractive to terrorists and other criminal actors such as those involved in OCSEA and ransomware, and legal records show that criminal actors are using them to conduct illicit activities. DeFi maintains the most attractive features of cryptocurrency for illicit actors—anonymity, poor regulation, untethered, easy to move, difficult to trace and confiscate—and scales them up, providing an actually anonymous and almost completely unregulated alternative.[75] It also facilitates the borrowing and lending of crypto, savings, investments, and more that cryptocurrencies alone do not.[76] DeFi already has vast links to money laundering, because users are not required to follow AML and KYC protocols.[77]

Bad actors are already mobilizing cryptocurrency networks and integrating elements of DeFi, which puts them on a trajectory to using DeFi as a primary financing tool. Regulating DeFi should, therefore, be a high-level priority for organizations

[71] United States Department of Justice (2020).

[72] United States of America v. 53 Virtual Currency Accounts (2020).

[73] Wagman (2022).

[74] Salami (2021); Aramonte et al. (2022).

[75] Aramonte et al. (2022).

[76] Salami (2021), p. 425.

[77] Ibid., p. 426.

mandated to develop effective counterterrorism and anti-money laundering protocols.[78] Even without DeFi, investigators in the Al-Qaeda campaign were unable to identify most actors involved in the network. In the Al-Qassam Brigades campaign, which operated in part in an internal network and did utilize DeFi in addition to cryptocurrency, there were even fewer identifiable actors. This anonymity likely explains, in part, the use of a civil prosecution against assets rather than criminal prosecution against individuals, which weakens the legal consequences suffered by the terror cell. Regulation needs to curtail the growth in DeFi as a financial alternative for criminals, notably expanding the FATF definition of VA's and VASP's to include more DeFi entities. Furthermore, crypto and DeFi entities that operate with high volumes of trade should have nuanced and appropriate KYC, CTF, and AML requirements.

6.2 *Criminal Behavior*

Geography is one explanatory variable for the use of cryptocurrency in these cases. Regions where groups involved in these cases operate are subject to several sanctions, as are the terrorist groups themselves. The Gaza Strip, for example, has been subject to sanctions from Israel[79] and the Palestinian Authority,[80] in addition to international sanctions on Hamas and other terrorist organizations within the region.[81] Syria as a whole, including Idlib, is also subject to sanctions[82] as are terrorist groups in Idlib.[83] Sanctioning and the remote location of these regions means travel is restricted and traditional financial infrastructures are inaccessible. The geographic location of these groups may, therefore, incentivize the use of virtual assets, as crypto is accessible where other forms of financing are not. Based on this observation, it seems plausible that groups cut off from other financing opportunities have an incentive to use cryptocurrencies.

Both case studies indicate that terrorist organizations have the capability to use third-party cryptocurrency networks and exchanges with ease, and at least in the case of the Al Qassam Brigades, they have the capability to build internal crypto networks. These internal crypto networks should be of concern, as they may be insulated from checks and balances that apply to public networks. The sophistication of these cases also indicates that terrorist organizations may, in some ways, be more

[78] Salami (2021).

[79] Weiner et al. (n.d.).

[80] Toameh (2018).

[81] United States Department of the Treasury (2015); Public Safety Canada (n.d.); Official Journal of the European Union (2022).

[82] Government of Canada (2023); United States Department of State (n.d.); Council of the European Union (2022).

[83] Official Journal of the European Union (2022); Public Safety Canada (n.d.).

skilled in the use of cryptocurrencies than other criminals. For example, in the Welcome to Video case of Online Child Sexual Exploitation and Abuse (OCSEA), the perpetrator left behind a trail of identifying information, including transfer funds to personal accounts registered in his own name.[84] The aforementioned terrorist financing cases do not make the same rookie mistakes. If these terrorist organizations are indeed more skilled than other criminal actors in cryptocurrency, then they may be the first to use DeFi as an illicit tool. This possibility is supported by the presence of DeFi in the Al Qassam Brigades case. Crimes in these case studies were largely perpetrated by organizations rather than individuals, save for the Welcome to Video case.[85] This suggests that organizations and individuals may interact differently with the illicit crypto economy, and that organizations may be more successful in evading identification and accountability as a result. Given the long reach and generally sophisticated structure of criminal organizations, better regulatory practices need to be applied and enforced equally across jurisdictions. Otherwise, as in the terrorist financing cases, criminal organizations will operate out of less developed regulatory jurisdictions, which sustains their activities while they evade prosecution.

The pattern of behaviour in these cases differs from traditional terrorist financing cases. The transfer network is more intricate with more nodes but requires fewer total actors, and the actors leverage social media to expand their reach. In addition to the use of social media, the Al Qassam Brigades case leveraged altcoins and DeFi. Patterns for sanctions evasions are similar.[86] Both terrorist financing cases and the sanctions evasion case study also used aspects of the traditional financial system as a complement to cryptocurrencies and DeFi, yet law enforcement still failed to identify them. This is unexpected, as DeFi and crypto provide anonymity that traditional financial institutions do not, and activities did not require the use of traditional financing pathways. That is, actors opted to use them despite their proficiency in a financial system more useful for their purposes. Understanding the relationship between traditional financing and DeFi or cryptocurrency warrants further investigation. The presence of partnerships between criminal groups in the Al-Qaeda case is also of interest, as this behaviour was observed less frequently in traditional terrorist financing cases. Ransomware shows similar traits: the Lazarus group partnered with other external groups.[87] In both cases, the collaboration between criminal groups made it difficult to shut down and mitigate criminal activity. These partnerships present an interesting and unexpected aspect of the crypto-crime nexus that warrants further research. Understanding how these relationships come about and how partnerships are negotiated matters to criminal intelligence and to developing effective regulation.

[84] Hamilton and Leuprecht (2023).

[85] Hamilton and Leuprecht (2023).

[86] Ibid.

[87] Ibid.

6.3 The Dark Web

Another explanatory variable for the use of cryptocurrency in these cases is a reliance on transboundary payments. The terrorist groups implicated in the case studies require large amounts of funding to meet their mandates. Owing to lack of prosperity or support among the population and the risk of detection by law enforcement, funding at this scale cannot be reliably collected through fiat currencies or from the region in which the group is operating. Transboundary payments allow the group to solicit more funds with greater discretion. Terrorist groups also require certain materials to meet their mandates, many of which can only be bought through transnational networks. In particular, terrorist groups engage in proliferation financing on the Dark Web, which necessitates transboundary payments.

Opportunities for proliferation financing resulting from crypto-terrorist financing include the Dark Web, which is an illicit marketplace platform that uses cryptocurrency and is frequented by terrorists.[88] As early as 2010, the cybersecurity firm Procysive estimated that upwards of 300 terrorist forums and 50,000 radical websites were operating on the Dark Web. The Dark Web provides a platform for the buying and selling of prohibited goods critical to terrorist mandates; including weapons of mass destruction (WMDs)[89] and chemical, biological, radiological, and nuclear (CBRN) materials.[90,91] While the financing networks discussed in this chapter were discovered and prosecuted before funds were used to perpetrate a terrorist attack, previous cases provide evidence that terrorists use the Dark Web to accumulate materials used in terrorist attacks. A 2016 attack in Paris by ISIS was perpetrated using assault rifles bought on the dark web, and at a Nuclear Security Summit in the same year, President Obama described how terrorists acquired radioactive isotopes from the Dark Web.[92] The cases discussed in this chapter represent an evolution through which terrorists can engage in proliferation financing more readily and discreetly. By soliciting donations directly through cryptocurrencies and DeFi, terrorist entities gain funds that are useful on the dark web without having to do the potentially traceable work of converting fiat currency into cryptocurrencies.

6.4 Interagency Cooperation

Interagency cooperation was critical to disrupting both terrorist financing cases. Interagency collaboration likely allowed law enforcement officials to identify the "big picture" of the crime, rather than remaining restricted by individual mandates

---

[88] Wang and Zhu (2021).

[89] Ibid.

[90] Ibrahim (2019).

[91] Ibrahim (2021).

[92] Ibid.

and resources. This indicates a larger need for interagency mandates and collaboration defined by regulations and legal frameworks. But while this works at the national level, transnational interagency collaboration across sovereign jurisdictions remains a challenge. FATF's recommendations highlight the necessity of cooperation and a collaborative approach between international and domestic actors to contain terrorist resourcing.[93] Lack of common standards and laws puts lightly-regulated jurisdictions at risk of being exploited by terrorist groups.[94]

In many circumstances intelligence identifies and tracks terrorist groups by analyzing clusters of payments between parties. In some circumstances analysts can apply social network analysis to identify individuals with more connections that are more centralized to the organizations.[95] Cryptocurrencies record transactions permanently and publicly, so once specific individuals are identified, their wallet transactions can be identified. Investigating these clusters is one of the most useful tools law enforcement agencies have in tracking down crypto-funded terrorist groups. Ergo, better network mapping and information sharing would beneficial investigators who are under-resourced or undertrained on virtual asset investigations.

6.5 *Legal & Regulatory Frameworks*

Three patterns emerge from the terrorist crypto-financing cases in this chapter. First, money laundering was required to make cryptocurrency donations useful to the group in both case studies. This overlap between criminal sectors means that terrorist financing regulation developed from AML protocols may be more effective when applied to crypto terrorist financing as opposed to traditional terrorist financing. Since traditional terrorist financing does not necessarily involve money-laundering, coupling traditional CTF to AML regulation is suboptimal.

Regulation is further complicated by the globalized and transboundary nature of cryptocurrency. Effective deterrence of illicit activities necessitates a coordinated international regulatory regime on cryptocurrency.[96] This grouped regulatory approach may be useful in identifying crypto terrorist financing given its apparent link to money laundering. To be useful, regulations must be properly adapted to apply to cryptocurrencies and universally implemented and enforced. That is, regulations must account for both cryptocurrencies and DeFi, including introducing and improving regulations around collecting identifying information. More importantly, proper adaptation requires appropriate enforcement. Given the globalized nature of DeFi and crypto, jurisdictional implementation and enforcement standards

[93] United States v. 155 Virtual Currency Assets (2021).

[94] Leuprecht et al. (2019).

[95] Leuprecht et al. (2017); FATF (2020, 2021a).

[96] Edwards et al. (2019), pp. 16–17.

need to be universal; otherwise, terrorist groups will sustain their operations in less stringent jurisdictions. Thus far, FATF standards are neither universally implemented nor are they universally enforced. Recommendations such as those for VASPs may, in some cases, pertain to DeFi, but are difficult to apply and limited in scope. FATF should, therefore, optimize current regulations around virtual assets, VASPs, and cryptocurrency transactions, and develop new ones that apply specifically to DeFi. In addition, local jurisdictions should ensure that current AML, KYC, and CTF obligations, to which DeFi may be subject due to the use of the blockchain, are met. Regulations should be appropriately nuanced, adopted universally and enforced evenly.

Second, in both terrorist financing cases in this chapter, as well as in cases of OCSEA, third-party software was instrumental to the investigative process. In cases involving cryptocurrency, software is complemented by the easily accessibly public ledgers that cryptocurrencies use. At least in these instances, criminal intelligence has visibility to identify criminal behaviour. Why they are not doing so is unclear, possibly for lack of staff, skills, or priorities. The need for third-party software in identifying crypto terrorist financing indicates that in cases of DeFi, third-party software is also likely to play a critical role. Without cooperation and consultation with third-party companies it may be difficult to develop investigative protocols that are effective against crypto and DeFi.

Finally, both terrorist financing cases in this chapter were tried in civil court. This is unusual. Terrorism financing cases brought by prosecutors tend to be criminal in nature, with indictments against actors in the network.[97] In these instances, indictments were brought against virtual assets rather than actors. This is telling: the legal system does not appear to have the means to prosecute these kinds of activities criminally. This may be in part due to a lack of evidence in crypto crime cases—an issue exacerbated by DeFi. The problem thus becomes not only how the legal system might adjust to prosecute such cases, but also how the type and quality of evidence can be improved. The largest obstacle in both terrorist financing cases was the anonymity and ability for terrorist groups to pivot and adapt their networks, such as moving a deposit from a US exchange to an internal network exchange, or the balance transfer of an initial repository to a central hub. Ergo, regulations around these aspects of cryptocurrency should be a priority. The fact that DeFi has perfected these aspects only makes the need for regulation more pressing.

7 Conclusion

This chapter has two key findings: the understanding of the role of DeFi in the crypto-crime nexus and within research is poor, and DeFi and crypto are indeed, being leveraged by bad actors in the illicit international political economy. The

[97] Leuprecht et al. (2019).

chapter contributes to the literature by establishing that DeFi is being weaponized by terrorist financing schemes, patterns of behaviour can be anticipated, and current regulation is insufficient and, in some ways, wholly lacking. The chapter has identified that an international, universal approach to CTF regulation is necessary to counter the risks of DeFi and crypto effectively as terrorist financing tools. For this to be possible, the entity which sets the standard for CTF protocols must have the ability to ensure the development and enforcement of said protocols. As such, FATF may be inappropriate as the international standard-bearer because of its lack of actual power in developing and enforcing regulation. Further, it would be disadvantageous to have counter crypto-terrorism be a single-entity effort overseen by a single body. Governments and law enforcement agencies should prioritize counter-crypto crime and counter-DeFi projects, and engage with regulatory bodies in efficient, meaningful ways.

The chapter identifies uneven regulatory development as an obstacle to effective CTF protocols. This uneven development is in part a result of ineffective interactions between organizations such as FATF and jurisdictions committed to upholding their standards. The lack of well-implemented regulation and enforcement indicates a disconnect between FATF expectations and government or law enforcement capabilities. Resolving these disparities will require better communication, collaborative development of recommendations, and swift responses to obstacles of enforcement or implementation. Private industry experts and technology firms should be part of a partnership with public entities, with a goal of developing useful and nuanced software that is capable of tracking virtual assets and decentralized finances. There must also be real consequences for states that do not comply with regulations, which puts the international financial system at risk by enabling proliferation and terrorist financing. For lack of a swift, adequate, and achievable regulatory framework, crypto and DeFi are bound to be leveraged by terrorist financing networks and other criminal actors with impunity to great effect.

Research for this article was supported by the Social Sciences and Humanities Research Council of Canada, Insight Grants 435-2022-0862 and 435-2019-1333 and Partnership Grant 895-2021-1007.

References

117th United States Congress, House of Representatives (2021) Terrorism and digital financing: how technology is changing the threat, before Subcommittee on Intelligence and Counterterrorism of the Committee on Homeland Security. https://www.congress.gov/event/117th-congress/house-event/113965/text. Accessed 21 Dec 2023

Andreas P (2004) Review: illicit international political economy: the clandestine side of globalization. Rev Int Polit Econ 11(3):641–652. https://doi.org/10.1080/0969229042000252936

Annison T (2023) What is... a Bridge? Elliptic Connect. https://hub.elliptic.co/learning/what-is-a-bridge/

Aramonte S, Doerr S, Huang W, Schrimpf A (2022) DeFi lending: intermediation without information? Bank for International Settlements Bulletin 57. ISSN: 2708-0420

Baron J, O'Mahony A, Manheim D, Dion-Schwarz C (2015) National security implications of virtual currency: examining the potential for non-state actor deployment. RAND Corporation, Santa Monica

Brill A, Keene L (2014) Cryptocurrencies: the next generation of terrorist financing? Defence Against Terrorism Rev 6(1):7–30. https://ssrn.com/abstract=2814914

Chainalysis Team (2022a) Crypto crime trends for 2022: illicit transaction activity reaches all time high in value, all-time low in share of all cryptocurrency activity. https://blog.chainalysis.com/reports/2022-crypto-crime-report-introduction/. Accessed 21 Dec 2023

Chainalysis Team (2022b) Ransomware revenue down as more victims refuse to pay. https://blog.chainalysis.com/reports/crypto-ransomware-revenue-down-as-victims-refuse-to-pay/. Accessed 21 Dec 2023

Chainalysis Team (2020) Chainalysis in action: Department of Justice announces takedown of two terrorism financing campaigns with help from blockchain analysis. https://blog.chainalysis.com/reports/cryptocurrency-terrorism-financing-al-qaeda-al-qassam-brigades-bitcointransfer/. Accessed 21 Dec 2023

Chainalysis Team (2023) OFAC sanctions Tornado Cash founder Roman Semenov, DOJ files charges against him and co-founder Roman Storm in coordinated action. https://www.chainalysis.com/blog/ofac-sanctions-roman-semenov-tornado-cash/. Accessed 21 Dec 2023

Ciaian P, Rajcaniova M, Kancs D (2018) Virtual relationships: short-and long-run evidence from Bitcoin and altcoin market. J Int Financ Mark Inst Money 52:173–195. https://doi.org/10.1016/j.intfin.2017.11.001

Clements R (2022) Commissioned Paper: cryptocurrency: challenges to conventional governance of financial transactions. Public Order Emergency Commission, Ottawa. https://publicorderemergencycommission.ca/files/documents/Policy-Papers/Cryptocurrency. Accessed 18 July 2023. Papers/Cryptocurrency Accessed 21 Dec 2023

Council of the European Union (2022) Syria: Council extends sanctions against the regime for another year. https://www.consilium.europa.eu/en/press/press-releases/2022/05/31/syria-council-extends-sanctions-against-the-regime-for-another-year/. Accessed 21 Dec 2023

Dion-Schwarz C, Manheim D, Johnston PB (2019) Terrorist use of cryptocurrencies: technical and organizational barriers and future threats. RAND Corporation, Santa Monica

Dyntu V, Dykyj O (2021) Cryptocurrency as an instrument of terrorist financing. Baltic J Econ Stud 7(5):67–72. https://doi.org/10.30525/2256-0742/2021-7-5-67-72

Edwards FR, Hanley K, Litan L, Weil RL (2019) Crypto assets require better regulation: statement of the financial economists roundtable on crypto assets. Financ Anal J 79(2):14–19. https://doi.org/10.1080/0015198X.2019.1593766

FATF (2019) Terrorist financing risk assessment guide. FATF, Paris, France. https://www.fatf-gafi.org/content/fatf-gafi/en/publications/Methodsandtrends/Terrorist-financing-risk-assessment-guidance.html

FATF (2020) Money laundering and terrorist financing red flag indicators associated with virtual assets. FATF, Paris, France. https://www.fatf-gafi.org/en/publications/fatfrecommendations/documents/second-12-month-review-virtual-assets-vasps.html

FATF (2021a) Ethnically or racially motivated terrorism financing. FATF, Paris, France. https://www.fatf-gafi.org/publications/methodsandtrends/documents/ethnically-racially-motivatedterrorism-financing.htm

FATF (2021b) Second 12-month review of the revised FATF standards on virtual assets and virtual asset service providers. FATF, Paris, France. https://www.fatf-gafi.org/en/publications/fatfrecommendations/documents/second-12-month-review-virtual-assets-vasps.html

FATF (2023a) Targeted update on implementation of the FATF standards on virtual assets/VASPs. FATF, Paris, France. https://www.fatf-gafi.org/en/publications/Fatfrecommendations/targeted-update-virtual-assets-vasps-2023.html

FATF (2023b) What we do. FATF, Paris, France. https://www.fatf-gafi.org/en/the-fatf/what-we-do.html

FATF (2023c) FATF Statement on the Russian Federation. FATF, Paris, France. https://www.fatf-gafi.org/en/publications/Fatfgeneral/fatf-statement-russian-federation.html

FATF (2023d) "Black and grey" lists. FATF, Paris, France. https://www.fatf-gafi.org/en/countries/black-and-grey-lists.html

Fletcher E, Larkin C, Corbet S (2021) Countering money laundering and terrorist financing: a case for bitcoin regulation. Res Int Bus Finance 56. https://doi.org/10.1016/j.ribaf.2021.101387

Georgiou GC (2020) Cryptocurrency challenges sovereign currency. World Econ 21(1):117–142

Goldbarsht D (2020) Global counter-terrorist financing and soft law. Edward Elgar Publishing, Cheltenham

Goldbarsht D (2024) Dancing in the dark: terrorist financing via the dark web. In: Goldbarsht D, de Koker L (eds) Financial crime and the law: identifying and mitigating risks. Springer. Chapter 7

Government of Canada (2023) Current sanctions imposed by Canada. https://www.international.gc.ca/world-monde/international_relations-relations_internationales/sanctions/current-actuelles.aspx?lang=eng. Accessed 21 Dec 2023

Haksar V, Bouveret A (2018) Back to basics: what are cryptocurrencies? Finance Dev 55(2):26–27. https://doi.org/10.5089/9781484357415.022

Hamilton R, Leuprecht C (2023) The Crime Crypto Nexus: nuancing risk across crypto-crime transactions. In: de Koker L, Goldbarsht D (eds) Financial technology and the law. Springer, Switzerland

Ibrahim SA (2019) Regulating cryptocurrencies to combat terrorism-financing and money laundering. Stratagem 2(1). http://journal.cscr.pk/stratagem/index.php/stratagem/article/view/38

Ibrahim SA (2021) Decrypting the risks of cryptocurrency: money laundering, terrorism financing, and proliferation financing. Pakistan Horizon 74(1). https://www.pakistan-horizon.piia.org.pk/index.php/pakistan-horizon/article/view/205/195

International Monetary Fund (2023) The IMF and the fight against money laundering and terrorism financing. https://www.imf.org/en/About/Factsheets/Sheets/2023/Fight-against-money-laundering-and-terrorism-financing. Accessed 21 Dec 2023

Jenkins C, Hamilton R, Leuprecht C (2023) Canadian cryptocurrency conundrums: a socio-technical systems analysis of crypto laundering in Canada. In: Leuprecht C, Ferrill J (eds) Dirty money: financial crime in Canada. McGill Queen's University Press, pp 322–341

King C, Walker C, Gurulé J (2018) Counter-terrorism financing: an overview. In: The Palgrave handbook of criminal and terrorism financing law, 1st edn. Palgrave, Basingstoke, pp 737–753

Kirimhan D (2023) Importance of anti-money laundering regulations among prosumers for a cybersecure decentralized finance. J Bus Res 157:1–10. https://doi.org/10.1016/j.jbusres.2022.113558

Krishnan A (2020) Blockchain empowers social resistance and terrorism through decentralized autonomous organizations. J Strateg Secur 13(1):48–58. https://www.jstor.org/stable/26907412

Legrand T, Leuprecht C (2021) Securing cross-border collaboration: trans governmental enforcement networks, organized crime and illicit international political economy. Policy Soc 40(4):565–586. https://doi.org/10.1080/14494035.2021.1975216

Leuprecht C, Walther O, Skillicorn DB, Ryde-Collins H (2017) Hezbollah's global tentacles: a relational approach to convergence with transnational organized crime. Terror Polit Violence 29(5):902–921

Leuprecht C, Cockfield A, Simpson P, Haseeb M (2019) Tracking transnational terrorist resourcing nodes and networks. Florida State Univ Law Rev 46(2):289–344. https://ssrn.com/abstract=3601189

Leuprecht C, Skillicorn DB, McCauley C (2020) Terrorists, radicals and activists: distinguishing between countering violent extremism and preventing extremist violence, and why it matters. In: Countering violent extremism and terrorism: assessing domestic and international strategies. McGill-Queen's University Press, Montreal, pp 18–46

Leuprecht C, Brunet-Jailly E, Hataley T, Legrand T (2021) Patterns in nascent, ascendant and mature border security: regional comparisons in transgovernmental coordination, cooperation, and collaboration. Commonwealth & Comparative Politics 59(4):349–375. https://doi.org/10.1080/14662043.2021.1997192

Leuprecht C, Jenkins C, Hamilton R (2022) Virtual money laundering: policy implications of the proliferation in the illicit use of cryptocurrency. J Financ Crime. https://doi.org/10.1108/JFC-07-2022-0161

Majumder A, Routh M, Singha D (2019) A conceptual study on the emergence of cryptocurrency economy and its nexus with terrorism financing. In: Das RC (ed) The impact of global terrorism on economic and political development. Emerald Publishing Ltd, Bingley, pp 125–138. https://doi.org/10.1108/978-1-78769-919-920191012

Normark M, Ranstorp M (2015) Understanding Terrorist Finance: Modus Operandi and National CTF Regimes. Swedish Defense University Report 46/2015. https://finansinspektionen.se/contentassets/1944bde9037c4fba89d1f48f9bba6dd7/understanding_terrorist_finance_160315.pdf

OECD (2022) Why Decentralised Finance (DeFi) matters and the policy implications. OECD. https://www.oecd.org/daf/fin/financial-markets/Why-Decentralised-Finance-DeFi-Matters-and-the-Policy-Implications.pdf

Official Journal of the European Union (2022) Document L:2022:025:TOC. https://eur-lex.europa.eu/legal-content/EN/TXT/?uri=OJ:L:2022:025:TOC. Accessed 21 Dec 2023

Phillips A (2004) Terrorist financing laws won't wash: it ain't money laundering. Univ Queensland Law J 23(1):81–101. http://classic.austlii.edu.au/au/journals/UQLawJl/2004/4.html

Public Safety Canada (n.d.) Currently listed entities. https://www.publicsafety.gc.ca/cnt/ntnl-scrt/cntr-trrrsm/lstd-ntts/crrnt-lstd-ntts-en.aspx. Accessed 21 Dec 2023

Salami I (2021) Challenges and approaches to regulating decentralized finance. Am J Int Law Unbound 115:425–429. https://doi.org/10.1017/aju.2021.66

Shukla S (2022) UN says crypto use in terror financing likely soaring, Bloomberg. Accessed 21 Dec 2023

Siripurapu A, Berman N (2023) Cryptocurrencies, digital dollars, and the future of money, council on foreign relations. https://www.cfr.org/backgrounder/cryptocurrencies-digital-dollars-and-future-money?gclid=Cj0KCQjwoK2mBhDzARIsADGbjeqobmm1YfaBaXOtJ9cSDRFCYrylBcA2hJYsSzwJ7tbfHcwtTEVOwwYaAqqqEALw_wcB

Toameh KA (2018) Palestinian authority rejects Israel, U.S. ideas to help Gaza. The Jerusalem Post. https://www.jpost.com/arab-israeli-conflict/palestinian-authority-rejects-israeli-us-ideas-to-help-gaza-560921. Accessed 21 Dec 2023

TRM (2023) Illicit crypto ecosystem report: a comprehensive guide to illicit finance risks in crypto. https://assets.website-files.com/6082dc5b670562332135887a4/649c21bd739a02564cea4abe_TRM_IllicitCryptoEcosystem_June2023.pdf?__hstc=19191463.57a7cd91dcffbd29cd7cace24ffc4337.1689017008773.1689017008773.1689017008773.1&__hssc=19191463.1.1689017008773&__hsfp=1150951002

Trozze A, Davies T, Kleinberg B (2023) Of degens and defrauders: using open-source investigative tools to investigate decentralized finance frauds and money laundering. Forensic Sci Int: Digit Invest 46:1–18. https://doi.org/10.1016/j.fsidi.2023.301575

United States Department of Justice Office of Public Affairs (2020) Global disruption of three terror finance cyber-enabled campaigns. https://www.justice.gov/opa/pr/global-disruption-three-terror-finance-cyber-enabled-campaigns. Accessed 21 Dec 2023

United States Department of State (n.d.) Syria sanctions. https://www.state.gov/syria-sanctions/. Accessed 21 Dec 2023

United States Department of the Treasury (2015) Treasury sanctions major Hamas leaders, financial facilitators and a front company. https://home.treasury.gov/news/press-releases/jl0159. Accessed 21 Dec 2023

United States Department of the Treasury (2023) Remarks by assistant secretary for terrorist financing and financial crime Elizabeth Rosenberg on DeFi Risk Assessment at the Atlantic Council | U.S. Department of the Treasury. https://home.treasury.gov/news/press-releases/jy1430

Velde F (2013) Bitcoin: a primer. Federal Reserve Bank of Chicago Essays on Issues 317. https://www.chicagofed.org/publications/chicago-fed-letter/2013/december-317

Wagman S (2022) Cryptocurrencies and national security: the case of money laundering and terrorist financing. Harv Natl Secur J 14:87–101. https://harvardnsj.org/wp-content/uploads/2022/12/Wagman_14-Harv.-Natl-Sec.-J.-87-2022.pdf

Wang S, Zhu X (2021) Evaluation of potential cryptocurrency development ability in terrorist financing. Policing: J Policy Pract 15(4):2329–2340. https://doi.org/10.1093/police/paab059

Weiner JR, Lindenfeld G, Binyamin I, Wanderman M, Lang J (n.d.) Israel and the Gaza Strip: why economic sanctions are not a collective punishment. Jerusalem Center for Public Affairs. https://jcpa.org/gaza-economic-sanctions/#9. Accessed 21 Dec 2023

Winer JM, Roule TJ (2002) Fighting terrorist finance. Survival: Global Polit Strategy 44(3):87–104. https://doi.org/10.1080/00396330212331343442

Ariel Burgess is a graduate student in War Studies at the Royal Military College of Canada. She holds a BAH in political studies and philosophy from Queen's University, where she works as a research coordinator at the Institute of Intergovernmental Relations. Her scholarly interests include proliferation financing, Canadian and American defence and foreign policy, the impact of counter-terrorism efforts on international relations, and the political-military nexus. She is also the recipient of a Social Sciences and Humanities Research Council (SSHRC) Graduate Student—Master's program grant and a Mobilizing Insights in Defence and Security (MINDS) scholarship initiative supplement

Rhianna Hamilton is a PhD student at the University of Adelaide and a research coordinator at Queen's University's Institute of Intergovernmental Relations. Her research interests include the study of illicit networks, with a specific focused on transnational environmental crimes like wildlife trafficking, money laundering, crypto crime, and the structures of networks engaging in crime.

Christian Leuprecht is Class of 1965 Distinguished Professor at the Royal Military College of Canada and Editor-in-Chief of the *Canadian Military Journal*. He also directs the Institute of Intergovernmental Relations in the School of Policy Studies and is an Adjunct Research Professor in the Australian Graduate School of Policing and Security at Charles Sturt University. A former Bicentennial Professor in Canadian Studies at Yale University (2009–2010), Matthew Flinders Fellow at Flinders University of South Australia (2017–2018), Eisenhower Fellow at the NATO Defence College (2019), and Fulbright Research Chair in Canada–US Relations at John Hopkins University's School for Advanced International Studies (2020), he is an elected member of the College of New Scholars of the Royal Society of Canada, recipient of the Cowan Prize for Excellence in Research at the Royal Military College of Canada and past president of the International Sociological Association's Research Committee 01: Armed Forces and Conflict Resolution.

Money Laundering Risks: The Case of Non-fungible Tokens—Key Recommendations for Australia

Samuel Orchard

Abstract As criminals continue to generate cryptocurrencies via fraudulent means, non-fungible tokens are well suited to act as vehicles to launder such funds outside of the regulatory oversight and protections of the Australian Transaction Reports and Analysis Centre. Unlike cryptocurrency exchanges, non-fungible tokens are currently not regulated directly under the Anti-Money Laundering and Counter Terrorism Financing Act 2006 (Cth). In August 2022, the newly elected Albanese Government announced an unprecedented 'token mapping' exercise in order to classify specific crypto assets and identify the gaps in the crypto asset regulatory market. This article aims to answer the question: How could the Australian anti-money laundering regulatory landscape be reformed in order to comply with updated global standards and adequately protect the non-fungible token ecosystem from money laundering exploitation? The first part of this paper presents a technical examination of non-fungible tokens and their ecosystem. Secondly, it is discussed whether non-fungible tokens are able to be utilised by criminals to launder illicit proceeds. Thirdly, drawing upon the normative system of recommendations and updated guidance as outlined by the Financial Action Task Force, Australia's existing crypto asset regulatory landscape is critically analysed insofar as illuminating a rigid reliance on traditional anti-money laundering measures incongruent with the nascent risks posed by non-fungible tokens and their associated markets. Finally, this paper analyses Australia's level of technical compliance with customer due diligence requirements and the Travel Rule and recommends incorporating select non-fungible token service providers as regulated entities, requiring the implementation of risk-based Know Your Customer processes informed by a de minimis threshold.

S. Orchard (✉)
Supreme Court of New South Wales, Sydney, NSW, Australia
e-mail: samuel.orchard@students.mq.edu.au

D. Goldbarsht, L. de Koker (eds.), *Financial Crime, Law and Governance*, Ius Gentium: Comparative Perspectives on Law and Justice 116,
https://doi.org/10.1007/978-3-031-59547-9_10

1 Introduction

1.1 Background

Money laundering is regulated in Australia under the *Anti-Money Laundering and Counter Terrorism Financing Act 2006* (Cth) (AML/CTF Act).[1] The absence of a specific regulation for, and a uniform definition of, crypto assets and their associated service providers (Crypto Asset Service Providers or CASPs) has led to actual and presumed regulatory gaps for anti-money laundering (AML) purposes.[2] In addition, the recent turmoil in crypto asset markets, losing approximately 63% of their value between November 2021 and January 2023,[3] highlights their volatility, structural vulnerability, and increasing interconnectedness with the traditional financial system, necessitating regulatory reform to ensure adequate levels of consumer protection and confidence.[4] Whilst awareness of non-fungible tokens (NFTs) is growing, consumer purchase of NFTs appears to be guided by mainstream media, desires to 'get rich quick', and a fear of missing out.[5] It follows that the NFT ecosystem is rife with 'bad actors', capitalising on the under-regulated market and underinformed, speculative investor in order to generate and launder illicit proceeds outside of law enforcement and regulatory oversight.[6]

NFTs present unique money laundering risks that have been overlooked by global and domestic regulators, resulting in a dearth of academic investigation.[7] The non-fungibility of NFTs distinguishes them from fiat (government issued) currency (such as Australian Dollars) as well as fungible crypto assets (such as Bitcoin) and may place them outside the scope of the AML/CTF Act. This ambiguity has allowed CASPs to capitalise on the minimal Know Your Customer (KYC) protections required to be implemented, challenging traditional AML regulatory efforts centred upon multinational banks and the identification of individual users, whilst profiting from their regulatory exclusion through smart contracts.[8] Furthermore, the proliferation of predicate offences including cyber extortion via ransomware or controlled malware, cyber-based fraud, and financial theft has increased the popularity of scams, victim payments, and illicit proceeds being generated in cryptocurrencies.[9] The use of anonymity-enhanced privacy coins and/or the use of anonymisation proxy services, such as TOR/I2P, has allowed criminals to buy, sell, and trade NFTs using illicitly generated cryptocurrencies without the need to provide

[1] *Anti-Money Laundering and Counter Terrorism Financing Act 2006* (Cth) ('*AML/CTF Act*').

[2] Wronka (2022a, b), p. 335.

[3] CoinGecko (2023).

[4] Financial Stability Board (2022).

[5] Sharma et al. (2022), p. 2.

[6] DeMatteo (2022) and McKay (2021).

[7] Schmidt (2021), p. 332.

[8] Ibid.

[9] Meland et al. (2020), p. 2.

verifiable identification documents.[10] Indeed, the nature of blockchain technology as involving pseudonymous distributed ledger technology (DLT) has inverted traditional AML concepts applied to financial markets, where the user is known and the transactions are hidden.[11] Accordingly, in April 2022 the Australian Transaction Reports and Analysis Centre (AUSTRAC), Australia's financial intelligence unit and AML regulator,[12] singled out NFTs as an emerging financial crime risk, with criminals attracted to their anonymity and volatile pricing.[13]

Within this context, in March 2022 the previous Australian Federal Government (the Morrison Government) proposed to carve out CASPs that engage with NFTs from critical AML reforms including KYC requirements.[14] KYC is one of the pillars of Australia's AML regime and acts as a frontline AML defence in regulated financial institutions to promote transactional accountability.[15] Whilst money laundering through NFTs represents a minimal proportion of global crypto laundering activity,[16] the Morrison Government's proposed amendments would likely result in significant opportunities for regulatory arbitrage, with high-value illicit NFT transactions being used as a means of circumventing enhanced AML regulations implemented elsewhere.[17] Furthermore, the lack of coherent regulatory guidance would likely stymie further development of Australia's fintech sector, as investors prefer the regulatory certainty of alternative jurisdictions.[18] Indeed, Australia's National Blockchain Roadmap confirms that "a regulatory environment that is conducive to innovation and growth is essential for Australia to take advantage of the blockchain opportunities available – including international investment".[19] Fortunately, the newly elected Federal Government (the Albanese Government) has announced that the Commonwealth Department of Treasury will undertake an unprecedented 'token mapping' exercise as a foundational step in a multi-stage crypto asset reform agenda, in order to identify the gaps in the existing regulatory landscape.[20] Accordingly, this article contributes to an area of immediate regulatory concern, as legislative bodies grapple with the appropriate regulatory framework needed for Australia to emerge as a global leader in crypto asset innovation, money laundering regulation, consumer protection, and investor confidence, to answer the question: How could the Australian anti-money laundering regulatory landscape be

[10] Dupuis and Gleason (2020), p. 63.

[11] Meland et al. (2020), p. 5.

[12] AUSTRAC (2022b), p. 3.

[13] AUSTRAC (2022a), p. 17.

[14] Commonwealth Department of Treasury (2022), p. 11.

[15] Chaikin (2009), p. 22; Al Shamsi et al. (2023), p. 8.

[16] Elliptic (2022).

[17] Evans (2019), p. 225.

[18] Marusevich (2021), p. 29.

[19] Commonwealth Department of Industry, Science, Energy and Resources (2020), p. 15.

[20] The Hon. Jim Chalmers MP and the Hon. Dr Andrew Leigh MP (2022).

reformed in order to comply with updated global standards and adequately protect the non-fungible token ecosystem from money laundering exploitation.

1.2 Structure

Following the introduction of several concepts integral to a technical understanding of crypto asset AML regulation and a summary of the relevant literature, part three of this paper will illuminate several methods criminals are able to utilise to launder illicit funds via NFTs, demonstrating the novel money laundering risks posed by an under-regulated NFT ecosystem. Part four will compare Australia's existing AML regulatory framework with the international best practices issued by the FATF. This will demonstrate that Australia has failed to implement critical updated guidance regarding crypto assets and their associated service providers and may be deemed non-compliant with specific FATF Recommendations. Finally, this paper will conclude by recommending the expansion of the AML/CTF Act to encompass crypto assets and suggest future research investigates the NFT service providers best placed to operate as reporting entities.

2 Money Laundering and the Blockchain Network

2.1 What Is Money Laundering?

Money laundering is defined by the *Criminal Code Act 1995* (Cth) as receiving, possessing, concealing, disposing, or engaging in a banking transaction with 'money or other property'[21] that is the proceeds of crime.[22] The ultimate goal of money laundering is not just to hide or obscure the proceeds of illegal activities, but to make them appear to have originated from legitimate, income generating sources and to render them re-usable for other purposes without drawing the attention of law enforcement agencies.[23] Traditionally, the money laundering process is comprised of three stages,[24] including:

1. *Placement*: the insertion of illicitly acquired proceeds into the financial system.[25] Typically, illicit funds will be divided into small amounts and deposited into

[21] '*Property*' means real or personal property of every description, whether situated in Australia or elsewhere and whether tangible or intangible, and includes an interest in any such real or personal property; *Criminal Code Act 1995* (Cth) s 400.1(1).

[22] *Criminal Code Act 1995* (Cth) s 400.3.

[23] Buchanan (2004), p. 117.

[24] Gilmore (1995).

[25] Sultzer (1995), p. 149.

various bank accounts across several financial institutions.[26] These accounts are usually set up using fraudulently-obtained identification documents or utilising strawmen to disguise the identity of the launderer.[27] Due to the requirement for verifiable identity documents to set up a bank account, as well as the central role of multinational financial institutions, AML regulatory efforts have typically been targeted towards identifying money laundering at the placement stage of the laundering process.[28]

2. *Layering*: the substantive stage of the money laundering process whereupon illicit proceeds are transferred or converted into alternate assets and subsequently sold for ostensibly legitimate proceeds.[29] This is typically achieved through the purchase and sale of various investments such as bonds, stocks, and cheques via a complex series of wire transfers between related accounts, financial institutions, and across jurisdictions to obscure any audit trails.[30]
3. *Integration*: the final stage of the money laundering process whereby the 'cleaned' funds are integrated back into the financial system through normal business operations, personal transactions, or through purchasing assets such as property or business ventures.[31] The effect of the integration stage is to render the laundered funds indistinguishable from legitimately derived income.

2.2 Blockchain Structure

Blockchain technology is an innovative and disruptive approach to the management of digital finance, smart contracts, and personal health records, with significant application within both the public and private sectors of computing applications. The blockchain relies on DLT which uses consensus validity, peer-to-peer network technologies, and cryptography to publicly store non-repudiable data without fear of reversal, deletion, or alteration.[32] The blockchain operates as a permissionless linear chain of cryptographically 'hashed' blocks, upon which individual transactions are timestamped and recorded, with individual user names removed.[33] Users are 'pseudonymous' within the blockchain as their personal identities are replaced with a public key.[34] Whilst the term 'wallet' and 'public key' are used interchangeably, a

[26] Ennis (2002), p. 639.

[27] Teichmann (2020).

[28] McCarthy (2018), p. 206.

[29] Ibid.

[30] Ibid p. 207.

[31] Mazorra et al. (2022), p. 949.

[32] Desmond (2020), p. 38.

[33] Sheth and Dattani (2019), p. 2.

[34] Li et al. (2019), p. 114; Osvald (2020), p. 17.

user's wallet represents the address to which payments are made, contracts are sent, and transactions occur.

Specifically, the blockchain is duplicated and stored locally across an entire network of 'nodes' (individual servers).[35] When a user initiates a transaction, the proposed block recording the details of that transaction is transmitted to all the nodes in the network who compete to 'witness' the accuracy of the transaction.[36] Once added, each node in the network updates its ledger to reflect the transaction, with the transaction becoming a non-repudiable and transparent part of the blockchain.[37] According to Al Shamsi et al., the potential for blockchain technology to offer consumers an unchangeable record of ownership has, in part, driven the popularity of NFTs.[38]

The increasing popularity of wallets has led to wallet services being offered by 'wallet providers', such as Coinbase, who store customer's crypto assets under their own keys. Wallets hosted by third-parties often do not require verifiable identity documents to set up and are independent of customer name, IP address, device details, and network connections, with no theoretical limit to the number of wallets a single user can control.[39] Accordingly, the 'traditional privacy model' in which centralised financial institutions obtain and accumulate intimate knowledge of their customers and the other party to a transaction, including via personal identification and transaction data, which is able to be provided to regulatory agencies to satisfy AML compliance obligations, is flipped, with all transaction data publicly available, the pseudonymity of individual participants maintained, and the centralised institution replaced with the Bitcoin Protocol.[40] However, as the transaction history of the blockchain is transparent to all network nodes, law enforcement authorities are theoretically able to track the chain of custody of a specific asset between identifiable accounts via an asset-tracing exercise.

2.3 Anatomy of Non-fungible Tokens

NFTs are stored on the blockchain and are digital certificates of ownership and authenticity of a specific underlying asset, such as a domain name registration or digital artwork,[41] which is stored separately.[42] NFTs are 'non-fungible' as they

[35] Osvald (2020), p. 23.
[36] Bhargava (2019), p. 12.
[37] Ibid.
[38] Al Shamsi et al. (2023), p. 2.
[39] Sedlmeir (2021), p. 605.
[40] Kyles (2022), p. 124.
[41] Bao and Roubaud (2022), p. 217.
[42] von Wachter et al. (2022), p. 1.

cannot be broken down into parts or exchanged equally for other NFTs.[43] The non-fungibility of NFTs distinguishes them from other crypto assets, such as Bitcoin, which have a fluctuating exchange rate, are indistinguishable from other Bitcoins, and can be exchanged with equivalence.[44] Rather, NFTs are considered provably unique digital assets whose transactional value is dependent upon a single exchange between buyer and seller, mediated via a fixed-price sale or auction.[45] Accordingly, the market value of an NFT is derived from its uniqueness, scarcity, and attractiveness to collectors and investors in the same sense as traditional artwork. NFTs can be purchased with cryptocurrencies, with users attaching a digital wallet to an NFT marketplace without being required to provide verifiable identity documents.

Ownership of NFTs is imputed via 'minting'.[46] Most NFTs are minted on the Ethereum blockchain, which allows for the use of smart contracts to impute predefined characteristics onto the block through metadata, such as owner identity, transaction history, and terms of use.[47] In addition, smart contracts may include terms equivalent to royalties, automating the payment of fees to the originating artist each time an NFT is traded on the open market. A smart contract is a program which verifies that the terms of a sale agreement have been met, executes the terms of the agreement, and transmits the terms of the proposed transaction to the network. Smart contracts are self-executing, cannot be deleted, and interactions with them are irreversible. Once minted, NFTs can be the object of transactions, which predominantly take place using the services of CASPs. CASPs are intermediary service providers who facilitate the storage, creation, exchange, and verification of crypto assets. Some CASPs generate revenue through fees associated with trading NFTs on their platform, such as OpenSea, the largest NFT marketplace, which generated USD$236M in trading fees from a trading volume of USD$3.5B in August 2021.[48]

2.4 Crypto Asset and Fintech Market in Australia

The crypto asset and fintech sectors in Australia continue to experience significant growth and transformation, described by the Hon. Dr. Jim Chalmers MP as a 'digital revolution'.[49] Substantial corporate investment in the fintech sector, totalling AUD$3.6B in 2021,[50] provides significant optimism for burgeoning start-ups

[43] Ibid.

[44] Jenson et al. (2021), p. 47.

[45] Wang et al. (2021), p. 3.

[46] Chiacchio et al. (2022), p. 4021.

[47] Wang et al. (2021), p. 3.

[48] Das et al. (2022), p. 1.

[49] The Hon. Jim Chalmers MP and the Hon. Dr Andrew Leigh MP (2022).

[50] KPMG (2022), p. 4.

seeking to attract local and international capital and established heavyweights looking to pivot, adapt, and deploy new technological solutions to their existing customer base. Similarly, emerging trends such as open banking and decentralised finance contribute to the development of nascent business models which challenge incumbent firms through attractive alternate financial services solutions and increased customer centricity.[51] In this vein, Australia's digital payments sector, including digital wallets and supply chain technologies, is forecast to have a total transaction value of AUD$135B in 2022,[52] with the number of users in the sector expected to exceed 21 million by 2026.[53] Furthermore, significant M&A activity, including Latitude's AUD$200M acquisition of Symple Loans and the AUD$39B acquisition of Afterpay by Block (formally Square), representing the largest takeover in Australian history, has placed the Australian fintech sector firmly on the global map.[54] NFTs remain central to the expansion of the crypto asset ecosystem due to their role in establishing proof of ownership in the Metaverse,[55] demonstrated by the meteoric growth to unicorn status of Australian NFT marketplace Magic Eden (raising AUD$187M at a AUD$2.3B valuation) in June 2022.[56]

2.5 *What Is the Financial Action Task Force?*

The FATF is an intergovernmental organisation comprised of 37 member-states and two regional organisations, representing most global financial centres,[57] of which Australia is a founding member. The FATF is widely recognised as promulgating the global standard in AML regulation through a series of non-binding recommendations regarded as soft international law, requiring member States to submit designated service providers to specified AML obligations including CDD and reporting requirements.[58] Nonetheless, according to Goldbarsht these recommendations have attained normative character and have achieved significant levels of implementation due to the rationality and self-interest of States.[59] Member States are motivated to incorporate the FATF Recommendations into their domestic regulatory frameworks through a system of peer-reviewal (Mutual Evaluation Reports (MERs) and Follow-up Reports (FURs)).[60] Each MER and FUR rates a countries' level of technical

[51] Ibid.

[52] Basul (2022).

[53] Ibid.

[54] KPMG (2022), p. 11.

[55] Abrahams (2022).

[56] Redrup (2022).

[57] Campbell-Verduyn (2018), p. 294.

[58] de Koker et al. (2022), p. 152; Campbell-Verduyn (2018), p. 294.

[59] Goldbarsht (2020), p. 8.

[60] Ibid 14.

compliance with each recommendation, ranging from complaint, largely compliant, partially compliant, or non-compliant. If a MER or FUR concludes that a country has strategic deficiencies in their AML/CTF regulatory regime, they may face a range of escalating consequences, including being placed on either the grey (where a country has committed to resolving swiftly the identified strategic deficiencies within agreed timeframes) or black (where the FATF calls upon all members to apply counter-measures to protect the international financial system) list.[61] The status of a country as non-compliant in certain regulatory areas and/or placement on either list can result in negative economic consequences including reducing foreign investment, restriction from certain financial markets, significant delays in international banking transactions, and sanctions.[62]

The FATF Recommendations combine a rule- and risk-based approach which prioritise preventative measures 'commensurate with the risks identified' and provide domestic regulatory bodies with significant discretion in implementing measures consistent with the common goal of eliminating money laundering.[63] The FATF 'rules' include a set of minimum requirements necessary to ensure the functioning of a global system of AML regulation, such as the requirement for members to identify and take action against money laundering risks,[64] to criminalise money laundering,[65] to adopt measures to enable the freezing, seizing, and confiscating of money laundering proceeds,[66] and to require designated service providers to carry out CDD measures when processing transactions above a minimum threshold of USD/EUR$15,000.[67] In contrast, the risk-based approach requires countries to identify, assess, and understand the unique money laundering risks they are exposed to and determine how it will assess those risks, allowing States to strengthen or weaken compliance requirements in higher- or lower-risk situations respectively.[68] However, 'risk' is not defined by the FATF, resulting in inconsistent global application of AML preventative measures and an overflow of useless AML information.

The FATF has issued several global standards to combat money laundering via crypto assets and has recommended that national authorities target the specific 'nodes' whose activities 'intersect with the fiat financial system'.[69] Crypto assets (or 'virtual assets') are defined by the FATF as 'digital representations of value that can be digitally traded or transferred and can be used for payment or investment

[61] Schmidt (2021), p. 349.

[62] Goldbarsht (2017), p. 129.

[63] Financial Action Task Force (2023a), p. 10.

[64] Financial Action Task Force (2023a), Recommendation 1.

[65] Financial Action Task Force (2023a), Recommendation 3.

[66] Financial Action Task Force (2023a), Recommendation 4.

[67] Financial Action Task Force (2023a), Recommendation 10.

[68] Financial Action Task Force (2023a), p. 8.

[69] Financial Action Task Force (2021), p. 10.

purposes'.[70] The FATF has recommended a broad reading of the definition of crypto assets and that domestic legislators take a 'functional' approach that is not confined by the nomenclature used by the issuer to describe its characteristics, insofar as, regardless of the technical specifications, there should not be a crypto asset that does not fall under the FATF Recommendations.[71] Similarly, the FATF has introduced a broad activity-based definition of CASPs, defined as 'any natural or legal person who, as a business, conducts one or more of the following activities for or on behalf of another natural or legal person:

1. Exchange between virtual assets and fiat currencies;
2. Exchange between one or more forms of virtual assets;
3. Transfer of virtual assets;
4. Safekeeping and/or administration of virtual assets or instruments enabling control over virtual assets; and
5. Participation in and provision of financial services related to an issuer's offer and/or sale of a virtual asset',[72]

including crypto asset exchanges, custodian wallet providers, and intermediaries that facilitate the transfer of crypto assets.

2.6 *Literature Review*

Traditional money laundering efforts have received considerable academic attention, including Ryder's cyclical theory,[73] Lilley's attention to criminal aims,[74] Robinson's historical analysis,[75] and Srivastava, Simpson, and Smith's professional guide for AML compliance.[76] Academics have long recognised the anonymity of cryptocurrencies and lack of regulatory oversight as a catalyst for laundering efforts.[77] In response, some researchers, such as Turner and Irwin, have attempted to de-anonymise cryptocurrencies through blockchain analytic technologies,[78] whilst others, such as Hillman, have examined whether specific crypto assets are able to be functionally tied to existing concepts of 'money'.[79] However, the non-fungibility of NFTs more appropriately equates the asset class to traditional

---

[70] Ibid.

[71] Ibid p. 22.

[72] Ibid p. 34.

[73] Ryder (2012).

[74] Lilley (2006).

[75] Robinson (1995).

[76] Srivastava et al. (2010).

[77] Stuhlmiller (2013) and Dostov and Shust (2014).

[78] Irwin and Turner (2018), p. 297.

[79] Hillman (2020), p. 108.

artwork through its subjectively fluctuating value and inability to be traded with equivalence and, in the absence of centralised institutions enforcing AML requirements,[80] has allowed the NFT ecosystem to 'neatly sidestep the plethora of anti-money laundering regulations developed over the past 25 years', a position endorsed by the FATF.[81] Indeed, on 30 June 2022 the FATF reported that feedback from FATF jurisdictions and open source data suggested criminals can misuse NFTs for illicit financial activities, including money laundering and wash trading.[82] To this end, Al Shamsi et al. utilised the Space Transition Theory to describe how NFTs can be used in the commission of financial crimes, including money laundering and crypto-fraud, recommending the incorporation of standard contractual forms into the blockchain records to reduce user pseudonymity and promote market transparency.[83]

Investigations of suspicious price patterns and suspected automated trading in NFT markets have confirmed patterns observed in nascent financial markets known for market abuse and price manipulation.[84] Wash trading is a stylised fact that poses a barrier to greater capital flow into the fintech industry, which promises to redress the drawbacks of the traditional financial system through transparency, democratisation, accessibility, and efficiency.[85] In response to a growing appreciation of the proliferation of cyber-fraud, academic literature has focused on developing blockchain data mining techniques to empower automatic detection systems.[86] Research by Tariq and Sifat, analysing the existence of wash trading in the NFT ecosystem, found a high probability of abnormal and computer-generated trades—both symptoms of wash trading and price manipulation.[87] Furthermore, research by Pelechrinis, focusing on transactions on the NFT exchange platform NBA TopShot, found clear signs of anomalous trades, both in terms of their expected profit and their underlying trade network structure.[88] Conversely, research by von Wachter et al., questioning the authenticity of NFT on-chain volumes and examining the existence of illicit trading patterns, suggested a predisposition for manual wash trading between few addresses, suggesting a viable lower bound estimate for NFT wash trading of approximately 2% of NFT sales.[89] Whilst acknowledging the ability for NFTs to operate as a vehicle for money laundering efforts, such studies are limited to data collection, aggregation, and analysis.

[80] Campbell-Verduyn and Goguen (2017), p. 74.

[81] Stokes (2013), p. 3; Financial Action Task Force (2023b).

[82] Financial Action Task Force (2022).

[83] Al Shamsi et al. (2023).

[84] Tariq and Sifat (2021).

[85] Ibid 3.

[86] Tiwari et al. (2023), p. 205.

[87] Tariq and Sifat (2021), p. 8.

[88] Pelechrinis et al. (2022), p. 1.

[89] von Wachter et al. (2022).

This paper builds on traditional AML proposals that a robust customer due diligence (CDD) process must involve comprehensive and all-encompassing risk-based KYC processes.[90] Previous research has cited the necessity for crypto exchanges (services that facilitate the exchange of fiat currency for cryptocurrencies (or vice versa)) to implement strong KYC measures, in line with traditional methods to combat the initial placement stage of money laundering.[91] However, illicit proceeds are increasingly being generated in the form of cryptocurrencies rather than fiat currency, undermining the necessity for criminals to utilise crypto exchange services.[92] Accordingly, previous proposals aimed at capturing specific crypto assets under existing AML regulatory approaches have neglected to examine the potential for various high-risk service providers to screen NFT users against politically exposed persons and sanctions lists or conduct adverse media monitoring, and, accordingly, fall short of the updated global standard in crypto asset AML regulation as outlined by the Financial Action Task Force (FATF).[93]

3 Money Laundering via NFTs

NFTs represent attractive vehicles for money laundering efforts due to the general volatility in price, the lack of an objective method for valuation, global tradability,[94] the general lack of technical knowledge of the NFT ecosystem required to authenticate the credibility of a project,[95] and the low barriers to entry.[96] Despite over US$17.7B in NFTs sold throughout 2021,[97] the value of NFTs remains largely driven by its online 'virality',[98] mediated by manipulable sources including social media presence, the involvement of celebrity influencers, and speculative trading.[99] In addition, certain NFT marketplaces incentivise the shaping of an ecosystem whereby NFTs are traded in quick succession, with many smart contracts containing clauses generating revenue for the marketplace each time a transaction involving the NFT is recorded on a blockchain.[100] As such, CASPs may be operating within an ecosystem where the incentive to transact is higher than the incentive to implement AML protections, and, as a corollary, it may not be feasible to conduct due diligence

[90] Chaikin (2009), p. 22.

[91] Dupuis and Gleason (2020), p. 70.

[92] Meland et al. (2020), p. 5.

[93] Financial Action Task Force (2023a).

[94] Wronka (2022a, b), p. 85.

[95] Al Shamsi (2023), p. 5.

[96] Wang (2022), p. 3.

[97] Elliptic (2022), p. 34.

[98] Roy et al. (2023), p. 2.

[99] Wang (2022), p. 4.

[100] Bao and Roubaud (2021), p. 45.

due to the frequency of transactions. However, the transparency of the blockchain necessitates that criminals seldom transfer criminal proceeds to centralised NFT marketplaces without obfuscating the source of their funds first. Accordingly, money laundering via NFTs (NFT Laundering) may consist of a series of sophisticated steps, detailed below, beginning with the acquisition of illicit proceeds in the form of cryptocurrencies via fraudulent means (for example, by executing a rug pull), followed by a series of obfuscation techniques designed to distance the illicit proceeds from the predicate crime and create a money trail that is impossible to track, and concluding with the introduction of the funds into the NFT ecosystem, allowing the criminal to capitalise on the subjective pricing of NFTs to legitimise the consolidation of illicit proceeds as trade-based profit.

Step 1: Rug Pull

A 'rug pull' refers to a social engineering scam whereby an NFT creator solicits investments and then abruptly abandons a project, fraudulently retaining project investors' funds without return.[101] Criminals will create an NFT project and leverage fraudulent marketing measures to promote interest and cultivate public confidence,[102] including strategies such as spruiking giveaways, 'sweepstakes', 'staking' opportunities, and exclusive rewards to purchasers. Criminals will develop sophisticated project roadmaps to entice potential purchasers and promise significant long-term investment returns or some form of good, service, or privilege, capitalising on the lack of centralised information about issuers of NFTs.[103] Whereupon customer interest has been generated to a significant extent, members of the public will be permitted to purchase the NFTs in exchange for Ethereum, which is deposited into a project wallet. After a certain amount of profit has been generated through NFT sales, the criminal will transfer the proceeds from the liquidity pool to various anonymous wallets under their control, rendering the NFTs untradeable and with zero economic value. This is achieved through the inclusion of a conditional withdrawal function in the smart contract of the NFTs, which, when executed by the criminal, directs the transferral of the proceeds to the criminal's private wallet(s).

Step 2: Obfuscated Sources

Obfuscation services include decentralised mixers who utilise publicly available smart contracts to mix customer funds, inhibiting attempts by law enforcement to trace identifiable cryptocurrencies to a specific wallet. This assists with laundering efforts by breaking the chain of custody of coin possession. According to a report by Elliptic, the recently sanctioned mixing service 'Tornado Cash' was the source of USD$137M of cryptocurrencies processed by NFT marketplaces and was the 'laundering tool of choice' for 52% of NFT scams in 2021.[104] Customers deposit equal amounts of Ethereum into a smart contract which pools the funds into a

[101] Mazorra et al. (2022), p. 950.

[102] Ibid.

[103] Jordanoska (2021), p. 718; Ellul and Revolidis (2023), p. 4.

[104] Elliptic (2022), p. 4.

consolidated asset pool.[105] Customers are then able to withdraw their funds into an alternate wallet by providing a zero-knowledge proof, returning mixed Ethereum minus a transaction fee.[106] The result is the creation of a single compound transaction that cannot be tied to a single wallet address, defining a customer's anonymity by the number of equal user deposits in a given pool. In addition, some mixers incorporate a time delay, use an escrow service, randomize fees, or redistribute the washed Ethereum in various amounts to further defeat asset-tracing efforts.

An alternate source of obfuscation is achieved through privacy coins, such as Monero. Privacy coins are built into their own blockchain to inhibit regulatory asset chasing and blockchain analytic efforts. Privacy coins embed privacy mechanisms into their transaction protocol through one-time addresses for the recipient, ring-confidential signatures for the sender, and confidential transaction amounts. One-time, or stealth, addresses are single-use wallet addresses that are randomly generated for each transaction to anonymise recipient identity insofar as multiple payments to the same wallet are not linked. Likewise, ring-confidential signatures employ a system of Multilayered Linkable Spontaneous Anonymous Group signatures involving a ring of public keys (the Ring) and a signature. The Ring contains a single private key and several indistinguishable public keys. When verifying a signature, nodes are able to identify which public key corresponds to the private key via a zero-knowledge-proof, restricting public identification of the sender to the extent that one of a fixed set of individuals initiated the transaction. Moreover, confidential transaction amounts conceal the value of the transaction on the public blockchain. This unique combination of cryptographic tools allows for the complete anonymisation of purchaser, seller, and transaction amount, frustrating asset-tracing efforts.

Step 3: Trade-Based Money Laundering

A simplified trade-based NFT laundering technique involves the purchase and sale of several NFTs as a means of layering illicit proceeds. A criminal can pseudonymously create and advertise a series of NFTs on an NFT marketplace, such as OpenSea, Rarible or Twinci, without providing verifiable identification documents or, in some cases, even an email address. The criminal will then create a second OpenSea account that is linked to a wallet containing obfuscated illicit proceeds, and purchase their own NFT series, legitimising the criminal proceeds with the NFT sale as proof of profits. Alternatively, a criminal can create and hold two pseudonymous crypto wallets, one containing illicit proceeds (wallet 1) and the other prepared to receive 'clean' funds (wallet 2). The criminal is able to link both wallets to anonymous OpenSea accounts and purchase several low-value NFTs using clean funds contained in wallet 2. The criminal may then re-list the NFTs at a marginally inflated price and purchase them using the illicit proceeds contained in wallet 1. The 'laundered' cryptocurrency is then deposited into wallet 2, giving the appearance

[105] Ibid, p. 34.

[106] Das et al. (2022), p. 6.

of legitimately acquired trade-based income. A criminal may also operate a legitimate NFT trading operation alongside laundering efforts and, in doing so, commingle legitimate trading income with illicit funds.

Step 4: Chain Hopping/Wash Trading
Wash trading refers to the activity of repeatedly trading assets between accounts controlled by a single proprietor for the purpose of generating a record of transactions on the blockchain and feeding misleading information, including asset price and trading volume, to the market.[107] NFT launderers are able to utilise chain hopping techniques to inhibit the ability for law enforcement agencies to trace the source of ownership throughout the blockchain as the unique qualities of the underlying asset are blurred, disguising the identity of participating buyers and sellers. The accumulation and self-trading of numerous low-value NFTs is a form of 'structuring'—spreading value across assets to disguise their illicit origin.[108] A criminal is able to open and chain together a large number of pseudonymous wallets, and cause NFTs to be transferred between such wallets in a cyclical or sequential manner at alternating intervals without relinquishing control, to create an artificial trading history and inflate the sale price of a once-worthless NFT or NFT collection. Price inflation is achieved in an incremental fashion to avoid suspicion (typically in a sequence to a maximum of 5% of the initial price[109]) to give the appearance of seemingly legitimate profits whilst maintaining ultimate control. Once an NFT's price is sufficiently inflated, the criminal will list the NFT on OpenSea utilising an anonymous account. As described above, the criminal will then purchase the NFT from themself using fraudulently obtained Ethereum, and 'laundered' Ethereum is transferred to the anonymous account. Alternatively, an innocent third party will purchase the NFT at the artificially inflated price, transferring clean Ethereum to the criminal's wallet.

4 Crypto Asset Anti-money Laundering Regulation

4.1 FATF Recommendations

FATF Recommendations 10–12 require financial institutions to have appropriate CDD systems in place in order to obtain and verify customer identities,[110] store and maintain all necessary records of domestic and international transactions,[111] and

[107] Grinblatt and Keloharju (2004), p. 51.
[108] von Wachter et al. (2022), p. 5.
[109] Jenson et al. (2021), p. 50.
[110] Financial Action Task Force (2023a), Recommendations 14–16.
[111] Ibid Recommendation 15.

determine whether a customer is a politically exposed person.[112] Reporting entities must obtain reliable, verifiable, and independent identification source documents from all new customers, and continue to apply these measures to existing customers on the basis of risk.[113] Enhanced CDD measures should be implemented before carrying out transactions of a value above a designated threshold, where there is a suspicion of money laundering, or if the veracity or adequacy of previously obtained identification data is questioned.[114] In 2019, the FATF expanded the scope of Recommendations 10–12 to any services that fall within the broad definition of a CASP.[115]

FATF Recommendation 15 provides that States should ensure CASPs are regulated for money laundering prevention, are licensed, and have implemented effective AML compliance and monitoring systems.[116] Recommendation 15 requires States to identify, assess, and understand the unique money laundering risks posed by novel crypto assets to their financial market segment.[117] Furthermore, Recommendation 15 requires States to ensure that CASPs apply a risk-based approach to AML initiatives and the identification of high-risk crypto asset transactions, emphasising factors that obfuscate the chain of custody or complicate customer identification, including the use of mixers and privacy coins.[118] The Interpretative Note to Recommendation 15 provides that CASPs should be licensed or regulated in the jurisdiction where they are incorporated, or, if they are a natural person, where their place of business is located.[119] However, States *may* extend their licensing regime to CASPs 'whose services can be accessed by, or are made available to, people residing or living within, or that have employees or management located in, their jurisdiction'.[120]

The application of Recommendation 15 to crypto assets presents several jurisdictional challenges to successful regulatory enforcement. Attempting to assert jurisdiction on the basis of the location of incorporation may give rise to jurisdiction shopping, as companies may incorporate holding entities in certain jurisdictions with a lack of regulatory oversight and operate their service in an alternate location. Similarly, the 'place of business' test is significantly undermined when considering a potential corporate structure involving employees spread across several jurisdictions accessing a centralised cloud-based server, or considering the potential for CASPs to operate under the control of a complex arrangement of non-corporate entities, joint ventures, or business trusts, undermining the ability of regulators to determine with

[112] Ibid Recommendation 16.

[113] Ibid Recommendation 14.

[114] Ibid.

[115] Financial Action Task Force (2019).

[116] Financial Action Task Force (2023a), Recommendation 17.

[117] Ibid.

[118] Financial Action Task Force (2020), p. 6.

[119] Financial Action Task Force (2023a), pp. 76–77.

[120] Ibid p. 127.

sufficient certainty the role, identity, or controlling rights of various companies involved in its management. Finally, attempting to establish jurisdiction on the basis of the location of users is undermined by the potential absence of assets or natural or legal persons able to be held accountable within that jurisdiction. However, whilst complex, the decentralised nature of the NFT corporate ecosystem does not exist independent or outside of applicable existing regulatory schemes and, despite being born amidst a culture of decentralisation, cannot replace the authority of the relevant legislative body.

FATF Recommendation 16, known as the Travel Rule, requires that States ensure that designated service providers collect, store, and exchange identification information about both parties to a transaction with a value of over USD$1000.[121] The Travel Rule aims to increase the amount of information available about individual users, improving sanction screening and asset tracing exercises.[122] Firms are required to maintain a record of their customers' name, account number, and unique identifiable information (such as address, national identity number, customer identification number, or date and place of birth).[123] For each transaction over the threshold amount, the transferor and beneficiary firms are required to transmit their customer's name and account number to the counterparty firm immediately and in a secured manner, and to make the information available to the appropriate authorities upon request.[124] Furthermore, firms are required to undertake a risk-based assessment prior to each transaction, requiring the exchange of increased counterparty information, such as national identity number, for high-risk, suspicious, or international transactions.[125] In 2019, the FATF confirmed that the Travel Rule applies to crypto assets, that all crypto asset transfers should be considered international transactions, and that CASPs should commence the 'immediate and secure' transferral of information.[126] However, on 30 June 2022 the FATF advised that only limited progress has been made regarding implementation and enforcement of Recommendation 15 and the Travel Rule and highlighted the immediate need for jurisdictions to accelerate compliance in this area through the passing of legislation and effective enforcement.[127]

The Travel Rule has certain limitations regarding its applicability to the crypto asset ecosystem which reflect the transplanting of traditional AML regulations into a nascent financial market. Counterparty identification requires that CASPs can identify with specificity the identity of the alternate transacting party. Contrary to a traditional financial transaction involving an International Bank Account Number (able to be attributed to a specific country, bank, and branch), the structure of a

[121] Financial Action Task Force (2023a), Recommendation 16.

[122] Ibid.

[123] Ibid.

[124] Ibid.

[125] Ibid.

[126] Financial Action Task Force (2019), pp. 28–31.

[127] Financial Action Task Force (2022), p. 23.

recipient's crypto wallet address is a string of randomly generated alphanumeric symbols. In this sense, from the perspective of a service provider instructed to transfer an NFT to a specified address, it is impossible to determine whether the recipient wallet is under the control of an individual or another service provider. Accordingly, as transfers involving wallets not under the control of service providers fall outside of the purview of the Travel Rule, the Travel Rule is likely only to be engaged in low-risk transactions between service providers with an existing business relationship. The FATF has specifically recognised the absence of any technically proven means of exhaustively, precisely, and accurately identifying the service provider that manages a recipient's wallet from their address alone.[128]

4.2 Australia's Regulatory Regime and FATF Compliance

Australia's money laundering prevention and detection measures are contained in the AML/CTF Act and overseen by AUSTRAC. The key preventative measures aimed at bringing Australia into line with international AML standards include customer identification and reporting obligations, which apply to 'reporting entities' that provide specific designated services which have the potential to facilitate, and are best placed to identify, money laundering, including financial services, the gambling sector, bullion dealers, and digital currency exchange sectors. These reporting entities are required to enrol with AUSTRAC,[129] establish and maintain an AML program to identify, mitigate and manage the money laundering risks the business faces, comply with initial and ongoing CDD requirements,[130] report transactions that exceed a stipulated value threshold of AUD$10,000 or are 'suspicious' to the AUSRAC CEO, and comply with record keeping obligations.[131] Reporting entities are required to obtain and verify identification details of all customers including their name, date of birth, and address.[132] In addition, each reporting entity must undertake a risk-based assessment to determine when additional CDD information is required and report transactions that are 'suspicious'.[133] Jurisdictionally, the AML/CTF Act applies to reporting entities whereupon:

1. The service is provided at or through a permanent establishment of the provider in Australia; or
2. The provider is a resident of Australia, and the service is provided at or through a permanent establishment of the provider in a foreign county; or

[128] Financial Action Task Force (2022), p. 62.

[129] *AML/CTF Act* s 51A.

[130] Ibid s 70.

[131] Ibid s 52.

[132] Ibid s 71.

[133] Ibid s 41.

3. The person is a subsidiary of a company that is a resident of Australia, and the service is provided at or through a permanent establishment of the person in a foreign country.[134]

A 'permanent establishment' of a person is defined as 'a place at or through which the person carries in any activities or business and includes a place where the person is carrying on activities or business through an agent'.[135] To this degree, Australia's most recent FUR, published in November 2018, prior to the FATF's 2019 amended and 2021 updated guidance on virtual assets, confirmed that Australia is compliant with Recommendation 15 and partially compliant with the Travel Rule.[136]

Whilst not attempting to undertake a full assessment of Australia's level of compliance, it is helpful to consider the extent to which Australia's regulatory landscape is consistent with the FATF's updated guidance on virtual assets. The AML/CTF Act extends only to 'digital currency', defined as a 'digital representation of value that functions as a medium of exchange, a store of economic value, or a unit of account which is not issued by or under the authority of a government body'.[137] The digital representation must be able to be used as consideration for the supply of goods or services, be generally available to the public without any form of restriction as to its use as consideration, and be interchangeable with fiat currency.[138] Whilst Australia's definition of 'digital currency' satisfied previous FATF definitions of 'virtual asset', the expansive language used in the FATF's 2021 updated guidance suggests that the Australian definition is unreasonably restrictive, resulting in assets falling outside of AML regulatory oversight. Under the AML/CTF Act, the definition of digital currency turns on the requirement for the transacted item to be used as consideration for the supply of goods and services.[139] NFT service providers may interpret this definition, and, as a result, the consequent reporting requirements, as not applying to NFTs. In this sense, consumers and service providers have received insufficient regulatory guidance as to the characterisation of NFTs as financial products (falling within the scope of s 763A of the *Corporations Act 2001* (Cth)),[140] digital currency under the AML/CTF Act, or neither. Regardless, as the FATF Recommendations apply with significant similarity to both class of assets and are intended to apply to all categories of crypto assets, the absence of any form of AML regulation or oversight of NFTs lends to the conclusion that Australia's AML regulatory landscape is inconsistent with the FATF's updated guidance.

As a corollary, the only CASPs currently regulated under the AML/CTF Act are digital currency exchange service providers that facilitate transactions involving fiat

---

[134] Ibid s 6(6).

[135] Ibid.

[136] Financial Action Task Force (2018), p. 3.

[137] *AML/CTF Act* s 5.

[138] Ibid.

[139] *AML/CTF Act* s 5.

[140] *Corporations Act 2001* (Cth) s 763A.

to crypto assets (or vice versa) and not crypto to crypto trades.[141] To this extent, Australia's regulatory regime, as it currently stands, extends only to item (1) of the FATF's activity-based definition of CASPs. It is relevantly apparent from the FATF's emphasis on the responsibility of each country to take a functional approach to determine whether an entity is undertaking the functions of a CASP, that the definition is intended to apply to all entities providing a qualifying service. Focusing regulatory attention on the on and off ramps of the crypto asset industry neglects the laundering potential of core 'nodes' integral to the NFT laundering ecosystem.[142] Accordingly, the limited scope of the AML/CTF Act, insofar as several CASPS, including custodial wallet providers, marketplaces, decentralised exchanges or platforms, and mixing and tumbling services, are not required to implement CDD systems, screen customers against politically exposed persons lists, or comply with the Travel Rule, is a consequence fundamentally inconsistent with the FATF's updated guidance.

An FATF FUR of Australia's current AML regulatory landscape would identify several weaknesses in the methodology and approach of Australia to the shared understanding of money laundering risk at a national level. An assessment of risk, coordination, and policy setting would conclude that Australia currently demonstrates a limited understanding of the emerging money laundering risks of crypto assets and that Australia's understanding of the relative scale of money laundering, as well as the vulnerabilities or channels exploited to launder criminal proceeds, is impaired by the lack of ongoing assessment of CASPs. The definition of 'money or other property' in the *Criminal Code Act 1995* (Cth) is broad enough to cover crypto assets, meaning that CASPs can engage in activities covered by the FATF's Glossary definition of CASPs in Australia. Accordingly, priority actions recommended to Australian authorities would include implementing specific procedures for licensing and regulating all CASPs, their activities, and their transactions, requiring CASPs take appropriate steps to identify, assess, manage, and mitigate their money laundering risks, and extending the definition of 'digital currency' under the AML/CTF Act to align with the FATF definition of virtual assets. The deficiencies relating to the lack of identification and assessment of the money laundering risks emerging from crypto assets and CASPs, and a lack of framework for the regulation and supervision of CASPs, would be considered important gaps and weighed significantly in the overall rating of Recommendation 15. The FUR would conclude that Australia has not demonstrated a thorough ongoing understanding of the modes, methodologies, and typologies of how money laundering threats manifest themselves in crypto assets and, ultimately, assess Australia as non-compliant with Recommendation 15.

[141] *AML/CTF Act* s 6(2) item 50A.

[142] Campbell-Verduyn (2018), p. 297.

5 Recommendation to Address Regulatory Gap

Classification of Australia's crypto asset regulatory landscape as requiring increased monitoring would likely result in the abandonment of foreign investment within the jurisdiction as a result of increased compliance costs and the potential exclusion of Australian crypto businesses from international markets as other jurisdictions advance their regulatory frameworks. Australia has concentrated critical AML regulatory measures, including CDD, at the on and off ramps of the crypto asset ecosystem. Whilst remaining technically compliant with the FATF Recommendations, the absence of regulatory reform to address the novel money laundering risks arising out new and emerging crypto assets has theoretically allowed criminals to utilise NFTs as a vehicle to generate, obfuscate, and withdraw proceeds of criminal actions without drawing the attention of regulatory or law enforcement agencies. To this end, the practice of applying existing regulatory measures to nascent financial markets is only successful if the money laundering threats mirror that of the traditional financial system.[143] In the case of NFT Laundering, criminals have sidestepped the presumed reliance on crypto asset exchange service providers, in the same sense, according to Schmidt, as how the cash economy cannot be regulated through financial surveillance.[144] Accordingly, future-proofing legislation applicable to crypto assets by expanding the definition of 'digital currency' to capture NFTs is the first step in creating concrete legal assurances, necessary to ensure Australia's AML regulatory regime keeps pace with the innovation and technical developments inherent in the crypto asset and fintech industry and to promote consumer and investor confidence.

The novel money laundering risks posed by an under-regulated NFT ecosystem suggest significant regulatory benefits in expanding the definition of reporting entities under the AML/CTF Act to include certain NFT service providers, including wallet providers and NFT marketplaces. The jurisdictional scope of the AML/CTF Act appears flexible enough to capture NFT launderers under its regime and would satisfy the FATF Interpretative Note to Recommendation 15, whilst acknowledging the FATF's guidance that individual nodes are best placed to understand their unique money laundering risks and to implement AML policies consistent with the service provider's business model. Future research is required to investigate the specific NFT service providers best placed to implement AML policies, including, at the customer intake stage, the verification and storage of CDD information and, prior to each transaction, undertaking a risk-based assessment according to a *de minimis* threshold and complying with the Travel Rule. This will require CASPs to develop a risk appraisal specific to each firm's product, business model, and customer base, as well as develop sector-specific tools in line with their risk profile. In this sense, a potential next step for the Albanese Government is to require AUSTRAC to supervise firms with significant crypto asset products or services in order to identify the

[143] Schmidt (2021), p. 340.

[144] Ibid.

specific crypto asset business models and sectors with heightened money laundering risks best placed to implement AML procedures.

Furthermore, the 'gatekeeper' nature of NFT marketplaces and wallet providers as facilitating the listing and exchange of NFTs between pseudonymous users could facilitate effective counterparty identification through a requirement for verifiable CDD information to be received upon the creation of an account or listing of an NFT, in addition to an ongoing risk-based appraisal of users for 'red flags', such as suspicious trading activity. The reporting of suspicious behaviour, high-risk transactions, and transactions above the threshold value to AUSTRAC, in combination with the introduction of record keeping obligations, would significantly increase the amount of consumer information available to assist regulatory and law enforcement bodies to undertake asset-tracing or user identification exercises. Furthermore, consumers accessing an NFT marketplace would participate with increased confidence knowing that participants are subject to regulatory measures to ensure they are sufficiently identifiable, and that user behaviour is subject to ongoing appraisal for fraud-related risk factors.

However, implementation of the Travel Rule for NFT service providers raises several complications regarding the use of non-custodial wallets. When applying a risk-based assessment to a transfer from a service provider to an unhosted wallet, service providers would be required to obtain baseline customer identification details of the recipient, in addition to applying enhanced CDD and risk-management measures commensurate with the heightened money laundering risks involved. Requiring verifiable documents from non-custodial counterparty wallets is impractical, primarily, due to the likely costs imposed upon service providers, in turn raising the costs of verification and potentially incentivising the transaction of NFTs between unhosted wallets. Whilst not suggesting a restriction on transfers involving non-custodial wallets, future research is required to determine the appropriate balance between permitting the natural expansion of the crypto asset and fintech industry through non-intervention and ensuring money laundering is curtailed to an extent permissible under the FATF Recommendations. Ultimately, whilst the FATF Recommendations contain several limitations regarding their suitability for the crypto asset ecosystem, the FATF has demonstrated a flexibility in its regulatory approach and, ultimately, it is in this sense that Australia's regulatory focus is lacking.

The implementation of an effective global system of AML regulatory measures is reliant upon a methodical process of updating international standards and regulatory governance. Whilst reliance on the FATF Recommendations, Interpretative Notes, and updated guidance is not mandatory, it is significant that the global standards required to address money laundering in nascent financial markets is within the remit of the FATF. Accordingly, consideration of whether Australia's current regulatory landscape is inconsistent with the FATF's most recent guidance is in important consideration in constructing a pathway for regulatory reform. The status of the FATF Recommendations as normative in nature provides significant confidence that global compliance is possible, albeit at an undeniably slower pace than criminal laundering strategies. However, for Australia to adapt its regulatory regime to combat the novel money laundering risks arising from NFTs, and remain compliant with the FATF Recommendations, it must avoid continuing to apply traditional regulatory measures to nascent financial markets.

6 Conclusion

Australia's reliance on transplanting a traditional regulatory model into a nascent financial market is incongruent with the pseudonymity inherent in the NFT ecosystem. This paper has demonstrated that in the absence of regulatory reform, NFTs will continue to present significant and novel money laundering risks. Firstly, fintech industries, of which NFTs play a fundamental role, will continue to experience significant growth as Australia pursues is digital revolution. Secondly, criminals are able to utilise NFTs at various stages of the money laundering process, including the acquisition of illicit proceeds through fraudulent activities, the structuring of proceeds to disguise their origin, wash trading to feed misleading information to the market, and trade-based laundering to legitimise the illicit proceeds for reintroduction to the traditional financial system. Thirdly, Australia's existing regulatory landscape does not extend to NFTs or their associated service providers and has neglected to implement critical regulatory reforms proffered by the FATF. Finally, a FUR of Australia's current AML regulatory landscape would likely conclude that Australia is non-compliant with Recommendation 15, a conclusion incompatible with Australia's desire to continue to attract significant international commercial investment. Ultimately, this paper argues that the current regulatory protections legislated under the AML/CTF Act must give way to innovative solutions commensurate with the novel money laundering risks posed by the crypto asset ecosystem and recommends that future research identify the specific NFT service providers best placed to implement critical AML regulatory measures, including CDD and KYC protocols. While the FATF Recommendations and associated updated guidance, in their current form, are insufficient to combat all of the money laundering risks posed by crypto assets, the necessity for a globally coordinated response affirms their position as the international benchmark in AML regulation, and, accordingly, provides the pathway for domestic regulatory reform.

References

Abrahams N (2022) There are six kinds of NFTs, and you still need to care. Australian Financial Review. https://www.afr.com/technology/there-are-six-kinds-of-nfts-and-you-still-need-to-care-20220622-p5avom. Accessed 21 Dec 2023

Al Shamsi M et al (2023) Space transition and the vulnerabilities of the NFT market to financial crime. J Financ Crime. https://doi.org/10.1108/JFC-09-2022-0218

AUSTRAC (2022a) Preventing the criminal abuse of digital currency. https://www.austrac.gov.au/business/how-comply-guidance-and-resources/guidance-resources/preventing-criminal-abuse-digital-currencies. Accessed 21 Dec 2023

AUSTRAC (2022b) Crypto asset secondary service providers: licensing and custody requirements: submission. https://treasury.gov.au/sites/default/files/2022-12/c2022-259046-austrac.pdf. Accessed 21 Dec 2023

Bao H, Roubaud D (2021) Recent developments in fintech: non-fungible token. FinTech 1(1): 44–46. https://doi.org/10.3390/fintech1010003

Bao H, Roubaud D (2022) Non-fungible token: a systematic review and research agenda. J Risk Financial Manag 15(5):215–224. https://doi.org/10.3390/jrfm15050215

Basul A (2022) Australia: home to a booming fintech industry. Bobsguide. https://www.bobsguide.com/articles/australia-home-to-a-booming-fintech-industry/. Accessed 21 Dec 2023

Bhargava R (2019) Blockchain technology and its application: a review. IUP J Inf Technol 15(1): 7–15. Available at SSRN: https://ssrn.com/abstract=3423915

Buchanan B (2004) Money laundering—a global obstacle. Res Int Bus Financ 18(1):115–127. https://doi.org/10.1016/j.ribaf.2004.02.001

Campbell-Verduyn M (2018) Bitcoin, crypto-coins, and global anti-money laundering governance. Crime Law Soc Chang 69:283–305. https://doi.org/10.1007/s10611-017-9756-5

Campbell-Verduyn M, Goguen M (2017) The mutual constitution of technology and global governance: bitcoin, blockchains, and the international anti-money laundering regime. In: Campbell-Verduyn M (ed) Bitcoin and beyond. Routledge, New York, pp 69–87

Chaikin D (2009) Risk-based approaches to combatting financial crime. J Law Financ Crime 8(2): 20–27

Chiacchio F et al (2022) A non-fungible token solution for the track and trace of pharmaceutical supply chain. Appl Sci 12(8):4019–4042. https://doi.org/10.3390/app12084019

CoinGecko (2023) Global cryptocurrency market cap charts. https://www.coingecko.com/en/global-charts. Accessed 21 Dec 2023

Commonwealth Department of Industry, Science, Energy and Resources (2020) The national blockchain roadmap: progressing towards a blockchain-empowered future. https://apo.org.au/sites/default/files/resource-files/2020-02/apo-nid276541.pdf. Accessed 21 Dec 2023

Commonwealth Department of Treasury (2022) Crypto asset secondary service providers: licensing and custody requirements. https://treasury.gov.au/consultation/c2022-259046. Accessed 21 Dec 2023

Das D et al (2022) Understanding security issues in the NFT ecosystem. Research report. Cornell University, New York

de Koker L et al (2022) Where's Wally? FATF, virtual asset service providers, and the regulatory jurisdictional challenge. In: Goldbarsht D, de Koker L (eds) Financial technology and the law. Springer, Cham, pp 151–183

DeMatteo M (2022) NFT scams: how to avoid falling victim. https://www.coindesk.com/learn/nft-scams-how-to-avoid-falling-victim/. Accessed 21 Dec 2023

Desmond D (2020) Cryptolaundering: optimising cryptocurrency laundering interventions. Thesis, University of the Sunshine Coast

Dostov V, Shust P (2014) Customer loyalty programs: money laundering and terrorism financing risks. J Money Laund Control 17(4):385–394. https://doi.org/10.1108/JMLC-06-2013-0021

Dupuis D, Gleason K (2020) Money laundering with cryptocurrency: open doors and the regulatory dialectic. J Financ Crime 28(1):60–74. https://doi.org/10.1108/JFC-06-2020-0113

Elliptic (2022) NFTs and financial crime. https://www.elliptic.co/hubfs/NFT%20Report%202022.pdf. Accessed 21 Dec 2023

Ellul J, Revolidis I (2023) Non-fungible tokens (NFTs), smart contracts and contracts: the need for legal and technology assurances

Ennis J (2002) Cleaning up the beaches: the Caribbean response to the FATF's review to identify non-cooperative countries or territories. Law Bus Rev 8(2):637–665. https://scholar.smu.edu/lbra/vol8/iss4/8

Evans T (2019) Cryptokitties, cryptography, and copyright. AIPLA Q J 47(2):219–266

Financial Action Task Force (2018) Australia's progress in strengthening measures to tackle money laundering and terrorist financing. https://www.fatf-gafi.org/en/publications/Mutualevaluations/Fur-australia-2018.html. Accessed 21 Dec 2023

Financial Action Task Force (2019) Guidance for a risk-based approach to virtual assets and virtual asset service providers. https://www.fatf-gafi.org/en/publications/Fatfrecommendations/Guidance-rba-virtual-assets.html. Accessed 21 Dec 2023

Financial Action Task Force (2020) Virtual assets red flag indicators of money laundering and terrorist financing. https://www.fatf-gafi.org/en/publications/Methodsandtrends/Virtual-assets-red-flag-indicators.html. Accessed 21 Dec 2023

Financial Action Task Force (2021) Updated guidance for a risk-based approach to virtual assets and virtual asset service providers. https://www.fatf-gafi.org/en/publications/Fatfrecommendations/Guidance-rba-virtual-assets-2021.html. Accessed 21 Dec 2023

Financial Action Task Force (2022) Targeted update on implementation of FATF's standards on Vas and VASPs. https://www.fatf-gafi.org/en/publications/Fatfrecommendations/Targeted-update-virtual-assets-vasps.html. Accessed 21 Dec 2023

Financial Action Task Force (2023a) The FATF recommendations. https://www.fatf-gafi.org/en/publications/Fatfrecommendations/Fatf-recommendations.html. Accessed 21 Dec 2023

Financial Action Task Force (2023b) Money laundering and terrorist financing in the art and antiquities market. https://www.fatf-gafi.org/content/fatf-gafi/en/publications/Methodsandtrends/Money-Laundering-Terrorist-Financing-Art-Antiquities-Market.html. Accessed 21 Dec 2023

Financial Stability Board (2022) FSB statement on international regulation and supervision of crypto-asset activities. https://www.fsb.org/2022/07/fsb-statement-on-international-regulation-and-supervision-of-crypto-asset-activities/. Accessed 21 Dec 2023

Gilmore W (1995) Dirty money: the evolution of money laundering counter-measures. Council of Europe Press, Paris

Goldbarsht D (2017) Who's the legislator anyway? How the FATF's global norms reshape Australian counter-terrorist financing laws. Federal Law Rev 45(1):127–151

Goldbarsht D (2020) Global counter-terrorist financing and soft law: multi-layered approaches. Edward Elgar, Cheltenham

Grinblatt M, Keloharju M (2004) Tax-loss trading and wash sales. J Financ Econ 71(1):51–76. https://doi.org/10.1016/S0304-405X(03)00180-6

Hillman H (2020) Money laundering through cryptocurrencies: analysing the responses of the United States and Australia and providing recommendations for the UK to address the money laundering risks posed by cryptocurrencies. Thesis, University of the West of England

Irwin A, Turner A (2018) Illicit bitcoin transactions: challenges in getting to the who, what, when and where. J Money Laund Control 21(3):297–313. https://doi.org/10.1108/JMLC-07-2017-0031

Jenson J et al (2021) An introduction to decentralised finance (DeFi). Complex Sys Informatics Modelling Q 26(1):46–54. https://doi.org/10.7250/csimq.2021-26.03

Jordanoska (2021) The exciting world of NFTs: a consideration of regulatory and financial crime risks. Butterworths J Int Banking Financ Law 10:716–718

KPMG (2022) Australian fintech survey report. https://assets.kpmg.com/content/dam/kpmg/au/pdf/2022/australian-fintech-survey-report.pdf. Accessed 21 Dec 2023

Kyles D (2022) Centralised control over decentralised structures: AML and CTF regulation of blockchains and distributed ledgers. In: Goldbarsht D, de Koker L (eds) Financial technology and the law. Springer, Cham, pp 121–150

Li Y et al (2019) Toward privacy and regulation in blockchain-based cryptocurrencies. IEEE Netw 33(5):111–117. https://doi.org/10.1109/MNET.2019.1800271

Lilley P (2006) Dirty dealing: the untold truth about global money laundering. Kogan Page, London

Marusevich A (2021) The uncertainty of cryptocurrency regulation. Law Soc ACT J 260:26–30

Mazorra B et al (2022) Do not rug on me: leveraging machine learning techniques for automated scam detection. Mathematics 10:949–973. https://doi.org/10.3390/math10060949

McCarthy K (2018) Money laundering market: regulating the criminal economy. Agenda Publishing

McKay T (2021) NFTs are crashing and who could have seen this coming other than basically anyone? https://www.gizmodo.com.au/2021/06/nfts-are-crashing-and-who-could-have-seen-this-coming-other-than-basically-anyone/. Accessed 21 Dec 2023

Meland PH et al (2020) The ransomware-as-a-service economy within the darknet. Comput Secur 92. https://doi.org/10.1016/j.cose.2020.101762

Osvald J (2020) Unjustly enriching the richer. Aust Natl Univ J Law Technol 1(1):16–34

Pelechrinis K et al (2022) Spotting anomalous trades in NFT markets: the case of NBA TopShot. Research report. Cornell University, New York

Redrup Y (2022) How three Aussies grew their NFT start-up to $2.3B in nine months. Australian Financial Review. https://www.afr.com/technology/how-three-aussies-grew-their-nft-start-up-to-2-3b-in-nine-months-20220621-p5avbb. Accessed 21 Dec 2023

Robinson J (1995) The laundrymen. Pocket Books, New York

Roy SS et al (2023) Demystifying NFT promotion and phishing scams. https://doi.org/10.48550/arXiv.2301.09806

Ryder N (2012) Money laundering—an endless cycle? A comparative analysis of the anti-money laundering policies in The United States of America, the United Kingdom, Australia and Canada. Routledge, London

Schmidt A (2021) Virtual assets: compelling a new anti-money laundering and counter-terrorism financing regulatory model. Int J Law Inf Technol 29(1):332–363. https://doi.org/10.1093/ijlit/eaac001

Sedlmeir J et al (2021) Digital identities and verifiable credentials. Bus Inf Syst Eng 63(5):603–613. https://doi.org/10.1007/s12599-021-00722-y

Sharma T et al (2022) "It's a blessing and a curse": unpacking creators' practices with non-fungible tokens (NFTs) and their communities. Research report. University of Illinois, Illinois

Sheth H, Dattani J (2019) Overview on blockchain technology. Asian J Convergence Technol 5(1): 1–3

Srivastava A et al (2010) International guide to money laundering law and practice. Bloomsbury Professional

Stokes R (2013) Anti-money laundering regulation and emerging payment technologies. Bank Financ Services Policy Rep 32(5):1–11

Stuhlmiller L (2013) Mitigating virtual money laundering: an analysis of virtual worlds and virtual currencies. Thesis. Utica College, Utica

Sultzer S (1995) Money laundering: the scope of the problem and attempts to combat it. Tennessee Law Rev 49:143–237

Tariq S, Sifat I (2021) Suspicious trading in nonfungible tokens (NFTs) evidence from wash trading. Research report. Radboud University, Nijmegen

Teichmann F (2020) Recent trends in money laundering. Crime Law Soc Chang 73:237–247

The Hon. Jim Chalmers MP and the Hon. Dr Andrew Leigh MP (2022) Work underway on crypto asset reforms. https://ministers.treasury.gov.au/ministers/jim-chalmers-2022/media-releases/work-underway-crypto-asset-reforms. Accessed 21 Dec 2023

Tiwari M et al (2023) Global money laundering appeal index: application of principal component analysis. J Money Laund Control 26(1):205–211

von Wachter V et al (2022) NFT wash trading quantifying suspicious behaviour in NFT markets. Research report. University of Copenhagen, Copenhagen

Wang Y (2022) Volatility spillovers across NFTs news attention and financial markets. Financ Anal 83. https://doi.org/10.1016/j.irfa.2022.102313

Wang Q et al (2021) Non-fungible token (NFT): overview, evaluation, opportunities and challenges. Research report. Southern University of Science and Technology, Shenzhen

Wronka C (2022a) Money laundering through cryptocurrencies—analysis of the phenomenon and appropriate prevention measures. J Money Laund Control 25(1):79–94. https://doi.org/10.1108/JMLC-02-2021-0017

Wronka C (2022b) "Cyber-laundering": the change of money laundering in the digital age. J Money Laund Control 25(2):330–344. https://doi.org/10.1108/JMLC-04-2021-0035

Samuel Orchard is a Tipstaff and the Equity Researcher at the Supreme Court of New South Wales. Samuel graduated from Macquarie University with a Bachelor of Arts (Psychology) and Laws (Honours) in 2022 and is currently a research assistant to the Financial Integrity Hub (FIH) at Macquarie Law School. Samuel has a broad research interest in the legal structures upholding Australia's anti-money laundering and counter-terrorism financing framework, specifically as it applies to new and emerging financial products and services.

The Legal Design of Domestic MLA Procedures in Southeast Europe: A Comparative Analysis of Serbia, North Macedonia and Bosnia and Herzegovina

Slobodan Tomic and Elizabeth David-Barrett

Abstract The chapter explores the domestic legal design of Mutual Legal Assistance (MLA) procedures, analysing individual forms of MLA such as extradition of suspects or convicts, takeover or surrender of prosecution, and execution of foreign judgments. The analysis compares legislation from three countries in Southeast Europe: Serbia, North Macedonia, and Bosnia and Herzegovina. It examines whether two key components of legal design, namely (1) the discretion granted to institutions within the criminal justice system and political establishment and (2) the presence of checks and balances systems within MLA procedures, have a positive or negative impact on MLA policy in practice. The analysis reveals that, although the three countries share many similarities in their legal arrangements pertaining to MLA procedures, there are some variations in specific forms of MLA, in terms of the discretion granted to domestic actors and the presence of checks and balances within the procedure. The findings show that significant discretion given to specific actors within the MLA policy can pave the way for harmful practices such as arbitrariness, uneven application of the law, and potential political abuse. The study also highlights the value of incorporating built-in checks and balances within the MLA procedure to ensure accountability and mutual control mechanisms, confirming that, where such mechanisms are not present, appropriate accountability and control safeguards are missing, enabling potential abuse of power or neglect in handling the MLA procedure. At the same time, it emerges that these checks and balances, whether they include internal review mechanisms, joint decision-making models, and/or approval powers ('de facto vetoing'), should not be excessive or burdensome to avoid obstructing the MLA processes.

S. Tomic (✉)
University of York, York, UK
e-mail: slobodan.tomic@york.ac.uk

E. David-Barrett
University of Sussex, East Sussex, UK

D. Goldbarsht, L. de Koker (eds.), *Financial Crime, Law and Governance*, Ius Gentium: Comparative Perspectives on Law and Justice 116,
https://doi.org/10.1007/978-3-031-59547-9_11

1 Introduction

Organised crime and corruption are increasingly transnational. To effectively tackle these issues, cross-border collaboration among states is essential.[1] The existing literature has mainly focused on the design of international instruments for Mutual Legal Assistance (MLA), which refers to the collaborative process where one state assists another in investigating and prosecuting crimes.[2] The design of states' legal frameworks governing MLA procedures has undergone less exploration. Yet the domestic legal framework crucially determines key operational aspects that can heavily influence whether cooperation succeeds. This chapter aims to address this scholarly gap by investigating how the domestic legal design of MLA procedures influences cross-border collaboration in combatting organised crime and corruption, with a focus on three transitional states—Serbia, Bosnia and Herzegovina, and North Macedonia—in Southeastern Europe or more specifically the Western Balkans.

The recognised forms of MLA include (1) evidence sharing, (2) extradition of a suspect, (3) surrender of a criminal prosecution, (4) takeover of a criminal prosecution, and (5) enforcement of a foreign judgment. The analysis unpacks the roles, duties, and powers of relevant institutions within the domestic criminal justice systems of these countries and assesses whether the existing legal design presents potential obstacles to efficient cross-border collaboration. We focus on the interdependence of key actors in the criminal justice system: prosecutors, police, courts, as well as political authorities such as the ministry of justice.

The chapter provides insights into how domestic legal design and procedure influences the handling and realising MLA. In doing so, it brings together literatures on criminal law and public administration. We focus on two concepts key to the wider study of legal design: institutional discretion, and checks and balances.

First, building on a broad literature about the importance of regulatory discretion,[3] we argue that the degree of discretion available to the key actors involved critically affects the scope for arbitrary decision-making in this highly sensitive area. This can lead to inconsistency and lack of uniformity in the implementation of law. Indeed, we contend that, in the context of MLA, discretion may be more detrimental than in other policy areas, including general judicial[4] and prosecutorial policy settings.[5]

---

[1] Dávid-Barrett and Tomić (2022).

[2] Gillmore (1995), p. 14.

[3] Schmidt and Scott (2021).

[4] O'Connor (1984).

[5] Herrmann (1973).

Second, building on literature which studies oversight mechanisms in various contexts, the regulation of power among various parts of the criminal justice system such as courts and prosecutors[6] or inter-governmental interactions[7] as well as 'veto-player' decision-making,[8] we compare systems of checks and balances in the MLA process. Our analysis reaffirms the value of having in-built internal checks and balances; without them, serious risks emerge concerning political abuse or neglectful use by actors in the criminal justice system. However, we also contend that checks and balances can become 'excessive'. For example, multi-tier review and/or veto-decision making arrangements may hinder or slow down the MLA procedure, or undue oversight powers may be strategically granted to particular actors who might leverage them to impede or obstruct the process rather than performing an accountability function.

2 Legal Design and Mutual Legal Assistance: The Role and Effects

There are various forms of MLA that one country can provide to or request from another country, including data sharing, joint investigation, extradition of a suspect, takeover or surrender of a criminal case or a convict,[9] and enforcement of a foreign judgment. The legal design establishes the rules, obligations, and power dynamics among criminal justice institutions who engage in MLA such as prosecutors, courts, police, domestic authorities such as ministries or the government, and foreign authorities. The MLA process stretches from the initial receipt and assessment of an MLA request from a foreign country, at which point it is necessary to determine eligibility for MLA provision, to subsequent decisions on whether to provide the requested assistance and how exactly to cooperate.

Our analysis focuses on two crucial aspects of legal design: (1) the scope for institutional discretion, determined by the comprehensiveness of regulation pertaining to the MLA process; and (2) the presence and adequacy of mechanisms of oversight, allowing for key institutions to be monitored and held accountable and therefore acting as a safeguard against the abuse of power.[10]

[6] See e.g., Epps (2021) and Brubacher (2004).

[7] Greene (1994).

[8] Tsebelis (1995).

[9] Gillmore (1995).

[10] Davis (1969); Black (2001), p. 2.

2.1 Institutional Discretion

Discretion is characterised as the "freedom to make choices" or the "power to choose".[11] While operating within prescribed criteria and directions for decision-making, discretion allows for individual judgement. In legal scholarship and public administration literature, ongoing discussions revolve around whether discretion in the hands of public authorities is inherently detrimental.[12] Earlier perspectives considered discretion to be detrimental to the rule of law, as it might lead to arbitrariness, legal uncertainty, and potential abuse of power.[13] However, contemporary understanding recognises that a degree of discretion is necessary and at times desirable, as it allows for contextual decision-making and equitable consideration of individual circumstances.[14]

Nevertheless, the positive function of institutional discretion is contingent upon the nature of specific policy sectors. The argument supporting a favourable role for discretion finds particular resonance in the context of "street-level bureaucracy" and sectors such as social services or welfare provision, where discretion is inevitable and potentially valuable.[15] Discretion can also play a positive role in the decision-making of prosecutors and even judges.[16]

However, within the realm of MLA, the potential risks of discretion multiply. MLA involves cooperation across borders, and hence raises thorny issues around national sovereignty. It also often pertains to very sensitive areas, particularly when used to investigate cases of corruption and organised crime. In such cases, state actors with decision-making influence may, at best, be unfamiliar with necessary procedures and, at worst, may have an interest in frustrating cooperation because they are implicated in corruption or embedded in organised crime networks. MLA policy can therefore give rise to numerous adverse outcomes when decision-making is left to discretion.

First, discretion in the MLA process can lead to arbitrary decision-making, as decision-makers are not bound by specific rules.[17] This creates potential to undermine the integrity of the MLA process, especially when decisions are influenced by political interests[18] or priorities other than justice and effective legal assistance. For instance, if political institutions such as the Ministry of Interior, Ministry of Justice, or the government more broadly hold considerable decision-making power within the MLA process, they can arbitrarily determine actions that may obstruct, delay, terminate, or even halt a specific investigation. This opens the door to politicisation

[11] Pratt and Sossin (2009), p. 221.

[12] Hawkins (1992) and Schmidt and Scott (2021).

[13] Black (2001), p. 2; Dicey (1982).

[14] McLachlin (1992), p. 168; Schmidt and Scott (2021).

[15] Evans and Harris (2004).

[16] Dworkin (1963) and Albonetti (1991).

[17] Black (2001), p. 2.

[18] Buromenskyi and Gutnyk (2019).

of the process, where political actors may protect or be involved in international criminal networks engaged in, for example, cross-border money laundering, human trafficking, or arms trafficking. In post-conflict contexts, as in the Western Balkans, elements within the political establishment may, for example, seek to protect war crimes suspects wanted by a neighbouring country, motivated by electoral pressures or in a bid to conceal their own involvement in crimes.[19]

Furthermore, the absence of detailed regulation in MLA procedures can result in inconsistent application of the law across different cases, thereby increasing legal uncertainty. This can undermine notions of justice and legal predictability and potentially impede the functioning of certain institutions within the "MLA chain" of decision-makers. Faced with differing approaches by other authorities compared to previous cases, the relevant authorities may experience a state of paralysis and reluctance to proceed.[20] Therefore, our working assumption is that granting broad discretion to national institutions involved in the MLA process is primarily a negative phenomenon with considerable potential for adverse effects. As legislation related to MLA should establish clear procedures and guidelines to ensure efficient and effective processing of requests for mutual legal assistance.

2.2 *Checks and Balances*

The other crucial aspect of legal design in the context of MLA proceedings relates to internal control mechanisms, i.e., whether the decisions of the relevant authorities with significant roles in the MLA process are subject to accountability mechanisms.[21] Such mechanisms include review instruments, such as judicial review over the decisions of prosecutors, courts, or ministries, oversight by one part of the criminal justice apparatus over another,[22] and "checks and balances" arrangements where one authority's decision requires approval or co-decision-making by another authority (e.g., a prosecutor's decision may be contingent upon approval from the competent ministry). These internal checks and balances, elsewhere called 'subconstitutional checks and balances'[23] distinct from the proverbial checks and balances among the three branches of power,[24] serve in criminal law systems to prevent misconduct or erroneous application of the law,[25] both of which can infringe upon individual rights, due process, and the rule of law. Implementing such "checks

[19] Radeljić (2013), p. 248; Radeljić and Đorđević (2020), p. 602.

[20] Eskridge Jr. and Frickey (1994).

[21] Davis (1969) and Lowi (1969).

[22] Brubacher (2004).

[23] Baughman (2016).

[24] Myers (2008).

[25] Epps (2021), p. 5.

and balances" within the criminal procedure is crucial, but a potential drawback is that they can hinder progress in the various stages of the MLA process or limit the autonomy and operational capacity of institutions whose ability to complete tasks is reliant on approvals from other institutions.

2.3 What Does an Adequate Legal Design Look Like in MLA?

An adequate legal design should prioritise and enhance the autonomy and capacity of prosecutors and other criminal policy institutions to conduct effective investigations. The importance of these factors has long been recognised in the success of anti-corruption and anti-crime policies.[26] Achieving this typically involves a legal design that simplifies the sequence of steps and establishes effective procedures within the MLA process.[27] This reduces the likelihood of certain decision-making actors within the domestic "MLA chain" undermining or obstructing cooperation.

Institutional autonomy for prosecutors refers to their ability to pursue policies independently, with minimal dependence on other actors, particularly political institutions. This means authority to utilise vital tools and instruments for investigative work, such deploying the police in gathering evidence, locating suspects, conducting investigations, and facilitating extraditions.[28] Unnecessary complexities arise when certain institutions, such as the court, relevant ministry, or police, possess "de facto veto powers" capable of significantly delaying or even halting an investigation. While these powers might be useful for internal checks and balances, excessive dependence on them hampers prosecutors' operational capacity to carry out their duties effectively.

A balance needs to be struck between the two sets of priorities: effectiveness and institutional autonomy, on the one hand, and institutional control and accountability on the other. Procedural simplicity and effectiveness should be pursued without compromising internal checks and balances, and internal control mechanisms should not suppress the autonomy and capacity of institutions involved in the MLA procedure, especially prosecutors.

---

[26] UNDP (2015).

[27] Swire et al. (2016).

[28] Tomic (2019), pp. 165–167.

3 Empirical Analysis

3.1 Serbia

Serbia is an unconsolidated, transitional democracy located in Southeastern Europe. Over the past two decades, the country has actively engaged in internationally promoted reforms, such as granting formal independence to non-political institutions,[29] as well as efforts to combat cross-border crime and corruption, becoming a member of international bodies and organisations and ratifying significant international conventions that facilitate and regulate cross-border cooperation, including MLA. Examples include the United Nations Convention against Transnational Organized Crime (UNTOC), also known as the Palermo Convention, as well as the European Convention on Mutual Assistance in Criminal Matters, to which Serbia has become a signatory as a member of the Council of Europe. Serbia has also participated in various other conventions on international cooperation in MLA, involving regions beyond its immediate vicinity, as well as regional multilateral and bilateral conventions within Southeast Europe.

Since 2011, Serbia has adopted the prosecutorial investigation model, whereby investigations are led and managed by a prosecutor, subject to court approval and oversight. The police are deployed and directed by the prosecutor to carry out investigations, rather than conducting investigations independently.

3.1.1 Determination of Jurisdiction

The primary legislation governing international legal assistance in criminal matters is the Law on International Legal Assistance in Criminal Matters (hereafter, Law on International Legal Assistance). This law is subsidiary in nature, giving priority to ratified international agreements, particularly bilateral agreements followed by multilateral agreements. Other relevant laws include:

1. the Law on International Legal Assistance in Criminal Matters;
2. the Law on the Organisation and Competence of State Authorities in Combating Organized Crime, Terrorism, and Corruption;
3. the Code of Criminal Procedure;
4. the Criminal Code;
5. laws regulating the work of the Ministry of Justice, Courts, Public Prosecution, Ministry of Internal Affairs, Ministry of Foreign Affairs; and
6. other statutory and regulatory provisions.

Serbia can provide MLA to another country under the following conditions (Article 7, Law on International Legal Assistance):

---

[29] Tomić and Jovančić (2012).

(a) The offense is considered a criminal offense in Serbia.
(b) The criminal proceedings in Serbia have not been concluded, and the criminal sanction has not been fully executed.
(c) The prosecution or execution of the criminal sanction is not excluded due to statute of limitations, amnesty, or pardon.[30]
(d) The request for assistance does not involve political offenses or offenses solely related to military duties.
(e) Assistance should not violate Serbia's sovereignty, security, public order, or essential interests.

The competent judicial authority decides on conditions a, b and c, while the Minister responsible for justice decides on conditions d and e or provides an opinion on them. In exceptional cases, MLA can be provided for crimes against international humanitarian law without any statute of limitations.

A Public Prosecutor in Serbia has discretionary power to initiate prosecution for a criminal offense committed on Serbian territory, even if another country has already initiated or completed criminal proceedings for the same offense.[31] If the perpetrator of the criminal offense is a foreign national, prosecution may be transferred to the foreign state, but reciprocity is required.[32] However, the law does not provide specific criteria for assigning prosecution; this lack of clear criteria can lead to jurisdictional conflicts and hinder cooperation between requesting and requested states. If the Republic of Serbia decides to transfer prosecution to another state, it is likely to provide MLA. However, if both states are conducting parallel criminal proceedings, creating a conflict of jurisdiction, inter-state cooperation is highly unlikely.

In cases of criminal offenses committed abroad that endanger the constitutional order and security of Serbia, such as terrorism, endangering persons under international protection, financing terrorism, terrorist association, or counterfeiting domestic currency, exclusive jurisdiction lies with the judicial authorities of Serbia.[33] Even if the offense falls under the jurisdiction of the requesting state's court according to Article 3 of the Law on International Legal Assistance, MLA will not be provided if the offense is one for which exclusive jurisdiction is granted to the authorities of Serbia under other laws. The list of offenses falling under exclusive jurisdiction may

[30] Note that statutes of limitations can vary in different national legislation. Additionally, amnesty and pardon are political acts specific to a particular state, applicable within that state's territory and made at a specific moment and for specific reasons. This may lead to denial of legal assistance if the conditions of the requesting state, which seeks to prosecute the perpetrator, do not align with the interests and stance of the state granting amnesty or pardon.

[31] Article 6, Criminal Code.

[32] Reciprocity is presumed unless information about its existence is unavailable (Article 8 of the Law). Procedurally, the criminal proceedings for the same offense must not have concluded in a domestic court, and the criminal sanction must not have been fully executed.

[33] Article 7, Criminal Code.

vary over time and differ between countries. In addition to meeting the jurisdiction requirement, there must be no other legal obstacles to international cooperation.

3.1.2 Conditions for Extradition

The extradition process in Serbia involves the requesting state submitting an extradition request to the Ministry of Justice in Serbia, which is then forwarded to the relevant court, where the investigating judge determines the extradition conditions and submits the case to a panel of three judges for a final decision.

The conditions are that the offense must be recognised under Serbian criminal law and carry a minimum prison sentence of 1 year (or the suspect is already sentenced to a minimum of 4 months). In addition, the following eight conditions must be met under the Law on International Legal Assistance in Criminal Matters: (1) the suspect is not a Serbian citizen; (2) the offense was not committed in Serbia; (3) no ongoing criminal proceedings exist in Serbia for the offense; (4) the proceedings can be retried domestically; (5) the identity of the requested person is established; (6) there is sufficient evidence to support the extradition request;[34] (7) guarantees are provided for repeat proceedings in the presence of the extradited person in case of conviction in absentia; and (8) guarantees are given that the death penalty will not be imposed or executed for the requested.

The panel of judges determines extradition conditions and issues a decision. An appeal can be made within 3 days. If extradition conditions are not met, judges dismiss the extradition and pass the decision to the higher court. The higher court assesses the case, hears from the prosecutor and defense counsel, and confirms, overturns, or modifies the rejection.[35] The final decision is conveyed to the Ministry of Justice, which notifies the requesting state. Extradition can be simplified with the accused's consent; in such cases, the panel of judges issues a non-appealable decision, followed by the regular process.[36]

The Minister of Justice receives the final decision and case files, and approves or rejects the extradition, informing relevant parties.[37] As such, the extradition request is decided by the court in various forms through a two-tiered procedure, but the final decision lies with the Minister of Justice. The Minister can approve, reject, or modify the court's decision without clear criteria, retaining ultimate authority in the extradition process.

[34] The interpretation of "sufficient evidence" for reasonable suspicion can be problematic as different stages of the criminal proceedings involve different degrees of suspicion, and the competent authority may arbitrarily determine that there is not sufficient evidence.

[35] Article 29, Law on International Legal Assistance in Criminal Matters.

[36] Article 30, Law on International Legal Assistance in Criminal Matters.

[37] Article 31, Law on International Legal Assistance in Criminal Matters.

3.1.3 Surrender of Prosecution

The conditions for surrendering the prosecution of a suspect, for a criminal offense falling under the jurisdiction of a Serbian court, are as follows:[38] (1) the accused must have a residence or domicile in the requesting state; and (2) the accused must be serving a prison sentence or another criminal sanction involving deprivation of liberty in the requesting state. The law does not obligate authorities to approve the surrender even when these prerequisites are met. There are no more detailed regulations governing the decision-making process for surrendering prosecution. This grants significant discretion to the authorities although they are required to provide explanations in case of rejection. If the criminal act has caused harm to the Republic of Serbia, its citizens, or a legal entity with its headquarters in Serbian territory, special consideration will be given to securing property claims and protecting the interests of the injured party in the decision-making process regarding the transfer of prosecution.

Surrendering criminal prosecution to a foreign state involves a broader level of cooperation compared to extraditing a person. It entails fully entrusting the proceedings and execution of judgment to the foreign state, thereby recognising its complete jurisdiction over the matter. However, the conditions for surrender are more restrictive and proportionally set than those for extradition, which is merely a presumption, and not a necessary requirement, for initiating criminal proceedings against an individual. Consequently, if Serbia is willing to surrender prosecution to another state, it should also be willing to extradite a perpetrator to that state.

The decision to initiate the transfer process of criminal prosecution is made by several authorities:

1. A public prosecutor, prior to the commencement of criminal proceedings.
2. An investigative judge, upon the proposal of a public prosecutor, until the indictment becomes legally binding.
3. A pre-trial chamber, after obtaining the opinion of the public prosecutor, until the commencement of the main trial.
4. The court panel, after obtaining the opinion of the public prosecutor, until the conclusion of the main trial.

Once the decision to initiate the transfer process for criminal prosecution is made, the domestic judiciary can only undertake procedural actions that cannot be delayed. In case of a decision to surrender criminal prosecution, the suspect has the right to object to the higher prosecutor within a three-day period. If the proceedings have already commenced, both the accused and the prosecutor have the option to appeal to the higher court within 3 days, as outlined by Article 52 of the Law on International Legal Assistance.

In sum, there exists a two-tier procedure with a built-in review mechanism that does not involve political authorities. This mechanism aligns with international

[38] Article 48, Law on International Legal Assistance in Criminal Matters 2009.

standards regarding the most suitable form of checks and balances within legal procedures.

3.1.4 Takeover of Prosecution

The competent public prosecutor has the authority to take over the prosecution of a suspect or accused individual for a criminal offense that falls under the jurisdiction of the requesting state's court. The takeover of prosecution can occur if the conditions outlined in Article 7 of the Law are met, along with one of the following:[39]

1. The individual has residence or is domicile in the Republic of Serbia.
2. The individual is serving a prison sentence or another criminal sanction involving deprivation of liberty in the Republic of Serbia.

These conditions are technical in nature and do not provide interpretative discretion to the prosecutor. In the next step, the Ministry of Justice forwards the request and criminal documents to the relevant public prosecutor,[40] and provides the competent public prosecutor with an opinion on the fulfilment of the conditions outlined in Article 7, paragraphs 1, points 4) and 5).

The procedure for the takeover of prosecution is not extensively regulated. While the necessary conditions for a takeover are prescribed, the decision-making process primarily rests with the prosecutor, with limited regulations governing the application of Serbian law and other technical aspects. There are no internal review mechanisms within the procedure. The prosecutor plays the key role, while the Ministry's involvement is mainly technical, with virtually no discretionary power to influence the process.

3.1.5 Execution of a Foreign Judgment

The criminal penalty imposed by the verdict of a competent court of the requesting state can be executed if the conditions set forth in Article 7 of the Law are met along with one of the following conditions:

1. the convicted person is a citizen of the Republic of Serbia;
2. the convicted person has residence or is residing in the Republic of Serbia;
3. the convicted person is serving a criminal penalty in the Republic of Serbia that consists of deprivation of freedom due to a previously imposed judgment.

The decision to reject a request for execution of a foreign verdict is made in the following circumstances: 1. If the prerequisites for executing a foreign criminal

[39] Article 43 of the Law on International Legal Assistance.

[40] This is the prosecutor in the jurisdiction where the accused individual resides, has domicile, or is serving a prison sentence or another criminal sanction involving deprivation of liberty.

judgment are not met; 2. If it can be reasonably concluded that the person was convicted based on race, religion, nationality, or political beliefs; if the judgment was delivered in the absence of the convict; 3. If the conditions for a fair trial were not fulfilled.

This legal solution contradicts other provisions of the law and other legislative regulations. Specifically, the execution of a foreign verdict is solely linked to the personal aspect of the convicted person, such as their citizenship, residence, or stay within the territory of the Republic of Serbia. It disregards the nature and type of the criminal offense, and the severity and type of the imposed criminal penalty. A request for execution of a foreign court judgment will be approved unless one of the conditions for rejection is met, namely if it can be reasonably concluded that the person was convicted based on race, religion, nationality, or political beliefs, if the judgment was delivered in the absence of the convict, or if the conditions for a fair trial were not met.

In practice, this means that if a foreign state convicts its citizen and imposes the death penalty, which is legally permissible in that country, Serbia will allow extradition provided the country guarantees that the penalty will not be carried out. However, if the same foreign state convicts its citizen who is present in Serbia, Serbia can approve the request to execute the death penalty on its territory, even though its own system does not recognise this penalty, providing the conditions for rejections are not met. While unlikely to occur in practice, this situation is legally possible. Additionally, trials in absentia are possible under certain conditions in Serbia, making it inconsistent to require that judgments not be delivered in absentia in other countries. Regarding the condition of a fair trial, although it should serve as a safeguard against decisions contradicting the fundamental principles of the requested state's legal order, the scope for interpretation gives further discretionary power to domestic approving authorities.

The Procedure for the Execution of a Foreign Verdict

The Ministry of Justice receives documentation from the foreign state and delivers the request along with a certified copy of the foreign judgment to a Serbian court, providing an opinion on the fulfilment of prerequisites (as described above). Subsequently, the investigative chamber of the competent court decides on the request during a council session, where the convicted person provides input regarding the fulfilment of prerequisites. The court then makes a decision to accept or reject the request. In this part of the process, there is no room for court arbitrariness or discretionary decision-making as the court is bound by the factual description of the criminal offense from the foreign criminal *verdict*. If the court accepts a foreign criminal request, it delivers a judgment following Serbian law that is not more severe than the original foreign sanction. Appeals are allowed, and any execution or parole follows Serbian law.

Overall, the process of executing foreign judgments is mostly technical. However, in the initial stages, the Ministry of Justice acts as gatekeeper with some discretion regarding interpretation of "political persecution" and "fair trial." In theory, this allows for arbitrary decision-making, although in practice the Minister rarely prevents requests from proceeding.

3.1.6 Execution Abroad of a Domestic Judgment

A local (Serbian) court can request the execution of a criminal sentence in a foreign country if the convict is a citizen of that country, resides or is domiciled there, or is serving a sentence in that country based on a prior verdict.[41] The criteria for executing a domestic criminal sentence align with those for a foreign sentence, and acceptance depends on the legislation of the receiving country.

In the procedure, a non-trial chamber of the original court, considering the public prosecutor's opinion, decides on executing a domestic sentence abroad, involving the internal review mechanisms of the non-trial chamber and the prosecutor's confirmation.[42] If the foreign country agrees to execute the sentence, Serbia suspends its process; otherwise, if the foreign sanction execution is evaded or not assumed, Serbia's procedure continues, and the Ministry of Justice updates foreign entities about decisions affecting domestic sentence execution.

Overall, the execution of a domestic judgment abroad is primarily a technical process, with the local court having discretion in deciding whether to request execution in a foreign state, while the Ministry of Justice serves a primarily technical role as a conveyer of the request. The existence and number of review mechanisms in the recipient state may vary, potentially introducing arbitrariness.

3.1.7 Concluding Remarks

The review of Serbia's legal framework for MLA reveals several key points:

- Lack of differentiation according to type of crime
- Inconsistent practices across varied MLA forms
- Inconsistencies with domestic legislation and practice
- Unclear criteria leading to discretionary power and uncertainty

The legal framework requires clarification, harmonisation, and simplification to address these shortcomings and inconsistencies. One option to increase efficiency would be to introduce a two-tier system assigning one institution to assess all conditions and another institution to review decisions based on appeals. This would ensure adequate internal control for each request, whilst reducing fragmentation.

[41] Article 72 of the Law on International Legal Assistance in Criminal Matters.

[42] In emergencies, the local court may seek detention in the foreign country before submitting the request, either directly, through the justice ministry, or via INTERPOL.

3.2 Bosnia and Herzegovina

Bosnia and Herzegovina (BiH) is a federal state comprising the Federation of Bosnia and Herzegovina and the Serb Republic, with the Constitution regulating the relationship between the central state and the federal entities, including the realisation of international and inter-entity criminal cooperation. Its Law on International Mutual Legal Assistance in Criminal Matters (hereafter, in this section, the Law) recognises various forms of MLA, such as extradition of suspects, surrender of criminal prosecution, and recognition and enforcement of foreign court decisions, with legally defined forms including procedural acts within criminal proceedings (Article 13). The Law applies throughout its territory, but each entity and canton can independently conclude international agreements that take precedence. One difference compared to Serbia is that, in urgent cases, MLA requests can be submitted through Eurojust, the EU Agency for Police and Judicial Cooperation, a procedure guided by instructions from the Minister of Justice.

3.2.1 Determination of Jurisdiction

When a foreign judicial authority submits a request, the competent domestic authority assesses whether or not to provide MLA based on domestic rules, regardless of the type of MLA. BiH adopts a more flexible approach than Serbia by considering assistance even without a formal agreement, as long as appropriate guarantees of reciprocity are given, while no guarantees are required for the service of documents. The conditions for denying MLA, exceptions, and the requirement for justification are comprehensively regulated. Bosnian legislation is more detailed than Serbia's.

3.2.2 Extradition of a Suspect or Convict

Under Article 34 of the Law, extradition is permitted for offenses punishable in both BiH and the requesting country, with a minimum 1-year sentence requirement and at least 4 months of the sentence remaining for those already serving. The following criteria apply:

- The individual must not be a Bosnian citizen.
- They cannot have asylum status or be seeking it in BiH.
- The offense must not have been committed in or against BiH or its citizens.
- The crime must be recognized in both countries and must not be political or military in nature.
- Domestic legal time limits should still be applicable.
- The individual's identity must be confirmed, and there should be substantial evidence of the crime or a final conviction.

- Extradition requests cannot be based on discriminatory reasons.
- Extradition is not permitted for offenses carrying the death penalty unless assurances are provided against its application.

Extradition Procedure
The extradition procedure differs from that in Serbia in three main ways:

1. In BiH, the court examines all presumptions, whereas in Serbia, this responsibility is split among the court and the Ministry of Justice.
2. In BiH, the decision of the Minister of Justice is final and cannot be appealed, while in Serbia, the decision can be appealed through an administrative procedure.
3. BiH has specific laws regulating provisional arrest and extradition custody, while in Serbia, the possibility of arrest under certain circumstances is only briefly mentioned.

Once received, the Ministry of Justice forwards a foreign state's MLA request to a competent prosecutor for completeness checks. The prosecutor can request temporary detention of the suspect(s), and an investigating judge makes a decision as to whether there is a danger of escape or hiding. The judge's decision on pre-trial detention can take up to 18 days initially, extendable by 40 days. This decision is then forwarded to the prosecutor's office and the Ministry of Justice, who can submit a formal extradition request to the issuing state. If the requesting state then fails to submit the request and necessary documents within the specified time, the court terminates the pre-trial detention, and it cannot be imposed again for the same request.

The pretrial judge, upon the prosecutor's proposal, can order extradition detention if there is a risk of evasion, destruction of evidence, or obstruction of proceedings by the person sought for extradition. The pretrial judge will not impose detention if the extradition request clearly lacks a basis. When extradition detention is imposed, the pretrial judge notifies the Ministry of Justice, and release from custody is granted when the grounds for detention are no longer present.

If it is determined that the person is a citizen of BiH based on an international arrest warrant, the requesting state and Interpol will be informed that extradition of Bosnian citizens is generally not possible unless specified by an applicable international agreement.

Thus, the court alone assesses the merits of an MLA application and its discretion in deciding whether to accept or reject is limited because criteria are clearly specified. The Ministry's role is limited to serving as a technical conduit for the application, while the prosecutor focuses on evaluating the technical aspects without considering its merits.

Bosnian Requests for Extradition from Another Country
In a situation where BiH conducts a criminal proceeding against an individual located in another country, or if a domestic court in Bosnia has imposed a prison sentence, the Minister of Justice can submit a request for the extradition of that individual. The Ministry sends the request through diplomatic channels or by other

means, as provided by international agreements—a technical role without discretionary power. In urgent cases where there is a risk of the individual escaping, the country can be asked to temporarily detain them before the request is formally submitted. Formal reciprocity is crucial to ensure equal conditions for extradition between BiH and the requested country. Since BiH, like many others, does not hand over its own citizens, requests seeking the extradition of a foreign citizen from BiH are unlikely to succeed.

3.2.3 Execution of a Foreign Judgment

In BiH, a domestic court can enforce foreign judicial judgments if they align with international treaties. Sanctions are carried out in accordance with local criminal law. Bosnian citizens and residents may be subject to the execution of foreign criminal judgments, particularly in cases related to imprisonment when the convicted person has a residence or sole residence in BiH but is unavailable in the requesting state.

The conditions for executing foreign criminal judgments include requirements such as finality, conformity with local criminal law, a remaining sentence of at least 6 months, consent from the convicted person, no previous conviction or ongoing proceedings for the same offense in BiH, and no time-barred sanctions. The execution of the judgment is denied if it contradicts local legal principles or if the offense is considered political or military in nature.

The Procedure

The Ministry of Justice forwards foreign judgment requests to a competent domestic authority, which consists of a three-judge panel that decides on recognition and execution. A recognised foreign judgment is executed similarly to a domestic one, without imposing harsher penalties. The final judgment is delivered through the Ministry to the sentencing state and relevant parties.

During the execution process, the sentencing state temporarily relinquishes the right to execute the judgment but regains this right if the individual flees the country. Information sharing between BiH and the sentencing state occurs regarding matters of evasion, amnesty, and pardon.

The domestic court will only consider a request from the sentencing state to enforce a criminal judgment if it is provided for in an international agreement. However, Bosnian judicial authorities can seek recognition and enforcement of a domestic criminal judgment from a foreign state.

Execution of a Domestic Judgment in a Foreign Jurisdiction

The initiation of the execution of a domestic criminal court judgment in a foreign state is done by the court. The court prepares a request for the enforcement of the sentence in the foreign jurisdiction, which is forwarded through the Ministry of Justice. Upon the foreign state assuming the enforcement of the sentence, the relevant judicial authority in BiH temporarily suspends the execution within its borders, following a reciprocal procedure but if the individual evades enforcement in the foreign jurisdiction, enforcement proceedings resume in BiH.

The court retains discretion regarding the delivery and timing of a potential request, as long as there is a sentence that qualifies for potential execution. No other authorities have powers to dictate the process and there are no internal review mechanisms. This arrangement is understandable because a judgment has already been rendered in a domestic trial, minimising the risk of significant violation of the defendant's rights or abuse of power. Additionally, any MLA request is subject to the approval of the requested state's authorities, which effectively serves as a "veto" mechanism on the other side of the MLA relationship.

3.2.4 Surrender of Criminal Prosecution

If a foreign individual commits a criminal offense in BiH, the criminal files may be transferred to the individual's country of residence for prosecution and trial, unless the foreign state objects. However, the transfer of prosecution and trial is prohibited if it would subject the foreign person to unfair trials, inhuman or degrading treatment or punishment. Additionally, the victim's property claims must be addressed before the transfer of prosecution is authorised.

The process for requesting the transfer of prosecution involves the foreign state's judicial authority submitting a request to the BiH Ministry of Justice. The Ministry then forwards the request to the competent authority of the requesting state and seeks feedback on the decision of the foreign judicial authority. If there are deficiencies in the request, the Ministry asks the requested authority to rectify them within 30 days; if they are not addressed, the request and files are returned.

The legal implications of accepting the surrender of criminal prosecution by a foreign state are governed by an international treaty if one exists. In the absence of a treaty, the requesting state is not allowed to proceed with the temporary prosecution of the individual until a decision is made by the Bosnian authorities. The law also outlines specific circumstances where it is considered that the requesting state has waived prosecution.

3.2.5 Takeover of Criminal Prosecution

A request for transferring criminal prosecution is made through a request letter, as outlined in Article 84 of the Law on International Legal Assistance in Criminal Matters. BiH has the authority to assume prosecution for offenses committed abroad, even without extradition, if the foreign authority assures that they will not prosecute further.

The Ministry of Justice forwards the request to the relevant prosecutor's office, which has the right to refuse taking over the prosecution if there are reasons that prevent proceedings from being conducted in BiH, as stated in Article 90 of the Law on International Legal Assistance in Criminal Matters.

The requesting state is informed of the decision, including refusal and final outcomes. If the request is refused, the reasons for refusal must be provided. Once the proceedings are completed, the authority informs the requesting state and shares the court decision through the Ministry of Justice.

In the transfer and takeover of criminal prosecution, there are no distinctions based on the type of criminal act, place and time of its commission, or the nationality of the suspect or perpetrator. Similar to Serbia, this form of legal assistance is less conditional compared to extradition, as implied in the legal text. The competent judicial authority in BiH can take over a criminal proceeding for a crime committed abroad, even if extradition from BiH is not permitted upon the request of a foreign state.

However, this arrangement presents certain problems. The decision on takeover or surrender of prosecution is made by a prosecutor's office rather than by a court. It lacks a clearly defined right to appeal or other legal remedies, a well-defined procedure, and clear conditions, although the prosecutor is obliged to provide a justification. Additionally, the issue of parallel criminal proceedings and their legal regulation are poorly specified in the legal text.

Overall, the takeover or surrender of prosecution, as specific forms of MLA, are not extensively regulated. This grants significant discretionary powers to local prosecutors in decisions regarding requests and approvals of prosecution transfers between BiH and another state, without inherent internal review mechanisms to ensure checks and balances.

3.2.6 Concluding Remarks

Key points are that:

- Jurisdiction for deciding on requests is uniform across types of MLA, as is the procedure for handling requests.
- The Law provides detailed conditions for refusing assistance and requires explanations for non-compliance.
- There are explicit criteria for decision-making by the relevant institutions involved in managing MLA processes as well as the state's obligations to inform the requesting state about the outcomes of the MLA request.

Overall, there is much less scope for arbitrary decision-making by the relevant domestic authorities compared to Serbia.

3.3 North Macedonia

North Macedonia is a transitional democracy in Southeast Europe, sharing a border with Serbia to the south. It is a unitary state with elements of power-sharing consociationalism at the central level, as established by the Ohrid Agreement. North Macedonia has actively integrated itself into the international community through joining organisations and agreements focused on transnational collaboration to combat such issues. The international agreements it has ratified are an integral component of the internal legal framework defined by its Constitution and cannot be altered by domestic law.

The Law on International Cooperation in Criminal Matters (hereafter, in this section, the Law) is the main relevant law, providing conditions and procedures for collaboration with other countries in criminal investigations and proceedings. However, ratified international agreements and legal acts governing criminal proceedings before recognised international courts take precedence. Notably, the extradition or surrender of North Macedonian citizens to other states is prohibited by the Constitution. This hierarchical legal structure is similar to the legal systems of Serbia and, to some extent, BiH, although the political structure of the latter adds additional complexities.

The Law covers various forms of MLA, including international legal assistance, assignment and extradition of criminal proceedings, extradition of suspects, execution of criminal verdicts, and transfer of convicted persons. It applies to criminal proceedings within the jurisdiction of the requesting state, including those before the European Court of Human Rights, the European Court of Justice, the International Criminal Court, and other international organisations of which North Macedonia is a member. The law also covers procedures involving minors.

Requests for international assistance are primarily handled by the Ministry responsible for justice affairs, except in urgent cases where international police cooperation channels are used. In the absence of a relevant international agreement, or if diplomatic channels are required, the Ministry of Foreign Affairs manages the transmission of requests. The law identifies grounds for refusing a request, such as contravening the Constitution, endangering sovereignty or security, involvement in political or politically-related crimes, breach of military duties, or a reasonable belief of discrimination based on race, nationality, social affiliation, or political or religious beliefs.

3.3.1 Determination of Jurisdiction

North Macedonia's law is distinctive in mandating that MLA requests related to crimes against humanity and international law, including attempts and complicity, cannot be denied (Article 18). This differs from the approach in Serbia and BiH. However, the Constitution's prohibition on extraditing its own citizens, even for severe international violations such as crimes against humanity and international law, raises concerns about consistent application.

Compared to the laws of Serbia and BiH, North Macedonia's law covers a broader range of specific actions subject to international legal assistance. It refers to "international legal assistance," while Serbia's law refers to "other forms of international assistance," and the Bosnian law refers to "general forms of providing international legal assistance." For other forms of international cooperation, except for the surrender of domestic citizens, domestic judicial authorities in North Macedonia are obliged to provide legal assistance to a foreign state in cases involving these crimes, even when it concerns citizens of North Macedonia. The law requires domestic judicial authorities to provide justification for rejecting a request or demand, unless otherwise specified by an international treaty.

Each form of cooperation has specified procedures, conditions, and criteria. If an MLA request is accepted by the domestic judicial authority, it will be carried out in accordance with the applicable domestic procedural law. However, they all share common features, such as undertaking specific procedural actions in criminal proceedings, a less formalised decision-making process compared to other forms of legal assistance, and involvement in a similar range of procedural actions.

Although North Macedonia's law specifies and regulates the broadest range of individual procedural actions, there is a slight weakness in that the list is defined as a closed circle. The implication is that legal assistance cannot be provided in cases beyond those explicitly mentioned.

3.3.2 Extradition of a Suspect or Convict

The regulation of extradition is detailed, particularly in comparison to procedures for the transfer and takeover of criminal prosecution. According to Article 50 of the Law, a person can be extradited based on an international warrant for crimes that carry a minimum punishment of 1 year's imprisonment or if they are sentenced to a 4-month term. Extradition is permissible only for crimes that are also illegal in North Macedonia. Conditions include the person not being a Macedonian citizen, verification of their identity, and ensuring that the crime was not committed against North Macedonia or its citizens. Additional criteria involve legal specifics, age at the time of the crime, and guarantees of fair trial procedures (Article 52). Extradition is not granted for political crimes, except for state leader assassination, terrorism, and international crimes. Military duty violations are not covered by these provisions.

The extradition procedure involves several steps:

- After establishing the person's identity and the presence of an international arrest warrant, the judge conducts preliminary investigative actions, a role that is purely technical without decision-making power.
- The competent public prosecutor then provides a written opinion on whether the legal prerequisites for extradition have been fulfilled, with limited discretion.
- The judicial panel must approve the prosecutor's decision, acting as a de facto check.

Both the defense attorney and public prosecutor can appeal to a higher court panel, providing a formal review mechanism to protect rights (Article 64). Decisions stating that the prerequisites for extradition are not met are automatically reviewed by the Supreme Court, creating a three-tier decision-making process in each specific case. The necessity of such a decision and whether it might be sufficient to allow review by the Supreme Court only when an authorised interested party requests legal remedy are debatable.

The final decision on extradition rests with the Minister of Justice and will not be permitted if the person has been tried in absentia and the requesting state does not provide guarantees for a retrial in their presence with respect for the right to defense; if there are substantial reasons to believe that the person would face torture, other forms of cruel or inhumane treatment, or be subject to the death penalty; or if, based on a Minister's proposal, there are particularly justified state interests (Article 65).[43]

Extradition Request by North Macedonia
If a criminal procedure is ongoing in North Macedonia against a person who is abroad, or if the person has been convicted by a domestic court, the Minister of Justice has the authority to submit an extradition request via diplomatic channels (Article 74). The judicial body that issued the international arrest warrant will send all necessary documents along with the request to the Ministry, which then approaches the foreign state through diplomatic channels, and the subsequent procedure regarding the request is determined by the regulations of that particular state.

In this process of requesting extradition from another country, the court holds arbitrary power to decide whether to issue an MLA request or not, as long as the statutory conditions are fulfilled. The Ministry, along with other domestic institutions, does not have a decision-making role, and there are no checks and balances.

3.3.3 Takeover of Criminal Prosecution

When it comes to the transfer and acceptance of criminal prosecutions, the law provides limited detail. A foreign competent authority seeking the takeover of criminal prosecution against a citizen of North Macedonia or a person residing in or visiting North Macedonia for a crime committed abroad directs the request to the competent public prosecutor (Article 42). Criminal proceedings will only commence if the crime falls under domestic legislation. If a procedure is initiated, it will be conducted in accordance with domestic law unless the law of the foreign state regarding the type and extent of the criminal penalty is more lenient (Article 43).

The procedure is that the competent public prosecutor examines the MLA request and makes a decision, immediately informing the foreign competent authority through the relevant ministry (Article 45). The entire procedure is minimally regulated, lacking clearer criteria regarding limitations on the prosecutor's discretion in responding positively or negatively to the request, other than the legally prescribed prerequisites that must be met for the request to be considered. There is second-tier review mechanism to oversee the prosecutor's decision.

[43] It is unclear which Minister can make such a proposal to the Government, whether any minister or only the one with the authority to make the final decision on extradition.

3.3.4 Surrender of Criminal Prosecution

When a foreigner commits a crime on the territory of North Macedonia and resides in a foreign country, the files and evidence for criminal prosecution and trial can be transferred to that foreign country under the conditions provided for extradition, if the foreign country does not object (Article 46). The transfer and takeover of criminal prosecution is a complex legal issue that requires careful regulation, yet the law contains very little detail on the topic. Only a few articles mention the authority responsible for making decisions regarding the transfer or takeover of prosecution, and no clear decision-making criteria or conditions are specified. Transfers are in principle allowed for crimes punishable by up to 10 years' imprisonment and crimes endangering public traffic.

The prosecutor plays a key role in this process too, having some discretion in determining whether and when to submit a request. Other authorities, such as the relevant ministry, have a technical role only. There is no second-tier review mechanism.

3.3.5 Execution of Foreign Criminal Judgments

Upon a request from a foreign state, the competent domestic court enforces a final judicial judgment by imposing a sanction equivalent to that imposed by the foreign or international court, ensuring that the punishment is not more severe than that of the foreign court. The domestic court receives the foreign judgment and then imposes the same sentence domestically.

The conditions for executing the judgment are:

- The judgment must be final and enforceable;
- The offense for which the judgment was rendered is also a criminal offense under domestic law.
- The judgment was rendered in the presence of the convicted person.
- The execution of the sentence is not time-barred under domestic law.

The domestic court executes the foreign judgment according to domestic law, treating it as a domestic judgment. The request for execution is submitted through the ministry. If accepted, the domestic court suspends execution as the foreign state carries out the judgment. The domestic court cannot execute the judgment if it has already been fully executed in the requesting state.

3.3.6 Concluding Remarks

Key Points

- The law contains a provision (Article 18) that sets strict conditions under which a request for assistance cannot be rejected, ensuring a credible commitment and limiting discretionary powers.

- The law encompasses a broader range of specific actions that can be subject to international legal assistance, although the closed nature of the list makes it inflexible.
- The extradition process includes automatic three-tiered review.
- the Government has discretion to declare a case relevant or sensitive for the 'national interest'.
- The regulations on the surrender and takeover of criminal prosecution lack clear criteria and conditions for decision-making.

4 Comparative Analysis and Discussion

The three states share the same tradition, having emerged from the same country, former socialist Yugoslavia (1945–1992), and the structure of their laws governing international legal assistance is similar. The scope of regulation, the legal institutions, and the types of assistance provided are almost identical across the three countries. Yet, key differences exist for specific forms of MLA, including in the two aspects of legal design—discretion and checks and balances-which constituted our primary focus (see Table 1).

Political authorities in all three states, primarily the Ministries of Justice, can invoke discretionary decision-making powers to reject or approve a foreign state's MLA request. This opens considerable space for arbitrariness and uneven application of law, which could be abused to advance interests other than those related to justice, including providing political protection to suspects or indictees, potentially those associated with war crimes or organised crime or corruption. However, there are also important differences among the three states.

One area of such differences relates to whether an international warrant is required in order to provide legal assistance. In North Macedonia, the international warrant necessitates cooperation, such that an MLA request cannot be rejected as long as it meets the legally defined conditions. However, in Serbia and BiH, the international warrant is treated only as a request for legal assistance, effectively granting domestic authorities greater discretion to withhold or reject assistance. This discretionary power provides room for arbitrary decision-making, and the risk that political authorities may abuse their power to obstruct the MLA process to further illicit interests, political agendas, or to favour their affiliated circles.

Significant differences also exist with regard to extradition across the three countries. In BiH, the minister's decision on extradition is final, making it the only country lacking internal checks, while the fact that the decision rests with a political authority leaves risk of politicisation. In North Macedonia, the Supreme Court examines whether the prerequisites for extradition are met, and the government can refuse extradition if there are justified state interests. While such 'state interests' are poorly defined, leaving scope for interpretation, a court may be less likely to stretch the meaning of national interest than a political institution, given the

Table 1 Summary of regulation of the various forms of MLA across Serbia, Bosnia and Herzegovina, and North Macedonia

Form of MLA	Serbia	Bosnia and Herzegovina	North Macedonia
Extradition (request directed to given country)	*Discretion* *SOME* • Ministry of Justice can ultimately approve, reject or modify court's decision *Checks and balances* *YES* • Conventional two-tiered legal procedure (court + panel of judges) • Minister of Justice; de facto veto player	*Discretion* *YES* • Final decision lies with Minister *Checks and balances* *YES* • Multiple points in procedural consideration of foreign request (court, prosecutor) * *Note: Bosnian citizens cannot be extradited, which significantly reduces scope*	*Discretion* *YES* • Government can invoke 'national interests' grounds for rejecting MLA request • Final decision rests with Minister of Justice *Checks and balances* *YES ('EXCESSVE')* • Three-tiered legal procedure (judge + judicial panel + supreme court) • 'De facto veto players': Ministry of Justice + Government as a whole (depending on interpretation of law)
Extradition requests from given country to another state	*Discretion* *YES* • Court *Checks and balances* *NO*	*Discretion* *YES* • *Court* *Checks and balances* *NO*	*Discretion* *YES* • *Court* *Checks and balances* *NO*
Surrender of prosecution	*Discretion* *YES* • Scantly regulated, no detailed regulations. Enables considerable arbitrariness to criminal justice actors + political authorities in approving/ rejecting MLA requests (on grounds of securing 'national interests') *Checks and balances* YES. Two-tiered legal procedure (court + panel of judges)	*Discretion* *YES* • Scantily regulated, leaving major discretion to local prosecutor timing and case launch-wise *Checks and balances* *NO*	*Discretion* *YES* • *Scantily regulated, leaving major discretion to local prosecutor timing and case launch-wise* *Checks and balances* *NO*
Takeover of prosecution	*Discretion* *YES* • Scantily regulated • Prosecutor enjoys extensive leeway in decision-making, timeing and case launch *Checks and balances* *NO* • Scantly regulated, no review mechanisms or 'de facto veto-players'	*Discretion* *YES* • Scantily regulated, leaving major discretion to local prosecutor regarding timing and case launch *Checks and balances* *NO*	*Discretion* *YES* • Scantily regulated, leaving major discretion to local prosecutor regarding timing and case launch *Checks and balances* *NO*

(continued)

Table 1 (continued)

Form of MLA	Serbia	Bosnia and Herzegovina	North Macedonia
Execution of a foreign judgment	*Discretion* *SOME* • Ministry as 'gate-keeper': It can 'stretch' the interpretation of a 'fair trial' and 'politicised' trial to justify a rejection Checks and balances *SOME* • Ministry as a 'gate-keeper' (hence: 'de facto veto player') + procedure subject to two-stage judicial process (court chamber + court) although this is automatised/technical	*Discretion* *SOME* • Three-judge panel appraises whether prescribed conditions are met *Checks and balances* *NO* * *note: If a requesting state has no international agreement with Bosnia and Herzegovina, MLA cannot be provided*	*Discretion* *NO* *Checks and balances* *NO*
Execution of a domestic judgment abroad	*Discretion* *SOME* • Court enjoys major leeway in decision-making, regarding timing and case launch *Checks and balances* *NO* • (Understandable given prior trail where verdict is delivered)	*Discretion* *YES* • Court enjoys major leeway in decision-making, regarding timing and case launch *Checks and balances* *NO* • (Understandable given prior trail where verdict is delivered)	*Discretion* *YES* • Court enjoys major leeway in decision-making, regarding timing and case launch *Checks and balances* *NO* • (Understandable given prior trail where verdict is delivered)

conservative nature of legal culture and less customary practice of expanding the understanding of national interest.

In Serbia, the responsibility for deciding extradition is jointly held by the court and minister, deciding respectively on different sets of conditions. Although this arrangement serves as a form of check on power, it also brings disadvantages. First, it complicates the process and results in inconsistent practices. The interpretation and decision of the court may be approved in one case but rejected in another, even when based on the same principles or arguments. Second, this arrangement allows for political influence where the legal conditions invoked by the ministry differ from those followed by the judiciary.

In the case of sending extradition requests to other countries, discretion is more 'innocuous' or could more easily be justified. In such situations, the local court might be best placed to appraise whether and how to respond, without detailed specific criteria; nevertheless, a general framework guiding the process, such as the level of preconditions and principles, would be welcome.

Courts tend to play a greater role in decisions related to the execution of foreign judgments than in extradition procedures, a role that is more technical since the prosecution has been completed elsewhere. In all three states, the relevant local prosecutor enjoys wide discretion in choosing whether and when to send an MLA request relating to the potential takeover of a prosecution, as well as whether and when a received request to surrender a case is acted on. This comes without any detailed regulation, leaving much scope for the prosecutor to slow down, halt, or neglect a case.

There is inconsistency regarding retrials for extradited persons convicted in absentia. All three countries permit trials in absentia under specific conditions. If the requesting state allows it, this should be recognised as a right. However, conditioning extradition on a retrial rejects the foreign court's decision based on its national legislation. This has indirect implications for other legal assistance and underscores the importance of extradition, which in Serbia and North Macedonia is limited to foreign nationals.

The provision of checks and balances varies according to the type of assistance requested. For dealing with received MLA requests for extradition, there are usually two tiers of judicial review, but for execution of a domestic verdict abroad, there are virtually no built-in internal checks and balances. For execution of a foreign judgment, no internal checks and balances exist in BiH or North Macedonia, while they are present in Serbia. For surrender of prosecution, Serbia features a two-tiered review procedure within its judicial system, whereas in BiH and North Macedonia, such internal review mechanisms are absent.

Overall, the presence of internal checks and balances provides a more robust system of control, ensuring better conditions for preventing power abuse or neglect by the involved authorities primarily relating to the protection of the rights of those who are the subject of MLA requests. Such better protection is ensured, for instance, in extradition procedures from certain countries to a foreign requester. In most other forms of MLA, though, internal checks and balances are much weaker, leaving scope for procedural misapplication or uneven application of law.

In some instances, we also observed 'excessive' checks and balances that go beyond the conventional two-tiered review system of judicial actors. One example is the three-tiered legal procedure for extradition in Bosnia and Herzegovina, which is redundant and cumbersome. Such an arrangement can endanger the capacity and autonomy of the institutions to effectively process MLA requests, with both classical review mechanisms and de facto 'veto player' points giving a certain institution too much the power to slow down or stall an MLA process through protracted approval or confirmation decisions.

Furthermore, interactions between discretionary power and oversight mechanisms should be considered. When political authorities are involved in the system of internal checks and balances, particularly where they command de facto veto powers and this is coupled with the ability to make arbitrary decisions because the law allows for interpretation, the risks mount. The latter kind of combination is often the case with requests for extradition, for example.

5 Conclusion

This chapter has examined the legal design of the MLA procedure in three Southeast European countries: Serbia, Bosnia and Herzegovina, and North Macedonia. The focus was on two key aspects: the level of detail and consequent extent of discretion granted to institutions involved, and the internal control and accountability procedures or "checks and balances." We now discuss the theoretical implications of our empirical findings.

Theoretical Implication 1: Discretion Is Neither Inevitable Nor Beneficial for MLA Procedures It is commonly observed that a degree of discretion built into institutional design is needed and plays a positive role in decision-making.[44] However, our analysis suggests that, in the specific area of MLA, discretion is neither a necessary[45] nor a-priori useful element of legal design. We identify specific examples where the significant discretion granted to authorities involved in MLA decision-making enables inconsistent application of the law, uneven legal practices and provides the potential for abuse of power or arbitrariness. We also note several examples where MLA procedures have been well-designed *without* granting major discretion to any of the authorities involved, as in all forms of MLA in BiH and in specific forms in North Macedonia and Serbia. We therefore contend that, in the context of MLA, discretion is closer to the "detriment" end of the benevolence vs. detriment spectrum. Clearly defined procedures in MLA are of paramount importance, and concerns that institutional discretion could lead to excess arbitrariness,[46] neglectful use and even political abuse,[47] are valid in the MLA context perhaps more than in most other policy areas.

In some aspects of MLA, reducing discretion and introducing more detailed and precise regulation of the powers and procedural obligations for respective authorities might significantly diminish arbitrary decision-making and opportunities for abuse of discretionary power. Each institution and step in the MLA procedure should rather adhere to clear criteria and conditions that guide decision-making. This applies to both criminal justice institutions (such as the police, court, or prosecution) and political authorities (e.g., ministries or the government).

Theoretical Implication 2: Built-in Checks and Balances Are Normatively Instrumental for MLA (As Long As They Are Not Multi-Tiered), Underpinning Control and Accountability Functions
The literature widely regards internal checks and balances as critical accountability and control devices that prevent erroneous and abusive decision making.[48] Our analysis revealed that all three states have some form of internal control mechanisms

[44] Dworkin (1963), Albonetti (1991), McLachlin (1992) and Evans and Harris (2004).

[45] Hawkins (1992) and Schmidt and Scott (2021).

[46] Black (2001), p. 2.

[47] Buromenskyi and Gutnyk (2019).

[48] Davis (1969); Lowi (1969); Brubacher (2004); Epps (2021), p. 5.

in most forms of MLA, although there are specific stages and aspects where sufficient checks and balances are lacking. However, we contend that not all checks and balances are equally effective and that, in the context of such a complex and contentious area as MLA, which requires cooperation across borders and among multiple institutions, internal control mechanisms may easily become excessive and dysfunctional unless carefully designed.

More specifically, we note that in certain stages of the MLA procedure, some states rely on a shared decision-making and approval system that effectively restricts the operational initiative and effectiveness of another institution, reducing its capacity and autonomy. Traditional two-tiered review systems may be more functional than checks and balances where multiple institutions possess de facto veto powers. Establishing appropriate checks and balances in the context of MLA is thus not only about having internal control mechanisms but also about adopting the right model that balances the need for control and accountability with operational effectiveness and institutional autonomy throughout the domestic MLA process.

Where possible, a two-tier review system may be more suitable rather than dividing powers among various institutions. If such a system is not feasible, to provide clarity and prevent undue delays or obstructions in the MLA process, detailed procedural regulations should specify decision-making procedures, set deadlines for completion of tasks, and establish mechanisms to address breaches of deadlines and ensure progress—as with the concept of "administrative silence".[49]

Acknowledgements Research for this project was supported by the Serious Organised Crime and Anticorruption Evidence research programme (SOC-ACE), which is part of the broader Anti-Corruption Evidence Programme funded by the UK government. We thank Professor Heather Marquette and Dr. Zenobia Ismail, and their colleagues from the University of Birmingham, for their support of this project.

References

Albonetti CA (1991) An integration of theories to explain judicial discretion. Soc Probl 38(2): 247–266

Baughman SB (2016) Subconstitutional checks. Notre Dame Law Rev 92:1071

Black J (2001) Managing discretion. *Unpublished manuscript, London School of Economics, UK*, 1–40

Brubacher MR (2004) Prosecutorial discretion within the international criminal court. J Int Criminal Justice 2(1):71–95

Buromenskyi M, Gutnyk V (2019) The impact of ECHR and the case-law of the Ecthr on the development of the right to legal assistance in international criminal courts (Icty, Ictr, Icc). Baltic J Eur Stud 3(9):188–204

Dávid-Barrett E, Tomić S (2022) Transnational governance networks against grand corruption: cross-border cooperation among law enforcement. SOC ACE research paper no. 8. University of Birmingham, Birmingham

[49] Marrara (2021).

Davis KC (1969) A new approach to delegation. Univ Chic Law Rev 36(4):713–733
Dicey AV (1982) [1885]. Introduction to the Study of the Law of the Constitution. Indianapolis Liberty Classics
Dworkin R (1963) Judicial discretion. J Philos 624:60
Epps D (2021) Checks and balances in the criminal law. Vanderbilt Law Rev 74(1):1–84
Eskridge WN Jr, Frickey PP (eds) (1994) Hart and Sack's the legal process: basic problems in the making and application of law. Foundation Press, Westbury
Evans T, Harris J (2004) Street-level bureaucracy, social work and the (exaggerated) death of discretion. Br J Soc Work 34(6):871–895
Gillmore (1995) Mutual assistance in criminal and business regulatory matters. xii
Greene AS (1994) Checks and balances in an era of presidential lawmaking. Univ Chi Law Rev 61: 123
Hawkins K (1992) The uses of discretion. Clarendon Press, Oxford
Herrmann J (1973) The rule of compulsory prosecution and the scope of prosecutorial discretion in Germany. Univ Chi Law Rev 41:468
Lowi T (1969) The end of liberalism
Marrara T (2021) Does the silence of the public administration mean consent? Decision duty, administrative silence and tacit approval. Adm Law Rev 280(2):227–264
McLachlin B (1992) Rules and discretion in the governance of Canada. Sask Law Rev 56:167
Myers RE (2008) Responding to the time-based failures of the criminal law through a criminal sunset amendment. BCL Rev 49:1327
O'Connor PA (1984) The judge, discretion and the criminal law. By rosemary Pattenden.[Oxford: Oxford university press. 1982. xv+ 299 pp.£ 20.]. Int Comp Law Q 33(3): 767–768
Pratt A, Sossin L (2009) A brief introduction of the puzzle of discretion. Can J Law Soc/La Revue Canadienne Droit et Société 24(3):301–312
Radeljić B (2013) Democratising and Europeanising the Western Balkans: contexts, challenges and prospects. East Eur Polit 29(2):245–251
Radeljić B, Đorđević V (2020) Clientelism and the abuse of power in the Western Balkans. J Balkan Near East Stud 22(5):597–612
Schmidt R, Scott C (2021) Regulatory discretion: structuring power in the era of regulatory capitalism. Leg Stud 41(3):454–473
Swire P, Hemmings JD, Vergnollie S (2016) A mutual legal assistance case study: the United States and France. Wis Int Law J 34:323
Tomić S (2019) Leadership, institutions and enforcement: anti-corruption agencies in Serbia, Croatia and Macedonia. Springer
Tomić S, Jovančić A (2012) Nastanak i nezavisnost regulatornih tela u Srbiji: domaće ili eksterne determinante? Polit Perspect J Polit Res 2(2):23–53
Tsebelis G (1995) Decision making in political systems: veto players in presidentialism, parliamentarism, multicameralism and multipartyism. Br J Polit Sci 25(3):289–325
UNDP (2015) Practitioner's guide: capacity assessment of anti-corruption agencies

Slobodan Tomic is a Lecturer in Public Administration and Management at the School of Business and Society, University of York, UK. His academic interests include all aspects of public administration and public policy, particularly where regulation is involved. His research has mainly focused on the analysis of integrity institutions and policies, which he has investigated both in OECD and non-OECD contexts, with a particular interest in how they manage institutional autonomy. He has worked on several projects with international organisations, including on civil service and autonomous agencies reform.

Elizabeth David-Barrett is Professor of Governance and Integrity and Director of the Centre for the Study of Corruption at the University of Sussex. Elizabeth has been researching corruption and anti-corruption mechanisms for 20 years, with particular interests in transnational cooperation, public procurement, and public ethics and integrity. She engages widely with policymakers and practitioners in international and national fora and has advised several governments on anti-corruption policy as well as working with private-sector organizations on improving integrity.

Public-Private Collaboration for Combatting Cyber Fraud

Daniel Halpin and Sheri Todd

Abstract It is estimated that Australians lost a staggering $3.1 billion to scams in 2022. This figure represents an alarming 80 percent increase compared with the total losses recorded in 2021. This figure is destined to increase in coming years due to the emerging popularity of the metaverse. The growing prevalence of scams in recent years has prompted government, law enforcement agencies, and the private sector to enhance their collaborative efforts in supporting the fight against these fraudulent activities. The current state of cooperation between Police and the private sector in Australia will be discussed, as well as the benefits of and barriers to collaborative work from a private investigations perspective. In addition, options for advancement of processes will be suggested, with a focus on continuing to improve the likelihood of asset recovery for victims. Ultimately, by strengthening the collaborative efforts of government, law enforcement, and the private sector, Australia can take significant strides in mitigating the impact of scams and ensuring the protection of its citizens against fraudulent activities.

1 Introduction

Cybercrime has become an increasingly significant threat to private individuals as well as public and private organisations in recent years. The term "cybercrime" comprises a broad variety of crime types,[1] referring to any criminal activity that is carried out using the internet or other computer-based or assisted technologies.[2] It is

[1] Anderson et al. (2019).

[2] United Nations Office on Drugs and Crime (2013).

D. Halpin (✉)
Cybertrace, Sydney, NSW, Australia
e-mail: dan.halpin@cybertrace.com.au

S. Todd
Sydney, NSW, Australia

D. Goldbarsht, L. de Koker (eds.), *Financial Crime, Law and Governance*, Ius Gentium: Comparative Perspectives on Law and Justice 116,
https://doi.org/10.1007/978-3-031-59547-9_12

generally sophisticated and complex, with a far wider impact than traditional crimes due to its ability to be conducted transnationally and target multiple victims simultaneously.

Cyber-dependent crimes are those committed using computers, networks, or other ICTs, including malware, ransomware, hacking, and denial of service attacks.[3] Cyber-enabled crimes, on the other hand, are traditional crimes, such as fraud, identity theft, and harassment, which do not rely on ICTs, but use them to enhance the scale or reach of the offence.[4] The increasing prevalence of cybercrime poses significant challenges to organisations, including financial losses, reputational damage, and legal liability.[5] Unfortunately, traditional law enforcement methods have been unable to effectively counter cybercrime.[6]

This chapter is based on the overall global impact of cybercrime and includes an overview of methods for combatting cybercrime, challenges for combatting cybercrime, and specifically, how Public-Private Partnerships (PPP) and Public-Private Collaboration (PPC) are the key to combatting cybercrime.[7]

Much of the discussion about PPC and PPP to date has necessarily focussed on cyber-dependent crimes and their associated cybersecurity issues. When criminals use digital technologies such as ransomware to engage in cyber warfare and target vital infrastructure, public safety and possibly national security is threatened.[8] Top-down approaches, such as national cybersecurity defence strategies are, of course, considered imperative for the prevention and mitigation of cyber threats. They also have limitations, however.

The current chapter proposes that bottom-up approaches, particularly those focussing on cyber-enabled crimes related to cryptocurrency fraud and investment scams, are equally crucial for combatting the growing onslaught from cyber criminals. Having robust services that can attend to and adequately assist individual cybercrime victims will have multi-faceted effects, including disrupting the activity of cybercriminals, collecting detailed intelligence regarding crime methodology, increasing public confidence in the government, and improving the financial and psychological well-being of victims.

The authors are employed in the Australian private cyber investigations industry and specialise in global cyber-fraud investigations. As a result of this unique insight into the issues surrounding the Australian response to cyber fraud, we have included Australia specific content in this article, along with more generalised global content.

---

[3] McGuire and Dowling (2013).

[4] Furnell and Dowling (2019).

[5] Taylor et al. (2019).

[6] Cross et al. (2021).

[7] U.S. Mission to International Organizations in Vienna (2021).

[8] US Mission Unvie (2021).

1.1 Increasing Threat of Cybercrime

The threat of cybercrime is increasing due to several factors. One of the primary reasons for this is the growing reliance on digital technologies. As more organisations, and in turn consumers, rely on digital systems and processes to conduct their operations, the potential for cybercrime increases. Moreover, the widespread adoption of internet-driven technologies, cloud computing, mobile devices, and social media has created new opportunities for cybercriminals to exploit vulnerabilities in organisational systems.

Another significant factor contributing to the increasing threat of cybercrime is the growth of the internet of things (IoT).[9] The IoT refers to the interconnected network of physical devices that are embedded with sensors, software, and other technologies that allow them to communicate with one another. The IoT has created new points of vulnerability for cybercriminals, as these devices are often poorly secured and can be exploited to gain access to other systems.

1.2 Increased Use of Digital Payments

The increasing use of digital payments is one of the main reasons why cyber fraud is impacting consumers globally. According to a report by Juniper Research, the value of digital payments is expected to reach \$6.7 trillion during 2023, up from \$3.9 trillion in 2020.[10] As more consumers switch to digital payments, cybercriminals are finding new ways to exploit vulnerabilities in the system. One of the most common types of cyber fraud associated with digital payments is phishing. Phishing involves the use of fraudulent emails, text messages, or websites to trick users into providing personal information, such as credit card details, and passwords.[11] Once cybercriminals have this information, they can use it to make unauthorised purchases or access bank accounts.

1.3 Lack of Consumer Awareness

Another reason why cyber fraud is impacting consumers globally is the lack of consumer awareness, also referred to as cyber literacy. Many consumers are not aware of the risks associated with digital payments and are not taking the necessary precautions to protect their personal information. This lack of awareness makes it

[9] Hilt et al. (2019).

[10] Juniper Research (2020).

[11] Federal Trade Commission (2022).

easier for cybercriminals to carry out their attacks.[12] According to the Australian Competition & Consumer Commission:

> While there is a great deal of work underway to disrupt scammers, our best defence against these types of scams is education.[13]

Despite our advancements in digitalisation, it is crucial to address the existing gap between digital consumption and digital literacy. To bridge this gap, certain banks have assumed the responsibility of educating their customers and enhancing their financial and digital literacy through targeted education and awareness campaigns for those at risk. Additionally, the government has implemented measures to detect and disrupt scams, minimise losses, and enhance public education. However, there is still much to be accomplished, and it is imperative that the education system takes on a greater role in preparing the next generation for a future heavily influenced by the digital realm. This involves integrating cyber literacy fundamentals into academic curricula to equip young individuals with the necessary knowledge to identify cyber threats.[14] While our journey with digital payments has made significant progress, it is important to recognise that as the world continues to embrace digitalisation, scams will become increasingly intricate and advanced.[15] Therefore, it is now more crucial than ever for the entire ecosystem to collaborate in combating digital threats.

1.4 Sophisticated Cybercriminals

The increasing sophistication of cybercriminals is another reason why cyber fraud is impacting consumers globally. Cybercriminals are becoming more skilled at developing new methods to deceive and defraud individuals and organisations.[16] Fraudsters are continuously seeking innovative methods to deceive their targets. These tactics involve the creation of counterfeit websites that bear a striking resemblance to legitimate ones, employing caller identity (ID) spoofing to conceal their real phone numbers, mislead recipients about the source of a call, and even utilising authentic hold music from company call centres. Consequently, customers are finding it increasingly challenging to discern between fraudulent activities and genuine ones. They may also use malware or ransomware to gain access to sensitive data or disrupt business operations.[17]

The use of advanced technologies, such as artificial intelligence and machine learning, is also making it easier for cybercriminals to carry out their attacks. These

[12] Cybercrime Getting More Sophisticated: How to Protect Your Business? (2022).

[13] ACCC (2022).

[14] Chiappini (2022).

[15] Henderson (2022).

[16] Cybercrime Getting More Sophisticated: How to Protect Your Business? (2022).

[17] Dunn and Gunson (2022).

technologies can be used to identify vulnerabilities in systems and networks and develop new attack strategies.[18]

2 Impacts

2.1 *Impacts on Consumers*

In recent years, cyber fraud has become a significant threat to consumers globally. Cyber fraud refers to the use of electronic communication to deceive and defraud individuals or organisations.[19] The rapid growth of e-commerce and digital payments has created new opportunities for cybercriminals to exploit vulnerabilities in the online environment.[20] Cyber fraud is impacting consumers globally due to the increased use of digital payments, the lack of consumer awareness, and the increasing sophistication of cybercriminals. As digital payments continue to grow in popularity, consumers must take the necessary precautions to protect their personal information. This includes regularly monitoring their bank accounts for fraudulent activity, using strong passwords, and avoiding public Wi-Fi networks.[21]

Considering the relentless and rapidly growing activities of cybercriminals, it is fundamental that governments and organisations work together to develop new technologies and strategies to combat cyber fraud and protect consumers from these growing threats.[22]

2.2 *Impact on Public and Private Organisations*

As with consumers, the impact of cybercrime on public and private organisations can be severe. One of the most significant impacts for an organisation in terms of cybercrime is direct or indirect financial loss. Cybercriminals can use a variety of tactics to steal money from organisations, including fraud, ransomware, and theft of sensitive financial information. The financial impact of cybercrime can be significant, with estimates suggesting that cybercrime costs organisations billions of dollars each year.[23]

---

[18] Halpin (2023).

[19] Federal Bureau of Investigation (2016).

[20] Smith and Johnson (2020).

[21] Study Shows High Level of Consumer Concern About Cyber Crime, Low Level of Action or Awareness About Safety Measures (2018).

[22] Cross et al. (2021).

[23] Australian Government (2023).

In addition to financial losses, cybercrime can also have a significant impact on the reputation of organisations. A cyber-attack can damage an organisation's reputation by exposing sensitive information or demonstrating a lack of security measures. The loss of customer trust that can result from a cyber-attack can be difficult to overcome and may result in decreased revenue and lost opportunities for growth.[24]

Cybercrime can also have legal and regulatory implications for organisations. If sensitive data is stolen during a cyber-attack, organisations may be held liable for any damages that result. Organisations may also face regulatory penalties for failing to comply with data protection and cybersecurity regulations. In addition, organisations that are found to be negligent in their cybersecurity practices may be subject to lawsuits from affected customers or stakeholders.[25]

2.3 *Australia-Specific Impacts*

Cyber fraud is impacting consumers globally, and Australia is no exception. The increasing use of digital payments, the lack of consumer awareness, and the increasing sophistication of cybercriminals are contributing to this growing problem. Consumers must take the necessary precautions to protect themselves, and governments and private organisations must work together to develop new technologies and strategies to combat cyber fraud. It is essential to continue to monitor the impacts of cyber fraud and adjust strategies accordingly to protect consumers, organisations, and the broader community.[26]

In 2019, the Australian Competition and Consumer Commission (ACCC) reported that Australians lost over $634 million to scams.[27] In April 2023, the ACCC published a paper titled, Targeting Scams: Report of the ACCC on Scams Activity 2022 which provides an overview of the scamming landscape in Australia in the year 2022.[28] The report highlights that scam activity has continued to rise, with over 246,000 reports made to the ACCC's Scamwatch in 2022, costing Australians a total of $.9 billion. The most reported scams included phishing, investment, and romance scams. The report also outlines the ACCC's efforts to combat scamming, including collaborations with law enforcement and financial institutions, and encourages individuals to remain vigilant and report any suspicious activity.

Recent reports from the Australian Cyber Security Centre (ACSC) indicate that almost 40% of the 76,000 reported cybercrimes for 2021 to 2022 were related to

[24] Daniels (2022).

[25] Gellman (2021).

[26] ACCC (2021).

[27] ACCC (2019).

[28] ACCC (2023).

investment or online fraud.[29] It is estimated, however, that only one fifth of cybercrime is actually reported.[30] This means that approximately 150,000 individuals per year are losing money to online scams in Australia, a figure that is only destined to increase. Given the high number of individuals impacted, the relatively low loss per individual, and the complexity of scams, it is considered highly unlikely that police would have the time, resources, or expertise to sufficiently investigate each case. In fact, cybercrime issues are described as being increasingly burdensome to police organisations. Harkin and colleagues conducted a survey and interviews of staff from two specialist Australian cybercrime units, identifying untenable workloads, inadequate resourcing, low institutional priority for cybercrimes, and insufficient training to respond to forthcoming challenges.[31]

The Australian government has taken steps to combat cyber fraud by implementing the Cyber Security Strategy 2020,[32] and more recently issued the Cyber Security Strategy Discussion Paper, as part of the process for updating the strategy. The strategy outlines a range of initiatives to protect Australians from cyber threats, including a $.67 billion investment in cybersecurity over the next ten years. The government has also established the ACSC to provide advice and support to government agencies and businesses on cybersecurity issues along with consumer cyber fraud reporting and awareness processes.[33]

2.4 Global Law Enforcement and Cybercrime

Despite sustained planning from governments worldwide, global law enforcement has been slow to adapt to the growing threat of cybercrime. The efficacy of proactive planning by governments, individuals and organisations is limited without genuine police action.[34] Police inaction, in fact, has been argued to directly encourage cybercrime. While specialist law enforcement agencies have made genuine efforts to bolster their response to cybercrime, under reporting persists, largely attributable to perceived police inaction.[35]

---

[29] ACSC (2022).

[30] UNSW (2021).

[31] Harkin et al. (2018).

[32] Australian Government Department of Home Affairs (2020).

[33] Australian Government Department of Home Affairs (2023).

[34] Broadhurst (2006).

[35] Broadhurst (2006).

3 Digital Crime Scene Analysis

Spurred on by the digital revolution, cybercriminals have readily adopted the internet in order to obtain both data and dollars from their victims.[36] Scams conducted online have rapidly increased in sophistication and are now so complex and multi-faceted that they are difficult to distinguish from legitimate business operations. Cryptocurrencies, which are widely regarded by cybercriminals as immune to international regulations, have also become entwined with cybercrime in order to conceal the source and destination of criminal proceeds.[37] Modern perpetrators of fraud and investment scams frequently create professional websites to create the illusion of a legitimate trading platform and encourage victims to invest via Bitcoin or other tokens, ultimately using commercial cryptocurrency exchanges to convert cryptocurrencies to fiat currency anonymously (also known as 'cashing out').

As a result of technological innovation, many crime scenes are digital rather than physical, and their investigation requires unique and dynamic skills that are not included as part of traditional police training, despite the frequency of cybercrimes. In interviews conducted by Harkin and Whelan in 2022 with three anonymous Australian cybercrime units, many staff members described their front-line colleagues in local area commands as being overwhelmed by the technological complexity of cybercrime, and consequently handing many 'trivial' matters to the specialist units.[38] In the same study, some specialist cybercrime officers reported receiving no specific training upon their recruitment, and expressed concern that a lack of understanding of cyber-related matters at an executive level was impacting strategic decision making. Another study found that officers with higher levels of education, who were comfortable with technology, or who had training in or previous exposure to cybercrime investigations were more willing to investigate cybercrimes.[39]

Two primary methods used to identify the offenders responsible for online fraud and investment scams are digital forensic analysis of websites and cryptocurrency tracing. Both approaches involve high levels of technical knowledge and analytical skills, as well as a sound understanding of cybersecurity and criminal justice.

Website forensic investigations involve examining and analysing the content, structure and history of a website in order to identify the individuals and criminal syndicates responsible for the cybercrime operation. Meticulous deconstruction of the website occurs, isolating and untangling webs of complex data associated with its source code, domain records, and hosting accounts. The information obtained is then expanded upon through searches of corporate and investigative databases,

---

[36] Schjolberg (2020).

[37] Maurushat and Halpin (2022).

[38] Harkin and Whelan. (2022).

[39] Cross et al. (2021).

social media accounts, and open-source records, as well as analysis of the identified documents.

Cryptocurrency tracing involves the tracking and analysis of cryptocurrency transactions. Popular cryptocurrencies such as Bitcoin, Ethereum, and Tether operate on their own unique blockchains, and act as a publicly available ledger protected by cryptography-based technology. Utilising highly sophisticated tracing software, it is possible to track a victim's funds through a maze of transactions, discerning suspicious patterns, ignoring decoys, and looking for links to criminal enterprises, dark markets, gambling sites and high-risk exchanges. While cryptocurrency transactions on the blockchain are anonymous, the points at which offenders 'cash out' their funds through cryptocurrency exchanges are not. Many exchanges comply with strict Know Your Customer (KYC) policies and Anti-Money Laundering (AML) regulations, requiring verification of customer accounts with government-issued identification, along with contact details such as email addresses and phone numbers. Furthermore, it is essential for an exchange to hold details of the bank account into which the customer's funds will be deposited. Therefore, personal and banking details for registered owners of addresses and wallets can be obtained through criminal warrants or civil subpoenas. Thus, the goal of cryptocurrency tracing is to identify the receiving wallet address and the exchange that hosts it.

Currently in Australia many victims of online scams have immense difficulty in having their cases investigated by local law enforcement, often feeling stigmatised, blamed, and dismissed. In a recent report released by the Australian state of New South Wales (NSW) Bureau of Crime Statistics and Research (BOSCAR), 71% of cybercrime reports made to the ReportCyber Application Platform (RCAP) between 1 July 2019 to 30 June 2022 were closed with no further investigation undertaken.[40] It is noted that the RCAP is only one method of reporting cybercrime in NSW and that this study consequently includes only a subsection of reported crime in NSW. Additional research suggests that the lack of clarity regarding who is responsible for investigating reported incidents results in victims of cybercrime in Australia feeling dissatisfied with responses from law enforcement agencies.[41]

Victims consequently turn to private investigation firms who have the skills to assist with tracing stolen cryptocurrency and conducting forensic website investigations, but do not have the jurisdiction to request records from exchanges or other internet-related service providers. Given the rapid development and dynamic nature of cybercrime, the proliferating number of scams and the burden these crimes create for law enforcement, it appears crucial that collaborative partnerships between private investigators and police are urgently established and consolidated.

[40] Klauzner and Pisani (2023).

[41] Cross (2018, 2020).

4 Current Public-Private Collaborations and Partnerships

4.1 The Importance of PPPs and PPC

There is a long history of private contractors being used by the government to ensure that delivery of public services is economical, efficient, and effective. PPP and PPC is one such type of arrangement that is characterised by long-standing agreements between the state and private contractors for the planning, development, and execution of large infrastructure projects (English 2006). The projects may target hard infrastructure such as roads, hospitals, and correctional facilities or soft infrastructure such as law enforcement, emergency services, or educational programs. These types of partnerships allow for projects to be accomplished within a shorter timeframe that would otherwise be possible, which is imperative when considering the current rates of cybercrime. Other benefits of PPC and PPPs include improving cost efficiency and sustainability, as well as harnessing innovation, sharing financial risk, and increasing corporate social responsibility.[42]

Because cybersecurity threats are continually evolving, public and private entities must acknowledge the importance of collaboration in combating cybercrime and work together to stay ahead of cybercriminals. Public entities can leverage the private sector's expertise in cybercrime investigation (including digital forensics), cybersecurity and technology, while private entities can benefit from the public sector's resources and legislative powers. Collaboration can also help bridge the gap between legal and technical expertise, essential for developing effective responses to cyber threats.[43] Furthermore, collaboration can promote information sharing and best practices, which enhances cybersecurity posture, as well as identifying and disrupting criminals before they can impact victims.

Public and private entities have different roles to play in combating cybercrime. Public entities, such as government agencies, are responsible for developing laws and regulations to protect against cybercrime. Private entities, such as businesses, are responsible for developing and/or implementing measures to protect their clients, systems, and data.[44] Furthermore, public entities have access to information that can help private entities investigate crime, collect intelligence, and protect technical systems. And, in turn, private entities have valuable intellectual property, including data and methodologies, that can help public entities identify emerging cyber threats and investigate cybercrime.[45]

Collaboration between public and private entities can take various forms, including sharing threat intelligence, participating in joint exercises, and coordinating incident response efforts. The U.S Government and international organisations

---

[42] Shaw (2015).

[43] US Missions to International Organizations in Vienna (2021).

[44] US Missions to International Organizations in Vienna (2021).

[45] Gordon et al. (2003).

such as Interpol and United Nations have been instrumental in the promotion of PPC and PPPs for cybersecurity and related fields such as cybercrime.

In April 2010, the Twelfth United Nations Congress on Crime Prevention and Criminal Justice culminated in the adoption of the Salvador Declaration, which appealed to Member States to engage in greater international cooperation to disrupt illegal activity and to adapt their criminal justice systems to the changing times. Paragraph 34 of the declaration focused specifically on PPPs emphasising that crime prevention and criminal justice must involve multi-sector cooperation.

> We recognize the importance of strengthening public private partnerships in preventing and countering crime in all its forms and manifestations. We are convinced that through the mutual and effective sharing of information, knowledge and experience and through joint and coordinated actions, Governments and businesses can develop, improve and implement measures to prevent, prosecute and punish crime, including emerging and changing challenges.[46]

4.2 International Examples of Public-Private Partnerships and Collaboration

Both the Federal Bureau of Investigation (FBI) and Interpol have a variety of well-established programs for collaboration with the private sector. Culturally, the FBI holds a strong and unwavering belief that cooperation with both government and private sector partners is essential for understanding, preventing, and responding to emerging threats.[47] Bilateral information sharing is seen as a mutually beneficial relationship and is appreciated as a vital resource for protecting U.S citizens and economy. Their services are also extended worldwide, with the International Operations Division being responsible for building relationships with the public and private sectors in order to eradicate terrorism, cybercrime, and organised crime.[48]

Likewise, Interpol capitalises on the cyber and technological proficiency of the private sector, claiming that their partnerships help to bridge gaps in knowledge and service, ultimately resulting in more comprehensive global responses to crime.[49] Interpol facilitates the Global Cybercrime Expert Group along with regional working groups, to engage in information sharing, strategy development, project implementation, and the formulation of policies to combat cybercrime.[50] The African Joint Operation against Cybercrime (AFJOC) is one recent example that demonstrates effective implementation of PPC. Interpol coordinated several operations between

[46] United Nations Office of Drugs and Crime (2010).

[47] FBI (n.d.-a).

[48] FBI (n.d.-b).

[49] Interpol (n.d.-a).

[50] Interpol (n.d.-b).

2021 and 2023 to boost the capacity of 49 African countries to fight cybercrime.[51] Private sector partners such as British Telecom, CyberTOOLBELT, TrendMicro, and Kapersky provided key intelligence to inform the investigations, which resulted in multiple arrests in relation to cryptocurrency, business email compromise, romance, and phishing scams.[52] Additionally, over 200,000 pieces of malicious infrastructure used to aid cybercrime across the continent were removed.

The National Institute of Standards and Technology (NIST) Cybersecurity Framework is an example of a collaborative effort between public and private entities to improve cybersecurity in the US.[53] The framework provides a set of guidelines that organisations can use to assess and improve their cybersecurity posture. Likewise, the U.S White House recognised the importance of PPC for combating cybercrime. In May 2021, President Joe Biden signed an executive order aimed at improving the nation's cybersecurity. The order called for increased collaboration between public and private entities to identify, detect, respond to, and recover from cyber threats.[54] Further, the United Nations has also recognised the importance of collaboration in combating cybercrime. The UN Global Programme on Cybercrime is a joint effort between the UN Office on Drugs and Crime and the International Telecommunication Union, which aims to assist countries in developing effective legal frameworks and technical capacity to combat cybercrime.[55]

Formalised collaborations, such as the NIST Cybersecurity Framework and the UN Global Programme on Cybercrime, can provide a framework for public and private entities to work together effectively. The NIST Cybersecurity Framework provides a set of standards, guidelines, and best practices to help organisations manage and reduce cybersecurity risk. The framework can be tailored to specific industries and organisations, making it a flexible tool for improving cybersecurity posture. The UN Global Programme on Cybercrime provides a platform for international cooperation and capacity building to combat cybercrime. The program facilitates information sharing, training, and technical assistance, helping countries build their capacity to prevent and investigate cybercrime.

Another prime example of effective PPPs in the United Kingdom (UK) is the National Cyber Security Centre (NCSC) which was established in October 2018. It operates as part of the National Crime Agency (NCA) and signified a crucial shift in the United Kingdom's approach to combating economic crime. In a pioneering move, the NECC consolidates law enforcement entities, justice agencies, government sectors, regulatory organisations, and private industries, all united under the collective aim of reducing the occurrence of serious, organised economic crime.[56] This endeavour is crucial not only for the protection of the public, but also for

[51] Interpol (n.d.-c).

[52] Interpol (n.d.-d).

[53] National Institute of Standards and Technology (2020).

[54] The White House (2021).

[55] United Nations (2021).

[56] National Crime Agency (n.d.).

maintaining the UK's standing and prosperity as an international hub for financial activities.

The Joint Money Laundering Intelligence Taskforce (JMLIT) is a member agency of the NCSC and is an exemplary PPP model. The JMLIT collaboratively integrates the expertise, capabilities, and resources of public entities and private corporations.[57] Through this coordinated approach, the JMLIT has amplified its capacity to detect, prevent, and prosecute money laundering and related financial crimes.[58] However, it's pertinent to note that these partnerships also bring challenges such as the potential for conflicts of interest, risks to privacy, and the need for regulatory oversight to ensure ethical operations.[59] Hence, while endorsing the merits of PPPs in money laundering intelligence, it is crucial to underscore the imperative for robust governance frameworks to maintain the credibility, legality, and efficacy of such partnerships.

Informal collaborations, such as public-private partnerships and information sharing networks, can also be effective in combating cybercrime. These partnerships can include joint exercises, information sharing, and coordinated incident response efforts. Information sharing networks are groups of organisations that share threat intelligence and best practices to enhance their cybersecurity posture. These networks can be industry-specific or cross-sector, and they can be facilitated by government agencies or private sector organisations.[60]

4.3 *Australian Examples of Public-Private Partnerships and Collaboration*

In 2013, the Australian Attorney-General's Department released the National Plan to Combat Cybercrime, outlining the need for a long-term, sustained response from Commonwealth, State, and Territory governments together.[61] Their mission to make Australia a more difficult target for cybercriminals included six priority areas, one of which was partnering with industry. The document states "Governments will continue to explore options for enhanced public/private information sharing on cybercrime, and for cooperation on mutually beneficial research and development initiatives designed at better understanding and minimising cybercrime".[62] Subsequently, the Australian Cyber Security Centre (ASCS), was established, bringing together the public and private sector for the purposes of education, information sharing, and cyber security threat response. Although the ACSC publicly announces

[57] The Royal United Services Institute for Defence and Security Studies (2017).

[58] HM Treasury (2020).

[59] Vogel (2022).

[60] European Union Agency for Network and Information Security (2017).

[61] Attorney-General's Department (2013).

[62] Attorney-General's Department (2013, p. 13).

the law enforcement authorities and government agencies with whom they partner, their private industry and academic partnerships are less clear.

An example of one project being implemented by the ACSC is the Cyber Threat Intelligence Sharing (CTIS) Program, a platform created in 2021 to share threat intelligence bilaterally between government agencies and multi-industry private sector organisations.[63] Following a successful pilot project rolled out by consulting firm Deloitte, the project was expanded significantly in scope and funding to meet escalating demands regarding cyber threats. By mid-2022 approximately 28,000 threat indicators had been shared, and by the beginning of 2023 around 100 partners had registered.[64]

In 2022 the Australian Federal Police (AFP) launched the Joint Policing Cybercrime Coordination Centre (JPC3). According to the National Plan to Combat Cybercrime the core functions of the centre are to combine capabilities from government agencies, state and territory law enforcement, and the private sector in order to gather intelligence, conduct research, and develop deterrence, prevention, and disruption strategies related to high volume cybercrime.[65] The creation of joint taskforces with police and industry partners was included in the plan to enhance the likelihood of successful outcomes[66] and the continued strengthening of partnerships between public and private sectors is seen as a key part of the Cybercrime Action Plan.[67] Due to the recent inception of the project, evaluative outcomes are not yet available.

It seems clear that collaboration between public and private entities is critical in combating cybercrime. The global nature of cybercrime requires a coordinated effort to identify and mitigate cyber threats effectively. Formalised collaborations, such as the NIST Cybersecurity Framework and the UN Global Programme on Cybercrime, can provide a framework for effective collaboration. Informal collaborations, such as public-private partnerships and information sharing networks, can also be effective in enhancing cybersecurity posture. However, collaboration requires trust, information sharing protocols, and incident response coordination to be successful. As the threat of cybercrime continues to evolve, organisations must be prepared to adapt and collaborate to protect themselves and their stakeholders.[68]

Collaboration between public and private entities is critical to combat cybercrime and a collaborative effort is required for it to be effectively addressed. Likewise, it is essential that organisations recognise the importance of collaboration to increase disruption activities and combat cybercrime. The need for collaboration will only

[63] Deloitte Australia (2022).

[64] Brookes (2023).

[65] Australian Government Department of Home Affairs (2022).

[66] AFP (n.d.).

[67] Australian Government Department of Home Affairs (2022).

[68] United Nations (2021).

continue to grow as the threat of cybercrime evolves, and organisations must be prepared to adapt to new challenges to protect themselves and their stakeholders.[69]

Significant steps are being taken by governments to establish, enhance, and broaden joint efforts between public and private sectors in the fight against cybercrime. The importance of such projects is palpable given the ongoing proliferation of deceptive online practices, and as they flourish or fail, it will be essential to evaluate their effectiveness to bolster the future of successful collaborative partnerships.

5 Case Study

Case study of a successful public-private collaborations for combatting cybercrime. Lessons learned from a successful collaboration.

At the time of publishing, this case was being actively investigated by international law enforcement, the author's private investigation company, and partners. Locations, names, investigative methodology and other sensitive details have been changed or removed to maintain the integrity of the investigation and pending prosecution. However, the level of public-private collaboration for this case is accurate.

This case study examines a large transnational criminal syndicate which has operated fraudulent websites since 2016. It is estimated by the author that approximately USD 150 million has been fraudulently obtained from its victims. The syndicate attracts new clients either directly or through affiliate advertisers who sell client data to the fraudsters. Affiliate advertising is a marketing model where one organisation pays another to advertise their products. This is a common method used by fraudsters to qualify and recruit victims.

The fraudsters use SQL injections, a common cyber-attack, to replace paid advertisements with fraudulent ones, often using botnets to distribute the content illegally in order to appear higher in Google rankings Botnets are used to distribute the content to millions—none of which is legal.[70] SQL injection is a common cyber-attack that uses malicious code for backend database manipulation.[71] Here, the injection was able to replace the paid advertisement on both the website and within Google search ad rankings with a fraudulent advertisement. The advertisements were usually relating to investments with get rich quick, or fake celebrity endorsement. For this case, the victims clicked on the advertisement and were redirected to a platform where they were required to submit their name and contact data to access the platform. This data was then on-sold to the fraudsters as qualified leads. The fraudsters employed hard-sell tactics to sell access to a proprietary platform, which

[69] European Parliament (2023).

[70] Maurushat (2011).

[71] SQL Injection (SQLi): How to Protect against SQL Injection Attacks (2022).

supposedly allows clients to gain access to restricted data for generating profit. However, the profit data was initially manipulated to encourage clients to invest more money for higher returns.

Most of the money paid by the victims, being cryptocurrency or fiat, was transferred internationally to the Ultimate Beneficiary Owners (UBO) via an elaborate money laundering network, with a small portion used to pay victim 'profits', boiler room staff wages and other operational expenses. This was a complex and highly professional criminal operation using traditional Ponzi scheme and Pig Butchering techniques. What makes this scam unique is that the fraudsters used a new type of commodity to attract and retain victims. They also created complex legal contracts where the victims would agree to terms and conditions with milestones and obligations that were not achievable. Most victims believed they had no option but to accept the determinations of the fraudsters, which in 100% of cases equaled a high loss. In reality, the legal contracts were not legally binding.

As this scam was operating in the early days of the COVID pandemic, the scammer used the international response to the pandemic as an excuse for closing their 'investment company' and offering victims between 2–3% of their money back as compensation. Based on the legal agreement signed by the victims, many believed that they had no other alternative but to accept some money back as a consolation. As a result, many victims did not initially report the scam as they were unaware that they had been scammed.

The scam was uncovered by the author's private investigation company initially through victim reporting and later through the recruitment of several informants. Information provided by the informants confirmed that the restricted data available in the scam platform was fake, along with the manipulated profit data. Shortly after the victims saw a manipulated account profit with high returns, the fraudsters would create cryptocurrency exchange wallets for clients to transfer payments via cryptocurrency. which were then laundered through complex transactions involving mixers to hide the funds' origin and destination. The author's private investigation company reviewed thousands of internal documents provided by the informants and were able to reverse engineer the scam, identify victims, addresses, offenders, and part of the money laundering network. A comprehensive brief of evidence was compiled including victim statements and supporting evidence. The brief of evidence was then submitted to the Australian Federal Police (AFP) and the African national law enforcement agency. Since this time, several other international law enforcement agencies have joined the investigation with the case being managed by Interpol at the time of writing.

Various laws, including those related to serious organised crime, fraud, money laundering/proceeds of crime, cybersecurity hacking provisions, and unauthorised access or modification of data or systems, may apply in this case. Other regulators, such as security commissions, tax authorities, and consumer authorities, may also prosecute those involved in fraudulent investment schemes.

This case exemplifies the effectiveness of public-private collaboration and partnerships. By combining the capabilities of both sectors, the outcome was significantly improved. It demonstrates how tasks can be allocated based on each partner's legal and operational abilities. Overall, this serves as a solid example of successful collaboration between the public and private sectors. In the past, it was highly unusual for a private company to launch a major international criminal investigation and remain actively involved with victim support, informant management, intelligence gathering, analysis, and dissemination; even after Interpol assumed management of the investigation. This kind of collaboration used to be entirely prohibited by law enforcement due to their lack of trust in outsiders, policing culture, and outdated policies and procedures.

The primary reason for the pre-arrest stages of this investigation being a major success was the willingness of the Australian Federal Police (AFP) to actively collaborate and partner with private industry. During 2020, and at the time of the initial conversation between AFP and the Author's private investigation company, PPC and PPP were not a priority for Australian Federal and State law enforcement. In this regard, the AFP is a leader for law enforcement PPC and the establishment of PPP in Australia. Although AFP was a proactive initiator for the PPC, other international agencies became active collaborators in this investigation and deserve recognition. These include the Federal Bureau of Investigation (FBI), United States (U.S.) Homeland Security, U.S. Secret Service, Interpol, Royal Canadian Mounted Police (RCMP), and the Israeli Police. This investigation has demonstrated the potential of PPC for the investigation of cybercrime and has set a positive precedence for future cybercrime investigations.

6 Challenges and Limitations

6.1 Challenges and Limitations in PPPs and PPC for Combatting Cybercrime

Various challenges related to the PPP model, such as their inherent complexity, unreliable mechanisms for sharing risk and responsibility, and inadequate monitoring and evaluation of processes apply across industries and project types and have been discussed extensively in the literature.[72,73] PPPs in the realm of cybercrime, however, require the consideration of a unique set of issues, which are primarily related to partnership trust, cultural differences between public law enforcement and private investigators, legal and regulatory barriers, and a lack of transparency.

[72] Batjargal and Zhang (2021).

[73] European PPP Expertise Centre (2015).

6.2 Partnership Trust

One of the biggest barriers to any type of collaborative work is trust. Particularly in an industry where confidentiality can be vital to ensure adherence to proper legal processes, public and private entities may be hesitant to share information with each other. Data privacy, security and the potential misuse of information are all valid concerns for both sides, with inappropriately disclosed information having the ability to significantly jeopardise investigations. Additionally, law enforcement agencies are understandably reluctant to advertise their investigative methods to prevent criminals from adapting their methodologies to become more proficient and more anonymous. The private sector, which typically drives innovation, has the added concern of intellectual property being disclosed to those outside the organisation. Such sharing essentially constitutes the revealing of trade secrets, potentially leading to an increase in competition and a resulting negative financial impact on the company. Public entities must assure private entities that sensitive information will be protected and not used against them, while private entities must be transparent about their security posture and vulnerabilities. Establishing trust takes time and effort, but it is crucial to the success of collaboration efforts.

A further hurdle to the establishment of trusting relationships between police and private investigations companies is the issue of training and qualifications. Historically, private investigators were unregulated until the 1950's when South Australia was the first state to begin the process of licencing.[74] Even with stricter regulations in place today regarding the training requirements necessary to become a private investigator, the licencing process remains rather basic. This results in private investigators having wildly disparate skill sets, with varied levels of investigative capability, ethical reasoning, and professionalism, making it difficult for those in the public service to determine who would be suitable for a partnership. PPPs are destined to fail, where requisite criteria are not established, and inadequate procedures are in place for selection of private partners.

6.3 Cultural Differences

Also central to the difficulties experienced when public and private entities join forces to fight cybercrime, are cultural differences between police and private investigators. While private investigators have traditionally been seen as working for profit and to have an agenda based on the goals of their clients, police are deemed to serve all members of the public equally and to focus on seeking truth and justice.[75] This apparent mismatch can create a moral and/or practical impasse, in which there may be conflict over the nature of the goals or the processes necessary to achieve

[74]Whitford (2015).

[75]Prenzler and Sarre (2012).

them. The difference in ethos is most apparent in the way law enforcement prioritises data collection and the investigation of crimes with high harm and volume, while private investigators will typically devote more time and attention to personal and civil matters. Traditionally, PPPs have also suffered from cultural issues related to differing organisational structures, processes, and communication styles, which must be addressed in the planning stages of a partnership.[76]

6.4 Legal and Regulatory Frameworks

The legal and regulatory frameworks that govern public and private entities may differ, creating additional challenges for the two sectors to work together smoothly. In some cases, laws and regulations may prohibit the sharing of certain types of information. However, this barrier can be overcome by all parties working together to establish information sharing agreements and protocols that comply with data protection regulations.[77] An example is a Memorandum of Understanding (MOU) which focuses on interagency cooperation and guides how staff from both sectors will work together. While MOUs can be incredibly useful for targeting cybercriminals, they are somewhat scarce and complicated to establish.

As information becomes more sensitive and confidential, it becomes essential for private investigators to obtain the necessary security clearances to effectively collaborate and share information with government authorities. Security clearances are granted by governments to individuals who meet specific criteria and demonstrate trustworthiness and reliability.[78] However, there are currently legal restrictions in place as private investigators generally do not hold government issued security clearances.[79] Security clearances provide a higher level trust and allow for efficient and legal information sharing. Firstly, it will ensure that sensitive information shared between government entities and private industry remains protected. By conducting thorough background checks and vetting processes, government authorities can assess an investigator's integrity, loyalty, and ability to safeguard classified information.[80]

In turn, the private industry often operates with commercial security classifications, non-disclosure agreements and legal caveats to protect intellectual property and sensitive client data. This is another legal consideration that will need to be overcome to ensure effective information sharing between public and private entities.

[76] Prenzler and Sarre (2012).

[77] Karaba et al. (2022).

[78] Australian Government-Attorney General's Department (2018).

[79] Australian Government – Defence (n.d.).

[80] Northrop Grumman (n.d.).

An additional important legal and regulatory aspect to facilitate effective PPC is the acknowledgment and admissibility of evidence gathered by private industry entities in criminal judicial proceedings. For privately collected evidence to be efficiently presented in court, legislative amendments may be necessary to establish a streamlined framework. Although there are currently procedures in place in most jurisdictions for private and expert evidence to be admitted, this process would need to be refined to allow for the high volume of cybercrime related cases being investigated. However, it is crucial to ensure that these changes are harmonised across both state and federal jurisdictions in countries such as Australia and the United States, to realistically implement a comprehensive national response to this matter.[81]

6.5 Lack of Transparency

Due to commercial confidentialities as well as the inherent privacy required in investigating and disrupting significant criminal networks, it is difficult to determine how successful or economically sound PPPs are, or to conduct an objective cost-benefit analysis in order to identify the areas in which the programs could be improved. A lack of transparency is a major issue for PPPs in general and is likely to be heightened in PPPs related to criminal investigations. Important consideration must be given to the fact that private partnerships with historically secretive organisations are occurring, creating a situation where the lack of communication of sensitive information must be re-evaluated.

7 Recommendations

We recommend the establishment of a national cyber police response agency that is primarily responsible for ensuring that all state and federal police agencies develop consistent police training, policy and procedure for reporting and investigating cyber fraud cases. Once a national coordination of policing jurisdictions is established, productive and efficient PPPs and PPC will naturally follow. The demand for police resources is high and it is unrealistic that police agencies alone will be able to address the rise of cybercrime as quickly as necessary. Formalised PPC supported by legislation will therefore be crucial to combatting cybercrime.

We recommend the establishment of qualification-based licensing for private investigation firms undertaking cyber based criminal investigations, including cryptocurrency tracing. The current qualification for licensed private investigators is not sufficient to demonstrate professional technical capability for investigating

[81] Australian Law Reform Commission (2010).

cybercrime. Especially where trust and cooperation with the courts, police, and prosecuting authorities is a primary activity. Licensed private cyber investigators will require sufficient technical education and/ or experience to demonstrate their capability. Their activities will be monitored and reviewed by an independent regulatory oversighting body to ensure adequate capability, and that best practice and professionalism are adhered to.

We further recommend that private cyber investigator licensing be bound by state and federal legislation to remove legal ambiguity. In turn, evidence identified and captured by private cyber investigators can be submitted directly to police agencies as evidence in support of formal criminal investigation. The introduction of licensed private cyber investigators will free up police resources and provide victims with the option to pay for expedited investigation of their case.

8 Conclusion

As cybercrime is a global issue that affects both public and private organisations, collaboration between public and private entities is essential for combatting this issue effectively. By sharing intelligence, participating in joint exercises, and coordinating incident response efforts, public and private entities can work together to identify and mitigate cyber threats. Collaboration can be formalised, such as with the NIST Cybersecurity Framework or the UN Global Programme on Cybercrime. These types of formalised collaborations can provide a framework for public and private entities to work together effectively, helping to establish common goals, streamline information sharing, and improve response coordination. Informal collaborations, such as PPPs and information sharing networks, can also be effective in combating cybercrime. Regardless of the form, collaboration between public and private entities is critical to combating cybercrime.

Several challenges unique to the creation of PPPs or PPC in the realm of cyber fraud were identified. Partnership trust, cultural differences between public law enforcement and private investigators, legal and regulatory barriers, and a lack of transparency are all issues that will need to be carefully considered prior to developing legislation regarding the formalisation of PPPs or PPC, in order to increase the probability of the partnerships being functional and effective.

The need for collaboration between public and private entities to combat cybercrime cannot be overstated. Cybercrime continues to pose a significant threat to organisations and individuals worldwide, and collaboration between public and private entities will help to improve cybersecurity awareness, enhance threat detection, and response capabilities, and foster information sharing and best practices.

Public and private entities must recognise the importance of collaboration in combating cybercrime. By collaborating, public entities can leverage the private sector's expertise in cyber investigation, cybersecurity, and technology, while private entities can benefit from the public sector's resources and access to privileged information. Furthermore, collaboration can help to bridge the gap between legal and technical expertise, which is essential in developing effective responses to cybercriminals.

References

Anderson R, Barton C, Bohme R et al (2019) Measuring the changing cost of cybercrime. The 18th Workshop on the Economics of Information Security (WEIS) 2019, Innsbruck, Austria. https://www.researchgate.net/publication/350793602_Measuring_the_changing_cost_of_cybercrime

Attorney-General's Department (2013) National plan to combat cybercrime. https://www.homeaffairs.gov.au/criminal-justice/files/national-plan-combat-cybercrime.pdf

Australian Competition and Consumer Commission (2019) Targeting scams: report of the ACCC on scams activity. https://www.accc.gov.au/about-us/publications/serial-publications/targeting-scams-report-on-scams-activity/targeting-scams-report-of-the-accc-on-scam-activity-2018

Australian Competition and Consumer Commission (2021) Targeting scams: report of the ACCC on scam activity 2020. https://www.accc.gov.au/about-us/publications/serial-publications/targeting-scams-report-on-scams-activity/targeting-scams-report-of-the-accc-on-scam-activity-2020

Australian Competition and Consumer Commission (2022) Scams Awareness Week 2022 empowers Australians to spot a scam. https://www.accc.gov.au/media-release/scams-awareness-week-2022-empowers-australians-to-spot-a-scam-0

Australian Competition and Consumer Commission (2023) Targeting scams: report of the ACCC on scams activity 2022. https://www.accc.gov.au/about-us/publications/serial-publications/targeting-scams-report-on-scams-activity/targeting-scams-report-of-the-accc-on-scams-activity-2022

Australian Cyber Security Centre (2022) ACSC Annual Cyber Threat Report, July 2021 to June 2022. https://www.cyber.gov.au/about-us/reports-and-statistics/acsc-annual-cyber-threat-report-july-2021-june-2022

Australian Federal Police (n.d.) Joint Policing Cybercrime Coordination Centre (JPC3). https://www.afp.gov.au/what-we-do/joint-policing-cybercrime-coordination-centre-jpc3

Australian Government Department of Home Affairs (2020) Cyber Security Strategy 2020. https://www.homeaffairs.gov.au/cyber-security-subsite/files/cyber-security-strategy-2020.pdf

Australian Government Department of Home Affairs (2023) 2023-2030 Australian Cyber Security Strategy Discussion Paper. https://www.homeaffairs.gov.au/reports-and-publications/submissions-and-discussion-papers/2023-2030-australian-cyber-security-strategy-discussion-paper

Batjargal T, Zhang M (2021) Review of key challenges in public-private partnership implementation. J Infrastruct Policy Dev 5:1378. https://doi.org/10.24294/jipd.v5i2.1378

Broadhurst R (2006) Developments in the global law enforcement of cyber-crime. Policing: Int J Police Strateg Manag 29:408–433. https://doi.org/10.1108/13639510610684674

Brookes J (2023) Cyber threat platform costing govt $59k a day. https://www.innovationaus.com/cyber-threat-platform-costing-govt-59k-a-day/

Chiappini T (2022) Developing digital literacy to keep consumers safe online. https://www.ejinsight.com/eji/article/id/3071748/20220317-Developing-digital-literacy-to-keep-consumers-safe-online

Cross C (2018) Expectations vs reality: responding to online fraud across the fraud justice network. Int J Law Crime Justice 55:1–12. https://doi.org/10.1016/j.ijlcj.2018.08.001

Cross C (2020) 'Oh we can't actually do anything about that': the problematic nature of jurisdiction for online fraud victims. Criminol Crim Justice 20:358–375. https://doi.org/10.1177/1748895819835910

Cross C, Holt T, Powell A, Wilson M (2021) Responding to cybercrime: results of a comparison between community members and police personnel. Report to the Criminology Research Advisory Council Grant: CRG 23/16–17

(2023) Cyber security and your business | business.gov.au. https://business.gov.au/online/cyber-security/cyber-security-and-your-business

(2022) Cybercrime Getting More Sophisticated: How to Protect Your Business?. https://threatpost.com/cybercrime-more-sophisticated/179676/

Daniels J (2022) The impact of cybercrime on company reputation: a 2022 update. In: Agility PR Solutions. https://www.agilitypr.com/pr-news/public-relations/the-impact-of-cybercrime-on-company-reputation-a-2022-update/

Deloitte Australia (2022) The importance of Public-Private Partnerships in Australian Cyber Resilience - Risk Advisory blog. https://www2.deloitte.com/au/en/blog/risk-advisory-blog/2022/importance-public-private-partnerships-australian-cyber-resilience.html

Department of Home Affairs (2022) National Plan to Combat Cybercrime 2022. Australian Government. https://www.homeaffairs.gov.au/criminal-justice/files/national-plan-combat-cybercrime-2022.pdf

Dunn P, Gunson T (2022) Scammers are getting smarter at targeting financial services, here's 5 ways to better guard against scams. https://www.pwc.com.au/financial-services/scammers-are-getting-smarter-at-targeting-financial-services.html

English LM (2006) Public private partnerships in Australia: an overview of their nature, purpose, incidence and oversight. UNSW Law J 29:250–262

European Parliament (2023) Public-Private Partnerships for Cybersecurity. https://www.europarl.europa.eu/legislative-train/carriage/public-private-partnerships-for-cybersecurity/report

European PPP Expertise Centre (2015) PPP motivations and challenges for the public sector. https://www.eib.org/attachments/epec/epec_ppp_motivations_and_challenges_en.pdf

European Union Agency for Network and Information Security (2017) Private-Public Partnerships (PPP) Cooperative Models. https://www.enisa.europa.eu/publications/public-private-partnerships-ppp-cooperative-models/

Federal Bureau of Investigation (2016) Cyber Crime. https://www.fbi.gov/investigate/cyber

Federal Bureau of Investigation (n.d.-a) How does the FBI interact with other federal law enforcement agencies? https://www.fbi.gov/about/faqs/what-is-the-fbi-doing-to-improve-its-interaction-with-other-federal-law-enforcement-agencies

Federal Bureau of Investigation (n.d.-b) International operations. https://www.fbi.gov/about/leadership-and-structure/international-operations

Federal Trade Commission (2022) Phishing scams. https://www.consumer.ftc.gov/articles

Furnell S, Dowling S (2019) Cybercrime: a portrait of the landscape. J Criminol Res Policy Pract 5:13–26

Gellman R (2021) Cybersecurity and privacy litigation: developments and trends. Commun ACM 64:52–57

Gordon LA, Loeb MP, Lucyshyn W (2003) Sharing information on computer systems security: an economic analysis. J Account Public Policy 22(6):461–485

Halpin D (2023) ChatGPT scam investigations. https://www.cybertrace.com.au/chatgpt-scam-investigation/

Harkin D, Whelan C, Chang L (2018) The challenges facing specialist police cyber-crime units: an empirical analysis. Police Pract Res 19:519–536. https://doi.org/10.1080/15614263.2018.1507889

Harkin D, Whelan C (2022) Perceptions of police training needs in cyber-crime. International Journal of Police Science & Management 24(1):66–76. https://doi.org/10.1177/14613557211036565

Henderson P (2022) Dark side of digital transformation: massive fraud. https://www.informationweek.com/big-data/the-dark-side-of-digital-transformation-massive-fraud

Hilt S, Kropotov V, Mercês F, Rosario M, Sancho D (2019) Uncovering IoT threats in the cybercrime underground. https://www.trendmicro.com/vinfo/us/security/news/cybercrime-and-digital-threats/the-internet-of-things-in-the-cybercrime-underground

HM Treasury (2020) UK national risk assessment of money laundering and terrorist financing. https://www.gov.uk/government/publications/national-risk-assessment-of-money-laundering-and-terrorist-financing-2020

Interpol (n.d.-a) Private sector partners. https://www.interpol.int/en/Our-partners/Private-sector-partners

Interpol (n.d.-b) Public-private partnerships. https://www.interpol.int/en/Crimes/Cybercrime/Public-private-partnerships

Interpol (n.d.-c) AFJOC - African Joint Operation against Cybercrime. https://www.interpol.int/Crimes/Cybercrime/Cybercrime-operations/AFJOC-African-Joint-Operation-against-Cybercrime

Interpol (n.d.-d) Operation across Africa identifies cyber-criminals and at-risk online infrastructure. https://www.interpol.int/en/News-and-Events/News/2022/Operation-across-Africa-identifies-cyber-criminals-and-at-risk-online-infrastructure

Juniper Research (2020) Digital Payment Value to Reach $6.7 Trillion by 2023, as New Players Follow Alipay and WeChat Pay's Lead. https://www.juniperresearch.com/press/press-releases/digital-payment-value-to-reach-$6.7-trillion-by-2023

Karaba F, Roehrich JK, Conway S, Turner J (2022) Information sharing in public-private relationships: the role of boundary objects in contracts. Public Manag Rev:1–25. https://doi.org/10.1080/14719037.2022.2065344

Klauzner I, Pisani A (2023) Trends in and characteristics of cybercrime in NSW. https://www.bocsar.nsw.gov.au/Publications/BB/BB165-Report-Cybercrime-in-NSW.pdf

Maurushat A (2011) Botnet Badinage: regulatory approaches to combating botnets. Thesis, UNSW Sydney

Maurushat A, Halpin D (2022) Investigation of cryptocurrency enabled and dependent crimes. In: Goldbarsht D, de Koker L (eds) Financial technology and the law: combating financial crime. Springer International Publishing, Cham, pp 235–267

McGuire M, Dowling S (2013) Cyber-dependent crimes. In: Cyber crime: a review of the evidence Research Report 75. https://assets.publishing.service.gov.uk/government/uploads/system/uploads/attachment_data/file/246751/horr75-chap1.pdf

National Crime Agency (n.d.) National Economic Crime Centre. https://www.nationalcrimeagency.gov.uk/what-we-do/national-economic-crime-centre

National Institute of Standards and Technology (2020) NIST Cybersecurity Framework. https://www.nist.gov/cyberframework

Prenzler T, Sarre R (2012) Public-private crime prevention partnerships. In: Prenzler T (ed) Policing and Security in Practice. Crime Prevention and Security Management series. Palgrave Macmillan, London. https://doi.org/10.1057/9781137007780_9

Schjolberg S (2020) The history of cybercrime, 3rd edn. Books on Demand, Norderstedt

Shaw M (2015) Public private partnerships & crime prevention. In: 13th UN Congress on Crime Prevention & Criminal Justice. International Centre for the Prevention of Crime, Doha, Qatar. https://www.unodc.org/documents/congress/workshops/workshop4/PDFs/Panel5/03_Shaw.pdf

Smith J, Johnson A (2020) Cybercrime and the rise of digital payments: exploring the expanding attack surface. Int J Cyber Criminol 14:77–92

(2018) Study Shows High Level of Consumer Concern About Cyber Crime, Low Level of Action or Awareness About Safety Measures. https://www.businesswire.com/news/home/20181018005770/en/Study-Shows-High-Level-of-Consumer-Concern-About-Cyber-Crime-Low-Level-of-Action-or-Awareness-About-Safety-Measures

Taylor RW, Fritsch EJ, Liederbach J (2019) Digital crime and digital terrorism, 3rd edn. Pearson, p 10

The Royal United Services Institute for Defence and Security Studies (2017) Public–Private Partnerships and Financial Crime: Advancing an Inclusive Model. https://www.rusi.org/explore-our-research/publications/commentary/public-private-partnerships-and-financial-crime-advancing-inclusive-model
The White House (2021) Executive order on improving the nation's cybersecurity. The White House. https://www.whitehouse.gov/briefing-room/presidential-actions/2021/05/12/executive-order-on-improving-the-nations-cybersecurity/
United Nations (2021) Global Programme on Cybercrime. https://www.unodc.org/unodc/en/cybercrime/global-programme-cybercrime.html
United Nations Office of Drugs and Crime (2010) Salvador Declaration. https://www.unodc.org/documents/crime-congress/12th-Crime-Congress/Documents/Salvador_Declaration/Salvador_Declaration_E.pdf
United Nations Office on Drugs and Crime (2013) Comprehensive Study on Cybercrime. https://www.unodc.org/documents/organized-crime/UNODC_CCPCJ_EG.4_2013/CYBERCRIME_STUDY_210213.pdf
UNSW (2021) Cybercrime an estimated $42 billion cost to Australian economy. https://www.unsw.adfa.edu.au/newsroom/news/cybercrime-estimated-42-billion-cost-australian-economy
US Mission Unvie (2021) The importance of strong public-private partnerships in the fight against cybercrime. In: U.S. Mission to International Organizations in Vienna. https://vienna.usmission.gov/the-importance-of-strong-public-private-partnerships-in-the-fight-against-cybercrime/. Accessed 21 Dec 2023
Vogel B (2022) Potentials and limits of public-private partnerships against money laundering and terrorism financing. EUCRIM J. https://doi.org/10.30709/eucrim-2022-002
What is a SQL Injection Attack? - CrowdStrike. In: crowdstrike.com. https://www.crowdstrike.com/cybersecurity-101/sql-injection/
Whitford T (2015) "A necessary but dangerous class": early private investigators in Australia. Salus J 3:28–39. https://researchoutput.csu.edu.au/ws/portalfiles/portal/11547383/80919_Published_Article_1000004763.pdf
Why technological growth leads to more cybercrime. In: Mycronic. https://www.mycronic.com/en/news/news-articles/why-technological-growth-leads-to-more-cybercrime/

Daniel Halpin with a distinguished 24-year career in the investigation and intelligence sectors, holds advanced credentials in policing, investigations, intelligence, and security. Currently, Dan is the Founder and Chief Executive Officer of private intelligence company, Cybertrace, and he is globally renowned for his pioneering work in cryptocurrency fraud detection. Dan's professional history is marked by positions with several major Australian institutions. These include the Australian Security Intelligence Organisation (ASIO), New South Wales (NSW) Police Force, Queensland Police Service, and the Australian Capital Territory (ACT) Department of Justice & Community Service. Notably, while serving as a NSW Police, Counter Terrorism Intelligence Officer, Dan was temporarily attached to both the Australian Federal Police (AFP) and NSW Crime Commission, offering crucial intelligence during the AFP Operation Pendennis Terrorism trial from 2007 to 2009 in Sydney. Moreover, in 2016–2017, he was engaged as a Consultant Advisor to the Department of Prime Minister & Cabinet to provide expert advice on matters relating to the Australian Public Service, Code of Conduct.

Dr. Sheri Todd holds a Doctorate in Clinical Psychology and worked extensively in tertiary mental health services, private practice, and training centres over a 15-year period. More recently a long-standing interest in crime and forensic psychology prompted a career change, leading her into the realm of private investigations and intelligence. Sheri is currently the Head of Cyber Investigations for a prominent Australian company specialising in international fraud and cybercrime.

Policy Conservatism and the Wirecard Scandal

Alfio Puglisi

Abstract Germany is considered the European FinTech champion. The recent Wirecard Scandal has raised concerns over Germany's financial policy approach and sheds light into how financial crime can be hidden behind innovation. The aim of this chapter is to explain why and when German officials have applied a conservative approach towards financial technologies both from an historical perspective and through policy analyses. In doing so, the chapter case study is the recent Wirecard Scandal. I apply a political economy framework to shed light on the influence of regulation on innovation and the tight network of regulators and financial actors in the innovation system of Germany. Results show that regulatory avoidance can be hidden behind German's regulatory architecture where the centralization of powers within BaFin supervisory authority limited the foresight of the Wirecard Scandal.

1 Introduction

The aim of this chapter is to examine the FinTech industry in Germany and explain why the German government has taken a conservative regulatory approach towards FinTech. Germany's idea is that government should remain neutral regarding which technologies will transform the banking system. German officials criticised the use of using a sandbox regime over other FinTech regulatory methods and demanded that technology neutrality must continue to play an important role in financial regulation. Historically, dominant actors gained influence in the German FinTech ecosystem because leading banks influence policymaking.[1] The 100 largest German companies averaged only 26 percent dispersed ownership, with 18 per cent of shares

[1] Höpner and Jackson (2001).

A. Puglisi (✉)
King's College, London, UK

D. Goldbarsht, L. de Koker (eds.), *Financial Crime, Law and Governance*, Ius Gentium: Comparative Perspectives on Law and Justice 116,
https://doi.org/10.1007/978-3-031-59547-9_13

held by families, 14 per cent by the state, and 17 per cent by foreign investors. Given the conflict between established, influential business actors and the government, Germany has picked national winners rather than opening markets to new entrants as occurs in other nations.

Scholars agree on the influence of regulation on innovation,[2] about the regulators' engagement with FinTech and the influence of banks on regulation.[3] This chapter argues that not only do regulator-business relationships affect regulatory innovation, but they also affect how the government approaches FinTech, given the political salience of regulatory avoidance and consumer data use.[4]

My first aim for this chapter is descriptive: I provide an overview of the institutions responsible for financial regulation and competition policy. I apply a political economy framework to explain the innovation ecosystem in Germany.

My second aim is to explain why Germany, with its regulatory policy approach of "picking up national winners" has demonstrated a deep regulatory commitment to addressing systemic risk and financial stability rather than promoting global competition and innovation. In the Wirecard scandal, the German government hide important information from the public.[5] This experience raised questions about policy makers' accountability and what role regulators should play in the innovation. The Wirecard scandal is considered as an exogenous shock that have occurred in the FinTech industry, and it calls into question the unconventional policy environment of private sector-led entrepreneurship rather than government-based innovation environment. My expectation is that market forces in the financial industry might have led the government to protect Wirecard at the expense of creating an inclusive digital ecosystem, in which other FinTech start-ups could have flourished. One of the main strengths of this approach is to move away from the regulatory scholarship that focuses on systemic risk and financial stability and instead look at how the German government can take an enabling role rather than acting as an industry player.[6]

This chapter presents three key findings: First, the German government has adopted a centralised model of financial regulation in which it strategically supports the business capacity of institutions posing a systemic risk, which triggered a distortion of trust in relation to the FinTech industry.[7] Second, German financial sector supervisors are mainly interested in financial stability and systemic risk because they face constitutional constraints, namely the lack of regulatory powers in the areas of competition and innovation.[8] Third, the Wirecard scandal, a surprising example of regulatory avoidance and regulatory failure, raises questions about how

[2] Arner et al. (2017); Zetzsche et al. (2017).

[3] Hardie and Howarth (2013).

[4] EBA (2017).

[5] Aßländer and Burkatzki (2023); Teichmann et al. (2023).

[6] Ranchordás (2015); Von Schomberg (2012); Sabel and Zeitlin (2010).

[7] Hardie and Howarth (2013); Friesendorf and Blütener (2023).

[8] Handke (2012); Hasan and Kruse (2023).

Germany can support innovation, given that the government created barriers to new entrants.[9]

This chapter is structured as follows: Sect. 2 explains Germany's financial market policy and the role of BaFin. Section 3 presents the Varieties of Capitalism perspective of the Germany's FinTech approach. It highlights differences with the UK's experimentalist regulatory style. Section 3 illustrates private-led entrepreneurialism in the German's banking system. Section 4 illustrates innovation in Germany's banking system with the examples of three leading banking groups. Section 5 develops a political economic argument regarding the politics of FinTech. Section 6 concludes this chapter.

2 Financial Market Policy

Germany's financial market policy relies on an apparent decentralised, complex and politically charged governance mechanism. The Ministry of Finance or "*Bundesfinanzministerium*" (henceforth BMF), is the central administrative body responsible for German financial market policy.[10] Financial regulation is somewhat decentralised but jointly executed by the BMF, BaFin and the Bundesbank (i.e. central bank). BMF and Bundesbank set standards and create new rules, whereas BaFin supervises and monitors financial activities.[11] Distinctive goals of the German financial market policy include financial market stability and integrity. Policy makers extensively regulate the banking, insurance and securities businesses. Following, the German Banking Act (Kreditwesengesetz, or henceforth KWG) and the Insurance Supervision Act (Versicherungsaufsichtsgesetz, or henceforth VAG), German financial market regulation has included disclosure requirements[12] and featured greater attention to risk regulation and risk management but not innovation. Supervision of financial markets accompanies BaFin's risk regulation and risk management.[13] FinTech entities embody systemic risk[14] and this has materialised in the pacing problem, in which innovation outpaces regulation.[15]

BMF plays a coordinating role, in which its specialised departments for every financial market subsector offer legal and technical oversight over BaFin.[16] Thus, BMF can formally decide on every single organisational or supervisory operation

[9] Aßländer and Burkatzki (2023).

[10] Handke (2012), p. 238.

[11] Hasan and Kruse (2023).

[12] E.g., article 26 of KWG; article 55 of VAG.

[13] Lindemann (2006).

[14] Cumming et al. (2019).

[15] Gary et al. (2011); Ranchordás (2015).

[16] Sec. 2 of the Act established BaFin FinDAG.

and any BaFin's policy.[17] BaFin is a de-facto autonomous organisation, however scholar Handke[18] argues that its independence depends on the weaknesses in the ministry's ability to exercise control over the agency and to formulate policies.[19] According to the Kreditwesengesetz (the German Banking Act) decisions such as dismissing managers[20] or assessing the provision of funds[21] are characterised by a trade-off between competition and consumer protection; this raises questions on wider question about competition and innovation in domestic markets. The relationship between BaFin and BMF is complex, and scholars have shown that BaFin does not have much discretionary policy-making power in banking regulation.[22] State capacity for regulatory action is lower in Germany than in the UK. BaFin insists that "its "supervisory activities are competition-neutral and technology-neutral. It is not one of BaFin's tasks to promote innovation or investment. Nor does it conduct industrial policy" in FinTech.[23]

Historically, Germany's banking, corporate governance and the overall financial system were characterised by a remarkable degree of stability[24] and competition.[25] However, technology has affected these strong features of the German's banking system. Germany is falling behind on consumer adoption of emerging financial technologies in Finance with just 14% of Germans using mobile payments, and two-thirds of the population claiming they are not considering adopting mobile payments with an increase in online payments and reduction of cash following the covid pandemic.[26] Jünger and Mietzner (2020) provide empirical evidence about the factors that may have caused German consumers to switch (at least part of their financial services) from traditional financial institutions to FinTech firms. One of the driving factors is higher customer satisfaction through better service offering (Jünger and Mietzner 2020). This finding is consistent with the first exercise mapping German FinTech activities, by Dorfleitner et al. (2017), which reports that digital banking and payments, P2P lending, and crowdfunding and digital financial-advisory services have grown into the largest segment of the banking infrastructure. Mietzner and Molterer (2018) examine discrepancies in Germany between the quality of financial advice and advisory commissions. They highlight that professional advice is no guarantee of a suitable match between investments and individual

[17] Handke (2012), p. 239.

[18] Handke (2012).

[19] "The government [can] override or preempt, at no cost to itself, supervisory actions directed at troubled banks, thus keeping such banks open and risking higher costs to society in the future" Quintyn Taylor, p. 7.

[20] § 36 KWG.

[21] § 10 KWG.

[22] E.g., Quaglia (2008).

[23] Leonhardt (2019).

[24] IMF (2011); Rothstein and Schulze-Cleven (2020); Hardie and Howarth (2013).

[25] Choulet (2016).

[26] Bundesbank (2021).

savings targets. The Commission of European Communities has stressed the need to improve financial advice and consumers' financial literacy. Technological solutions can address some of these concerns with innovation designed for consumers. BaFin (2016) recently launched an internal project group for FinTech to review new developments in the area of digitalization.

Institutional legitimacy. In Contemporary Germany, institutions and their associated practices have been described as 'fluid',[27] meaning that political economic models present market-driven and government-led structures driving institutional changes. There have been recent theoretical accounts of institutional change in labour markets[28] and European industrial relations. Yet, analysts have not analysed how FinTech challenges long-standing industrial structures and market relationships. The relationship between the market and institutions is a politically salient topic. The debate is between bank-based and market-based systems. The empirical evidence on which system is preferable is limited and has reached mixed results. Levine's (2002) analysis of the relationship between economic performance and financial structure and whether national market institutions are bank-based or market-based can shed light on the path of evolution of financial markets. The bank-based view of the Germany's market highlights how banks are equipped to address asymmetric information problem, improve capital allocations, and strengthen corporate governance.[29] Moreover, considering the market as a group of banks, liquidity risk is spread across several banks, which enhances investment efficiency and economic growth.[30] This may help mobilise capital and exploit economies of scale.[31] However, the empirical evidence demonstrates that the government played a limited role in mitigating these risks by taking a nation-based view of markets with established players. Market-modifying and market-correcting political intervention were neglected by focusing on competitive markets such as the car-manufacturing sector[32] or focusing on national champions. The main issue was not on banks or markets but rather on market-modifying structures and an environment in which new FinTech intermediaries and markets would provide innovative based solutions and sound financial services. The politics of FinTech is about clear patterns of developments within an ecosystem and how institutions acquire legitimacy through patterns of coalition and cooperation.[33] The technical environment concerns the development of products, services and technologies before they reach the market. Capital market constraints are easily adapted to business influence and that labour can accommodate some new distributional constraints within the existing CME institutional framework. However, in FinTech, governance of innovation is

[27] E.g., Streeck (2009); Baccaro and Benassi (2017).

[28] Thelen (2004).

[29] Diamond (1984); Ramakrishnan and Thakor (1984).

[30] Allen and Gale (1999); Bencivenga et al. (1995).

[31] Sirri and Tufano (1995).

[32] C.f. Hildermeier and Villareal (2011).

[33] Maggio and Powell (1991).

centralized[34] and not treated as a political objective. Technology and increasing digitalisation of business organisational structures shaped how capital is treated by the German government and firms in the process of corporate governance and employment relationship.[35] Banks still provide substantial long-term investment support, and they act as stable shareholders, and protect companies against hostile takeovers.[36]

These limited changes to the German banking system were conditioned by the country's overarching institutions and mediated through market forces of the leading financial institutions. For example, the German Startup Association, established in 2012, stated that FinTech was their priority in the digitalisation banking debate. At the EU level, the European FinTech Association also coordinated with their national counterparts. FinTech companies also joined the Association of German Banks. The ministry of Germany operates a 'Digital Finance Forum', which has about 40 individual (mainly private sector) members. Formerly named the 'Fintech Council', the forum has working groups in fields such as payments, insurance, blockchain and investment. Typically officials of BaFin and supervisory authorities are included on cross-cutting topics of relevance to their mandates.".[37]

The institutions that matter in the politics of FinTech reflect the German model of capitalism.[38] In my account, the political institutions that are mostly significant are those political institutions which do not have the constitutional legitimacy over the market.[39] Private institutions coordinate their business activities with banks and scale-up their operations for experimentation. Their policy-making processes are structured and ad hoc, and they focus on financial stability among their participants. Two leading banks, DZ Bank and WGZ Bank, cooperated in a private innovation hub initiative and since 2023 they now have emerged. While institutions may experiment with innovation at the firm-level, platform capitalism is moving towards greater support of FinTech start-ups. While Germany mainly focuses on the private digitalisation of the banking system, the experimentation is limited. Germany's government instituted local innovation hubs in accordance with the European Commission's strategy on innovation. It did not engage in any thoughtful discussion of innovation with firms or the public but rather consulted with the FinTech high level panel and issued reports on innovation[40]. The 2021 McKinsey Report on the status of the German banking infrastructure highlights that commercial banks are

[34]Friesendorf and Blütener (2023).

[35]Jackson et al. (2004).

[36]Jackson et al. (2004), p. 1.

[37]Federal Ministry of Finance (2019).

[38]Hall and Soskice (2001); Thelen (2004).

[39]For example, in commercial law, recent regulatory experiments faced regulatory challenges in the application of the Trade Regulation Act (Federation), "The governments of the Lander (local government) shall be authorised to issue ordinances to test out simplifications, particularly to facilitate start-ups and take-overs of companies" BMWI, p. 80 Annex.

[40]Bafin (2022).

experiencing a decline in institutional legitimacy as demand for their products and services decreases. Big banks are facing the challenge of a shift of customer preferences towards tailored financial products and efficient decision-making. The reluctance of the German government to change the current FinTech institutional structure shows that the traditional bank-fee model, in which banks pursue profit and saving banks serve small and medium-sized enterprises and private customers, is a plausible way to slow change in the FinTech sector and in regulatory experimentation.

3 The German's Banking System Is Experiencing Structural Changes Yet Remains Conservative

The German banking system is a universal banking system. Banks are permitted to offer payments, lend money, and offer a wide range of financial services and products to their clients. While they dominate the market, legal regulations in place have prevented oligopoly to a certain extent.[41] The German banking market is rather fragmented and has been called the 'three pillar banking system', consisting of private banks, state-owned banks, and cooperative banks,[42] though it also includes international universal banks (Deutsche, Dresdner and Commerzbank). About 20 percent of all German banks are public savings banks and about 60 per cent are cooperative banks.[43] Cooperative banks were set up as part of the broader project of the welfare in Germany in the nineteenth century it observe the demands of the rural population and of the working class.[44] Cooperative banks attained as a competitive advantage in a banking system in which private banks focused on large projects such as steel and railway investments and served the needs of the wider German's industry. Clergymen or teachers supervised the activities of cooperative banks members.[45] Cooperative banks emerged as secure debtors. While cooperative banks today have been merged into bigger organisations, they retain the original business model in which the 'customer is a shareholder' and 'shareholder is a customer'. The co-operative banking s sector has steadily increased its market share at the expense of other types of banks, and it has resisted structural changes in the global economy. Deeg (1999) demonstrates that despite capital-market harmonisation and despite the convergence of various models of capitalism, the German economy has benefited from globalisation and capital-market integration. Choulet (2016) highlights that the German banking system remains very

[41] Hackethal (2005).

[42] Behr and Schmidt (2015); Choulet (2016).

[43] Hackethal (2005).

[44] Deeg (1999, 2001).

[45] Deeg (2001).

concentrated. Private banks take on international projects and serve global markets, whereas cooperative and savings banks pursue local and national financing strategies. According to the Bundesbank, there were 1533 credit institutions, including 377 savings banks, 815 cooperative banks (Volks und Raiffeisenbanken), and 1 central cooperative bank (DZ Bank AG) as of 2021. This model of capitalism is now being challenged by technology. According to a 2021 McKinsey report on German banking, banks remain at the heart of the economy, as they provide vital financial services, manage risk, and have led the economy through the pandemic. Moreover, Germany's banks provide standard products at relatively low cost by international standards.[46] While German banks have succeeded at retail banking and corporate banking, they show weaknesses in technology, demographics, and ESG-related emissions and sustainability targets.

Germany's abstention from financial deregulation in the 1990s and 2000s reflected its status as a CME.[47] As of 2018, Germany had more than 1500 banks.[48] The structure of the German banking system—with commercial banks, cooperative banks, and public saving banks—has attracted the interest of the institutionalist approach to political economy and governance,[49] which emphasises the role of competition. Rather than seeing competition as an individualist view of competition, institutions frame competition as 'group competition'.[50] Each group of banks has its own objective, legal structure, and corporate organisation. The three types of banks avoid competition,[51] and the government favors public saving banks and cooperative banks through the principle of regional competences. In principle, public saving banks and cooperative banks serve small and medium-sized companies in what is known as the 'Sparkassen' model. The success of these companies depends on avoiding competition with each other.[52] Stakeholders in the German banking system coordinate to offset the pressures of global competition and support long-term investments in strategic areas of the economy. The success of the Sparkassen model of savings and public banks rests on undermining competition[53] rather than introducing innovative products.

The structure of the German banking industry has been questioned by the European Union, especially as EU rules have been harmonized.[54] The harmonisation sought to lead political actors to assimilate the EU governance framework into national legislation on financial innovation and on international payments.

---

[46] McKinsey (2021).

[47] Hall and Soskice (2001), pp. 59–60.

[48] Statista Research Department (2023).

[49] Deeg (2001); Grossmann (2006).

[50] Deeg (1998).

[51] Langenohl (2008).

[52] Deeg (2001); Langenohl (2008).

[53] Choulet (2016).

[54] Choulet (2016).

Technology has allowed firms to strengthen their operational infrastructure (Rothstein et al. 2017). Payment services represent an area with severe structural challenges. Since payment services became subject to different rules following the implementation of the EU's first Payment Services Directive, banks have come to favour a fee-based model. Thus, it has become more common for banks to license specialised payment institutions by appealing to Germany's Banking Act.[55] This political-economy account of the changes in the German banking system is very useful for understanding the institutional discourse about FinTech policy in Germany. For example, Flogel and Beckamp (2019) explore the relationship between FinTech companies and regional banks serving small to medium-sized enterprises (SMEs) by focusing on the relationships of institutions with their consumers in both digital and physical environments. Their findings demonstrate that FinTech addresses financial inclusion and that FinTech start-ups and traditional banks can support the real economy, as their operations and organisations complement each other. Regional banks can strengthen their relationships, improve the validity of information, and cut costs by deploying technology-based solutions. However, as FinTech displaces the relationship banking of regional banks, policies such as regulatory sandboxes are needed to facilitate growth.[56] Jackson and Thelen (2015) explain stability and change in CMEs by focusing on corporate governance and industrial relations in Germany. Patient capital that supports markets in CMEs is grounded in cooperative relations with unions by supporting investments in human capital and allowing firms to retain workers in the face of economic shocks such as labour-market shocks. With FinTech shocking the labour market and social structures, Germany may be equipped to adapt to these changes.

Competition in the banking system. Evidence on competition and market power is limited, despite the political salience of banks' market power.[57] The important finding of what studies there are on the topic is that interest rates and capital ratios affect competition in retail banking. Courvoisier and Gropp (2002) show that Germany is as one of the most competitive markets in Europe. De Bandt and Davies (2000) demonstrate that larger banks are more competitive than smaller ones and private banks are more competitive than savings banks or credit cooperatives. These findings indicate that smaller banks—both savings banks and credit cooperatives—exercise market power because they have their strong competitive position in local retail markets.[58] While regulators have addressed market imbalances, the German banking system is characterised by competition among groups of banks. Empirical challenges exist in assessing the overall system because of the peculiarity and structural adjustments[59] that followed the Banking Act of 1961. The Act introduced limits on banking activities and restrictions on bank branching. These

[55] Haag (2020).

[56] Flogel and Beckamp (2019).

[57] C.f. Aßländer and Burkatzki (2023).

[58] Fischer and Pfeil (2004).

[59] Kreditwesengesetz, or KWG.

measures differed from those of other countries, in which these regulations were abolished much earlier. Reforms of the Banking Act in the 1990s were undertaken by necessity to apply EU directives to German law.

The relative importance of cooperative banks, public banks, and private banks relates to the stability of the banking system. Germany's banking associations have coordinated the industry and its interactions with regulators.[60] Questions of competition and market concentration in the German banking industry are open to debate. The evidence is mixed, and scholars often present anecdotal evidence.[61] Goodhart and Shoemaker (1993) note, "It is the German tradition which exhibits the greatest concern about conflicts of interest, and the greatest desire for separation of responsibilities; yet it is the German system, dominated by an oligopoly of enormously powerful universal banks, with relatively underdeveloped, competitive wholesale financial markets, in which such "conflicts" of interest will be least bothersome." This quotation reflects the separation of powers between the Bundesbank and the supervisory authority. Moreover, Westrup (2007) argues that concerns about the competitiveness of Germany as a financial center contributed to the establishment of BaFin. During the process of regulatory reform and in the negotiation processes that led to BaFin's establishment, Westrup explains, the Bundesbank sought control over the regulation and supervision of the banking system in Germany; the Vorstand member responsible for regulation, Edgar Meister, affirmed that "banking oversight is not suitable for the business of politics".[62] Eventually, BaFin was created, but it retained close ties to the Bundesbank due to its political influence on regulatory reforms.[63]

The German's banking system has been characterised by a strong relationship between firms and banks.[64] One of the crucial advantages of this relationship is banks' involvement in companies, which provides an efficient way of monitoring markets and sharing information between industry and banks. Banks can exert influence in the governance of the large, listed firms not only by having ownership stakes but also by exercising authority over elected supervisory-board representatives.[65] Recent developments in financial markets have raised a couple of questions about whether the German bank-based model is efficiently serving the real economy. The literature reaches mixed results. Edwards and Fischer (1994) demonstrate that firms in a bank-based system do not depend on capital markets more than firms in a market-based system. While this can be crucial for supporting FinTech start-ups, it does not show why the government has not been active in supporting a FinTech

[60] Krahnen and Schmidt (2004).

[61] Krahnen and Schmidt (2004).

[62] FAZ 1/26/01 in Westrup (2007), p. 27.

[63] Busch explains the challenge of German unification and European integration. He highlights the regulatory relationship between the Bundesbank and BaFin, especially during the regulatory reform that concluded the establishment of BaFin.

[64] Cable (1985); Dyson (1986); Shonfield (1965).

[65] Owners of German corporations very often turn over control rights to financial institutions in the form of proxy voting rights.

ecosystem. The German government did not focus on steering markets, because it could control firms via corporate governance measures.[66] The role of the government was marginal in innovation in financial services. The government favoured domestic competition.[67]

Governments have an incentive to support sectors when companies and other economic actors invest within the governments' jurisdiction. The domestic context can affect regulation and is often influenced by cooperation among dominant actors. The competitiveness of the bank-based system has been celebrated by both firms and government and has often been used as an 'escamotage' for regulatory avoidance, especially in areas in which regulators's competence is limited.[68] Wade (2020) highlights how officials emphasise the competitiveness of domestic industry and an aging society's need to diversify investments.[69] It is explained as the commitment to certain regulatory policies through reaching agreements between governments and firms and through bringing trade unions into crisis management.[70] Studies of Germany's political economy analysing industrial relations include those written by Markovits (1982, 1986), who looked at how trade unions challenged dominant political and authority structures and the complex strategic thinking behind those structures. More recent institutional accounts look at the capacity of local coalitions of public sector banks and state governments to veto policies that may be detrimental to German public banks in the domestic market.[71] Streek analysed the growing importance of international markets, the competitiveness of newly industrialised economies, and the veto in German politics. Feldenkirchen highlights the relationship between banks and industry in Germany's political economy. While the governments have been actively involved in managing the banking relationship among relevant actors, the focus of the German government has been on protecting national champions.

4 The Varieties of Capitalism Perspective

Capitalism differs across countries and exhibits different institutional patterns. This chapter focuses on Germany, a leading CME and how its postwar domestic and foreign economic policy and its strategy for European integration[72] affected

[66] Jackson and Thelen (2015). This is valid for the oversight of Wirecard corporate governance.

[67] Eyre and Lodge (2000).

[68] Gary et al. (2011).

[69] "Apologists argue that German officials cannot increase domestic investment because the state has an unusually small role in investment or has recently constitutionalized debt brakes that further limit its fiscal space or has a set of ordo-liberal beliefs that amount to prohibitions on certain policy actions or even 'sticky' consumption levels that don't respond to increased household income" Wade (2020), p. 504.

[70] Crouch (1985).

[71] Massoc (2020), p. 138.

[72] Zimmerman (2010); Streeck (2009); Vitols (2001).

innovation in domestic markets. Stimulating entrepreneurial activities has become an important goal of governments.[73] Instead of developing a national sandbox devoted to the financial-services industry, a political majority in Germany has always declined to take any steps in this direction.[74] Bundesbank and BaFin have stated on multiple occasions that the concept of the regulatory sandbox is not something they would support.[75] In 2018, Felix Hufeld, head of German regulator BaFin has said he does not want to give FinTech startups "little buckets and spades" to avoid the regulatory burden of financial rules.[76] In this section I elaborate on why innovation has occurred at the firm level in the form of incremental innovation and digitalisation of business models rather than in the form of radical innovation framed as a public good. This outcome is puzzling, considering the national debate on the usage of data and the emergence of data capitalism in Germany.[77] Streeck (2009) argues coordinated capitalism is disappearing in Germany as entrepreneurial capitalism materialises. This shift is valid for the private-based-innovation model of entrepreurialism in Germany. At the federal level, the prevailing viewpoint among policy makers, regulators, and supervisors is that private innovation and experimentation matters. For example, empirical evidence demonstrates that innovation is likely to be more deeply embedded in the structure and strategy of small German firms than small UK firms. Innovation does not just define the object of regulation. Individuals are required to manage their own risks and opportunities. The general perception is that the government should be less active in the economy and the market[78] reflecting the belief that experimentation and competition should come from individuals and companies who will act on their own initiatives. German's ordo-liberalism justifies a regulatory economic model where a strong state is the political form of free markets.[79] Bonefeld (2012) argues the strong state can promote enterprise and secure the role of the entrepreneurs. Thus, liberalism does not demand 'weakness from the state, but only freedom for economic development under state protection', to prevent 'coercion and violence'.[80] The state is 'strong and neutral guardian of the public interest'. The political economy of innovation in Germany embraces the country's political culture of defending individual rights and responsibilities for entrepreneurship. For the Germans, entrepreneurship is not something that is 'naturally given' but is constructed in markets in which the government plays an important role by facilitating knowledge creation and sharing (Bonefeld 2012).[81]

[73] Stam and Garnsey (2007); Haddad and Hornuf (2019).

[74] BMWI Report (2021).

[75] Reuters (2020).

[76] Jones (2018).

[77] Lutz (2020).

[78] Vogelsang (1989).

[79] Bonefeld (2012).

[80] Hayek (1972), p. 66.

[81] In the German context, Joseph Keith, the director of policy studies, argues that 'responsible policies, which work with and through the market to achieve [the] wider social aims' of a well-integrated society (Joseph 1975, p. 3).

If one looks at the reasons why innovation occurs in specific countries but not others, innovation in financial markets is often the result of how well institutions have filled their roles in serving the markets and carrying on long-standing banking traditions.[82] Historically, Germany had intense competition in domestic banking and had a bank-based system that served the demands of local economies and societies and supported their close relationships with the Mittelstand.[83]

The key features of the German banking market are the very large number of credit institutions (just over 2700 as of December 2000 and 1458 as of 2022) and the relatively high market shares of the public and cooperative banking subsectors. However, Hempell (2002) analyses domestic bank competition for the period 1993–1998 and rejects the hypothesis of perfect competition. He highlights the role of cooperative banks in benefiting from government measures and socio-economic structures based on protection. While EU regulatory changes such as the introduction of the Payment Services Directive and Electronic Money Directive have challenged the national banking system, industry observers agree that banking all over Europe, including Germany, has not changed much. German supervisors might be biased towards domestic banks rather than foreign banks, which represents a problem that is high on the agenda at the EU level.[84] Previous studies highlighting monopolistic competition in banking include Lang and Bikker and Groeneveld (2000), which demonstrate the presence of coercive government. Seikel (2017) depicts Germany as having avoided the competition reform in which private banks are not allowed to acquire public banks. For example, a law on bank mobility was introduced in 2016 Barth et al. demonstrate that Germany has a bank-based financial system.

5 Innovation in German's Banking System

Experimentation clauses and recognition of existing projects for innovation represent two barriers to innovation in Germany. The lack of interest in regulatory discovery and the pace and impact of digitisation have divided the innovation system between private and public initiatives with different public objectives being pursued. Public objectives may improve access to financial services, and many prove the provision of government services in the transportation and logistics systems and in the health sector. In what follows, I focus on the initiatives in the financial services industry.

---

[82] Barba Navaretti et al. (2018); Cantner and Kösters (2009); Earl and Gault (2006); Muniesa and Lenglet (2013).

[83] Krahnen and Schmidt (2004); Rostow (1959).

[84] For example, "national supervisors tend to be biased. They tend to be a little too soft on: "their domestic banks and sometimes a bit too protective. European banking supervision balances this bias" Nouy (2017).

Private initiatives. A study, conducted on behalf of the Federal Ministry of Finance, found 346 active FinTech firms. Their financing and wealth management segments totaled was 2.2 billion EUR in 2015.[85,86] The market is growing both domestically and internationally, and the German FinTech sector is led by private sector entrepreneurs. In Germany, private sector-led entrepreneurship takes the form of a network of firms, regulators and leading players and is known as a private innovation hub. CommerzBank, DZ Bank and Landesbank Baden-Württemberg, three leading financial institutions, have all set up an innovation hub to understand and improve the efficiency of their distinctive business models.

Commercial Bank. Commerzbank AG is a major commercial bank in Germany with branches and associates in domestic and foreign finance and banking. With its headquarters in Frankfurt, the bank was established in 1870 as the Commerz-und Disconto-Bank in Hamburg. Deutsche Börse and Commerzbank are entering a strategic partnership with FinTech 360X to develop a new blockchain-based digital marketplace.[87]

Cooperative Bank. DZ Bank established its innovation lab in 2018 in order to experiment with emerging technologies in finance. The lab was designed as a platform on which German firms can interact as well as experiment with new banking products and services. The lab is composed of four key strategic departments that have helped 26 businesses to innovate via the following methods: design sprint, rapid prototyping, design thinking, and hackaton of emerging technologies. The lab also introduced and the Innovation Round Table (a platform for transparency and the networking of knowledge), and the Innovation Radar (a digital platform for joint trend scouting) and Fintech Cooperative entities (e.g. TechQuartier and Plug'n'Play) which are integrated into the the Innovation LAB.

Savings banks. Landesbank Baden-Württemberg (LBBW) is a universal bank that acts as the Landesbank for some federal states of Germany (Baden-Württemberg, Rheinland-Pfalz, Sachsen). As of 2016, it was considered Germany's biggest state-backed landesbank lender. The creation of the innovation lab was a joint project of Capgemini and BW Bank in which they coordinated on the strategic direction of the project.[88]

Public initiatives. In Germany, the organisation of FinTech and in general the management of innovation policy comprises four layers and reflects a national policy-making and regulatory framework that is coordinated and decentralised across federal institutions.[89] This framework works from the bottom up: private actors coordinate in business and regulatory processes via private innovation hubs.

---

[85] Dorfleitner et al. (2017).

[86] A total of 433 FinTech businesses with operations in Germany were identified. The other 87 businesses either did not begin their operations before 2016 or else are no longer active. The study was conducted between between 2007 and the end of 2015 (Dorfleitner et al. 2017).

[87] Bartel (2021).

[88] Capgemini (2020).

[89] E.g., for an overview of German's public administration please consult Jann (2003).

Germany's education partners have also played an important role. The first layer focuses on educational initiatives concerning the risks and opportunities of emerging technologies. The Ministry of Research and Education and the Max Planck Institute developed the national strategy for FinTech and shaped how research institutes invest in new technologies.[90] The second layer involves advisory and coordinating bodies and creates partnerships between SMEs, corporations, and the latest innovators. The third layer is made up of administrative bodies such as federal ministries and BaFin, which provide information-gathering and feedback mechanisms to market participants and other political authorities. They focus on issues dealing with the future of various disciplines from engineering to science to ethics to health. The network—which comprises the most important academic and nonacademic associations, including Acatech—German Academy of Science and Engineering, Building Ministers' Conference, and German Ethics Council—brings together excellent researchers and offers the business and academic worlds a forum for exchanging ideas and information. The fourth layer, which oversees all other activities, comprises the federal parliament, which coordinates local, regional, and national activities, together with the regional parliaments.

Germany's political-economy framework has influenced how the government has approached FinTech. One of the main objectives of the German government has been to create the right institutions for innovation by creating a holistic framework of innovation.

Initiatives for FinTech in the public sphere are very limited. In 2018, the Federal Ministry for Economic Affairs and Energy designated finleap as one of the 12 digital hubs. As of 2020, finleap had established 17 FinTech ventures with spurious politicians' comments on FinTech to attract investment in Germany and replace London with Berlin as the post-Brexit FinTech capital. Cornelia Yzer, senator for Economics, Technology and Research—in a public event in London promised "We will win (UK start-ups) for Berlin".[91]

Local agencies and the municipalities have pursued few experiments in regulatory sandboxes, such as the promotion of innovation, advancement of regional policy goals for economic growth, the promotion of sustainable mobility and logistics, or environmental and energy policy goals.[92,93] The authorities often note

[90]Investments were mainly concentrated in the area of Blockchain.

[91]Chazan (2016).

[92]BMWI (2019).

[93]Dr. Jorg Kukies, State Secretary, of the Federal Ministry of Finance states: "A healthy innovation culture needs opportunities to test out new technologies and processes. The handbook is an important tool to give security to decision-makers in companies and administrations as they deal with experimental spaces. Confidence in the content, purpose and scope of statutory experimentation clauses plays a crucial role in decisions to invest in innovative solutions" (BMWI 2019, p. 21). What does experimentation look like in practice? The e-government project of Saxon supports the electronic delivery of services. In this project, the experimentation clause in Section 20 of the eGovernment Act of Saxony authorised start-up and small firms' exemptions from the application of various rules of Saxony on administrative procedures to develop the e-Government project (BMWI 2019).

that the experimentation clauses are narrowly defined and do not support the application of regulatory innovation and often in conflict with EU legislation.[94] Government officials have now started to apply these experimentation clauses in practice, but regulatory challenges still exist.[95]

The aims of these collaborative-based hubs are many: from developing new digital technologies focused on regional and local existing demand to removing institutional barriers that may hold back Industry 4.0.[96] The Innovation hub aligns the interests of the local FinTech firms to FinTech and Industry 4.0 by offering technological support to developing new technologies to facilitate the digital transition and change. These examples show an important mechanism that defines the development of institutional change in Germany: 1) the interlocking of organisational models within the German banking market in which each pillar focuses on its strengths but seeks to create synergies with actors in the innovation and collaboration economy.[97] The legitimization of new digital paradigms in their focal regions required the German's government to strengthen the CME[98] by promoting close networking and coordination among all members of the network of cooperative and savings banks.[99] These institutional changes in the pursuit of innovation were mediated by both markets' forces. Digital technologies impacted the business models of banks and were conditioned by overarching institutions. Private sectors entrepreneurs operate innovation hubs. While commercial, co-operative and savings banks embrace innovation via the creation of innovation hubs, the legitimacy of these changes were mediated by their target audience and business scenarios as highlighted in chapter three. Examples include how innovation hubs have investigated not only how to streamline their cost organisation structure, but also on how to reinvent banking, as they are looking for new ways to provide novel services to customers, such as fully digital financing or investment solutions.[100] Still, it is striking that these institutional changes have increased the homogeneity of the financial sector in Germany by strengthening the roles of the relationship and cooperative nature of digital and traditional banking. For example, FinTechs began as regular start-ups but eventually obtained a bank licenses (e.g., solaris Bank) or founded a bank as a spin-off of their FinTech.[101] These FinTech-banks coordinated their business models and almost exclusively saw banking as a service or banking as a platform.[102] They partnered with bigger players, who leveraged the FinTech technological infrastructure. Banks such as Santander and

[94] BMWI (2019).

[95] Aßländer and Burkatzki (2023).

[96] Capgemini (2020).

[97] See Hall and Soskice (2001); Deeg (2001).

[98] Hall and Soskice (2001); DZ Bank (2015).

[99] DZ Bank (2015).

[100] DZ Bank (2015); BMWI (2019).

[101] E.g., FinTech AG—biw Bank für Investments und Wertpapiere, Brandl and Hornuf (2020).

[102] Brandl and Hornuf (2020).

Commerzbank largely acquired start-ups from the financial industry, whereas traditional banks, including Hypo Vereinsbank and Deutsche Bank, are more cautious about investing in FinTechs.[103] The last example shows how commercial banks find themselves in an institutional environment in which change is defined by the legitimacy of institutional structures. The cultural dimension of institutional entrepreneurship was considered essential to competition and innovation. Competition would have disintermediated firms to create a more specialised market for FinTech. The digital market that would have emerged from FinTech would have not occurred overnight but would have been built from traditional market services that are disentermediated by market forces and innovation.

5.1 Methodology

The methodology of this chapter is composite: it includes the WireCard scandal as the main case-study to explain the corrupt scandal occurred in Germany due to the limited supervisory powers and a set of interviews to uncover the implicit mechanisms of powers between private and public actors. In what follows, I explain the case study and the set of interviews (Bennet Moses 2017; George and Bennet 2005).

5.2 WireCard Scandal

The Wirecard Scandal involved a well organised plan of business financial reporting that led to the insolvency of Wirecard, a leading FinTech company-based Germany, offering payment services to financial institutions Davis (2014)[104] The company was funded in 1999 with headquarter in Munich, Germany, part of the DAX Financial Index since 2018. The company was structured in payment services and acquired a banking license. Ernest and Young, a long-time auditor of the company, did not follow the International Financial Reporting Standards, resulting in inflated earnings and cash flows figures. In 2021, Pav Gill, Wirecard's senior legal counsel from the Singapore Office decide to reveal the malpractice of Wirecard and provided documents to the UK Press and the Financial Times.

Germany presents an intriguing case study for understanding the emergence of innovative forms of regionalisation and territorial policy.[105] I analyse the regulatory preferences and policy tools of Germany regarding FinTech and how FinTech has accelerated the pace of policy decentralisation. Regulatory preferences are the preferences not only of regulators but also the policy makers who set the national

[103] Brandl and Hornuf (2020).

[104] Aßländer and Burkatzki (2023); Teichmann et al. (2023).

[105] Gualini (2004); BMWI (2019):;

strategy for innovation. Regulatory preferences are situated within a framework of innovation, which includes not only competitive markets and consumer-centered innovation but also decentralisation and integration of national and international markets. Germany also represents a leading example of experimental governance in regional policy in areas such as the environment, and energy system but not FinTech.[106] Its regulatory model explains how its financial regulation impacts the economy. The German case study explains the emerging relationship between regulated entities and regulators, especially with respect to FinTech.

I collected data from three main sources: 1) archival material 2) interviews and 3) research of supervisors' CV. First, I gathered a unique set of more than 100 documents published between 2008 and 2020 including policy documents and statements issued by regulators, supervisors, governments and civil society actors on the topic of FinTech and financial technology in Germany. This collection of documents sheds lights not only on the regulatory preferences but also on the interaction of old and young technology companies in Germany. Second, I have also conducted four elite interviews in a variety of four contexts with supervisors, regulators, private sector actor, and expert in order to understand their legal mandate, supervisory objectives, business objectives and opinions respectively. These interviews allowed me to explore the underpinnings of the governments' supervisory and regulatory mandates as well as learning how official's educational background might have impacted their decisions on the politics of FinTech. Interviews were conducted via telephone and videoconferencing with open-ended structure and notes were digitally recorded.

5.3 Analysis

Regarding FinTech in Germany, politics justifies the regulatory mandate over financial services. It is similar to what Hardie and Howarth (2009) have observed about the financial crisis: the German system has been protectionist, as it adopted a neo-mercantilist mode of policymaking and is anti-competitive in many ways.[107] There are different degrees and forms of regulatory, market-based interventions which seem politically salient in Germany.[108] For example, digital banking—an innovative area of research in universities—has been promoted as an area of study in a few research centers. These explanations do not reveal enough explanatory power. We need to unpack the causal relationship between FinTech and regulatory

[106] Gualini (2004).

[107] See Simonis (1998). The German government, the Association of German Banks, the European Commission and the Bundesbank all support the elimination of the three-pillar German system, but change has been strongly resisted by Land governments (Hardie and Howarth 2009).

[108] Hardie and Howarth (2009).

processes. Having conducted four elite-interviews[109] with German regulators and supervisors and having read key policy documents issued by BaFin and Bundestag, I see that FinTech regulation is supported on three key pillars:

1. Regulation as public good for citizens: risk is perceived as both object of regulation and justification for intervention in regulatory clauses.
2. Regulation as a coordination mechanism between firms and government; This pillar illustrates how the construction and distribution of interests is important in explaining how regulatory regimes are shaped by dominant actors such as cooperative and savings banks.
3. Regulatory sandboxes reflect the government's preferences as a regulatory sandbox for firms to innovate rather than a tool for government to innovate. Institutional constraints shape the regulatory processes and regulatory attention is now turned towards crisis management of political and economic events and towards instituting innovation-based practices for the economy.

Whilst the German government used public law and experimental clauses to institute soft regulation, including Blockchain and Artificial Intelligence guidelines, it also used its powers to focus on systemic risk posed by FinTech entities. In contrast to other jurisdictions in the EU, Germany has encouraged its key stakeholders, such as BaFin and the federal ministries, to act according to their specific mandates of financial stability and mitigation of systemic risk.[110] They are meant to assess the impact of FinTech on systemic risk to society and the wider economy. As such, the Bundestag has not granted new powers or mandates to BaFin or the federal ministries, but has limited their actions on innovation, as it views FinTech as a politically salient threat to individual digital rights. BaFin applied the EU approach to technological neutrality and proportionality,[111] in the following manner: small firms are eligible for exemptions regarding their technology requirements, and BaFin supervises technology by looking at the risks. This approach to financial regulation embodies two mechanisms: First, when technology changes, regulators do not have the right set of skills, competences, and powers to develop a regulatory framework suitable for emerging technologies[112] and protecting consumers.[113] Second, regulatory avoidance of FinTech showed that hidden conflicts arise between governments and the banking system.[114] For example, La Porta et al. (2002) show that the share of government ownership in Germany was 51.90 per cent in 1970 and

[109]Elite interviews is a form of data to collect information or context whereby the researcher conducts interviews with experts and high-level profile individuals on specific subject matters about events and processes.

[110]Hardie and Howarth (2009).

[111]EC (2017).

[112]Gary et al. (2011); Brandl and Hornuf (2020).

[113]C.f. Massoc (2020); Mitchell (2016).

[114]La Porta et al. (2002); Kane (1988).

36.36 per cent in 1995 and it has not increased post-2007.[115] BaFin, unlike its international counterparts, made clear that supervised financial entities are expected to ensure sound IT governance in their institutions. This approach is a specific example of regulatory avoidance and mismatch between the institutional environment of German regulators and the innovative structure of private German firms. The public protection of legitimacy structures governing the banking system is also important: the government's reluctance to inform the public about future regulation allowed regulators to hide information.[116] Regulatory reputation can translate into institutional risks, but in Germany, the regulatory reputation risk was used to hide information from the public. There is also the risk that regulators will not comply with their organisational objectives.[117] While institutional risks may limit what regulators can and cannot do, they can limit oversight of new business models.[118] If Germany does not keep up with the pace of technological innovation, institutional risk can have detrimental effects for consumers.[119] This process of regulatory consequentialism suggests that FinTech requires agile regulatory structures to monitor and supervise financial innovation.[120] Claims about the essential functions of regulation concern how regulators communicate their actions to the public. Communications about regulatory risk to market participants showed the importance of insulating regulatory decisions from industry influence and demonstrating how regulators and supervisors see FinTech as a regulatory risk. If regulatory perception of market participants is a politically salient topic, the German government had a relationship with established financial institutions and politicians.[121] BaFin failed to point out publicly the shortcomings of Wirecard, instead hiding numerous cases of financial misreporting about capital on the balance sheet (Interview conducted online with anonymous participant 2020).

6 Conclusion

The recent Wirecard scandal has taught us that the unknown risks of FinTech appear in the intra-industry relationships between regulated entities and regulators. Regulatory avoidance is a topic that has been widely discussed among regulatory scholars and political scientists. German's regulatory architecture allowed both the centralisation of powers within BaFin supervisory authority and decentralisation of regulatory processes among administrative bodies, federal and regional parliament

[115] Seldeslachts et al. (2017).
[116] Hardie and Howarth (2009).
[117] Black (2002).
[118] Rahman and Thelen (2019); Cumming et al. (2019); Arner et al. (2016).
[119] Gary et al. (2011).
[120] Zetzsche et al. (2017).
[121] Mitchell (2016).

authorities who are in charge of monitoring FinTech. Trust in the system had an impact on Germany's reputation as a regulator.[122] In Germany, a close-knit group of politicians, regulators and supervisors managed FinTech's policy.[123] This strategy, pioneered by BaFin and the German Parliament, has benefited one big financial institution at the expense of FinTech start-ups; it has raised question about the regulatory accountability and transparency of BaFin.

This chapter warns us about a few policy implications. Digital transformation will accelerate in the next few years, governments need to further pursue legitimate political goals in competition which may or may not stifle innovation in markets[124] and institute more with experimental clauses. Historical approaches to regulation can help us explain the un-observable regulatory practices[125] especially considering the Wirecard scandal. In the future, regulatory studies should be combined with industrial policy, to understand how regulation can address the economic and social organizational problems of innovation. Most global policy problems will not be addressed by a single institution, but effective cooperation across organisational boundaries is now required.

References

Allen F, Gale D (1999) Diversity of opinion and financing of new technologies. J Financ Intermed 8:1–22

Arner DW, Barberis J, Buckley RP (2016) FinTech, RegTech, and the reconceptualization of financial regulation. Northwest J Int Law Bus 37:371–431. https://heinonline.org/HOL/LandingPage?handle=hein.journals/nwjilb37&div=17&id=&page

Arner DW, Barberis J, Buckley RP (2017) FinTech and RegTech in a nutshell, and the future in a sandbox. CFA Institute. https://www.cfainstitute.org/-/media/documents/article/rf-brief/rfbr-v3-n4-1.ashx. Accessed 21 Dec 2023

Aßländer MS, Burkatzki E (2023) The financial fraud of the German Fintech Company WireCard: structural causes and failures of the supervisory authorities. In: Dion M (ed) Sustainable finance and financial crime. Sustainable finance. Springer, Cham. https://doi.org/10.1007/978-3-031-28752-7_15

Baccaro L, Benassi C (2017) Throwing out the ballast: growth models and the liberalization of German industrial relations. Soc Econ Rev 15(1):85–115

BaFin (2016) FinTechs: young IT companies on the financial market. Expert Article 29 January

Bafin (2022) Future without supervision? Decentralized finance as a challenge for financial supervision. Online resource available at https://www.bafin.de/SharedDocs/Veroeffentlichungen/DE/Fachartikel/2022/Kurzkommentare_BaFinTech2022/fa_bj_2203_Kurzkommentar_Rodolphe.html. Accessed Dec 2023

Barba Navaretti G, Calzolari G, Mansilla-Fernandez JM, Pozzolo AF (2018) Fintech and Banking. Friends or Foes? (January 10, 2018). Available at SSRN: https://ssrn.com/abstract=3099337 or https://doi.org/10.2139/ssrn.3099337

[122] Aßländer and Burkatzki (2023).

[123] Teichmann et al. (2023).

[124] Zetzsche et al. (2017).

[125] Davis (2014); Totterman and Sten (2005).

Bartel (2021) Online resource. Available at https://www.deutsche-boerse.com/dbg-en/media/press-releases/Deutsche-B-rse-and-Commerzbank-jointly-invest-in-new-digital-marketplaces-of-the-future-2629326. Accessed Jan 2024

Behr P, Schmidt RH (2015) The German banking system: characteristics and challenges, SAFE White Paper, No. 32. Goethe University Frankfurt, SAFE - Sustainable Architecture for Finance in Europe, Frankfurt a. M., http://nbn-resolving.de/urn:nbn:de:hebis:30:3-391178

Bencivenga VR, Smith BD, Starr RM (1995) Transactions costs, technological choice, and endogenous growth. J Econ Theory 67:53–177

Bennett Moses L (2017) Regulating in the face of sociotechnical change regulating in the face of sociotechnical change. In: Brown Sword R, Eloise S, Karen Y (eds) The Oxford handbook of law, regulation and technology. Oxford University Press, pp 1–24

Bikker J, Groeneveld JM (2000) Competition and concentration in the EU banking industry. Kredit und Kapital 33(1):62–98

Black J (2002) Critical reflections on regulation. Crime Regul 4:15–49

BMWI (2019) Regulatory Sandboxes – Testing Environments for Innovation and Regulation. Online resource: https://www.bmwi.de/Redaktion/EN/Dossier/regulatory-sandboxes.html--

BMWI Report (2021) Online report. Available at https://www.startbase.com/downloads/fintech-report/2021/fintech-report.pdf. Accessed Feb 2024

Bonefeld W (2012) Freedom and the strong state: on German Ordoliberalism. New Polit Econ 17(5):633–656. https://doi.org/10.1080/13563467.2012.656082

Brandl B, Hornuf L (2020) Where did FinTechs come from, and where do they go? The transformation of the financial industry in Germany after digitalization. Front Artif Intell. https://doi.org/10.3389/frai.2020.00008

Bundesbank (2021) Payment behaviour in Germany in 2021. Online resource https://www.bundesbank.de/en/press/press-releases/payment-behaviour-in-germany-in-2021-894120. Accessed 23 Dec 2023

Cable J (1985) Capital market information and industrial performance: the role of West German Banks'. Econ J 95(1):118–132

Cantner U, Kösters S (2009) Picking the winner? Empirical evidence on the targeting of R&D subsidies to start-ups (No. 2009, 093). Jena Economic Research Papers

Capgemini (2020) BW Bank digital.lab schafft Innovation. Online report: https://www.capgemini.com/consulting-de/wp-content/uploads/sites/32/2017/08/bw_bank_digital.lab_schafft_innovation.pdf

Chazan (2016) Berlin bids to replace London as post-Brexit FinTech capital. Financial Times, 6 July

Choulet C (2016) German Sparkassen: a model to follow? BNP-Paribas Conjoncture, 16

Courvosier S, Gropp R (2002) Bank concentration and retail interest rates. J Bank Financ 26:2155–2189

Crouch C (1985) The conditions for trade union wage restraint'. In: Lindberg L, Maier C (eds) The politics and sociology of world inflation. Brookings Institution, Washington

Cumming DJ, Johan S, Pant A et al (2019) Regulation of the crypto-economy: managing risks, challenges, and regulatory uncertainty. J Risk Financ Manag 12(3):126–139. https://doi.org/10.3390/jrfm12030126

Davis S (2014) Branson gives backing to money transfer start-up. Transfer Wise. Financial Times 9 June

De Bandt O, Philip E (2000) Davis Competition, contestability and market structure in European banking sectors on the eve of EMU. J Bank Financ 24(6):1045–1066. ISSN 0378-4266. https://www.sciencedirect.com/science/article/pii/S037842669900117X. https://doi.org/10.1016/S0378-4266(99)00117-X

Deeg R (1998) What makes German Banks different. Small Bus Econ 10(2):93–101. http://www.jstor.org/stable/40228540

Deeg R (1999) Finance capitalism unveiled: banks and the German political economy. University of Michigan Press

Deeg R (2001) Institutional change and the uses and limits of path dependency: the case of German finance. (MPIfG, discussion paper 01 and 06). Max Planck Institute, Koln
Diamond D (1984) Financial intermediation and delegated monitoring. Rev Econ Stud 51:393–414
Dorfleitner G, Hornuf L, Schmitt M, Weber M (2017) The FinTech Market in Germany. In: FinTech in Germany. Springer, Cham. https://doi.org/10.1007/978-3-319-54666-7_4
Dyson K (1986) The state, banks and industry: the West German Case. In: Cox A (ed) State, finance, and industry. St. M, New York
DZ Bank (2015) Rethinking Banking annual report. Z_BANK_Group_magazine_accompanying_annual_report_2015.pdf
Earl L, Gault F (2006) National innovation, indicators, and policy. Edward Elgar, Cheltenham
Edwards, Fischer (1994) Banks, finance and investment in Germany. Cambridge University Press, Cambridge UK
European Banking Authority (EBA) (2017) Discussion Paper on the EBA's approach to financial technology (FinTech). EBA Discussion Paper 2017 (2)
European Commission (2017) Summary of contributions to the 'Public Consultation on FinTech: a more competitive and innovative European financial sector'. https://ec.europa.eu/info/sites/default/files/2017-fintech-summary-of-responses_en.pdf
Eyre S, Lodge M (2000) National tunes and a European melody? Competition law reform in the UK and Germany. J Eur Public Policy 7(1):63–79
Federal Ministry of Finance (2019) Online resource https://www.globalgovernmentfintech.com/global-government-fintech-lab-2023-delaney-krasovska-voelkl/
Flogel F, Beckamp M (2019) Will FinTech make regional banks superfluous for small firm finance? Observations from soft information-based lending in Germany. Economic Notes
Friedrich C (1955) The political thought of neo-liberalism. Am Polit Sci Rev 49(2):509–525
Fischer K, Pfeil C (2004) Regulation and competition in German banking: an assessment. In: Krahnen JP, Schmidt RH (eds) The German financial system. Oxford University Press, Oxford
Friesendorf C, Blütener A (2023) Centralized Finance. In: Decentralized Finance (DeFi). Business Guides on the Go. Springer, Cham. https://doi.org/10.1007/978-3-031-37488-3_2
Gary M, Braden A, Herkert J (2011) The growing gap between emerging technologies and legal-ethical oversight the pacing problem. Springer. ISBN 978-94-007-1355-0
George AL, Bennett A (2005) Case studies and theory development in the social sciences. MIT Press, Cambridge
Goodhart CAE, Shoemaker (1993) Institutional Separation between Supervisory and Monetary Agencies (1993). In: The Central Bank and the Financial System (1995). Palgrave Macmillan, London. https://doi.org/10.1057/9780230379152_16
Grossman E (2006) Europeanization as an interactive process: German public banks meet EU state aid policy. J Common Mark Stud 44:325–348. https://doi.org/10.1111/j.1468-5965.2006.00625.x
Gualini E (2004) Regionalization as 'experimental regionalism': the rescaling of territorial policy-making in Germany. Int J Urban Reg Res 28(2):329–353
Haag S (2020) Bridging the postcolonial political-economy divide. Towards a theoretical framework
Hackethal A (2005) German Banks and Banking Structure. Chapter 3. In: Krahnen JP, Schmidt RH (eds) The German Financial System. Oxford University Press, Oxford
Haddad C, Hornuf L (2019) The emergence of the global fintech market: economic and technological determinants. Small Bus Econ 53:81–105. https://doi.org/10.1007/s11187-018-9991-x
Hall Peter A, Soskice D (eds) (2001) Varieties of capitalism: the institutional foundations of comparative advantage. Oxford University Press, New York
Handke S (2012) A problem of Chief and Indian—the role of the supervisory authority BaFin and the ministry of finance in German financial market policy. Policy Soc 31(3):237–247
Hardie I, Howarth D (2009) Die Krise but Not La Crise? The financial crisis and the transformation of German and French Banking Systems. J Common Mark Stud 47(5):1017–1039

Hardie I, Howarth D (eds) (2013) Market-based banking and the international financial crisis. Oxford University Press, Oxford

Hasan R, Kruse O (2023) The impact of regulatory requirements on German financial institutions' outsourcing arrangements. J Financ Regul Compliance, Vol. ahead-of-print No. ahead-of-print. https://doi.org/10.1108/JFRC-03-2023-0033

Hayek F (1972) Individualism and economic order. Mises Institute, Auburn

Hildermeier J, Villareal A (2011) Shaping an emerging market for electric cars: how politics in France and Germany transform the European automotive industry. European review of industrial economics and policy

Höpner M, Jackson G (2001) An emerging market for corporate control? The Mannesmann takeover and German corporate governance (MPIfG Discussion Paper 4). Max-Planck-Institut für Gesellschaftsforschung, Köln. https://hdl.handle.net/10419/43731

IMF (2011) Germany financial stability assessment report. Online resource available at: https://www.imf.org/external/pubs/ft/scr/2011/cr11169.pdf. Accessed 21 Dec 2023

Jackson G, Thelen K (2015) Stability and change in CMEs: corporate governance and industrial relations in Germany and Denmark. In: Beramendi P, Häusermann S, Kitschelt H, Kriesi H (eds) The politics of advanced capitalism. Cambridge University Press, Cambridge, pp 305–330. https://doi.org/10.1017/CBO9781316163245.013

Jackson G, Hopner M, Kurdelbush A (2004) Corporate governance and employees in Germany: changing linkages, complementarities, and tensions. In: Gospel H, Pendleton A (eds) Corporate governance and labour management in comparison. Oxford University Press

Jann W (2003) State, administration and governance in Germany: competing traditions and dominant narratives. Public Adm 81:95–118. https://doi.org/10.1111/1467-9299.00338

Jones H (2018) EU guidelines on fintech to include 'sandbox' design recommendations. Online article Reuters. https://www.reuters.com/article/us-eu-banks-regulator/eu-guidelines-on-fintech-to-include-sandbox-design-recommendations-idINKCN1LM25V/. Accessed 21 Dec 2023

Joseph K (1975) Freedom and order. Centre for Policy Studies, London. Retrieved from Cadmus, European University Institute Research Repository, at: http://hdl.handle.net/1814/4038

Jünger M, Mietzner M (2020) Banking goes digital: the adoption of FinTech services by German households. Finance Res Lett 34:101260. https://doi.org/10.1016/j.frl.2019.08.008. ISSN 1544-6123. Accessed 21 Dec 2023

Kane EJ (1988) Interaction of financial and regulatory innovation. Am Econ Rev 78(2):328–334. http://www.jstor.org/stable/1818145

Krahnen JP, Schmidt RH (2004) The German Financial System. Oxford University Press, Oxford

La Porta R, Lopez-de-Silanes F, Shleifer A (2002) Government ownership of banks. J Finance 57: 265–301

Langenohl A (2008) How to change other people's institutions: discursive entrepreneurship and the boundary object of competition/competitiveness in the German banking sector. Econ Soc 37(1): 68–93. https://doi.org/10.1080/03085140701760882

Leonhardt F (2019) Evolutionary influence of fintech on the financial sector. BaFin Expert Articles, 15 November

Lindemann G (2006) Lebensmittelsicherheit in der EU und in Deutschland – Vom Acker oder Stall bis zum Tisch des Verbrauchers. Journal für Verbraucherschutz und Lebensmittelsicherheit 1(2):71–72

Lutz C, Hoffmann CP, Ranzini G (2020) Data capitalism and the user: an exploration of privacy cynicism in Germany. New Media Soc 22(7):1168–1187. https://doi.org/10.1177/1461444820912544

Maggio, Powell (eds) (1991) The new institutionalism in organisational analysis. Chicago University Press, Chicago and London, pp 41–66

Markovits A (ed) (1982) The political economy of West Germany: modell Deutschland. Praeger Publishers, New York

Markovits A (1986) The politics of the West German trade unions: strategies of class and interest representation in growth and crisis. Cambridge University Press, New York

Massoc E (2020) Banks, power, and political institutions: the divergent priorities of European states towards "too-big-to-fail" banks: the cases of competition in retail banking and the banking structural reform. Bus Polit 22(1):135–160. https://doi.org/10.1017/bap.2019.18

McKinsey & Company (2021) Perspective: German banking returns to the playing field. Online report available: https://www.mckinsey.com/industries/financial-services/our-insights/german-banking-returns-to-the-playing-field. Accessed 21 Dec 2023

Mietzner M, Molterer M (2018) You might not get what you need: the discrepancy between financial advice and commissions in Germany. Econ Lett 162:167–170. ISSN 0165-1765. https://www.sciencedirect.com/science/article/pii/S0165176517304597. https://doi.org/10.1016/j.econlet.2017.11.004

Mitchell C (2016) Saving the market from itself: the politics of financial intervention. Cambridge University Press, Cambridge

Muniesa F, Lenglet M (2013) Responsible innovation in finance: directions and implications. In: Owen R, Bessant J, Heintz M (eds) Responsible innovation: managing the responsible emergence of science and innovation in society. Wiley, London, pp 185–198

Nouy D (2017) European banking supervision – a necessary innovation. Speech. Online resource available: https://www.bankingsupervision.europa.eu/press/speeches/date/2017/html/se170118.en.html. Accessed 21 Dec 2023

Quaglia L (2008) Setting the pace? Private financial interests and European financial market integration. Br J Polit Int Relat 10(1):46–64

Rahman, Thelen (2019) The Rise of the platform business model and the transformation of twenty-first-century capitalism. J Polit Soc 47(2):177–204

Ramakrishnan RTS, Thakor AV (1984) Information reliability and a theory of financial intermediation. Rev Financ Stud 51:415–432

Ranchordás S (2015) Innovation-friendly regulation: the sunset of regulation, the sunrise of innovation. Jurimetrics 55(2):201–224. http://www.jstor.org/stable/24395571

Reuters (2020) Online source. Available at https://www.thomsonreuters.com/en/press-releases/2020/december/thomson-reuters-2021-report-on-fintech-regtech-and-the-role-of-compliance.html. Accessed Feb 2024

Rostow W (1959) The stages of economic growth. Econ Hist Rev New Ser 12(1):1–16

Rothstein H, Demeritt D, Paul R, Beaussier A-L, Wesseling M, Howard M, de Haan (2017) Varieties of risk regulation in Europe: coordination, complementarity and occupational safety in capitalist welfare states. Socio-Econ Rev:1–28

Rothstein Sidney A, Schulze-Cleven T (2020) Germany After the social democratic century: the political economy of imbalance. Ger Polit 29(3):297–318. https://doi.org/10.1080/09644008.2020.1752677

Sabel CF, Zeitlin J (eds) (2010) Experimentalist governance in the European Union: towards a new architecture. Oxford University Press, Oxford

Seikel D (2017) Savings banks and Landesbanken in the German political economy: the long struggle between private and public banks. In: Public banks in the age of financialization. Edward Elgar Publishing

Seldeslachts J, Newham M, Banal-Estanol A (2017) Changes in common ownership of German companies, DIW Economic Bulletin, ISSN 2192-7219. Deutsches Institut für Wirtschaftsforschung (DIW), Berlin, vol 7, iss 30, pp 303–311

Shonfield A (1965) Modern capitalism: the changing balance of public and private power. Oxford University Press, Oxford

Simonis G (1998) Das Modell Deutschland. In: Simonis G (ed) Deutschland nach der Wende. Neue Politikstrukturen [Germany after the Turn. New political structures]. Leske+Budrich, Opladen, pp 257–284

Sirri ER, Tufano P (1995) The economics of pooling. In: Crane DB et al (eds) The global financial system: a functional approach. Harvard Business School Press, Cambridge, pp 81–128

Stam E, Garnsey E (2007) Entrepreneurship in the knowledge economy. Centre for Technology Management (CTM) Working Paper, No. 2007/04. Available at: https://doi.org/10.2139/ssrn.1923098

Statista Research Department (2023) Online data. https://www.statista.com/statistics/667710/fintech-investmentsquarterly/. Accessed Feb 2024

Streeck W (2009) Re-forming capitalism: institutional change in the German political economy. Oxford University Press, Oxford

Teichmann FMJ, Boticiu SR, Sergi BS (2023) Wirecard scandal. A commentary on the biggest accounting fraud in Germany's post-war history. J Financ Crime, Vol. ahead-of-print No. ahead-of-print. https://doi.org/10.1108/JFC-12-2022-0301

Totterman H, Sten J (2005) Start-ups: business incubation and social capital. Int Small Bus J 23:487–511. https://doi.org/10.1177/0266242605055909

Thelen K (2004) How institutions evolve: the political economy of skills in Germany, Britain, the United States, and Japan. Cambridge University Press, New York

Vogelsang I (1989) Price cap regulation of telecommunications services: a long-run approach. In: Crew MA (ed) Deregulation and diversification of utilities. Topics in regulatory economics and policy, vol 3. Springer, Boston, MA. https://doi.org/10.1007/978-1-4684-6897-7_3

Vitols S (2001) Varieties of corporate governance: comparing Germany and the UK. In: Hall PA, Soskice DW (eds) Varieties of capitalism—the institutional foundations of comparative advantage. Oxford University Press, Oxford, pp 337–360

Von Schomberg R (2012) Prospects for technology assessment in a framework of responsible research and innovation. In: Dusseldorp M, Beecroft R (eds) Technikfolgen abschätzen lehren. VS Verlag für Sozialwissenschaften. https://doi.org/10.1007/978-3-531-93468-6_2. Accessed 21 Dec 2023

Wade J (2020) Surplus Germany. German Polit 29(3):498–521. https://doi.org/10.1080/09644008.2019.1707188

Westrup J (2007) The politics of financial regulatory reform in Britain and Germany. West Eur Polit 30:1096–1119

Zetzsche DA et al (2017) Regulating a revolution: from regulatory sandboxes to smart regulation. Fordham J Corp Financ Law 23:31–103. https://news.law.fordham.edu/jcfl/wp-content/uploads/sites/5/2018/01/Zetzsche-et-al-Article.pdf. Accessed 21 Dec 2023

Zimmerman H (2010) Varieties of global financial governance? British and German approaches to financial market regulation. In: Heilleiner E, Pagliari S, Zimmerman H (eds) Global finance in crisis: the politics of international regulatory change. Routledge, London, pp 135–150

Alfio Puglisi studies the interaction of political and economic systems of financial innovations (i.e. Blockchain applications for financial services). He is also interested in how scholars construct explanations and make inferences in the social sciences. He is an advisor to universities, regulatory bodies, start-ups and investment funds working in the distributed ledger technologies (DLT) space. He taught International Economics at Fordham University, King's College London and the University of Lisbon. He worked at the European Banking Authority as a Policy Analyst in the Financial Innovation Unit and advised the European Commission in the area of Blockchain Technology. He holds a PhD from King's College London, Department of Political Economy, Master of Sciences in European Public Policy from University College London, and Master of Arts with honours in Economics from The University of Edinburgh.

Global Standard-Setting on Financial Crime: Navigating Challenges

Doron Goldbarsht and Louis de Koker

Abstract The chapter considers some of the challenges relating to global standard-setting to combat financial crime. It identifies the need for research about the drivers behind the standard-setting processes, the abuse of global standards by authoritarian governments to justify oppressive measures, and challenges regarding enforcement of compliance.

1 Introduction

The emergence of global standard-setting to coordinate measures to combat transnational financial crime is outlined in Chapter 1 ('Towards a Global Approach to Combating Financial Crime') of this collection.[1] The collection itself highlights a range of national perspectives regarding the implementation of these standards. This chapter considers some of the challenges regarding global standard-setting in this space and identifies areas for future research.

The global standard-setting process has resulted in a fairly uniform set of laws and structures to combat money laundering, terrorist financing and proliferation financing globally. Although many countries are not yet appropriately compliant with the global standards, it is important to appreciate that the strategy has delivered significant levels of technical compliance.[2] Actual effectiveness level are however lagging and may remain modest for many small, lower capacity jurisdictions.

[1] De Koker and Goldbarsht (2024a).

[2] FATF (2022).

D. Goldbarsht (✉)
Macquarie University, Macquarie Park, NSW, Australia
e-mail: doron.goldbarsht@mq.edu.au

L. de Koker
La Trobe Law School, Melbourne, VIC, Australia

D. Goldbarsht, L. de Koker (eds.), *Financial Crime, Law and Governance*, Ius Gentium: Comparative Perspectives on Law and Justice 116,
https://doi.org/10.1007/978-3-031-59547-9_14

The standards themselves mirror some of the complexity of international relations. The anti-money laundering and combating terrorism and proliferation financing (AML/CTF/CPF) standards of the Financial Action Task Force (FATF) are underpinned by a risk-based approach. They operate, however, in a context of international conventions and sanctions that are rule-based. This gives rise to effectiveness and efficiency challenges that are not trivial. Interpretation of global rules and standards is also challenging given different legal interpretations and cultures globally. Risk-based standards and regulations therefore need to be accompanied by an increasing amount of guidance to align interpretations, ensure sufficient standardisation across different political and legal contexts, and prevent unintended negative consequences.

This chapter considers a few specific challenges regarding global standard-setting, in particular, the drivers behind the standard-setting processes, abusive practices by authoritarian governments that justify oppressive measures as responses to global standards, and challenges regarding enforcement of compliance. It identifies a range of areas for future research in this space.

2 The Weakest Link Theory

Global crime combating standards are informed by the fear that non-compliant countries will introduce risk into the system and weaken the efforts of compliant countries. This is the so-called 'weakest link' theory that holds that international action against crime is only as strong as the weakest link in the crime control chain. This argument is, for example, often raised in relation to FATF standards[3] and was expressed in 2010 as follows in its global threat assessment:[4]

> Because a chain is only as strong as its weakest link, the international community must rely on all countries to establish effective AML/CTF regimes that are capable of successfully preventing, detecting, prosecuting and imposing sanctions on ML/TF in order to counter the negative consequences of these criminal activities.

FATF representatives commonly stress the risks relating to the 'weakest links'. Bjørn Aamo, FATF president 2012–12, for example warned that 'The chain we

[3]See also David Lewis, FATF executive secretary: 'Anti-money laundering and counter-terrorist financing measures are only as strong as the weakest link' (Lewis 2016); FATF (2010) par 72: 'It was highlighted that there are different levels of AML control in Transaction Monitoring (TM) across jurisdictions and, therefore, the network is as strong only as its weakest link,' (FATF 2021a); Labori (2019): 'He also noted that criminals will always attempt to find the weakest link, exhorting jurisdictions to broadly and aggressively update the financial crime compliance standards up to FATF levels, which in recent years have shifted from a focus on technical compliance with recommendations to effectiveness, meaning concrete, measurable progress in fighting financial crime. 'The United States calls on all nations to join us in ensuring the FATF's standards are implemented globally, and standing together against those who threaten the security of the international financial system,' Mnuchin said.'

[4]FATF (2010), par 8.

build is only as strong as its weakest link',[5] Roger Wilkins, FATF president 2014–15, addressing a committee of the United Nations Security Council, said that: 'Everybody needs to do their part; otherwise money will continue to flow through the weakest link'.[6] Marcus Pleyer, FATF president 2020–22 stated in an interview that:[7]

> No country in the world can afford to ignore where the money comes from. Money - which includes dirty money - flows to those parts of the world where the legal regimes are weak or the legal regimes are applied ineffectively. Because money can enter the financial system through these loopholes, even small jurisdictions can provide a gateway.

The theory is clearly well-entrenched and drives the FATF's global standard-setting and review of compliance and effectiveness of all jurisdictions. Yet it has not been subjected to much critical analysis. This may be because it holds some truth. Criminals do exploit weaknesses in country-level AML/CTF/CPF measures by transacting in countries that allow significant illicit funds to flow through their systems with limited control measures or that enable criminals to hide their beneficial ownership of illicit assets. It is important to remember that the FATF standards were drafted at a time when many small island jurisdictions acted as criminal havens by registering shell banks and shell corporations and by adopting laws that provided criminals with measures to protect their identity.[8] As illustrated by the Pandora Papers[9] and similar scandals such measures are still in place in a number of jurisdictions, albeit with higher levels of technical sophistication.

Furthermore, conditions to put the theory to a practical test have not been put in place yet. After more than 30 years the AML/CTF/CPF framework is still a work in progress. To date, no country has achieved a perfect FATF-compliance scorecard on both technical compliance and effectiveness.[10] While many countries adopt technical compliance measures, the level of effectiveness of these measures globally is still fairly low.

It is submitted, however, that the 'weakest link' theory is too general to be appropriately meaningful in this context. It holds that the AML/CTF/CPF measures of developed economies will fail when even the smallest country with the weakest financial sector fails to adopt and implement similar AML/CTF/CPF measures. It is, however, unlikely that every weak link will undermine the effectiveness of the measures taken by other states. Much would depend on the type of weakness, on the economy of the country concerned, on the sophistication of its financial and legal system, and on its linkages to the global financial system.

Nauru may serve as a case in point. With a population of about 13,000 and a GDP of US$ 130 million this remote Pacific Island jurisdiction may not appear to pose any

---

[5] Aamo (2013).

[6] UNSC Counter-Terrorism Committee Executive Directorate (2014).

[7] Finance Malta (2023).

[8] Blum et al. (1998).

[9] Bhuiyan (2023).

[10] FATF (2022).

significant global integrity risks and yet, for a period of its history, it did. During the 1990s Nauru was a criminal haven that sold shell bank licences and passports.[11] It is estimated that in 1998 alone about US $70bn in Russian criminal funds were processed through Nauru's banks.[12] The FATF added Nauru to its list of Non-Compliant Countries and Territories in 2000[13] and Nauru responded fast by repealing its criminal haven laws and adopting FATF-compliant measures. Despite adopting key AML/CTF measures, it is unlikely to be assessed as fully compliant in its current mutual evaluation process. Key technical deficiencies and effectiveness challenges relating to corruption controls were, for example, identified in a 2021 UN report.[14]

The last mutual evaluation report on Nauru by the Asia/Pacific Group on Money Laundering followed on a visit by assessors to the country in 2011.[15] At the time of the onsite visit by the assessors, Nauru had no operational bank and there was no financial institution offering financial services beyond one Western Union branch, operating from a hardware store.[16] The economy of Nauru was entirely cash based, using the Australian dollar as its currency.[17] After the abolition of the offshore banking sector in 2004, there was only a relatively small offshore company registry operating in Nauru. Only 59 corporations were registered under Nauru law, with a number of those pending slated to be deregistered. The report held that the "remaining offshore companies and trusts represent a residual risk that Nauruan legal persons or arrangements could be used for laundering the proceeds of foreign offences, although the very low rate of company and trust formation in the sector may indicate that the risks are relatively low."[18]

Since the publication of that report Australia's Bendigo Bank entered into a special project with Nauru's Ministry of Finance to open an agency branch in Nauru in June 2015. The agency operates under the Australian AML/CTF regulatory regime and is supervised by AUSTRAC, the Australian AML/CTF regulator.[19] The agency can transfer funds to and from Australia only. Restrictions imposed by

[11] Sharman (2005), p. 313.

[12] Van Fossen (2003).

[13] Other small jurisdictions that were added to the list include Antigua and Barbuda, Bahamas, Belize, Bermuda, British Virgin Islands, Cayman Islands, Cook Islands, Cyprus, Dominica, Gibraltar, Guernsey, Isle of Man, Israel, Jersey, Lebanon, Liechtenstein, Malta, Marshall Islands, Mauritius, Monaco, Nauru, Niue, Panama, Philippines, Russia, Samoa, Seychelles, St. Kitts and Nevis, St. Lucia, St. Vincent and the Grenadines, and Vanuatu.

[14] Implementation Review Group (2021).

[15] Asia/Pacific Group on Money Laundering (2012).

[16] Asia/Pacific Group on Money Laundering (2012), par 3.

[17] Asia/Pacific Group on Money Laundering (2012), par 4.

[18] Asia/Pacific Group on Money Laundering (2012), par 6.

[19] International Monetary Fund (2021), p. 15.

Bendigo Bank's correspondent banks prevent the flow of funds to and from other countries, notably the USA.[20] In 2023, however, Bendigo Bank informed Nauru that it will close this branch in December 2024.

During the period that Nauru offered offshore banking services, it posed a significant risk to the global community by assisting offshore criminals to hide the beneficial ownership of accounts and transactions. Once the relevant laws were repealed and the system was dismantled, the risk profile of Nauru changed. While they continue to have a small number of offshore companies a level of risk remains as those companies may allow foreign criminals to abuse the companies to hide their control of illicit transactions and wealth. That risk is however low as banks globally employ enhanced due diligence measures in relation to such offshore companies. In addition, Nauru's very weak links to the global financial system should be considered. Should the onshore AML/CTF/CPF control measures of Nauru fail, the ability to transact more than a few million is limited by the nature of its correspondent banking relationships. The small size of its economy further restricts the value of illicit funds that may be processed through the jurisdiction.

In the case of Nauru it would seem as if the most important achievement of the international standard setting processes to date was the dismantling of Nauru's offshore banking system.[21] Many AML/CTF/CPF weaknesses still remain in the system of Nauru. Due to the economic situation of Nauru, it is submitted, however, that these compliance weaknesses do not pose a significant risk to the global financial system. While the 'weakest link' concerns applied while its offshore banking system was fully operational, it seems less appropriate to argue that the remaining weaknesses in the current system of Nauru or Nauru's generally weak AML/CTF/CPF control measures continue to pose a significant risk to the global AML/CTF/CPF system.

Another example of a type of country that may not be appropriately compliant with the FATF standards but may not pose a significant risks to the global AML/CTF/CPF system is a developing economy with strict exchange control measures and limited liquidity. An African supervisor from a country with those features once remarked in relation to their jurisdiction: 'We are a broken washing machine. You can invest your dirty money in our country, but you can't get it out again.' The fact that the political elite at that time engaged in nationalisation and the appropriation of foreign investments added to the unattractiveness of the country for money laundering purposes by foreign criminals.

The sophistication of a country's legal system should also be considered. It is unattractive for investors and criminals to transact in jurisdictions where the rule of law is under pressure and where legal redress when reasonable sought, might not be available. At face value such a country's lack of compliance with global standards may be viewed as inviting criminal abuse. Other country-related factors may

---

[20] Asian Development Bank Pacific Liaison and Coordination Office (2019); International Monetary Fund (2021), p. 15.

[21] Gustitus et al. (2001).

however limit the potential for such abuse. Legal certainty and protection add to the attractiveness of the USA, UK and Europe as money laundering destinations.

The introduction of a mandatory risk-based approach in the FATF standards in 2012, replacing the rule-based approach (which unfairly became associated with a one one-size-fits-all approach),[22] provided space to develop an improved understanding of risks and how they differ globally. That opportunity has not been fully exploited yet. Even in relation to the FATF standards the opportunities to shape different approaches in and to different jurisdictions remain limited as many of the elements of the standards, especially the laws and structures each jurisdiction must have in place, are not subject to a risk-based approach.

It is submitted that the "weakest link" theory should receive more critical attention, especially from Global South scholars. Countries with small formal economies, generally included on the United Nations list of Least Developed Countries,[23] often feature high on lists such as the Basel AML Index.[24] Whether that is sensible should be considered. There is a real risk of policymakers losing sight of the more complex global crime risk picture when the narrative is that the protection of all jurisdictions is dependent on full and effective compliance with global standards by all small jurisdictions, regardless of their context and infrastructure. Not all AML/CTF/CPF weaknesses give rise to similar levels of risk. An improved understanding of the weaknesses that require more attention from global standard-setters may inform a more focused, effective and efficient approach to combating economic crime globally.

3 Abuse of Global Crime Combating Standards by Authoritarian Governments

Global standard-setting in the AML/CTF/CPF context aims to ensure that countries comply with minimum standards. This is a strength of the standards, especially when combined with a proportional risk-based approach. This approach allows countries to respond appropriately to the standards and to their own contexts. In some cases that means that they may go beyond the standards to respond to domestic risks.

The UK, for example, has positioned itself ahead of the global standard in terms of its AML regulation in the art market. The inclusion of art market participants under the purview of criminal offenses related to money laundering dates to 2002, through the Proceeds of Crime Act (POCA). Additionally, as of January 2022, art market participants in the UK involved in trading or facilitating transactions for art valued at €10,000 or more are mandated to undertake additional measures to prevent

[22] De Koker and Goldbarsht (2024b), p. 227–8.

[23] United Nations (2023).

[24] Basel Institute of Governance (2022).

money laundering.[25] This proactive approach by the UK demonstrates that jurisdictions can implement more stringent measures than the global standard when there are valid reasons to do so.

That strength however comes at a cost. The standards as well as the measures to ensure that countries comply with the standards do not have appropriate mechanisms to effectively prevent the adoption of oppressive measures ostensibly to combat money laundering or terrorist and proliferation financing. As a result, authoritarian governments can use compliance with the FATF's standards as a political excuse and defence when they adopt enhanced surveillance and control measures.

When the FATF reviewed the unintended consequences of the implementation of their standards in relation to not for profit organisations (NPOs) they found evidence of 'intrusive supervision of NPOs; restrictions on NPOs' access to funding and bank accounts; and forced dissolution, de-registration or expulsion of NPOs.'[26] Regarding due process rights they also found evidence of issues relevant to investigation and prosecution of terrorist financing and money laundering offences, such as the presumption of innocence and a person's right to effective protection by the courts and 'excessively broad or vague offences in legal counterterrorism financing frameworks'.[27] Measures in relation to NPOs can be abused by authoritarian governments to suppress civil society while overly-broad definitions of terrorism can be used against political opponents.[28]

Russia provides a continuing case study in this regard. Russia's inclusion on the FATF's Non-Compliant Country and Territory list in 2000 triggered significant regulatory responses within the country. The Russian Government saw this blacklisting as arbitrary, noting that while other post-Soviet states lacking AML measures were not listed (except Ukraine), Russia was. The decision by the FATF was interpreted by Russia as the result of a smear campaign originating in the United States.[29]

Despite this, the Russian Government expressed a strong desire to be delisted. They therefore enacted FATF-compliant AML laws that aligned with international standards in August of the same year. However, due to a lack of conclusive evidence regarding implementation, Russia remained on the FATF list. Subsequently, Russia ratified the 1999 UN Convention on the Suppression of Terrorist Financing and joined the Egmont Group of financial intelligence units. Finally, in October 2002, Russia was removed from the list and less than a year later, it became a full member of the FATF.[30]

---

[25] British Art Market Federation (2022).

[26] FATF (2021b), p. 4. Also see Hayes (2012).

[27] FATF (2021b), p. 6.

[28] Reimer (2022); Halliday et al. (2020), pp. 76–77; Yansura (2022).

[29] Favarel-Garrigues (2005a), p. 535.

[30] This membership is often ascribed to political reasons relating to the invasion of Iraq rather than Russia's AML leadership at that stage.

Orlova, however, pointed to the disconnect between the Russia's formal AML/CTF/CPF regime and actual practices of courts and the Central Bank, raising questions about the true purpose of these regulations in Russia.[31] It was suggested that the AML framework was employed as a convenient instrument in the Kremlin's efforts to expand its domestic economic and political control.[32] These concerns endure. Questions were raised for example about the law enforcement measures against Alexei Navalny, Kremlin critic and opposition leader, on fraud and money laundering charges.[33] Despite concerns about the application of FATF standards in the country, Russia assumed the presidency of the FATF in 2013–14. In 2023 the FATF suspended the membership of Russia as a result of its 'unprovoked and unjustified full-scale military invasion of Ukraine', and its actions that "unacceptably run counter to the FATF core principles aiming to promote security, safety, and the integrity of the global financial system.[34] Yet, Russia's mutual evaluation of 2019 found that it 'has an in-depth understanding of its money laundering and terrorist financing risks and has established policies and laws to address these risks'.[35]

The FATF's mutual evaluation process and its interpretation of its standards may also compel countries to broaden the footprint of some of their most oppressive laws. At the time the FATF was considering the unintended consequences of its standards,[36] its mutual evaluation process was putting pressure on South Africa to broaden its terrorism definition. The definition in South Africa's Protection of Constitutional Democracy Against Terrorist and Related Activities Act 33 of 2004 (POCDATARA) was carefully crafted to navigate South Africa's political history. The governing party, the African National Congress, was declared to be a terrorist organisation by the apartheid government, and its leaders, including, former president Nelson Mandela, were on the US terrorist watchlist until 2013. FATF mutual evaluation criticism of the limited definition of terrorism in POCDATARA in 2021 led to amendments to the definition in 2022. The general consequence is that the concept of "terrorist activity" in South Africa is now much broader than envisaged by the South African Parliament in 2004 and arguably defines acts of violence by the African National Congress as freedom fighter organisation in the twentieth century and of its leaders such as former President Nelson Mandela, together with a host of non-political offences, as terrorist activity.[37]

Another example of FATF pressure to increase the scope of anti-terrorism legislation can be found in the impact of a FATF mutual evaluation on the Australian CTF regime. The 2005 mutual evaluation[38] found that, although the

---

[31] See Orlova (2008); Favarel-Garrigues (2005b).

[32] Favarel-Garrigues (2005b).

[33] European Human Rights Advocacy Centre (2023).

[34] FATF (2023).

[35] FATF (2019).

[36] FATF (2021a).

[37] De Koker et al. (2023a) par 4.01. The assessors also required an increase in penalties for offences under the Act. For criticism see De Koker et al. (2023a), par 4.11.

[38] FATF (2005).

range of offences and definitions were quite broad, the Australian legislation did not specifically criminalise the collection or provision of funds for an individual terrorist. The Australian authorities noted to the FATF evaluation team that the Criminal Code refers not only to recklessness in funds being used to engage in a terrorist act, but also to facilitating a terrorist act. Therefore, according to Australian authorities, providing or collecting funds where the person is reckless as to whether they will be used to facilitate a terrorist act, covered 'the collection of funds for a terrorist organisation' and 'the collection or provision of funds for an individual terrorist'. However, the evaluation team did not agree that this sufficiently covered the provisions of the standard and recommended that Australia specifically criminalise the collection of funds for an individual terrorist.[39] Australia, despite asserting that there was no need to change the Criminal Code, proceeded to implement the FATF recommendation and amendments two months later in the Criminal Code, explaining that the amendments strengthened the existing terrorist financing offences and confirmed Australia's commitment to the principles behind the FATF's (then) Special Recommendations on Terrorist Financing.[40] The Security Legislation Review Committee's responded that 'it is difficult [on the above analysis] to see how this could be so';[41] and as Professor George Williams summarises, 'having... parallel offences in fact only muddies the waters. These offences complicate the domestic terrorist financing regime and make it more difficult for people to understand their legal obligations.'[42]

Both the South African and Australian examples are cases where the FATF has pushed sensitive laws beyond what policymakers in the countries felt comfortable with or deemed necessary. The impact of such actions and signals on policy decisions of oppressive regimes have not yet been studied appropriately.

Despite warnings over years that FATF standards can be abused by oppressive regimes unless the FATF framework has controls to ensure an appropriate emphasis on human rights and especially privacy protection,[43] FATF references to human rights remain limited. The concept is referenced three times in the full set of FATF Recommendations, Interpretive Notes and Glossary[44] and only once in its mutual

[39] Goldbarsht (2017), p. 141.

[40] Parliament of Australia (2005) Sch 3 item 3.

[41] House of Representatives Security Legislation Review Committee, Parliament of Australia, Report of the Security Legislation Review Committee (2006), p. 160.

[42] Lynch et al. (2015), p. 67.

[43] E.g. De Koker (2011), p. 382: 'Civil society should, for example, question whether the FATF framework has appropriate controls to ensure that law enforcement objectives are balanced with an appropriate emphasis on human rights and especially privacy protection. The exposure of new, vulnerable financial services clients to breaches of international human rights standards by oppressive regimes acting ostensibly in furtherance of AML/CTF and financial inclusion, would be unconscionable.' See also De Koker and Jentzsch (2013), p. 278.

[44] FATF (2012–2023).

evaluation methodology, as an example of a specific factor that could be considered in relation to asset forfeiture.[45]

The improved alignment between technical standards to combat financial crime and international human rights require more research attention. Observance of the rule of law and international human rights can of course be incorporated into international financial crime combating standards. The dilemma for the FATF is that it will make it much more difficult to reach agreement about the standards. Many countries, including some G20 countries, may re-think their support for the standards. Unfortunately, actions aimed at increasing financial transparency to combat crime, terrorism and proliferation cannot be divorced from their political and human rights contexts. Research that explores ways to align financial integrity and good governance goals will be required to inform appropriate policy positions in global standard-setting.

4 Compliance Enforcement

Global standard-setting processes require some means to ensure compliance. In the late twentieth century and early twenty-first century the leading economies secured global endorsement of the FATF standards by threatening exclusion from the global financial system by those who failed to commit to implementing the standards. This entailed the use of peer review mechanisms backed by black- and greylisting to move most countries to higher levels of compliance.

The processes are however not without challenges and complications. Peer review mechanisms are resource intensive. The FATF's third round of mutual evaluations that assessed countries against its revised 2021 standards has taken more than a decade to complete.

Blacklisting has furthermore failed to move Iran, North Korea and, more recently, Myanmar to appropriate levels of compliance. The FATF's listing design and procedures around blacklisting have furthermore thwarted attempts to have Russia blacklisted after its 2021 invasion of the Ukraine. During this period Russia for example actively collaborated with Iran on armed drones and engaged and supported North Korea. This undermines the FATF's blacklisting of those countries and raise concerns about proliferation financing.[46] Black- and greylisting processes are however designed to follow on mutual evaluations that identified strategic AML/CTF/CPF deficiencies in AML/CTF/CPF frameworks of countries. In Russia's case its 2019 mutual evaluation[47] did not produce those results and hence the FATF could only suspend its membership in 2022.

[45] FATF (2013–2023).

[46] See Alsancak (2023); Vasylevska-Smahliuk (2023).

[47] FATF (2019).

Greylisting, on the other hand, is also imperfect. It may, for example, impact negatively on listed countries at a time when they are actively and constructively working with the FATF to address any remaining strategic deficiencies in their AML/CTF/CPF regimes.[48] There is furthermore a growing number of countries that were greylisted more than once. Some countries have entered the lists now for the third time. The Philippines, e.g., listed from 2000–2005 and from 2010–2013 was again listed in June 2021. Myanmar, listed from 2001–2006 and from 2010–2016 was blacklisted in June 2021. Nigeria, listed from 2001–2006 and from 2010–2013 was re-listed in February 2023.

Listing is supposedly a mechanism to secure political commitment of countries to compliance with FATF standards. Where countries are listed more than once either political support is not consistent, or the country lacks capacity to comply with the global standards. The current remedial and delisting processes do not seem adequate to address the underlying problems.

A further aspect of concern regarding listing is that nearly a half of the world's jurisdictions have now been listed by the FATF for compliance failures since it launched its listing processes in 2000. How global are the standards if the FATF had to use the pressure of a listing process to improve global implementation levels at that scale?

The listing processes themselves are not viewed as fair and the Global South often raises questions about transparency, participation, reasoned decision, legality, and effective review.[49] Normally, if decisions of a similar kind were reached at the state level, they would be subject to judicial review and could thereby be overturned.[50] The AML/CTF/CPF regime has no such mechanism. These problems raise a genuine concern that if the powers of the FATF are not aligned correctly with the rule of law, the unique characteristics that make its compliance mechanisms so effective may be viewed increasingly negatively by a growing number of countries.

There is therefore a need for further research to improve mechanisms that will support the procedural legitimacy of the FATF[51]. This research should probe how accountability could be strengthened.

[48] De Koker et al. (2023b). It's worth noting that greylisting can also have a positive impact on compliance. For instance, it appears that one of the primary drivers for the Australian government to consider revising its AML/CTF regime, and to comply with FATF Rec 22 and 23 by the inclusion of lawyers, accountants, trust and company service providers, real estate agents, and dealers in precious metals and stones (referred to as tranche-two entities) is influenced by the concern of being greylisted: 'Australia will undergo its next Mutual Evaluation between 2025 and 2027 and is at risk of receiving low ratings and potential grey listing if we do not undertake significant reform. Greylisting could result in significant economic costs for Australia', see Attorney general, Modernising Australia's anti-money laundering and counter-terrorism financing regime - Consultation paper on reforms to simplify and modernise the regime and address risks in certain professions (April 2023), p. 19.

[49] See Goldbarsht (2018), p. 233. See also Littrell (2024) who raises concern about demographic biases in FATF-related mutual evaluation results.

[50] Goldbarsht and Harris (2022).

[51] Goldbarsht and Harris (2020).

Participation in decision-taking also requires more attention. The members of the FATF are wealthier countries that have dominated the formulation of policies and recommendations, while less developed countries have relatively little, if any, influence over outcomes. This structure presents a serious challenge to legitimacy[52] and will continue to generate unintended consequences. In relation to the FATF, those who actually negotiate the standards are a limited number of officials of member states. They have no clear responsibilities to the public except that of the member state that they represent. In many cases governments do not fully appreciate the impact of the standards their FATF delegations endorse. As there is no formal negotiation process and ratification procedure required, the draft standards do not require the formal blessing of any national elected non-member officials. The system is designed to minimise friction and enable the adoption of technical standards. The standards and their effects are however also political in nature, and this needs to be better reflected in the FATF processes.

5 Conclusion

The concerns raised in this chapter have been voiced for three decades but we seem to have entered a new phase that requires deeper analysis of the strategy to date. The future direction of global standard-setting and compliance enforcement is less clear in an increasingly complex global political context. The level of global agreement that helped the FATF to adopt most of its standards has declined. Geopolitical tensions are on the rise. The US is decoupling key industries from China and that holds implications for the global financial services too. The sanctions imposed on Russia after its 2014 annexation of Crimea escalated dramatically when it launched its full-scale invasion of Ukraine in 2022. As discussed in 4 above, Russia is openly working and trading with FATF blacklisted jurisdictions, and China has not adopted an explicitly pro-FATF approach in this regard.

There is therefore a real risk of fragmentation of the international financial system, accompanied by a loss of traction and scope of the current international financial standards and the standard-setting process as a whole. This increases the need for muti-disciplinary research to outline policy options and inform appropriate policy decision in the current fluid context.

References

Aamo (2013) Statement by FATF President Bjørn S. Aamo at the EU Conference "Fighting money laundering and terrorist financing - New framework, future challenges" 15 March. https://www.fatf-gafi.org/en/publications/Fatfgeneral/Effectivenesshasmovedtothetopofthefatfagenda.html

[52] See Goldbarsht (2020), p. 235.

Alsancak F (2023) The Financial Action Task Force's Challenge with Russia. 9 May 2023. https://rusi.org/explore-our-research/publications/commentary/financial-action-task-forces-challenge-russia

Asia/Pacific Group on Money Laundering (2012) Mutual Evaluation Report: Anti-Money Laundering and Combating the Financing of Terrorism - Republic of Nauru. APG, Sydney. https://apgml.org/includes/handlers/get-document.ashx?d=585e21ee-0c23-40cb-93fd-e1562267298e

Asian Development Bank Pacific Liaison and Coordination Office (2019) Nauru. Pacific Finance Sector Briefs. ADB, Sydney. https://www.adb.org/sites/default/files/publication/530246/pacific-finance-sector-nauru.pdf

Basel Institute of Governance (2022) Basel AML Index 2022: 11th Public Edition Ranking money laundering and terrorist financing risks around the world. https://index.baselgovernance.org/api/uploads/221004_Basel_AML_Index_2022_72cc668efb.pdf

Bhuiyan S (2023) The pandora papers opens up pandora's box: integrity in crisis. Public Integr 25(2):245–256

Blum JA, Levi M, Naylor RT, Williams P (1998) Financial havens, banking secrecy and money laundering. Trends Org Crime 4:68

British Art Market Federation (2022) Guidance on anti-money laundering for UK art market participants. https://tbamf.org.uk/wp-content/uploads/2022/07/BAMF-HMT-AML-Guidelines-30-June-2022.pdf

De Koker L (2011) Aligning anti-money laundering, combating of financing of terror and financial inclusion: questions to consider when FATF standards are clarified. J Financ Crime 18(4):361–386

De Koker L, Goldbarsht D (2024a) Towards a global approach to combating crime. In: Goldbarsht D, De Koker L (eds) Financial crime, law and governance: navigating challenges in different contexts. Springer, Cham

De Koker L, Goldbarsht D (2024b) FATF's risk-based approach: has the pendulum swung too far? In: Goldbarsht D, De Koker L (eds) Financial crime and the law: identifying and mitigating risks. Springer, Cham

De Koker L, Jentzsch N (2013) Financial inclusion and financial integrity: aligned incentives? World Dev 44:267–280

De Koker L, Basson M, Smit P, Symington J (2023a) Money laundering and terrorist financing: law and compliance in South Africa. LexisNexis, Durban

De Koker L, Howell J, Morris N (2023b) Economic consequences of greylisting by the Financial Action Task Force. Risks 11(5):81

European Human Rights Advocacy Centre (2023) Navalny/FBK case. http://ehrac.org.uk/en_gb/key-ehrac-cases/navalny-fbk-case/

FATF (2005) Summary of the Third Mutual Evaluation Report: Anti-Money Laundering and Combating the Financing of Terrorism – Australia. https://www.fatf-gafi.org/content/dam/fatf-gafi/mer/MER%20Australia%20ES.pdf.coredownload.pdf

FATF (2010) Global Money Laundering & Terrorist Financing Threat Assessment A view of how and why criminals and terrorists abuse finances, the effect of this abuse and the steps to mitigate these threats. FATF, Paris. https://www.fatf-gafi.org/content/dam/fatf-gafi/reports/Global%20Threat%20assessment.pdf

FATF (2012–2023) International Standards on Combating Money Laundering and the Financing of Terrorism & Proliferation. FATF, Paris. www.fatf-gafi.org/recommendations.html

FATF (2013–2023) Methodology for Assessing Compliance with the FATF Recommendations and the Effectiveness of AML/CTF Systems. FATF, Paris. http://www.fatf-gafi.org/publications/mutualevaluations/documents/fatf-methodology.html https://www.fatf-gafi.org/en/publications/Mutualevaluations/Fatf-methodology.html

FATF (2019) Anti-money laundering and counter-terrorist financing measures: Russian Federation Mutual Evaluation Report. https://www.fatf-gafi.org/content/dam/fatf-gafi/mer/Mutual-Evaluation-Russian-Federation-2019.pdf.coredownload.inline.pdf

FATF (2021a) High-Level Synopsis of the Stocktake of the Unintended Consequences of the FATF Standards. FATF, Paris. https://www.fatf-gafi.org/en/publications/Financialinclusionandnpoissues/Unintended-consequences-project.html

FATF (2021b) High-Level Synopsis of the Stocktake of the Unintended Consequences of the FATF Standards. https://www.fatf-gafi.org/en/publications/Financialinclusionandnpoissues/Unintended-consequences-project.html

FATF (2022) Report on the State of Effectiveness and Compliance with the FATF Standards. https://www.fatf-gafi.org/content/dam/fatf-gafi/reports/Report-on-the-State-of-Effectiveness-Compliance-with-FATF-Standards.pdf.coredownload.pdf

FATF (2023) FATF Statement on the Russian Federation. https://www.fatf-gafi.org/en/publications/Fatfgeneral/fatf-statement-russian-federation.html

Favarel-Garrigues G (2005a) Domestic reformulation of the moral issues at stake in the drive against money laundering: the case of Russia. Int Soc Sci J 57(185):529–540

Favarel-Garrigues G (2005b) Domestic reformulation of the moral issues at stake in the drive against money laundering: the case of Russia. Blackwell Publishing Ltd, Oxford

Finance Malta (2023) Malta: FATF reforms will improve fight against money laundering and terrorism financing – Pleyer, Mondaq, 18 January 2023. https://www.mondaq.com/financial-services/1272034/fatf-reforms-will-improve-fight-against-money-laundering-and-terrorism-financing%2D%2Dpleyer

Goldbarsht D (2017) Who's the legislator anyway? How the FATFs global norms reshape Australian counter terrorist financing laws. Fed Law Rev 45(1):127–151

Goldbarsht D (2018) Multi-layered approaches to counter terrorist financing: norm development and compliance. Doctoral dissertation, UNSW Sydney

Goldbarsht D (2020) Global counter-terrorist financing and soft law. Edward Elgar Publishing, Cheltenham

Goldbarsht D, Harris H (2020) Transnational regulatory networks: a study in compliance and legitimacy in counter-terrorist financing. Journal of Financial Crime 27(3):855–870

Goldbarsht D, Harris H (2022) Check the balance: is the doctrine of separation of powers sufficient in the context of intergovernmental organisations? A case study of Australia's AML/CTF financing framework. Federal Law Review 50(4):527–557. https://doi.org/10.1177/0067205X221126558

Gustitus L, Bean E, Roach R (2001) Correspondent banking: a gateway for money laundering economic. Perspectives 6(2):26–29

Halliday T, Levi M, Reuter P (2020) Why do transnational legal orders persist? The curious case of money-laundering controls. In: Shaffer G, Aaronson E (eds) Transnational legal ordering of criminal justice. Cambridge University Press, Cambridge, pp 51–83

Hayes B (2012) Counter-terrorism, policy laundering, and the FATF: legalizing surveillance, regulating civil society. Int J Not-for-Profit Law 14:5–48

Implementation Review Group (2021) State of Implementation of the United Nations Convention against Corruption: Nauru. Twelfth session Vienna, 14–18 June 2021, CAC/COSP/IRG/2021/CRP.2. https://www.unodc.org/documents/treaties/UNCAC/WorkingGroups/ImplementationReviewGroup/14-18June2021/CAC-COSP-IRG-2021-CRP.2_V2103650.pdf

International Monetary Fund (2021) Republic of Nauru: 2021 Article IV Consultation-Press Release; Staff Report; and Statement by the Executive Director for the Republic of Nauru. IMF, Washington DC. https://www.imf.org/en/Publications/CR/Issues/2022/02/07/Republic-of-Nauru-2021-Article-IV-Consultation-Press-Release-Staff-Report-and-Statement-by-512874

Labori D (2019) FATF must move to enforcer, not just standard setter, of global AML recommendations: Mnuchin. ACFCS, 21 June. https://www.acfcs.org/fatf-must-move-to-enforcer-not-just-standard-setter-of-global-aml-recommendations-mnuchin/

Lewis D (2016) Remarks for the Opening Ceremony of FATF TREIN. https://www.fatf-gafi.org/en/publications/Fatfgeneral/David-lewis-trein-opening-ceremony.html

Littrell C (2024) Economic and demographic biases in FATF mutual evaluation results. In: Goldbarsht D, de Koker L (eds) Financial crime and the law. Ius Gentium: Comparative perspectives on law and justice, vol 115. Springer, Cham. https://doi.org/10.1007/978-3-031-59543-1_8

Lynch A, McGarrity N, Williams G (2015) Inside Australia's Anti-Terrorism Laws and Trials. New South Publishing

Orlova AV (2008) Russia's anti-money laundering regime: law enforcement tool or instrument of domestic control? J Money Laund Control 11(3):210–233

Parliament of Australia (2005) Explanatory Memorandum, Anti-Terrorism Bill (No 2) 2005 (Cth)

Reimer S (2022) Authoritarian abuses: the weaponisation of anti-financial crime. RUSI. https://rusi.org/explore-our-research/publications/commentary/authoritarian-abuses-weaponisation-anti-financial-crime

Sharman JC (2005) South Pacific tax havens: from leaders in the race to the bottom to laggards in the race to the top? Account Forum 29(3):311–323

United Nations (2023) LDCs at a Glance. https://www.un.org/development/desa/dpad/least-developed-country-category/ldcs-at-a-glance.html

UNSC Counter-Terrorism Committee Executive Directorate (2014) Interview with Roger Wilkins, President of the Financial Action Task Force (FATF): "We need to focus on concrete things that we can achieve together". https://www.un.org/securitycouncil/ctc/news/interview-roger-wilkins-president-financial-action-task-force-fatf%E2%80%9Dwe-need-focus-concrete

Van Fossen AB (2003) Money laundering, global financial instability, and tax havens in the Pacific Islands. Contemp Pac:237–275. https://scholarspace.manoa.hawaii.edu/server/api/core/bitstreams/655f86e8-f7f7-4f3e-8ba6-a99514d6eac8/content

Vasylevska-Smahliuk O (2023) Blacklisting Russia should be a priority for the FATF. 16 June 2023. https://www.rusi.org/explore-our-research/publications/commentary/blacklisting-russia-should-be-priority-fatf

Yansura J (2022) CTF is meant to counter terrorists, not democratic opposition. Global Financial Integrity. https://gfintegrity.org/CTF-is-meant-to-counter-terrorists-not-democratic-opposition/

Doron Goldbarsht LLB, LLM (HUJI), PhD (UNSW), is the Director of the Financial Integrity Hub (FIH) and an Associate Professor at Macquarie Law School, where he teaches banking and financial crime. He is an authority on anti-money laundering and counter-terrorist financing (AML/CTF) regulations, with expertise in the related fields of compliance and financial innovation, with over 20 years of experience in the field. His recent books *Financial Crime and the Law: Identifying and Mitigating Risks* (Springer 2024, co-edited), *Financial Crime, Law and Governance: Navigating Challenges in Diverse Contexts* (Springer 2024, co-edited), *Financial Technology and the Law: Combating Financial Crime* (Springer, 2022 co-edited), and *Global Counter-Terrorist Financing and Soft Law: Multi-Layered Approaches* (Edward Elgar, 2020), as well as journal and chapter publications, focus on international AML/CTF standards and the mechanisms for their effective implementation and compliance at the national level.

Louis de Koker LLB LLM (UFS) LLM (Cantab) LLD (UFS) FSALS, is a Professor and Associate Dean: Research and Industry Engagement at the La Trobe Law School (Australia), an Extraordinary Professor at the Faculty of Law of the University of the Western Cape (South Africa) and a Board member with the Financial Integrity Hub (FIH) at Macquarie Law School. From 2014 to 2019 he was the national program leader of the Law and Policy research program of the Australian government-funded Data to Decisions Cooperative Research Centre. Louis is an expert on anti-money laundering and counterterrorist and proliferation financing, and especially the relationship between financial integrity and financial inclusion policies and regulations. Louis has worked with the Consultative Group to Assist the Poor, the World Bank, the OECD, the Asian Development Bank regulators and financial service providers on the design and implementation of appropriate integrity and inclusion over the past two decades. He has advised on a range of laws and regulations and his research on integrity laws and their impact on financial inclusion has been cited in publications of various international bodies including the World Bank, IMF, the Financial Action Task Force (FATF) and the Basel Committee on Banking Supervision.

Printed in the USA
CPSIA information can be obtained
at www.ICGtesting.com
CBHW071608200924
14498CB00037B/164

9 783031 595462